A comprehensive guide to future-proofing public sector communication and increasing citizen satisfaction

How to communicate with the citizens of the future? Why does public sector communication often fail? *Public Sector Communication* combines practical examples from around the world with the latest theoretical insights to show how communication can help bridge gaps that exist between public sector organizations and the individual citizens they serve. The authors—two experts in the field with experience from the public sector—explain how public entities, be they cities, governments, foundations, agencies, authorities, municipalities, regulators, military, or government monopolies and state owned businesses can build their intangible assets to future-proof themselves in a volatile environment.

The book examines how the recent digitalization has increased citizen expectations and why one-way communication leaves public sector organizations fragile. To explain how to make public sector communication antifragile, the authors map contributions from a wide variety of fields combined with illustrative examples from around the world. The authors propose a research-based framework of different intangible assets that can directly improve communication in the public sector.

This important resource:

- Helps explain the sector-specific conditions and why communication is often challenging in the public sector
- Summarizes all relevant literature on the topic across disciplines and includes the most popular management ideals of the recent decades
- Explores how public sector organizations can increase citizen satisfaction with effective communication
- Presents new approaches to both the study and practice of communication in the public sector
- Provides international examples of successful public sector communication
- Offers realistic guides to building intangible assets in practice

Written for advanced undergraduate and graduate students, as well as public managers and leaders, *Public Sector Communication* offers an illustrative, research-based guide to improving communication and engaging citizens of today and the future.

María-José Canel, Complutense University of Madrid, Madrid, Spain

Vilma Luoma-aho, University of Jyväskylä, Jyväskylä, Finland

Public Sector Communication

Closing Gaps Between Citizens and
Public Organizations

María-José Canel and Vilma Luoma-aho

WILEY Blackwell

Registered Office(s)
John Wiley & Sons, Inc., 111 River Street, Hoboken, NJ 07030, USA

Editorial Office
101 Station Landing, Medford, MA 02155, USA

For details of our global editorial offices, customer services, and more information about Wiley products visit us at www.wiley.com.

Wiley also publishes its books in a variety of electronic formats and by print-on-demand. Some content that appears in standard print versions of this book may not be available in other formats.

Library of Congress Cataloging-in-Publication Data: applied for
9781119135616 [Hardback]
9781119135579 [Paperback]

Cover Design and Image: © Vilma & Leo Luoma-aho;
(back cover image) © OnstOn/iStockphoto

Set in 10/12 pt WarnockPro-Regular by Thomson Digital, Noida, India

Printed and bound in Singapore by C.O.S. Printers Pte Ltd

10   9   8   7   6   5   4   3   2   1

Table of Contents

Part I

1

What Is Changing in Public Sector Communication?

> *Budgets are cut, lines get longer and citizens voice their dissatisfaction real time*
> (A civil servant describing the change)

Public sector organizations have traditionally been blamed for bureaucracy, slowness, inefficiency, and corruption. These apparent failings have resulted in poor relationships between the public sector and citizens. Furthermore, many efforts aimed at improving the public sector seem to fail due to reasons that include a lack of understanding of citizens' changing expectations and an absence of strategic and planned communication. In response to a context of global economic and financial crisis and of the rise of new and social media, this book focuses on how communication can help to bridge the gap that exists between public sector organizations and the individual citizens whom they serve.

Recognizing that public sector communication cannot operate outside a political environment, this volume focuses on the apolitical function of communication undertaken by different public sector organizations, including governments, public foundations, agencies, authorities, regulators, and entities involved in joint public–private sector operations such as state monopolies and businesses.

The first part of this introductory chapter describes the changing context in which the public sector operates today, and it pays special attention to the transformations, problems, and challenges that require new approaches to both the study and practice of communication. The second part sets out the framework for the book. After exploring different contributions from research disciplines and areas that we judge to be of use in the study of public sector communication, the book's underlying rationale and structure are presented.

1.1 The Change: Identifying the Gaps with Citizens

1.1.1 What Is Changing?

1.1.1.1 Change in Everyday Practice

On a global level, change appears to be the new normal for public sector organizations today. Although not every change is radical in nature or overturns all established processes, incremental change has become a daily practice for public sector employees. Reforms as intentional changes on a smaller scale are typical (Pollit and Bouckaert, 2011) as the speed of societal change is understood to be accelerating, and public sector organizations are being reconceived and reorganized to serve citizens better. Public sector managers and employees are learning to deal not only with changes in citizens' needs but also with the continuous pressure being placed on them to develop, measure, and improve their services and organizations. The complex setting in which public sector organizations exist today requires public sector organizations to be connected, departments to be influential, and authorities to be ambitious in their work (Tench et al., 2017).

As recent decades of public sector reform have focused mostly on savings and efficiency (Kuipers et al., 2014), more value-based ideals to guide change have been called for (White, 2000; Andrews, 2012). If one takes into account the finding that almost 70% of change initiatives in organizations fail (Higgs and Rowland, 2005, p. 121), a top priority is to better understand the actual needs and values behind change processes. Doing so is especially vital for efficiency, which remains one of the central mantras of the public sector globally.

Much of the research on public sector change has focused on the need for and the organization and processes of change, but there remains a lack of contextual consideration and understanding of the microlevel processes of change for individuals (Kuipers et al., 2014). In their review of change management in public organizations, Kuipers et al. noted that most public sector change remains "top-down, planned change, i.e. changes that are 'made to' organizations rather than changes made by and within organizations" (Kuipers et al., 2014, p. 15). These practices appear to ignore the vital role of employees' and citizens' engagement in making change successful. In fact, engagement is understood as a "vehicle for co-production, co-creation and co-innovation of public goods" (Bourgon, 2009, p. 230).

1.1.1.2 Answering the Most Important Question

In line with the central idea of this book, it is generally agreed that there is an increasing need for public managers "to know how to interact with the public" (Thomas, 2013, p. 786). Reasons for public sector change that have been voiced recently include citizens' needs evolving as a result of private sector standards of service (Thijs and Staes, 2008). There has been an overall change from what Mary P. Follett describes as holding power *over* citizens to what she views as holding power *with* citizens (Thomas, 2013). This new focus on relationships is urgently needed because recent decades of focusing on productivity have made public sector organizations increasingly dependent on the scientific management paradigm. Public sector organizations will remain fragile as long as the illusion persists that their operating environment is predictable, that change can be controlled, and that ex post adaptations are sufficient (Bourgon, 2009, 2011).

As citizens have begun to receive services and goods almost instantly elsewhere, their expectations of public sector organizations have also risen. These expectations are also empowered by new technological developments and the rise of mass self-communication (Castells, 2009), through which individual citizens are equipped to voice their opinions and experiences in real time to mass audiences without the traditional journalism processes of fact checking, editing, or gatekeeping.

Whether change takes the form of wholesale transformations to structures or governments or merely involves reorganizing or introducing new procedures or tools, the once-stable environment of public sector organizations appears to remain only in myths put forward in public sector literature. Communication plays a key role in times of change, as public sector employees and citizens alike want an answer to the most important question that arises when change occurs: What will happen to me? The only way to ensure successful change is to answer this question, which requires the ability to communicate effectively with citizens.

Recent research suggests that there is no single event alone that is the cause of changes in the public sector. Instead, changes occur on all the societal, governmental, organizational, and individual levels simultaneously. In fact, most of the external drivers for change are complexly intertwined within larger contextual developments that affect not just a few but many organizations at once (Kuipers et al., 2014).

1.1.1.3 Changing Values?

When it comes to change in the public sector, several factors are considered important by both researchers and practitioners. First, while the context of change matters, so too does the content of what is changing. Second, it is agreed that the process through which change occurs is highly significant, as is the leadership of the change process. Perhaps too much emphasis is often placed on the outcomes of change, even though these may change over the course of the process (in a manner similar to the ways in which budgets have to be revised), and they might sometimes be difficult to grasp directly.

Change and organizational functions are guided by societal values, as values reflect what citizens want. Along with the introduction of new principles borrowed from management literature, the traditional values of public sector organizations are slowly changing (Pollit and Bouckaert, 2011). "Equity" is being replaced by "efficiency of services," as legitimacy – the license to exist – is now more dependent on the effectiveness of services (Kuipers et al., 2014). Moreover, there is an increasing emphasis on the utility and value that citizens receive from services, and even "fairness" as a value is being replaced by "transparency." Furthermore, the traditional value of "reliability" is partly being replaced by "frugality" as financial factors gain increasing importance. Only the core values of "safety" and "due process," the key elements for trust within democratic societies, seem to be holding their ground (Rothstein, 2001).

We will next look at public sector change from two complementary levels that in practice often overlap: (i) changes in individual citizens and their communication patterns and habits (including those of public sector employees) and (ii) changes in public sector organizations and their management and organization.

1.1.2 Changes in Individuals: Citizens, Stakeholders, Customers, and Partners

There is a common agreement that public sector organizations should be "more responsive to society's needs and demands" (Thijs and Staes, 2008, p. 8). At the same time, however, the public that they serve is more complex than ever (Thomas, 2013). There are numerous reasons for changes in the nature of citizenship, but previous studies seem to confirm the significance of four areas of rapid change in this domain that have affected public sector organizations: citizens' demands and expectations, citizens' communication practices, citizens' diversity, and new citizen roles. The following subsections elaborate on each of these areas of change.

1.1.2.1 Changes in Citizens' Demands and Expectations

As public sector organizations develop, "the place and the role of the citizen/customer have become of very high importance in these changes and reforms" (Thijs and Staes, 2008, p. 1). Despite the fundamental public value of serving, citizens' and public servants' experiences and expectations are often overlooked in public sector development (Pekkarinen et al., 2011), and change management continues to be a hot topic of public sector development. In fact, in previous literature on public sector change, the micro-view of individuals has been overshadowed by the overwhelming attention paid to change outcomes and processes (Kuipers et al., 2014).

Citizen expectations arise as a result of combining citizens' personal experiences with what the public sector communicates. As service design becomes more popular in the business sector (Whicher and Cawood, 2013), citizens are starting to expect a similar level of service delivery from public sector organizations. Previous research suggests that citizen expectations are formed based on a combination of previous experiences, personal needs, word of mouth, and the implicit and explicit communication emanating from the public service (Thijs and Staes, 2008). Citizen satisfaction differs from customer satisfaction in the respect that whereas customer satisfaction focuses purely on service quality, citizen satisfaction must also assess individual services on a relative basis. It poses the question: With the funding available, which services should be prioritized?

1.1.2.2 Citizen Communication Practices

As traditional mass communication has been partly replaced by social networks (Castells, 2009), the logic of citizen engagement has changed. Public organizations are now challenged to reach individual citizens within their cultural bubbles (Sloterdijk, 2011). These bubbles let in only the communication that citizens actively choose for themselves. And instead of comprising traditional mass media content, they often consist of streams and feeds that citizens select from an array of potential messages. Moreover, as citizens are able to communicate their needs and experiences online in real time and to massive audiences, stories and reports of individual experiences are gaining in importance.

New sociological research suggests that the contemporary existence of citizens within these individual bubbles is an isolated one, and that together these bubbles do not make up a network (which is too geometric and point oriented) or a society (which is too restricted in its container form), but rather a plurality of spheres – a kind of "social foam" (Sloterdijk, 2011). In this foam, citizens are simultaneously interconnected and isolated, and several different conditions and atmospheres shape their behavior and expectations.

With these changes in the nature of society and citizens, there is an urgent need to shift from a "culture of controls" to a citizen-centered engagement (Bourgon, 2011).

1.1.2.3 Citizen Diversity

Citizens today are not a homogenous group by any measure. Diversity understood merely through ethnicity and location is becoming outdated; citizen "superdiversity" is becoming the norm (Vertovec, 2007). Superdiversity refers to the wide scale of variance available in today's multigroup relationships (Vertovec, 2007). On the level of organizations and institutions, decisions are globally interconnected, and so single policies and actions may have new and unexpected multicultural impacts (Luoma-aho and Paloviita, 2010). A shift from citizen categorization to temporal and dynamic citizen roles and identities is currently under way. In practice, when public sector organizations address citizens, they can no longer categorize them according to ethnicity; they must instead consider a range of factors that is based on citizen identities, locations, histories, trajectories, and expectations.

Moreover, as superdiverse citizens mix together into the new social foam, unintended misunderstandings that further challenge the work of public sector organizations may occur. As a result of diversity, the importance of the messenger and the priming of messages in a culturally suitable way become highlighted.

1.1.2.4 Changing Citizen Roles

Along with the introduction of NPM (new public management), new roles for citizens have emerged. The use of the word "citizen" is becoming controversial, as many individuals living within national borders do not have citizenship. In this book, we use that word loosely to refer to those individuals within the jurisdiction of the public sector organizations we discuss. In addition to the traditional view of citizens as taxpayers and contributors and as individuals with rights and responsibilities, new roles that shape the way in which public sector organizations can address citizens are also emerging. One central role attributed to citizens today is that of "beneficiaries." This role emphasizes the right to certain services or goods. Similar to this role of beneficiary is that of customer or client. These roles emphasize choice, and they highlight citizens' ability to choose between different public services. For citizens, this means changing expectations, as the assumption is that comparisons and options are available. These newer citizen roles emphasize exchange and demands for quality: if a certain sum of money is paid (whether through taxes or fees), the quality of the service should be higher (Thijs and Staes, 2008). Moreover, as public services continue to be developed and service design becomes more common, citizens also become producers and cocreators in the context of public sector services. As a result, more emphasis is placed on the nature of engagement between citizen and organization (Bowden, Jana, and Naumann, 2016). Each role carries with it certain citizen expectations regarding interaction with public sector organizations.

1.1.3 The Traditional Gaps that Citizens Perceive When Assessing the Public Sector

1.1.3.1 Citizens Are from Venus, Public Authorities Are from Mars?

Although all parties involved in public sector services agree that the final product of public sector organizations is a successful society consisting of satisfied citizens, several communication hurdles must be overcome if this aim is to be achieved. Whereas authorities construct their communication and key messages based on their aims and correct procedures, citizens assess communication from authorities based on whether it meets their needs and answers their questions. Whereas organizations look at the bigger picture, citizens often take an individual view. In addition, the political nature of public sector organizations and their leadership sometimes complicates communication.

The assessment of public sector performance differs from the assessment of private sector goods and services. In the public sector, assessments need to include, in addition to the operational objective of "doing things right," the more existential and often-political question of "doing the right things" (Thijs and Staes, 2008, p. 9).

Communication between authorities and citizens online is not without challenges. Lack of common viewpoints and the legal constraints that guide all authorities' communication online have been noted as challenges to interaction (Tirkkonen and Luoma-aho, 2014). This book is focused on bringing citizens and public sector organizations closer together by closing the following gaps that are emerging in the new communication environment.

1.1.3.2 Gap 1: Speed: Bureaucracy versus Postbureaucracy

Public sector organizations are still for the most part guided by the scientific management paradigm's principles of efficiency and structure, and accordingly procedure often overtakes flexibility. This causes what citizens perceive as slowness – for example, when a simple request goes through a long bureaucratic route. Such a path produces a gap in the expectations of citizens who are living in a postbureaucratic environment in which traditional modes of managerial authority are obsolete owing to "a range of pressures commonly associated with globalization and technological advance" (Johnson et al., 2009, p. 37). In short, citizens are able to receive fast services elsewhere online, and as a result they are beginning to expect similar service from a sector that in their view they fund through their taxes. Citizens find it difficult to understand why they can sign up to a new credit card immediately online and have it delivered to their house the next day but may when renewing their driver's license have to make a personal visit to the department issuing the document, wait several weeks to receive the new license, and sometimes even submit additional paperwork or take medical tests.

1.1.3.3 Gap 2: Privacy: Public versus Private Communication

As we will discuss in Chapter 2 of this book, the borderline between what is considered public and what is considered private has continued to blur as connectivity has increased. This phenomenon is being accentuated by the trend of public sector employees bringing their own devices to work, the extension of work into leisure time, and the increasingly diverse range of actors comprising the body of public sector workers. There are no longer purely private messages intended for employees only; any message can potentially become public. This is highlighted during crises (Frandsen and Johansen, 2010, p. 432), when communication straddles the traditional distinctions of "what is public (i.e., the public sphere of the media), semipublic (networks), or private (inside the organization)." The traditional division of public sector communication as targeted for either internal personnel or external stakeholders now seems naïve, as potentially private messages may end up in public forums through both intended and unintended information leaks, hacks, and sharing on social media. The question of privacy also relates to which channels and media can be officially used by authorities, and which channels would be most likely to reach individual citizens in their communication bubbles. When Australian immigration officers make a decision to refuse to grant asylum for an individual, the individual can publicly disagree and argue his or her case on social media, whereas the authorities are required to keep the process private and are hence unable to release, for example, the records that would explain their decision.

1.1.3.4 Gap 3: Viewpoints: Process versus Answers

Authorities and citizens take different viewpoints when dealing with issues that require solutions. As authorities are often experts in their field, they use exact definitions and concepts that are accurate but seldom easily understood. In contrast, citizens are still often effectively lay people when it comes to administrative processes, and what they look for are answers that fit their individual challenges or questions. They may find it difficult to identify an answer to their query within a detailed procedural description that makes use of technically correct descriptions, and as a result they may resort to alternative outlets where clear questions are given clear answers – for example, online discussion forums (Tirkkonen and Luoma-aho, 2011, 2014). Their need to feel that they have a clear answer overpowers the need for technical precision, and ultimately the clear answer that citizens end up with from unofficial sources may contain false information and create a false sense of having had the question answered. An illustrative example of this is the global discussion about vaccinations for children. When the authorities stick to vague recommendations based on statistical probabilities of being affected by a disease, citizens search for strong opinions to confirm their own thinking via online discussion forums, where "people like me" share their views and experiences. As will be shown, intangible assets help to elaborate narratives that bridge these different viewpoints.

1.1.3.5 Gap 4: Context: Single Events versus General Attitude

For authorities dealing with citizens' needs and emerging issues, individual crises are put into the context of otherwise-successful public administration, and so citizens' problems or complaints are therefore treated as one-off events. However, from the citizen's perspective, there is an impression of recurrent failures. In fact, because negative reports are viewed as more credible than positive ones (Chen and Lurie, 2013), citizens are hard wired to remember public sector failures and arrange them into a narrative of ongoing problems. This contributes to a widespread negative attitude toward the public sector in general. Studies suggest that despite a negative attitude to the public sector at large, citizens may simultaneously value and appreciate individual public services provided to them (Thijs and Staes, 2008). The challenge of communicating with regard to a single event and explaining its context becomes difficult if there is a general attitude of hostility or negativity. Whereas authorities saw the floods caused by Hurricane Katrina in the United States as a single disaster, for citizens they were merely one more example of a failure by the public services to help when needed. Citizens saw the hurricane in the context of other disasters and added it to their list of other incidents such as forest fires and other hurricanes.

1.1.3.6 Gap 5: Perceptions: Perception versus Performance

The whole public sector, including authorities and employees, is subject to a sector-wide reputation that has been established over time and that is hence quite stable (Luoma-aho, 2008). The public sector is often linked with negative traits, including bureaucracy, slowness, unreliability, and inefficiency (Wæraas and Byrkjeflot, 2012), despite quite successful renewals and practices. In fact, the public sector's actual performance is something individual citizens can seldom evaluate for themselves, and the more complex the service process, the more difficult its evaluation becomes (Thijs, 2011). This is frustrating for public sector employees, who often feel their efforts yield no results. Furthermore, public sector organizations rightly often focus on more pressing issues in their communication than their own development and successes, and this choice of focus exacerbates the gap. Research shows that even major improvements and renewals may leave organizational reputation untouched (Luoma-aho and Makikangas, 2014), as perceptions overtake even the best attempts at improving. When neighbors tell stories of, for example, long lines for water purification services at a local plant after a flood that may have polluted the local water supply, the fact that every single affected household may have been successfully assisted within a reasonable time frame may not resonate as a victory. Personal experiences, emotions, and perceptions rule over performance reports.

1.1.3.7 Gap 6: Roles: Obligations versus Rights

Citizens can focus on their own rights, whereas authorities need to consider the full impact of individual choices for society at large. Procedures originally intended for citizen protection seem to have created a gap between citizens and public sector organizations. For example, frustration may arise when a citizen moves to a new city and the public health officials there are unable to see his or her medical records produced by medical practitioners in the previous city of residence. Although citizens do in principle understand the importance of protecting data and adhering to procedures, when it comes to simple requests and answers they sometimes feel frustrated by the slowness of the process (Thijs and Staes, 2008). Any perceived experiences of unfair treatment or not getting what is rightfully theirs have the potential to escalate into bigger crises owing to the fact that citizens are now empowered to voice their misfortunes via media platforms such as YouTube videos. In such an environment, public sector organizations are automatically cast in the role of Goliath – the big, evil system – with the individual citizen playing the role of a small, brave David. A recent example of this is an angry Nordic parent who filmed and posted on YouTube the process of a child protection services worker coming to take his child into custody. Without any context and background information, it appears as though his rights were violated, when in fact he was severely neglecting his welfare obligations to the child. He had a right to tell his story publicly; the authorities had the obligation to not tell their story in public.

1.1.3.8 Gap 7: Media Use: Controlled versus Real Time

Changes to the arena in which communication takes place have raised an important question: Is there a single arena that is controlled and set by the authorities, or do citizens choose their own communication arena? Many public sector organizations still function in a world in which media is exclusively of the owned (for example, agency websites), earned (for example, news articles covering agency decisions), and paid varieties (for example, social advertising and campaigns). Here, the focus is on providing information through one-way websites and press releases and on the nurturing of traditional print or broadcast media relations. These channels are controllable and allow a message to be broadcast uninterruptedly, but they do not always match citizens' media use and consumption habits, or their actual information needs. However, in the citizen's world, alongside owned media (such as websites and physical formats), earned media (such as messages via press releases and pitching to journalists), and paid media (such as advertising and public service broadcasts), there are also in fact several other forms of media. These include searched media (such as questions to which citizens seek answers via search engines), shared media (content that citizens share with one another), hacked media (such as hijacked hashtags for campaigns that do not resonate with citizens' experiences), and – the most recently developed form – mined media (such as data that have been collected from several sources with a view to answering complex questions). To give a practical example of this gap, boat-owning citizens who hold a permit to moor their vessels may find it difficult to understand why the city authorities do not approach them via Facebook or email when their transaction has not been processed and their permit runs the risk of expiring, but instead post a paper warning on the vessel itself. The practices of public sector communication suggested in this book seek to interact with citizens where they prefer to be.

Although these gaps may not comprehensively address all the challenges that citizens perceive in relation to public administration or those which public administrators perceive in relation to communication with citizens, they appear to be among the most dominant challenges on a global level. They are the gaps that we attempt to address in this book through adopting a citizen-centered approach to public sector communication.

1.2 Framework for the Book

To set the framework for the book, we next explore existing knowledge on public sector communication and the different fields contributing to its development.

1.2.1 What Has Been Done on Public Sector Communication?

1.2.1.1 Earliest Works

The earliest sources that we could find regarding public sector communication go back to a book chapter by McCamy published in 1939 (McCamy, 1939). Framing his chapter on the notion of public relations (its title is "Public Relations in Public Administration"), he focuses on the external communications undertaken by public administrations. Years later, in 1957, based on the assumption that administration is essentially a form of decision making that can be viewed in terms of communication phenomena, Dorsey (Dorsey Jr., 1957) provided a model to analyze administrative communication. But here the word "administration" is broadly understood as the processes of decision making, and its use is not necessarily confined to political contexts and settings. A similar approach was adopted by Redfield (*Communication in Management: The Theory and Practice of Administrative Communication*) in 1953 (Redfield, 1958) and by Thayer (*Administrative Communication*) in 1961 (Thayer, 1961). The first work to be more fully focused on public sector communication was the volume published in 1965 by Highsaw and Bowen (1965), which is entitled *Communication in Public Administration*.

1.2.1.2 Little Development despite the Relevance of the Topic

On the whole, research on public sector communication is still limited in terms of quantity. Despite the key role that communication plays in the provision of public services and goods, it has not yet been fully analyzed, and more research is needed to address the challenge that public sector organizations face globally to reach citizens, engage them in administrative processes, and maintain their trust (Grunig, 1992; Garnett, Marlowe, and Pandey, 2008; Glenny, 2008; Bourgon, 2009; Lee, Fairhurst, and Wesley, 2009; Lee, 2010; Gelders and Ihlen, 2010a; Strömbäck and Kiousis, 2011; Wæraas and Byrkjeflot, 2012; Sanders and Canel, 2013; Valentini, 2013; Luoma-aho and Makikangas, 2014; Bowden et al., 2016).

1.2.1.3 Nomenclature

The expression "public sector communication" has to date seldom been used, and until 1992, no book had dealt specifically with the topic by that name (Graber, 1992). Very few scholars or works use this expression to refer precisely to what we describe in this book. Nevertheless, various authors have discussed aspects of what we would define as "public sector communication." In Table 1.1, we have compiled different expressions used by scholars to refer directly or indirectly to communication emanating from the public sector. We have sorted them into three main levels: government, public administration, and public sector.

Overall, the longest list of works falls under the term "government communication." Under the level of "government," few studies refer to government information management or to government public relations, and there is also only one term ("government reputation") that deals specifically with intangible assets.

The term "public administration" is very scarcely used to refer to the topic that we discuss in this book, and there has not yet been a book whose title incorporates the term "public administration communication." There are some studies on communication and public administration (most of which are from the mid-twentieth century). However, "administrative communication," which was coined by Garnett (see for instance Garnett and Kouzmin, 1997 and Garnett, 1997), is a well-established term, and it has been used in the most systematic and extensive studies on communication beyond the unit of government. Interestingly, there has been no study explicitly on "public relations in public administration" since McCamy's initial volume.

Finally, the broader label of "public sector" has been used in conjunction with "reputation" (Luoma-aho, 2008; Luoma-aho and Canel, 2016), "branding" (Wæraas, 2008, p. 205), "public relations" (Valentini, 2013), "communication management" (Gelders et al., 2007), and "mediatization" (Lee, 1999; Schillemans, 2012; Thorbjornsrud et al., 2014; Fredriksson, Schillemans, and Pallas, 2015). The term "public sector communication" has only been used by Graber (1992), Pandey and Garnett (2006), Glenny (2008), and Canel and Luoma-aho (2015).

1.2.1.4 Mapping Contributions from Different Fields to the Study of Public Sector Communication

We will now provide a brief review of the scholarly contributions to public sector communication from the fields of government communication, public relations, corporate communication, and public administration studies.

As already mentioned, the major scholarship at the level of government that is related to public sector communication uses the label "government communication." The most up-to-date and systematic analysis of government communication is the volume edited by Sanders and Canel (2013). This work, which draws comparisons between different countries, identifies common trends, issues, and challenges of government communication worldwide, and it concludes that government communication depends on the surrounding society. In a later piece of cross-disciplinary comparative research, Canel and Sanders conclude that while political communication research has quite rightly highlighted the political purposes of government communication, concepts offered by other research disciplines complement this view by suggesting avenues of study directed at what they see as the *civic* purposes of government communication: "Building long-term relationships, mutual understanding and citizen engagement become part of what

Table 1.1 Nomenclature used by authors who focus on topics related to public sector communication.

Government					
Government information management/provision	Government communication	Government public relations	Political public relations	Government policy communication	Government reputation
Édes, 2000 Gelders, 2005	Heise, 1985 Garnett, 1992, 1997 Gregory, 2006 Vos, 2006 Fairbanks, Plowman, and Rawlins, 2007 Glenny, 2008 Vos and Westerhoudt, 2008 Howlett, 2009 Gelders and Ihlen, 2010a, 2010b Liu et al., 2012 Canel and Sanders, 2012, 2015 Heinze, Schneider, and Ferié, 2013 Ponce, 2013 Sanders and Canel, 2013 Laursen and Valentini, 2014	Grunig and Jaatinen, 1999 Lee, 2001, 2007, 2009a Motschall and Cao, 2002 Sanders, 2011 Hong et al., 2012	Froehlich and Rüdiger, 2006 Strömbäck and Kiousis, 2011	Gelders and Ihlen, 2010a Gelders and Ihlen, 2010b	Da Silva and Batista, 2007
Public administration and management		**Government news management management** Pfetsch, 2008			
Communication and public administration Dorsey Jr., 1957 Highshaw and Bowen, 1965 Bacharach and Aiken, 1977 Garnett, Marlowe, and Pandey, 2008 Canel, 2014	**Public agency communication**	**Public relations in public administration** McCamy, 1939 Lee, 1999, 2002, 2009b	**Administrative communication** Thayer, 1961 Garnett and Kouzmin, 1997 Garnett, 1997, 2009	**Public institutions communication** Canel, 2007	
	Avery et al., 2009 Avery, Lariscy, and Sohn, 2009				
Public sector	**Public sector branding** Wæraas, 2008	**Public sector public relations** Valentini, 2013	**Mediatization of the public sector** Schillemans, 2012 Fredriksson et al., 2015 Thorbjornsrud, Figenschou, and Ihlen, 2014	**Communication management in the public sector** Gelders et al., 2007 Gelders, Bouckaert, and van Ruler, 2007	**Public sector communication** Graber, 1992 Pandey and Garnett, 2006 Glenny, 2008 Canel and Luoma-aho, 2015
Public sector reputation Luoma-aho, 2008 Luoma-aho and Canel, 2016 Wæraas and Maor, 2015					

is understood to be government communication and understanding how they are helped and hindered then becomes part of the research agenda" (2014, p. 101).

This cross-disciplinary approach has been used to put forward and explore the notion of professionalism in the context of government communication, an undertaking that has revealed diverse understandings according to country and theory perspectives (Sanders et al., 2011; Sanders and Canel, 2013; Canel and Sanders, 2014). This line of research reveals that a systemic approach to political communication (which emphasizes systems and power) should incorporate a public relations approach (which throws the spotlight on practice, values, and occupational legitimacy) in examining professionalism as an institutional process and as a dynamic "community of practice." One major conclusion in this regard is that the professionalization of government communication involves an increase in both strategic and civic capacities (Canel and Sanders, 2014), a finding that introduces new (albeit contested) ways of looking at communication undertaken by governments and that is helpful for addressing critical issues in public sector communication.

The fields of public relations and corporate communication have provided studies that deserve inclusion here. Hong et al. (2012) focus on the segmentation of the general public for the purpose of conducting government public relations; Gelders and Ihlen (2010b) provide a "gap analysis" framework to analyze possible gaps between governments and citizens in communicating public policies; and Liu and Horsley (2007) propose a model for analyzing the relationship between governments and publics that has subsequently been applied to compare government and corporate communication practices (Horsley, Liu, and Levenshus, 2010; Liu, Horsley, and Yang 2012). Canel and Sanders (2014) point out that in an attempt to identify and establish professional standards, public relations research tends to stress the effective practice of communication, seeking out precise and tangible measures of internal efficiency and external effectiveness. For example, Gregory (2006) provides a competencies framework for government communicators that is designed to improve performance and the functional consistency of communication across a given government; Pandey and Garnett (2006) have tested a model for measuring public sector communication performance; Luoma-aho (2007) has developed a barometer for public sector stakeholder experiences and reputation; and Vos (2006) has designed a model to measure the efficiency of government communication and, together with Westerhoudt, has applied it to the Netherlands to establish the current state of the practice of government communication (Vos and Westerhoudt, 2008). Krey (2000), Hong (2013), and Lee (2007), meanwhile, have elaborated on the tools to improve the practice of government public relations.

In the field of public administration studies, the most prolific author who takes a communication-oriented approach to the public sector is James L. Garnett. In 1992, he published *Communicating for Results in Government: A Strategic Approach for Public Managers*, a highly systematic work that features many useful insights into both prescriptive and descriptive accounts of communication emanating from US public agencies (Garnett, 1992). Together with Kouzmin, Garnett edited the *Handbook of Administrative Communication* (Garnett and Kouzmin, 1997), the first and to date only work of its kind. It is a thorough, multidisciplinary, and inspiring handbook that encompasses organizational and public management theory and practice in its exploration of the field of public management communication research, and it examines specific communication issues in specialized arenas.

Building on a previous volume entitled *Public Sector Communication* (Garnett, 1992), *The Power of Communication: Managing Information in Public Organizations* (Graber, 2003) is one of the few systematic and comprehensive analyses of communication in the public sector. It focuses on information management in US government agencies by analyzing the nature of information flows and communication problems. This work combines both scholarly perspectives (grounded principally in approaches to organizational behavior and decision making from the fields of sociology, communication, and political science) and practical aspects of communication in public agencies to analyze the structure of communications networks within public agencies from a system-communication-flow perspective, in order to explain how research findings can help government officials meet the challenges that they face.

To the extent that public sector organizations and public services are principally led by politicians within an increasingly mediated environment, political communication research helps to address different political constraints on public sector communication. Some scholars try to establish boundaries between political/propaganda communication and the more apolitical/nonpartisan communication undertaken by civil servants when providing public services (Glenny, 2008; Gelders and Ihlen, 2010a). Looking at the communication undertaken by civil servants in Australia, Glenny (2008) distinguishes communication activities that serve the purpose of governing of the nation from those which promote a political party and/or politician in order to win electoral support. A related issue is that of how citizens ought to be included in public sector communication. In relation to this question, an analysis by Heinze, Schneider, and Ferie (2013) of the use of direct communication instruments by German governments, in which they note that most research centers on the exchange between mass media and government without systematically including citizens, also contains a call for a form of communication that helps to foster a greater proximity to citizens.

In our view, such a call has to be complemented by Waymer's warning that one must take into account the fact that there are segments of the public, and particularly segments of the government's audience, who have no desire for a relationship. Based on this observation, Waymer argues for a broader understanding of what democratic public relations comprise (Waymer, 2013). It is a suggestion that we believe should be taken into account with regard to public sector communication research in order to refine the interactions that civil servants should aim to bring about in relation to the publics that they serve. The audience that this present book takes into consideration includes not just those who are able to engage in perfectly rational deliberation but rather encompasses all public sector stakeholders and end users of public services, regardless of whether or not they are willing to be involved in public discussion. In this regard, contributions such as that of Simmons (2014) or the book coedited by Falconi et al. (2014) on how to manage stakeholder relationships provide information on best practices for public sector organizations in implementing a continued, integrated, multichannel, and multistakeholder reporting activity in order to foster a culture of listening.

A final theme that we consider to be of key importance for the field of communication research is organizations' management of intangibility – that is, the immaterial aspects that enable an organization to function, such as its reputation. The building up, management, and measurement of intangible assets, as well as the role that communication plays in them, are issues that appear to offer new perspectives for public sector communication research. One of the core arguments of this book is that they open up new opportunities to close gaps between public organizations and citizens.

1.2.2 The Three Pillars of this Book

In this book, we propose that communication is at the core of democracy and public sector operations, and we see communication as playing a crucial role in bridging gaps and in addressing the challenges and problems described above. The framework for this book is based on the three major aspects that make up our approach to public sector communication: the need to manage public sector intangibles, the need to combine theory with practice, and the need to see public sector organizations from an international perspective.

1.2.2.1 The Intangible Nature of Public Sector Management

This book argues that only by understanding the intangible assets apparent in relationships between citizens and public sector organizations can we begin to close existing gaps between the two sides of the relationship. In our view, intangible assets hold the key to measuring future success for the public sector.

Nowadays, the productivity of organizations and institutions is increasingly built on intangible assets (Sztompka, 2000). Intangible capital can be understood as immaterial aspects that enable the organization to function. In addition to human capital, these include, among others, social capital, acquired knowledge and relationships, quality, trust, and reputation.

While in the private sector there is an increasing awareness and active discourse about the economic role of intangible assets and their consequences (Lev and Daum, 2004), the public sector remains slightly apprehensive about measuring them (Cinca, Molinaro, and Queiroz, 2003; Da Silva and Batista, 2007), and it was only recently that public sector organizations started to think about intangibles.

But this gap is a paradoxical one, since intangibility is even more important in public organizations than it is in profit-making ones (Cinca et al., 2003; Queiroz et al., 2005). Whereas quantifiable objectives are key within the private sector, dominated as it is by profitability and the generation of value for shareholders, public administrations work predominantly with nonmonetary aims and intangible resources. Rather than capital, machines, and raw materials, the public sector principally uses knowledge and human resources. And the outcomes of the public sector – public services – are closely linked to intangibility.

During the last 10 years, an emerging trend in governments from different countries has been to establish units to allocate functions related to intangibility management. For instance, some countries such as Kenya have introduced citizen engagement into their constitution. In the United States, there is an Office of Public Engagement, which was created by the Obama administration (https://www.whitehouse.gov/engage/office). The federal government of Canada has a similar office (http://www.ope.gov.nl.ca/office/contact.html), and an office for the intangible asset of corporate responsibility has been established by the government of the United Kingdom (https://www.gov.uk/government/consultations/corporate-responsibility).

To summarize previous research, it seems that the most developed intangible assets in the public sector are intellectual and social capital, followed by trust and reputation. Ours is the first book that provides a systematic account of the development of different intangible assets in the public sector. Importing the notion of intangible assets from the private sector to the public sector requires reconceptualization, classification, building, and evaluation of intangibility, and this is what we do in this book. Through this focus on intangible assets, we show how communication can create value for both public sector organizations and citizens by placing emphasis on relationships and strategic communication. By taking this approach, the book moves closer to the daily practice of public sector organizations and further away from political communication perspectives that are focused on image management, spin doctoring, and political campaigns.

1.2.2.2 Knowledge for Practice, Practice for Knowledge

This book has three aims. First, it provides academic readers with a comprehensive multidisciplinary map of concepts, theories, perspectives, and cases in order to navigate through this emerging field. Second, it provides students (undergraduate and graduate) with a textbook that systematizes and classifies knowledge, thus helping them to understand, from a communication perspective, the complexities involved in public sector management. Finally, the book also provides practitioners (for example, public sector managers, civil servants, and politicians) with deeper understanding and tools that may assist them in addressing the rapid changes that they face in reaching out to citizens and stakeholders and establishing realistic and feasible goals that do not lead to frustration.

The whole book is about combining theory with practice. The first part of this book charts what is already known about "public sector communication." The chapters in the second part of the book each introduce one specific intangible asset and specify why building the intangible asset in question might solve problems that cause gaps between public sector organizations and citizens. In the second part of the book, several practical examples or case studies are provided from different cultural settings. To make our research concrete, at the end of each chapter in the second part of the book, there is a route guide for building in practice the specific asset focused on in the chapter.

1.2.2.3 Considering Public Sector Communication from an International Perspective

This book embraces the international scope of public sector communication. It concentrates on Western democracies and OECD-type countries, which feature established public sectors. Practical cases have been selected from different cultural contexts and continents.

The challenges public sector organizations face seem to be globally similar. In this book, we identify and address these problems (including the key issue of plummeting trust in public sector organizations). We move away from a country-specific focus and adopt an approach that focuses on common problems and challenges.

Drawing on a review of the relevant literature and based on an analysis of actual practical cases, practices, and experiences, the book will elaborate theoretical profiles of different situations that practitioners might face. But unlike many academic volumes, we go beyond this to provide general guidelines for addressing these challenges on the general level.

1.2.3 Plan of the Book

In this first part of the book, we establish the central concepts and describe the changing operating environment of public sector organizations. We identify gaps and highlight the fragility of public sector organizations. Chapter 1 pinpoints the gaps that exist between public organizations and citizens. Chapter 2 explains what is so special about public sector communication, and what should be taken into account when importing concepts and practices regarding intangible assets from the private sector. Chapter 3 looks into what is making public sector organizations fragile. Finally, Chapter 4 introduces how public sector organizations can become more robust through "antifragile communication."

The second part of the book introduces the different intangible assets needed to close the gaps between citizens and public sector organizations. Each chapter refers to one intangible asset; these have been selected to meet existing needs. The chapters build on previous studies and practical cases within which the same issue has already been addressed somewhere in the world. The following intangible assets are addressed: satisfaction, organizational culture, reputation, legitimacy, intellectual capital, engagement, social capital, and trust. A final chapter serves as a summary of the suggestions made in the book to close the gaps.

As has already been mentioned, we combine our theoretical approach with a very practical one. We aim to answer questions on the practice of communication such as: How should public sector organizations consider and plan their communication? How should they establish relationships with their stakeholders? There is more than one answer to each of these questions throughout the book.

References

Andrews, R. (2012). Social capital and public service performance: a review of the evidence. *Public Policy and Administration* **27** (1): 49–67.

Avery, E.J., Lariscy, R.W., and Sohn, Y. (2009). Public information officers' and journalists' perceived barriers to providing quality health information. *Health Communication* **24** (4): 327–336.

Bacharach, S.B. and Aiken, M. (1977). Communication in administrative bureaucracies. *Academy of Management Journal* **20** (3): 365–377.

Bourgon, J. (2009). New directions in public administration: serving beyond the predictable. *Public Policy and Administration* **24** (3): 309–330.

Bourgon, J. (2011). *A New Synthesis of Public Administration: Serving in the 21st Century*. Washington, DC: McGill Queen's University Press.

Bowden, L.-H., Jana, V.L., and Naumann, K. (2016). Developing a spectrum of positive to negative citizen engagement. In: *Customer Engagement Contemporary Issues and Challenges*, 1st ed. (ed. R.J. Brodie, L. Hollebeek and J. Conduit), 257–277. London: Routledge.

Canel, M.-J. (2007). *Comunicación de las Instituciones Públicas*. Madrid: Tecnos.

Canel, M.-J. (2014). Reflexiones sobre la reputación ideal de la administración pública. In: *Escribir En Las Almas. Estudios En Honor de Rafael Alvira* (ed. M. Herrero, A. Cruz, R. Lázaro and A. Martínez), 69–88. Pamplona: Eiunsa.

Canel, M.-J. and Luoma-aho, V. (2015). Building intangible assets in the public sector: an introduction. Paper Presented at the Annual Convention of the International Communication Association, Puerto Rico (21–25 May 2015).

Canel, M.-J. and Sanders, K. (2012). Government communication: an emerging field in political communication research. In: *Handbook of Political Communication*, vol. 23 (ed. H.A. Semetko and M. Scammel), 85–96. London: Sage.

Canel, M.-J. and Sanders, K. (2014). Is it enough to be strategic? Comparing and defining professional government communication across disciplinary fields and between countries. In: *Comparing Political Communication across Time and Space: New Studies in an Emerging Field* (ed. M.J. Canel and K. Voltmer), 98–116. London: Palgrave.

Canel, M.-J. and Sanders, K. (2015). Government communication. In: *The International Encyclopedia of Political Communication*, 3 Volume Set, vol. 1 (ed. G. Mazzoleni, K. Barnhurst, K. Ikeda et al.). Boston: Wiley-Blackwell.

Castells, M. (2009). *Communication Power*. Oxford: Oxford University Press.

Chen, Z. and Lurie, N. (2013). Temporal contiguity and negativity bias in the impact of online word of mouth. *Journal of Marketing Research* **50** (4): 463–476.

Cinca, C.S., Callén, Y.F., and Molinaro, C.M. (2003). An approach to the measurement of intangible assets in dot com. *The International Journal of Digital Accounting Research* **3** (5): 1–32.

Dorsey, J.T. Jr. (1957). A communication model for administration. *Administrative Science Quarterly* **2** (3): 307–324.

Édes, B.W. (2000). The role of government information officers. *Journal of Government Information* **27** (4): 455–469.

Fairbanks, J., Plowman, K.D., and Rawlins, B.L. (2007). Transparency in government communication. *Journal of Public Affairs* **7** (1): 23–37.

Falconi, T., Grunig, J.E., Zugaro, E.G., and Duarte, J. (2014). *Global Stakeholder Relationships Governance: An Infrastructure*. New York, NY: Palgrave Macmillan.

Frandsen, F. and Johansen, W. (2010). Crisis communication, complexity and the cartoon affair: a case study. In: *The Handbook of Crisis Communication*, 1st ed. (ed. T. Coombs and S.J. Holladay), 425–448. Wiley-Blackwell.

Fredriksson, M., Schillemans, T., and Pallas, J. (2015). Determinants of organizational mediatization: an analysis of the adaptation of Swedish government agencies to news media. *Public Administration* **93** (4): 1049–1067.

Froehlich, R. and Rüdiger, B. (2006). Framing political public relations: measuring success of political communication strategies in Germany. *Public Relations Review* **32** (1): 18–25.

Garnett, J.L. (1992). *Communicating for Results in Government. A Strategic Approach for Public Managers*. San Francisco: Jossey-Bass.

Garnett, J.L. (1997). Administrative communication: domain, threats, and legitimacy. In: *Handbook of Administrative Communication*, Public Administration and Public Policy, 63, 1–20. Marcel Dekker.

Garnett, J.L. (2009). Administrative communication (or how to make all the rest work): the concept of its professional centrality. In: *Public Administration: Concepts and Cases*, 242–256. Boston: Wadsworth.

Garnett, J.L. and Kouzmin, A. ed. (1997). *Handbook of Administrative Communication*. New York: Marcel Dekker.

Garnett, J.L., Marlowe, J., and Pandey, S.K. (2008). Penetrating the performance predicament: communication as a mediator or moderator of organizational culture's impact on public organizational performance. *Public Administration Review* **68** (2): 266–281.

Gelders, D. (2005). Public information provision about policy intentions: the Dutch and Belgian experience. *Government Information Quarterly* **22** (1): 75–95.

Gelders, D. and Ihlen, Ø. (2010a). Government communication about potential policies: public relations, propaganda or both? *Public Relations Review* **36** (1): 59–62.

Gelders, D. and Ihlen, Ø. (2010b). Minding the gap: applying a service marketing model into government policy communications. *Government Information Quarterly* **27** (1): 34–40.

Gelders, D., Bouckaert, G., and van Ruler, B. (2007). Communication management in the public sector: consequences for public communication about policy intentions. *Government Information Quarterly* **24** (2): 326–337.

Glenny, L. (2008). Perspectives of communication in the Australian public sector. *Journal of Communication Management* **12** (2): 152–168.

Graber, D.A. (1992). *Public Sector Communication: How Organizations Manage Information*. Washington, DC: CQ Press.

Graber, D.A. (2003). *The Power of Communication: Managing Information in Public Organizations*. Washington, DC: CQ Press.

Gregory, A. (2006). A development framework for government communicators. *Journal of Communication Management* **10** (2): 197–210.

Grunig, J.E. (1992). *Excellence in Public Relations and Communication Management*. Abingdon, UK: Routledge.

Grunig, J. and Jaatinen, M. (1999). Strategic, symmetrical public relations in government: from pluralism to societal corporatism. *Journal of Communication Management* **3** (3): 218–234.

Heinze, J., Schneider, H., and Ferié, F. (2013). Mapping the consumption of government communication: a qualitative study in Germany. *Journal of Public Affairs* **13** (4): 370–383.

Heise, J.A. (1985). Toward closing the confidence gap: an alternative approach to communication between public and government. *Public Administration Quarterly* **9** (2): 196–217.

Higgs, M. and Rowland, D. (2005). All changes great and small: exploring approaches to change and its leadership. *Journal of Change Management* **5** (2): 121–151.

Highsaw, R.B. and Bowen, D.L. (1965). *Communication in Public Administration*. Bureau of Public Administration, University of Alabama.

Hong, H. (2013). Government websites and social media's influence on government–public relationships. *Public Relations Review* **39** (4): 346–356.

Hong, H., Park, H., Lee, Y., and Park, J. (2012). Public segmentation and government–public relationship building: a cluster analysis of publics in the United States and 19 European countries. *Journal of Public Relations Research* **24** (1): 37–68.

Horsley, J.S., Liu, B.F., and Levenshus, A.B. (2010). Comparisons of U.S. government communication practices: expanding the government communication decision wheel. *Communication Theory* **20** (3): 269–295.

Howlett, M. (2009). Government communication as a policy tool: a framework for analysis. *Canadian Political Science Review* **3** (2): 23–37.

Johnson, P., Wood, G., Brewster, C., and Brookes, M. (2009). The rise of post-bureaucracy: theorists' fancy or organizational praxis? *International Sociology* **24** (1): 37–61.

Krey, D. (2000). *Delivering the Message: A Resource Guide for Public Information Officials*. Sacramento, CA: California Association of Public Information Officials.

Kuipers, B.S., Higgs, M., Kickert, W. et al. (2014). The management of change in public organizations: a literature review. *Public Administration* **92** (1): 1–20.

Laursen, B. and Valentini, C. (2014). Mediatization and government communication: press work in the European Parliament. *The International Journal of Press/Politics* **20** (1): 26–44.

Lee, M. (1999). Public relations in public administration: a disappearing act in public administration education. *Public Relations Review* 24 (4): 509–520.

Lee, M. (2001). The image of the government flack: movie depictions of public relations in public administration. *Public Relations Review* 27 (3): 297–315.

Lee, M. (2002). Intersectoral differences in public affairs: the duty of public reporting in public administration. *Journal of Public Affairs* 2 (2): 33–43.

Lee, M. (2007). *Government Public Relations: A Reader*. Washington, DC: CRC Press.

Lee, M. (2009a). Origins of the epithet 'government by public relations': Revisiting Bruce Catton's *War Lords of Washington*, 1948. *Public Relations Review* 35 (4): 388–394.

Lee, M. (2009b). The return of public relations to the public administration curriculum? *Journal of Public Affairs Education* 15 (4): 515–533.

Lee, M. (2010). Government public relations during Herbert Hoover's presidency. *Public Relations Review* 36 (1): 56–58.

Lee, M.-Y., Fairhurst, A., and Wesley, S. (2009). Corporate social responsibility: a review of the top 100 US retailers. *Corporate Reputation Review* 12: 140–158.

Lev, B. and Daum, J.H. (2004). The dominance of intangible assets: consequences for enterprise management and corporate reporting. *Measuring Business Excellence* 8 (1): 6–17.

Liu, B.F. and Horsley, J.S. (2007). The government communication decision wheel: toward a public relations model for the public sector. *Journal of Public Relations Research* 19 (4): 377–393.

Liu, B.F., Horsley, J.S., and Yang, K. (2012). Overcoming negative media coverage: does government communication matter? *Journal of Public Administration Research and Theory* 22 (3): 597–621.

Luoma-aho, V. (2007). Reputation formation of innovations. *Innovation Journalism* 4 (2).

Luoma-aho, V. (2008). Sector reputation and public organisations. *International Journal of Public Sector Management* 21 (5): 446–467.

Luoma-aho, V. and Canel, M.J. (2016). Public sector reputation. In: *Sage Encyclopedia of Corporate Reputation* (ed. C. Carroll), 597–600. Sage Publications.

Luoma-aho, V. and Makikangas, M. (2014). Do public sector mergers (re)shape reputation? *International Journal of Public Sector Management* 27 (1): 39–52.

Luoma-aho, V. and Paloviita, A. (2010). Actor-networking stakeholder theory for today's corporate communications. *Corporate Communications: An International Journal* 15 (1): 49–67.

McCamy, J.L. (1939). Public relations in public administration. In: *Current Issues in Library Administration* (ed. C.B. Joeckel), 31–39. Chicago, IL: Chicago University Press.

Motschall, M. and Cao, L. (2002). An analysis of the public relations role of the police public information officer. *Police Quarterly* 5 (2): 152–180.

Pandey, S.K. and Garnett, J.L. (2006). Exploring public sector communication performance: testing a model and drawing implications. *Public Administration Review* 66 (1): 37–51.

Pekkarinen, S., Hennala, L., Harmaakorpi, V., and Tura, T. (2011). Clashes as potential for innovation in public service sector reform. *International Journal of Public Sector Communication Management* 24 (6): 507–532.

Pfetsch, B. (2008). Government news management: institutional approaches and strategies in three Western democracies reconsidered. In: *The Politics of News the News of Politics* (ed. D. Graber, D. McQuail and P. Norris), 71–97. Washington, DC: CQ Press.

Pollit, C. and Bouckaert, G. (2011). *Public Management Reform*. Oxford: Oxford University Press.

Ponce, M. (2013). Reglas del juego y comunicación de gobierno: propuesta de un nuevo marco analítico. *Contratexto* (21): 43–62.

Queiroz, A.B., Callén, Y.F., and Cinca, C.S. (2005). Reflexiones en torno a la aplicación del capital intelectual en el sector público. *Spanish Journal of Finance and Accounting/ Revista Española de Financiación y Contabilidad* **34** (124): 211–245.

Redfield, C.E. (1958). *Communication in Management: The Theory and Practice of Administrative Communication*. Chicago, IL: University of Chicago Press.

Rothstein, B. (2001). Social capital in the social democratic welfare state. *Politics and Society* **29** (2): 207–241.

Sanders, K. (2011). Political public relations and government communication. In: *Political Public Relations: Principles and Applications* (ed. J. Strömbäck and S. Kiousis), 254–273. London and New York: Routledge.

Sanders, K. and Canel, M.-J. ed. (2013). *Government Communication Cases and Challenges*. London: Bloomsbury Academic.

Sanders, K., Canel, M.J., and Holtz-Bacha, C. (2011). Communicating governments: a three-country comparison of how governments communicate with citizens. *The International Journal of Press/Politics* **16** (4): 523–547.

Schillemans, T. (2012). *Mediatization of Public Services: How Organizations Adapt to News Media*. Frankfurt: Peter Lang.

da Silva, R. and Batista, L. (2007). Boosting government reputation through CRM. *International Journal of Public Sector Management* **20** (7): 588–607.

Simmons, P. (2014). Challenges for communicators in future Australian local government. *Procedia-Social and Behavioral Sciences* **155**: 312–319.

Sloterdijk, P. (2011). *Bubbles, Spheres*. Cambridge, MA: MIT Press.

Strömbäck, J. and Kiousis, S. ed. (2011). *Political Public Relations: Principles and Applications*. Taylor & Francis.

Sztompka, P. (2000). Cultural trauma: the other face of social change. *European Journal of Social Theory* **3** (4): 449–466.

Tench, R., Vercic, D., Zerfass, A. et al. (2017). *Communication Excellence: How to Develop, Manage and Lead Exceptional Communications*. Cham, Switzerland: Palgrave Macmillan.

Thayer, L.O. (1961). *Administrative Communication*. Homewood, IL, R. D. Irwin.

Thijs, N. (2011). *Measure to Improve: Improving Public Sector Performance by using Citizen-User Satisfaction Information*. Brussels: EUPAN/EIPA.

Thijs, N. and Staes, P. (2008). *European Primer on Customer Satisfaction Management*. Brussels: EUPAN/EIPA.

Thomas, J.C. (2013). Citizen, customer, partner: rethinking the place of the public in public management. *Public Administration Review* **73** (6): 786–796.

Thorbjornsrud, K., Figenschou, T.U., and Ihlen, Ø. (2014). Mediatization in public bureaucracies: a typology. *Communications: The European Journal of Communication Research* **39** (1): 3–22.

Tirkkonen, P. and Luoma-aho, V. (2011). Online authority communication during an epidemic: a Finnish example. *Public Relations Review* **37** (2): 172–174.

Tirkkonen, P. and Luoma-aho, V. (2014). Authority crisis communication vs. discussion forums, swine flu. In: *Ethical Practice of Social Media in Public Relations*, 1st ed. (ed. M. DiStaso and D.S. Bortree), 192–204. Routledge.

Valentini, C. (2013). Public relations in the public sector. The role of strategic communication in the Italian public administration. *Sinergie Rivista Di Studi E Ricerche* 93–113.

Vertovec, S. (2007). Super-diversity and its implications. *Ethnic and Racial Studies* **30** (6): 1024–1054.

Vos, M. (2006). Setting the research agenda for governmental communication. *Journal of Communication Management* **10** (3): 250–258.

Vos, M. and Westerhoudt, E. (2008). Trends in government communication in The Netherlands. *Journal of Communication Management* **12** (1): 18–29.

Wæraas, A. (2008). Can public sector organizations be coherent corporate brands? *Marketing Theory* **8**: 205–221.

Wæraas, A. and Byrkjeflot, H. (2012). Public sector organizations and reputation management: five problems. *International Public Management Journal* **15** (2): 186–206.

Wæraas, A. and Maor, M. (2015). Understanding organizational reputation in a public sector context. In: *Organizational Reputation in the Public Sector*, 1–14. New York, NY: Routledge.

Waymer, D. (2013). Democracy and government public relations: expanding the scope of 'relationship' in public relations research. *Public Relations Review* **39** (4): 320–331.

Whicher, A. and Cawood, G. (2013). *An Overview of Service Design for the Private and Public Sectors*. Cardiff, Wales: SEE Network.

White, L. (2000). Changing the "whole system" in the public sector. *Journal of Organizational Change Management* **13** (2): 162–177.

2

What Is So Special about Public Sector Communication?

> *Public sector employees should always be thinking about the citizen*
> (From a citizen focus group)

This chapter clarifies what is meant by "public sector communication." Before providing a definition of this term, the meaning of "public" is discussed in order to identify what type of organizations fall under the remit of this book. We end this chapter by suggesting different contingencies, challenges, and opportunities related to the study and practice of public sector communication.

2.1   What Is the Public Sector?

2.1.1   Initial Basic Definitions

When it comes to making society work, "state bodies and authorities are just some of the actors; sometimes they are the most relevant and powerful ones and at others the least" (Thoenig, 2006, p. 250). We start by identifying three major ideas that basic definitions of "public sector" provided by dictionaries, encyclopedias, and public bodies refer to:

- *First, the idea of economic development*: "The part of an economy that is controlled by the state" (Oxford English Dictionary, 2015); "A portion of the economic system" (Whatis.com, 2015); "The part of the economy concerned with providing basic government services" (Investorwords, 2015); "The part of an economy that consists of state-owned institutions" (Collins English Dictionary, 2015).
- *Second, the idea of control*: "The area of the nation's affairs under governmental rather than private control" (Word Reference, 2015); "Controlled by the State" (Oxford English Dictionary, 2015); "State-owned institutions" (Collins English Dictionary, 2015). All these include the idea of state/government ownership and state/government control.
- *And finally, the idea of public purpose*: "The term 'public sector' refers broadly to the entities that exist and people employed for public purpose" (Public Sector Commission, 2014).

Public Sector Communication: Closing Gaps Between Citizens and Public Organizations, First Edition.
María-José Canel and Vilma Luoma-aho.
© 2019 John Wiley & Sons, Inc. Published 2019 by John Wiley & Sons, Inc.

Boundaries between the public and the private sector are blurring, and there is a growing debate among scholars about what criteria should be applied to disentangle the complex myriad of organizations and determine what belongs to the public sector. For an initial basic definition, we will say here that the public sector can be considered as comprising public organizations, owned and controlled by the government, at local, regional, national, and international levels. It supports all three arms of the government: the "executive" arm (the government), the "legislature" (parliament), and the "judiciary" (judges of various courts). To the extent that the public sector has to do with satisfying public needs, its core role is the provision of public services regarding common needs (i.e. for instance, mobility – public roads and public transit).

The public sector overlaps with the private sector in providing certain goods and services – for example, waste and water management, social and health care, and security services. Governments also usually outsource, hiring private corporations to provide goods and services for the public sector. Such a relationship can be found, for example, in the construction and maintenance of roads, freeways, bridges, parks, aircrafts, and so forth.

The spectrum of organizations that could be taken to be part of the public sector goes from core governmental departments (including ministries and public administrations) to companies that deliver services such as nationalized industries (for instance, in some countries railway transportation is provided by a public company) and public corporations (for instance, broadcasting corporations in some countries). Even other entities further away from the core such as quangos and executive agencies could also be regarded as part of the public sector.

2.1.2 Is This Public or Private?

Among scholars who focus on political science and public administration, there is a long debate about the weakness of definitions of publicness (Thoenig, 2006) and the blurring of boundaries between the private and public sectors (Bozeman and Bretschneider, 1994; Antonsen and Jørgensen, 1997; Boyne, 2002). In fact, different entities overlap in providing public services, and as a consequence, establishing a clear frontier between what is, for instance, publicly or privately controlled becomes a more complex task. The US Postal Service, for example, is owned by the US government but derives the overwhelming portion of its revenues from sale of its services to the public in a competitive setting (Meier and O'Toole, 2011, p. i284). This complexity in distinguishing the private sector from the public sector has increased as a result of the more unstable economic climate that has prevailed since 2008. For instance, private banks have increasingly been subjected to a greater level of political control (Meier and O'Toole, 2011, p. i284).

Our first step in examining this discussion is to note that the main conventional distinction between public and private organizations is their ownership: private firms are owned by entrepreneurs or stakeholders, and public agencies are collectively owned by members of political communities. Two further distinctions are linked to this initial one: public agencies are largely funded by taxation (rather than by fees paid directly by customers), and they are controlled by political forces and not by market ones (Boyne, 2002). The most commonly accepted criteria to define publicness include ownership, source of financial resources, and control (Perry and Rainey, 1988). Thoenig (2006) takes a broader approach and sets four traits for publicness: social impacts, policies legitimized by governmental authority, multiple and divergent indicators of success and failure, and nonspontaneous self-assessment.

What makes an organization more likely to respond to public needs? This is a question that is of interest to practitioners and scholars alike. Given that this book on public sector communication assumes that communication plays a crucial role in providing public services, we must clearly establish what we understand by "publicness."

2.1.3 Scholarly Approaches to Establishing Criteria of Publicness

Ultimately, all organizations are subject to influences on publicness and privateness, and they vary in the degree to which they are subject to each. Because the three criteria of ownership, resources, and control are not perfectly correlated and thus often create situations in which the public or private nature of a given organization is ambiguous, scholarly debate revolves around what has been referred to as the "public puzzle" (Bozeman and Bretschneider, 1994; see also Antonsen and Jørgensen, 1997; Moulton, 2009; Meier and O'Toole, 2011).

To solve the puzzle, Bozeman and Bretschneider (1994) have differentiated the core approach (which puts forward a categorical yes/no legal definition of what is public) from the dimensional approach (which takes publicness as a continuum and gradable variable). In 1987, Bozeman (1987) synthesized the three variables of ownership, resources, and control into what he called the "dimensional" model of publicness: instead of a categorical definition, both government agencies and private firms can be arrayed on the three dimensions of publicness. Applying Bozeman's dimensional approach, other scholars have introduced the "public purpose" criteria. Publicness is measured by the number and type of values both adhered to and instilled by public organizations. Antonsen and Jørgensen (1997), for example, take as a basis for their classification of organizations the degree to which the latter adhere to public sector values (for example, democratic accountability, production of collective goods, and compliance with due process). Consequently, what is important here is not the tasks performed but the values that employees of these organizations feel obligated to adhere to while undertaking those tasks.

Publicness is thus indicative of a process of public values as inputs that results in public values as outcomes (Antonsen and Jørgensen, 1997; Moulton, 2009; Meier and O'Toole, 2011). We take the view that communication enables values – which although unseen are expressed in opinions, attitudes, preferences, and choices (Meier and O'Toole, 2011) – to become manifest in organizations. As will be discussed in the second part of this book, the challenge of building intangible assets in the public sector has to do not only with tangible outcomes (for instance, mortality rates in hospitals) but also with the values subscribed to in the process of producing those outcomes (for example, the intangible democratic accountability of the process through which hospitals are regulated).

In 2011, Bozeman and Moulton (2011) suggested an "integrative publicness model" to combine empirical and normative considerations; the model "provides a field-level depiction of the empirical and normative publicness of policy environments that can be useful for long-range strategic planning to achieve public value outcomes" (Bozeman and Moulton, 2011, pp. 375–376).

In the introductory article to a 2011 *Journal of Public Administration Research* special issue on this topic, Walker and Bozeman identified the global financial crisis (they pinpoint the subprime mortgage crisis that would mutate into a global recession) as the cause of increasingly blurred boundaries between public policy making, public management, and business practice. At the time of writing, the publicness map of much of the world was, they argued, very different to that prior to the recession, and

> in the middle of 2010, patterns of publicness have changed in unanticipated ways as banks, the bastions of privateness, have been subjected to greatly increased external political control and publicness (Moulton, 2009). Institutions of private financial might have become reliant on tax dollars and new forms of regulation are being developed to restrain the "pure privateness" of unfettered markets.
>
> *(Walker and Bozeman, 2011, p. 1)*

How this new publicness affects and determines the conceptualization, analysis, and practice of communication and intangible assets is the concern of this book.

2.1.4 The Rings of Publicness

The Institute of Internal Auditors (2011) suggests that an organization belongs to the public sector if some of the following criteria are met:

- it delivers programs, goods, or services that can be considered a public good or that are established by government policy;
- substantially all of its funding is provided by government or determined by government policy;
- it is accountable to and reports directly to the government, including a government department or agency, or a minister of the government;
- it has a board of directors, commission, or similar appointed body, to which the government controls a majority of appointments;
- (for organizations with share capital) the government is the majority shareholder;
- its employees are members of the public service, are subject to public service rules, and receive public service benefits;
- overall, the government controls, directly or indirectly, the organization's policies, operations, administration, or service delivery;
- there is a legislative requirement for the organization to be audited by a government auditor or supreme audit organization.

Applying these criteria, organizations are arrayed within rings, with those exhibiting the most public character located at the core (Institute of Internal Auditors, 2011, p. 5). Organizations that clearly belong to the public sector (core government, agencies, and public enterprises) fall within the three central rings. Outside this central area, there is a gray zone, to which state businesses and public contractors belong.

2.1.5 The Publicness Fan

We describe the publicness of public sector organizations through a fan (see Figure 2.1) that shows a continuum of various degrees of publicness that are subject to change during the lifespan and morphosis of a given public sector organization. The fan

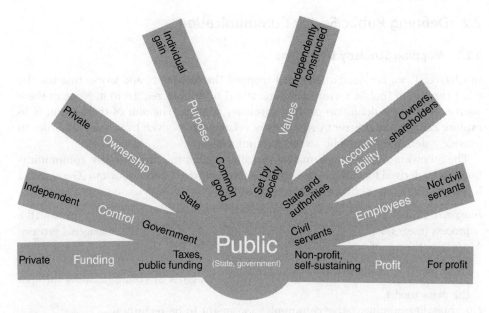

Figure 2.1 The publicness fan showing continuums of what is considered public in relation to different organizational characteristics.

structure implies that actors involved in a specific communication situation or action could have different degrees of publicness. The center of the fan represents the "purely" public organizations (that is, state or government ones; for instance, a ministry – a governmental institution – has the highest level of publicness in all variables), and the degree of publicness diminishes toward the outskirts of the fan.

We take the view that publicness consists of several variables. The first three of these are the classic variables already mentioned: funding, control, and ownership. We are aware that there is some overlap between these variables and the next three. For instance, "employees" (whether they are civil servants or not) could be taken as a feature that derives from "ownership"; "profit" (non- vs for-) relates to "funding"; and "accountability" is connected with the "control" that an organization submits to. Nevertheless, our publicness fan keeps these latter variables separate to give this tool the greatest possible analytical power. Finally, the variable "purpose" measures how oriented an organization and service are to the common good or conversely to individual gain, and the variable "values" measures to what extent the values that guide an organization are set by society as opposed to their being independently constructed.

This analytical tool allows us to set research questions such as the following:

- Are there differences in how an intangible asset is managed depending on the publicness level?
- Would it be possible to establish a type of intangible asset as the best fit for each type of publicness level/organization type?

We are aware that these questions are difficult to answer without data specifically collected for such a purpose, but in this book, we will use our case studies to explain the logic behind specific intangibles and how they match different organizations.

2.2 Defining Public Sector Communication

2.2.1 Mapping Scholarly Definitions

In Chapter 1, we provided a table that mapped the sources of and works that use the exact concept of "public sector communication" or notions related to it. None of these sources provides a definition of the expression as such. The aim of this section is to explore and analyze different definitions of related topics given by scholars in order to provide a definition of public sector communication.

The following somewhat normative variables related to administrative communication can be derived from the *Handbook of Administrative Communication* (Garnett and Kouzmin, 1997, pp. 3–6; see also Garnett, 1997):

Impact: communication that is to be considered of an administrative nature has impacts on the process (means) and/or goals (ends) of administration. It affects the managerial process.

Media use: the use of mass media should be included within the scope of administrative communication, recognizing that administrators in government, business, or non-profit organizations often pursue their managerial goals by communicating through the mass media.

Directionality: administrative communication ought to be reciprocal.

Boundedness: administrative communication supersedes organizational boundaries to include not only internal but also external communications.

Intentionality/purpose: administrative communication refers to acts intended to affect managerial processes and goals.

Utility: administrative communication must be constructive.

Although Garnett's focus in his handbook does not fully coincide with ours, his delimited variables are a helpful guide for processing the different scholarly contributions to defining the terms that are related to public sector communication. In this book, we highlight impact on the managerial process, directionality, and boundedness and intentionality.

Table 2.1 offers a compilation of the definitions provided by scholars. We have included authors who either provide a definition of a related term or at least the ideas from which a definition can be inferred.

There are not many definitions on which to build. Definitions come from different research areas (organizational studies, political communication, public relations, and organizational communication), with no one research area clearly predominating. Reflecting on Garnett's variables above:

Impact on the managerial process: only Graber (1992, 2003) and Howlett (2009) refer to the impact that communication might have on the managerial process, with both authors referring to communication as a function or tool that helps in achieving organizational goals.

Directionality: there are no explicit references to the directionality of communication, though implicit references to one direction could be taken in several definitions (see Froehlich and Rüdiger, 2006; Pfetsch, 2008). Similarly, implicit references to two-way communication can be found in other works (see Graber, 1992, 2003; Garnett, 1997; Canel, 2007; Lee, 2007; Strömbäck and Kiousis, 2011; Canel and Sanders, 2013).

No definition refers to boundaries, probably because the internal and external delimitations are no longer in use.

Table 2.1 Definitions of public sector communication and related terms.

Source	Concept/term	Definition	Area
Graber, 1992, 2003	Public sector communication	The use of symbols in public organizations to coordinate work in order to achieve goals (this definition is not provided by the author but has been elaborated based on Graber's text)	Public administration organizational studies
Garnett, 1997	Administrative communication	The communication undertaken by public organizations, which can be one way or two way; intentional or unintentional; and functional or dysfunctional in terms of impact on the management process (elaborated based on Garnett's text)	Organizational studies
Froehlich and Rüdiger, 2006, p. 90	Political public relations	The use of media outlets to communicate specific political *interpretations* of issues in the hope of garnering public support for political purposes	Political communication
Canel, 2007	Communication of public institutions	The transactional process of symbols exchange between public institutions and their stakeholders	Political communication and PR
Lee, 2007, p. 6	Government public relations	Managing different kinds of communication relationships with different kinds of publics	Public relations
Glenny, 2008	Communication in the public sector	The apolitical or nonpartisan communication activities of the executive arm of government (distinguished from the communication activities that serve the purpose of promoting a political party and/or politician in order to win electoral support)	Public relations
Pfetsch, 2008, p. 90	Government news management	A strategic variant of public information whereby governments manage communication in order to influence public opinion by controlling the news media agenda	Political communication
Howlett, 2009, p. 24	Government communication	Policy tool or instrument to give effect to policy goals and to influence and direct policy actions through the provision or withholding of information or knowledge from societal actors	Public relations
Strömbäck and Kiousis, 2011, p. 8	Political public relations	The management process by which an organization or individual actor for political purposes, through purposeful communication and action, seeks to influence and to establish, build, and maintain beneficial relationships and reputations with its key publics to help support its mission and achieve its goals	Political communication and PR
Canel and Sanders, 2013, 2014, 2015	Government communication	Communication directed and seeking to influence key publics, in the pursuit of both political and civic purposes, carried out by executive politicians and officials, usually in a managed way, to establish and maintain beneficial relationships to build reputation and to gain support from and interact with citizens, using the tools and strategies of PR and corporate communication	Political communication and PR

Purpose: almost all definitions refer either explicitly or implicitly to the purpose of communication, but in very different terms. Graber (2003), Lee (2007), and Howlett (2009) refer to purpose in terms of helping in the achievement of policy goals. Most definitions from the political communication research field refer to purpose explicitly, identifying it as a political one: influencing public opinion to gain or maintain power (see Froehlich and Rüdiger, 2006; Pfetsch, 2008). Only one definition refers to purpose explicitly in terms of the establishment of intangible assets (Strömbäck and Kiousis, 2011).

The only source entitled "public sector communication" is Graber's, and she does not provide a definition of the term as such. Rather, she deals separately with the two components of the expression. With regard to "communication," she draws on Lasswell's classic conceptualization of the communication process and the major elements included in it (sources, messages, channels, receivers, effects, and, added subsequently by scholars, feedback). Graber's work focuses on the relations between the message (words, gestures, and symbols) transmitted and the message received. Communication is the use of symbols to share information. When information becomes an organized body of thought it constitutes knowledge, which allows for a clear perception of a particular situation. Graber focuses more specifically on information and communication management as vital to the public sector. Garnett concludes wisely: "Our evolving understanding of communication in general and administrative communication in particular will produce evolving definitions of these phenomena" (Garnett, 1997, p. 3).

2.2.2 Some Insights from Practice

Before providing our definition of public sector communication, we feel that it is pertinent to mention that, in contrast to scholarly sources, professional practices seem to have been concerned with a definition. An online search for "public sector communication" returns quite a few sources that come from practice. There is an interesting contribution from New Zealand's government (2010, February) on the definition of public sector communication, in which a thorough and systematic approach is provided, including answers to all the variables suggested by Garnett. According to the New Zealand Government, public sector communication is

> a function that enables the effective flow of information and ideas between an agency and its internal and external publics, to facilitate participation, service delivery, and informed decision making, and to build accountability and trust in government. This is achieved by developing, delivering and evaluating public agency communications based on good practice communications techniques, supported by the principles of integrity and neutrality of the public service (The New Zealand Government, http://www.psnetwork.org.nz/).

Before we provide our official definition of public sector communication, we should comment that we are aware that in practice public sector communication still poses several challenges for many public sector organizations. With this in mind, we would suggest that a definition of how public sector communication practices really work at present might be: one-way, randomly issued messages and unemotional listings of facts that consecutively contain several difficult words as a result of unclear processes that reflect organizational challenges; such communications are sent out before employees are informed of political leaders' whims and ignore stakeholders' current needs; their purposes are to impress the local media, maintain the individual and organizational benefits achieved to date, and attempt to sound important.

In the process of collecting feedback and comments from practitioners for our definitions, one major Nordic ministry's chief communication officer replied, "I do not see that much humor in this definition. This summarizes the whole core challenge of our situation." This book attempts to move public sector communication beyond such tragedies and suggests that intangible assets management entails a strategic approach to communication that can help to address the problems involved in this "realistic" definition. With this pinch of realism in mind, we next move to our official definition of public sector communication.

2.2.3 Our Definition of Public Sector Communication

We understand public sector communication to be:

> *Goal-oriented communication inside organizations and between organizations and their stakeholders that enables public sector functions within their specific cultural and/or political settings, with the purpose of building and maintaining the public good and trust between citizens and authorities.*

Therefore:

- organizations are defined based on a wide, dimensional approach so that they include organizations owned and controlled by the state/government, plus any organization involved in the provision of public services;
- "public sector communication" is understood to be a broader term than "administrative communication," "government communication," or "government public relations";
- this definition entails a conceptualization of communication intrinsically linked to the creation of values, and it thus attributes to communication the role of helping values to be manifested;
- to the extent that we understand the public sector to be defined by the "amount" of publicness that each specific organization, situation, and activity could entail, we understand this definition to be open to the changing boundaries of the sectors that building intangible assets in practice might imply.

This definition depicts a multipurpose, multistakeholder, and multiorganizational public sector (one that is not confined purely to state organizations), and it is open to descriptive, prescriptive, and normative approaches.

2.3 Looking at Public Sector Communication from the Publicness Fan

2.3.1 Different Communication?

The question of whether there are differences between managing purely public organizations and purely private ones should now become the following: Does publicness make a difference in the way in which communication is managed? Following Walker and Bozeman's approach to cross-sector comparative analysis (Walker and Bozeman, 2011), the pertinent research questions regarding the analysis of communication could be put as follows: What are the specific constraints to which the public sector (as compared to the private sector) is subject with regard to communication and intangible assets management? What are the problems, challenges, and opportunities that comparisons between public and private sectors reveal?

The literature yields mixed results and offers contradictory views with regard to differences between the private and public sectors. Boyne (2002) contends that the two sectors are not fundamentally dissimilar in all important respects. In his empirical observation of the United Kingdom, he found only three differences: public organizations are more bureaucratic, public managers are less materialistic, and public managers have a weaker organizational commitment than their private sector counterparts. But Van der Wal et al. (2008) found that in the Netherlands, contrary to a body of literature that presupposes the intermixing of value systems, there are relevant differences despite the presence of common core values that have been shown to be crucial to both sectors (those commonly found are accountability, expertise, reliability, efficiency, and effectiveness): for employees from the private sector, the values of profitability, innovativeness, and honesty are most important, whereas for those from the public sector, values such as lawfulness, incorruptibility, and impartiality take priority.

Several scholars have focused on the differences in communication management by comparing both sectors (Grunig and Jaatinen, 1999; Lee, 2002; Gelders, Bouckaert, and van Ruler, 2007; Liu, Horsley, and Levenshus, 2010; Canel and Sanders, 2012; Carpenter and Krause, 2012; Wæraas and Byrkjeflot, 2012). Despite Grunig and Jaatinen's argument (1999) that the traditional models of public relations (primarily conceptualized for the private sector) are also valid for the public sector, most of the studies argue that there are relevant differences (Canel and Sanders, 2012; Sanders and Canel, 2013) and claim to elaborate public relations models that are better adapted to the public sector (Valentini, 2013).

Gelders et al. (2007) focus on the constraints and opportunities involved in managing public communication carried out by politicians in relation to policy intentions. They argue that government officials are confronted with four main constraints that are typical of the public sector but not of its private counterpart: a more complicated and unstable environment, additional legal and formal restrictions, more rigid procedures, and more diverse products and objectives. These constraints have implications for the practice of communication. For instance, ministers communicating policy intentions face specific communication issues such as intensive political and media interference and more rigid timing and budget constraints (Gelders et al., 2007, p. 326).

Liu et al.'s (2010) survey data from the United States found that there are differences between the public and private sectors in terms of budgets, political influence, communication frequency, public pressure, interaction with other organizations, media coverage frequency, media coverage evaluation, and the impact of legal frameworks. However, no significant differences were found with regard to the diversity of audiences, opportunities for professional development, participation in organizational leadership, and management support for communication. The literature's findings are therefore mixed, and of course differences can vary across country and time, meaning that analyses should be tailored on an ad hoc basis.

2.3.2 How Public Is This and Hence How Should Intangibles and Communication be Managed?

How does management of intangibles and communication change as publicness increases? In Table 2.2, we identify the constraints associated with each variable (grouped in logical, interrelated pairs) of the publicness fan that might have an impact on intangibles and communication management. In the second column, we list the implications that these lead to. The assumption is that they are two-sided implications,

Table 2.2 The implications of publicness on building intangibles and communication management.

	Constraint based on the amount of publicness	Implications: challenges and opportunities
Funding/ profit	More rigid budgets More formal procedures More risk averse Lower competition Challenging uniqueness	Emerging needs have to be satisfied without the required flexibility Reputation is perceived suspiciously Intangibles management is needed to address an overall negative prejudice The ideal reputation of the public sector needs to be rethought
Ownership/ employees	State ownership Bureaucratic structures Shorter time horizons Mishmash of permanent civil servants with political appointees	Positive connotations of the neutrality of the state need to be explored and taken advantage of Identity, brand promise, reputation, and communication aims have to be defined in a changing context Organizational culture programs are needed to align aims and increase pride in belonging New institutional arrangements to prevent public sector messages from partisanship need to be explored The paradox of better perceived public services provided by a more poorly perceived public administration has to be addressed from a communication perspective
Control/ accountability	Less decision-making autonomy Less flexibility to address changes More demanding transparency More rigid legal framework More public and media scrutiny	Innovative ways of implementing transparency Public organizations have to be prepared for deliberation on public policies in public fora Communication includes ongoing monitoring of citizens' expectations and perceptions of public performance
Purpose/ values	Multiple different goals that are more vaguely defined Multiple values Multiple stakeholders Heterogeneous markets Different products	Communication is needed to reconcile conflicting objectives Measures of intangible assets are needed to better calibrate the public value Ways of segmenting the message according to different public audiences are required Intangible assets management is needed for the challenge of message coordination

meaning that negative and problematic implications entail opportunities for intangibility management.

2.3.2.1 Funding and Profit

Publicness is gradable based on the places that organizations receive funding from and the profit that they aim for. To the extent that public sector organizations are not submitted to market forces and have fixed resources regardless of profit, the more public the organization, the less openness there is to competing in the market, to reducing costs, and to being concerned with consumer preferences (Boyne, 2002; Canel and Sanders, 2012). Moreover, the more public the organization, the more formal procedures for decision making become and thus the less flexible and more risk averse organizations become (Gelders et al., 2007).

The implications of these constraints on the building of intangibles and communication management can been discussed at different levels. First, at a structural level, public organizations have more rigid budgeting systems, with fewer margins for innovative communication approaches and practices. In fact, as a previous study shows, governments in most countries are still trapped with traditional advertising campaigns and not yet involved in intangible assets programs (Sanders and Canel, 2013). There are countries in which implementing a government reputation program would be perceived with suspicion as a poor investment of public resources.

Second, there are also problems concerning the negative perception that people have of the public sector, which is seen as in need of drastic reform and as too big and wasteful of the public funds that it receives (Wæraas and Byrkjeflot, 2012). Therefore, public sector communication has to overcome negative prejudices on a continuous basis.

The more public the organization, the more difficult it is to gain a competitive advantage that could help secure allocated funding. In building a competitive advantage, public organizations need to deal with the tension of combining the requirement to conform to the norms of their sector (and thus to be similar, but not so similar that they cannot be distinguished) with the requirement to be distinguished (and thus to be different, but not so different that they are expelled from the sector) (King and Whetten, 2008; Canel, 2014). As Wæraas and Byrkjeflot (2012) argue, for most people, public organizations probably seem more similar than unique, given the common traits of political, hierarchical, and rule-oriented entities. But at the same time, they struggle to communicate their differences and ultimately themselves in a conformity trap, unable to capitalize on their uniqueness.

This problem is associated with that of excellence building, as has been very cleverly analyzed by Wæraas and Byrkjeflot (2012, p. 200). Due to their common mission of serving the public good, public organizations need to share similar characteristics. But at the same time, they seek to establish excellent reputations, something which might imply competition within the sector and, probably, with organizations with the same ownership. This dynamic has led Luoma-aho to suggest that public organizations should aim (no more and no less) to have a "neutral" reputation, because of both contextual factors (the economic crisis makes it more difficult to permanently cultivate a high-cost excellent reputation) and structural ones (because of the lack of competition, there is no need to be distinguished: there is only one Ministry for Education). Such neutrality enables a critical operating distance (Luoma-aho, 2007, p. 124).

This issue taps into the debate about similarities and differences between reputation and legitimacy (Deephouse and Suchman, 2008; King and Whetten, 2008), a matter that is more complex in the context of the public sector, given the stronger expectations of similarity in services and quality, as well as the higher requirements of equity and solidarity that it is subject to (Wæraas and Byrkjeflot, 2012). In discussing the ideal reputation that a public administration should aim for, Canel (2014) has suggested exploring in more depth the value of state neutrality on the basis of the state's significance as representative of all citizens.

2.3.2.2 "Ownership" and "Employees"

At the most public extreme in the ownership variable of the publicness fan is the state. Although the state may be a stable entity, it nevertheless involves an unstable context due to changing political mandates and policies; the more public an organization is, the more its dynamics are subject to governmental term lengths, which are usually no longer than four years (Boyne, 2002; Canel, 2007).

This short termism has clear implications for building intangible assets and communication management. On the one hand, state ownership might imply what Wæraas and Byrkjeflot call the "charisma problem" (public entities must serve everyone and be for all citizens rather than choosing their followers). But on the other, there is an implicit opportunity here since, at the same time, the reputation of public organizations is bound up with the legitimacy of the state (Wæraas and Byrkjeflot, 2012). This is something that can be taken advantage of, as research has shown that positive connotations of statism help governmental messages to be more inclusive, neutral, and nonpartisan (Canel, 2007). Intangibles management should explore the positive connotations that the neutrality of the state can impress upon public sector messages.

State ownership is linked to a specific type of employees and, more specifically, the more public an organization is, the greater the extent to which communication is managed by two different types of people. There are, first of all, heads of communication in government ministries, agencies, and institutions who are political appointees and may have been assigned to their posts on the basis of partisan rather than professional criteria. Second, there are civil servants who belong to civil service bodies (in some countries such as the United Kingdom, there are specific civil service bodies for communication) that have specific criteria for recruitment, training, promotion, and the formulation of the values and principles that should prevail in government communication (Sanders and Canel, 2013). How the combination of these two types of employees operates in communication management has been widely discussed in the literature (Canel, 2007; Garnett, 2009; Sanders and Canel, 2013), and one of the critical issues revealed in cross-national analyses of governments' communication is the role that should be assigned to public administration bodies in government communication (Sanders and Canel, 2013).

Ownership also presents challenges for the management of organizational culture as an intangible asset. Gelders et al. (2007) point out that civil servants are subjected to a greater extent to penalties for violation of established procedures and receive fewer rewards and incentives than do employees in the private sector, something which has been measured in the case of the United States by Liu et al. (2010). As a result, employees become more focused on rules and processes than on results, outcomes, service provision, and end users, something which could be a cause of citizens' distrust, cynicism, and contempt (Wæraas and Byrkjeflot, 2012, pp. 186–187). Paradoxically, most people are quite satisfied with the services that they receive from the public sector, which demonstrates the image problem that public organizations have (Wæraas and Byrkjeflot, 2012). Again, here an important challenge is to manage the organizational culture asset to bridge gaps with citizens.

2.3.2.3 Control and Accountability

Public sector organizations have to operate within a more rigid legal framework. There are stronger hierarchies and lower levels of discretion in terms of personnel issues (due to inflexible rules on hiring, firing, and promotion and to less flexibility to address changes) (Gelders et al., 2007; Canel and Sanders, 2012; Wæraas and Byrkjeflot, 2012).

This circumstance has two conflicting implications with regard to communication. On the one hand, the greater the level of an organization's publicness, the more it is submitted to requirements for transparency (Canel and Sanders, 2012). This is a phenomenon that most democratic countries are going through, particularly with the approval of transparency and freedom of information laws (Sanders and Canel, 2013), and that might encourage public sector communicators to look for new and innovative ways of establishing relations with citizens. On the other hand, and precisely because of these laws, governments might ultimately become too rigid and, as Liu et al. (2010) argue, less able to communicate fully and openly. There are also statutory constraints and exceptions within the public sector regarding freedom of information – for example, civil servants' freedom of speech in relation to ongoing policy issues (Gelders et al., 2007, p. 331). According to Graber (2003, p. 247), these laws often hamper creativity and can also encourage government communicators to be too careful about how they document their strategic planning. Ultimately, it may be the case that public organizations do not release all information but simply adapt their communication to media and specific public information requests. Intangibles management is needed to allow innovative ways of implementing transparency.

Public sector organizations are also required to have a high degree of accountability to political and public constituencies at the two levels of the media and citizens. A basic duty is to report decisions and actions to the public via the media (Liu et al., 2010), and this is a relevant constraint that determines a communication strategy (timing, content of messages, information release, and so forth), and even policy measures and outcomes. Negative coverage might block a governmental program, and in searching for positive news, government communicators might end up being too technical, stiff, and unappealing in emotional terms. Gelders et al. (2007, p. 330) point out a further difference relative to the private sector with regard to accountability before the media: the deliberative process of public policies is more public than in the private sector, where it is an internal matter. But again, here there is an opportunity for intangible assets, since public organizations need to be prepared for deliberation on public policies in public fora, something to which strategies for the intangible asset of legitimacy contribute.

Finally, public organizations have to face the problem of continuous "societal" scrutiny, which very easily results in poor public perceptions, which, as Vos (2006) argues, can weaken the success of their communication. The public is often cynical about government communication however honest governmental messages might be (Liu and Horsley, 2007). And as a recent study has shown in relation to Spain, citizens become suspicious about governments' intentions when the latter professionalize their communication (Sanders and Canel, 2015). For communication performance to succeed, there seems to be a need for an ongoing monitoring of citizens' expectations and perceptions, something which is at the core of intangible assets management.

2.3.2.4 Purpose and Values

Pursuing the "public good" is one of the distinctive features of the public sector, whereas individual gain is the focus of corporations. But the meaning of "public good," which is usually phrased in terms of "serving citizens," "social purpose" (Liu et al., 2010), and so forth, is certainly vague. This vagueness is due, in part, to the politics involved in the public sector: public authorities have to be able to balance and reconcile conflicting objectives (Gelders et al., 2007).

Different purposes, aims, and goals go hand in hand with the existence of different and diverse sectors of the public, each of which places demands and constraints on managers. Furthermore, the requirements of the various external constituencies are likely to conflict with each other (for example, those of taxpayers relative to those of service recipients, or those of consumer groups relative to those of producer groups) (Gelders et al., 2007). Public sector organizations serve as legislators, officials, regulators, educators, and development and research centers, and as such they cannot always please all stakeholders (Luoma-aho, 2008). This constraint shapes communication management and, as Carpenter and Krause (2012) discuss, dictates that the public administrator, when speaking or presenting policies, should refrain from committing to a specific interpretation, from favoring one audience over another, and from committing forcibly to a future course of action (p. 29). However, this constraint also entails the challenge of developing new ways to subsequently segment the message.

If the public sector has to deal with different sectors and goals, it has also to deal with different products. As Gelders et al. (2007, p. 332) argue, the political product is complicated and intangible, in clear contrast with the homogeneous perception of product characteristics in consumer markets.

How many goals/values/sectors of the public/products there should be, what different dimensions they should have, how much each of them should weigh, and who is entitled to determine all of these criteria are critical issues that, under the perspective of "the public value," have received extensive attention (for example, Bozeman and Sarewitz, 2011; Meynhardt and Bartholomes, 2011; Bozeman and Johnson, 2015; Bryson, Crosby, and Bloomberg, 2015). In Chapter 3, we will examine this paradigm, and in Chapter 4, we will elaborate on the relations between public value and intangible assets. For now, however, it is sufficient to mention that making progress in the great challenge of finding the best formulae, methods, and techniques to measure intangible assets in the public sector would contribute to the development of the "public value" paradigm and hence better calibrate the value provided by public management.

The mixed nature of values in the public sector has implications for the management of reputation. One of these has to do with coordination. As Wæraas and Byrkjeflot (2012) point out, different elements and types of communication need to be united into one single expression of identity (p. 195). Doing so is particularly difficult since within a single public organization there might be different institutional structures intervening, and so communicators face the challenge of coordinating across different units in order to gain and keep the consistency of the message. Building intangible assets such as those of organizational culture, legitimacy, and intellectual capital might help in this challenge of message coordination.

We see in what has been called the "public service ethos" (Pratchett and Wingfield, 1996) a possibility for strengthening the implantation of intangible assets: as research has shown, public managers are believed to be less materialistic than their private counterparts, to have a stronger desire to serve the public (contrasting with the desire of private firms to meet the demands of individual customers), and to be driven by a strong sense of vocation and concern regarding the promotion of public welfare (Boyne, 2002). These seem to be well-consolidated values in public employees, and hence it is reasonable to end this chapter by stating that there is a great opportunity for the public sector to build on intangible assets to bridge gaps with citizens.

To conclude, this book:

1) examines, under the legal approach, organizations legally owned by government departments and public administrations;
2) takes, under the dimensional approach, publicness as a gradable variable that goes beyond governments and public administrations;
3) incorporates the "public purpose" criteria, including those organizations which subscribe to, infuse, and/or are inspired by public values to create intangible assets that are beneficial for both organizations and stakeholders;
4) elaborates analytical tools that are of use for the management and assessment of intangible assets in the public sector.

With these in mind, we next analyze the causes for fragility in public sector organizations.

References

Antonsen, M. and Jørgensen, T.B. (1997). The 'publicness' of public organizations. *Public Administration* **75** (2): 337–357.

Boyne, G.A. (2002). Public and private management: what's the difference? *Journal of Management Studies* **39** (1): 97–122.

Bozeman, B. (1987). *All Organizations are Public: Bridging Public and Private Organizational Theories*. San Francisco: Jossey-Bass.

Bozeman, B. and Bretschneider, S. (1994). The 'publicness puzzle' in organization theory: a test of alternative explanations of differences between public and private organizations. *Journal of Public Administration Research and Theory* **4** (2): 197–223.

Bozeman, B. and Johnson, J. (2015). The political economy of public values a case for the public sphere and progressive opportunity. *The American Review of Public Administration* **45** (1): 61–85.

Bozeman, B. and Moulton, S. (2011). Integrative publicness: a framework for public management strategy and performance. *Journal of Public Administration Research and Theory* **21** (suppl 3): i363–i380.

Bozeman, B. and Sarewitz, D. (2011). Public value mapping and science policy evaluation. *Minerva* **49** (1): 1–23.

Bryson, J.M., Crosby, B.C., and Bloomberg, L. (2015). Introduction. In: *Public Value and Public Administration* (ed. J.M. Bryson, B.C. Crosby and L. Bloomberg), xvii–xxvi. Washington, DC: Georgetown University Press.

Canel, M.J. (2007). *Comunicación de las Instituciones Públicas*. Madrid: Tecnos.

Canel, M.-J. (2014). Reflexiones sobre la reputación ideal de la administración pública. In: *Escribir En Las Almas. Estudios En Honor de Rafael Alvira* (ed. A.M. Herrero Cruz, R. Lázaro and A. Martínez), 69–88. Pamplona: Eiunsa.

Canel, M.-J. and Sanders, K. (2012). Government communication: an emerging field in political communication research. In: *Handbook of Political Communication*, vol. 23 (ed. H.A. Semetko and M. Scammel), 85–96. London: Sage.

Canel, M.-J. and Sanders, K. (2013). Introduction: mapping the field of government communication. In: *Government Communication: Cases and Challenges* (ed. K. Sanders and M.J. Canel), 1–26. London: Bloomsbury.

Canel, M.-J. and Sanders, K. (2014). Is it enough to be strategic? Comparing and defining professional government communication across disciplinary fields and between countries. In: *Comparing Political Communication across Time and Space: New Studies in an Emerging Field* (ed. M.J. Canel and K. Voltmer), 98–116. London: Palgrave.

Canel, M.-J. and Sanders, K. (2015). Government communication. In: *The International Encyclopedia of Political Communication*, 3 Volume Set, vol. 1 (ed. G. Mazzoleni, K. Barnhurst, K. Ikeda et al.), 1–8. Wiley-Blackwell.

Carpenter, D.P. and Krause, G.A. (2012). Reputation and public administration. *Public Administration Review* **72** (1): 26–32.

Collins English Dictionary (2015). *Collins English Dictionary*. HarperCollins Publishers https://www.collinsdictionary.com/dictionary/english/public-sector.

Deephouse, D.L. and Suchman, M. (2008). Legitimacy in organizational institutionalism. In: *The Sage Handbook of Organizational Institutionalism*, 49–77. London: Sage Publications.

Froehlich, R. and Rüdiger, B. (2006). Framing political public relations: measuring success of political communication strategies in Germany. *Public Relations Review* **32** (1): 18–25.

Garnett, J.L. (1997). Administrative communication: domains, threats, and legitimacy. In: *The Handbook of Administrative Communication* (ed. J.L. Garnett and A. Kouzmin), 3–20. New York: Marcel Dekker.

Garnett, J.L. (2009). Administrative communication (or how to make all the rest work): the concept of its professional centrality. In: *Public Administration: Concepts and cases*, 242–256. Boston: Wadsworth.

Garnett, J.L. and Kouzmin, A. (1997). *Handbook of Administrative Communication* (ed. J.L. Garnett and A. Kouzmin). New York: Marcel Dekker.

Gelders, D., Bouckaert, G., and van Ruler, B. (2007). Communication management in the public sector: consequences for public communication about policy intentions. *Government Information Quarterly* **24** (2): 326–337.

Glenny, L. (2008). Perspectives of communication in the Australian public sector. *Journal of Communication Management* **12** (2): 152–168.

Graber, D. (1992). *Public Sector Communication: How Organizations Manage Information*. Washington, DC: CQ Press.

Graber, D.A. (2003). *The Power of Communication: Managing Information in Public Organizations*. Washington, DC: CQ Press.

Grunig, J.E. and Jaatinen, M. (1999). Strategic, symmetrical public relations in government: from pluralism to societal corporatism. *Journal of Communication Management* **3** (3): 218–234.

Howlett, M. (2009). Government communication as a policy tool: a framework for analysis. *Canadian Political Science Review* **3** (2): 23–37.

Institute of Internal Auditors (2011). What is the public sector. https://na.theiia.org/standards-guidance/Public%20Documents/Public%20Sector%20Definition.pdf (accessed 29 September 2017).

InvestorWords (2015). Public sector. http://www.investorwords.com/3947/public_sector. html (accessed 29 September 2017).

King, B.G. and Whetten, D.A. (2008). Rethinking the relationship between reputation and legitimacy: a social actor conceptualization. *Corporate Reputation Review* **11** (3): 192–207.

Lee, M. (2002). Intersectoral differences in public affairs: the duty of public reporting in public administration. *Journal of Public Affairs* **2** (2): 33–43.

Lee, M. (2007). *Government Public Relations: A Reader*. Boca Ratón, FL: CRC Press.

Liu, B.F. and Horsley, J.S. (2007). The government communication decision wheel: toward a public relations model for the public sector. *Journal of Public Relations Research* **19** (4): 377–393.

Liu, B.F., Horsley, J.S., and Levenshus, A.B. (2010). Government and corporate communication practices: do the differences matter? *Journal of Applied Communication Research* **38** (2): 189–213.

Luoma-aho, V. (2007). Neutral reputation and public sector organizations. *Corporate Reputation Review* **10** (2): 124–143.

Luoma-aho, V. (2008). Sector reputation and public organisations. *International Journal of Public Sector Management* **21** (5): 446–467.

Meier, K.J. and O'Toole, L.J. (2011). Comparing public and private management: theoretical expectations. *Journal of Public Administration Research and Theory* **21** (suppl 3): i283–i299.

Meynhardt, T. and Bartholomes, S. (2011). (De)composing public value: in search of basic dimensions and common ground. *International Public Management Journal* **14** (3): 284–308.

Moulton, S. (2009). Putting together the publicness puzzle: a framework for realized publicness. *Public Administration Review* **69** (5): 889–900.

Oxford English Dictionary (2015). *Public Sector*. Clarendon Press.

Perry, J.L. and Rainey, H.G. (1988). The public-private distinction in organization theory: a critique and research strategy. *Academy of Management Review* **13** (2): 182–201.

Pfetsch, B. (2008). Government news management: institutional approaches and strategies in three Western democracies reconsidered. In: *The Politics of News the News of Politics* (ed. D. Graber, D. McQuail and P. Norris), 71–97. Washington, DC: CQ Press.

Pratchett, L. and Wingfield, M. (1996). The demise of the public service ethos. In: *Local Democracy and Local Government* (ed. L. Pratchett and D. Wilson), 106–126. London: Macmillan Education.

Public Sector Commission (2014). *Public Sector*. Public Sector Commission.

Sanders, K. and Canel, M.-J. ed. (2013). *Government Communication Cases and Challenges*. London: Bloomsbury Academic.

Sanders, K. and Canel, M.J. (2015). Mind the gap: local government communication strategies and Spanish citizens' perceptions of their cities. *Public Relations Review* **41** (5): 777–784.

Strömbäck, J. and Kiousis, S. (2011). *Political Public Relations: Principles and Applications*. New York: Routledge.

Thoenig, J.C. (2006). El rescate de la publicness en los estudios de la organizacion? *Gestion y Politica Publica* **15** (2): 229–258.

Valentini, C. (2013). Public relations in the public sector: the role of strategic communication in the Italian public administration. *Sinergie Rivista Di Studi E Ricerche* **92**: 93–113.

Van der Wal, Z., De Graaf, G., and Lasthuizen, K. (2008). What's valued most? Similarities and differences between the organizational values of the public and private sector. *Public Administration* **86** (2): 465–482.

Vos, M. (2006). Setting the research agenda for governmental communication. *Journal of Communication Management* **10** (3): 250–258.

Wæraas, A. and Byrkjeflot, H. (2012). Public sector organizations and reputation management: five problems. *International Public Management Journal* **15** (2): 186–206.

Walker, R.M. and Bozeman, B. (2011). Publicness and organizational performance. *Journal of Public Administration Research and Theory* **21** (suppl 3): i279–i281.

whatis.com (2015). *Public Sector*. Whatis.com.

WordReference (2015). *Public Sector*. WordReference.

3

Fragile Public Sector Organizations

The more complex the system, the more fragile it becomes
(Nassim Taleb)

This chapter looks at how the public sector has become what it is today and at how a changing environment is leaving traditionally stable public sector organizations vulnerable. We analyze some of its history and the globally most popular management ideals of the recent decades. We look at the causes of public sector organizations' fragility, and we explore changes in expectations placed on public sector organizations.

3.1 A Brief History of Public Sector Organizations' Development

Public sector organizations have often developed over time and in conjunction with the society and environment to which they belong. The traditional definition of an organization as "a complex set of independent parts that interact to adapt to a constantly changing environment in order to achieve its goals" (Kreps, 1990, p. 94) is a good description of public sector organizations today. As societies become increasingly complex, there is not one but several theories and models of what good public sector organizations should consist in (Jawahar and McLaughlin, 2001, p. 412).

Public sector organizations represent "a specific identity of professional knowledge, routines, and value perceptions, rooted in the organization's production processes and history" (Jørgensen et al., 1998, p. 502). Public sector organizations are often some of the oldest existing forms of organizing within society, and hence they often represent quite formal organization types. Formal organizations are systems of "coordinated and controlled activities that arise when work is embedded in complex networks of technical relations and boundary-spanning exchanges," which arise in highly institutionalized contexts (Meyer and Rowan, 1977, p. 430). Although the formal organization model seems to be the status quo for many public sector organizations, this may be changing as citizen orientation becomes a goal (Bourgon, 2011).

Although the development and environmental factors of each public sector organization are historically shaped and context dependent, several common stages can be distinguished. Current organizational trends also shape how public sector organizations

Public Sector Communication: Closing Gaps Between Citizens and Public Organizations, First Edition.
María-José Canel and Vilma Luoma-aho.
© 2019 John Wiley & Sons, Inc. Published 2019 by John Wiley & Sons, Inc.

and their employees see citizens, and they guide the attitude toward serving the public. In the 1960s, public sector organizations largely followed the traditional public administration paradigm, whereas the ideal of efficiency began to take over in the 1970s and 1980s (Cheung, 1996). Management by objectives was among the early signs of the public sector's shift toward building on private sector management models, followed by management by results. The biggest wave of the 1990s was total quality management, which turned within public administration into new public management and later into new public service (Denhardt and Denhardt, 2000). The twenty-first century has brought with it clearer measurement guidelines and processes and a focus on intangible assets such as reputation (Luoma-aho, 2008; Wæraas and Maor, 2015), citizen satisfaction, and trust (Thijs and Staes, 2008; Thijs, 2011). The current trends of the 2010s are behavioral economics (Dolan et al., 2010) and service design (Whicher and Cawood, 2013) as well as public value (Cordella and Willcocks, 2010).

The format for organizing public sector organizations mirrors societies, times, and cultures (North, 1990; Putnam, 1993). Classic organizational thinkers Meyer and Rowan (1977) see the structure of organizations as having been adopted for institutional congruence rather than for mere efficiency. Public sector organizations are often referred to as institutions, and institutionalization is a process whereby "obligations or actualities come to take on a rule-like status in social thought and action" (Meyer and Rowan, 1977, p. 341). In fact, recent findings suggest that the traditional hierarchies of public sector organizations may restrain development (Nederhand, Bekkers, and Voorberg, 2016). This is often visible even on the level of individual citizens through their practical experiences of bureaucracy or "red tape." Public sector organizations often resemble the organization format of the industrial age, relying as they do on hierarchy and bureaucracy (Lipnack and Stamps, 1994).

As society evolves into the network society (Castells, 2009), the traditional hierarchies of public sector organizations often restrain development. Public sector organizations try to function with a nineteenth-century chassis (in the form of bureaucracy and even hierarchy) in a twenty-first-century world of networks and empowered publics (Lipnack and Stamps, 1994). In terms of the life-cycle theory, many public sector organizations have reached the mature or revival stages of their development, where the focus is more on serving than it is on establishing the organization and its functions (Jawahar and McLaughlin, 2001). It could be argued that intangible assets were not as crucial in the golden era of bureaucracy, but in the current era of empowered publics, public sector organizations depend more on intangible assets not only for their daily operations but also for legitimacy and efficiency (Wæraas and Sataøen, 2015).

3.2 Global Trends in Public Sector Management: An Overview

There are certain global trends apparent in public sector organizations and their development in recent decades. Public sector organizations often turn to popular management models and techniques, partly due to their promised results, but simultaneously also due to an isomorphic imitation of other organizations. Interestingly, organizations associated with new management techniques have been shown to gain in intangible assets such as reputation and legitimacy (see Staw and Epstein, 2000). Overall, there has been a shift for public sector organizations from the traditional "bureaucratic culture" to the new citizen-oriented culture of serving and engagement (Claver et al., 1999, p. 459; Bourgon, 2009; Wæraas, 2014). This new culture tends to include directing the tasks and activities of public agencies solely toward efficiently serving citizens, with an emphasis on quality and engagement (Bowden, Luoma-aho, and Naumann, 2016). This change is especially visible through the changing focus of public sector communication, where a shift is occurring from mere one-way information provision and influence toward citizen cocreation and dialogue (Canel and Sanders, 2015; Luoma-aho and Canel, 2016).

Overall, there has been a clear global need in recent decades for administrative change to emerge in the public sector, as the bureaucracy that Weber originally meant for good has in many public sector organizations become a restriction on ordinary affairs. Public sector organizations are under constant pressure to change and improve: "Administrative reforms represent continuing efforts to maintain a satisfactory balance in governance – in relation to both the external societal forces as well as the internal institutional elements" (Cheung, 1996, p. 38). Ideas from managerialism and neoliberal thinking have brought with them a constant stream of new management ideals and models for the public sector. Some of the most influential ones originate from neoliberal thinking and include "public choice theory," as institutional economists label it, as well as the commonly known concepts of "managerialism," "new public management," "market-based public administration," and "entrepreneurial government" (Cheung, 1996, p. 38). Citizens have learned about these through the practical forms of application that they have taken, including the principles of new public management and total quality management or the measurement systems of process thinking, the balanced scorecard or, Six Sigma (Kaplan and Norton, 1996). Many of these models and ideals merely mention intangible assets, and hence they require tailoring to fit the needs of the mostly intangible services provided by public sector organizations (Cinca, Molinero, and Queiroz, 2003).

There is also another side to the development of public sector organizations: as public services improve, citizen expectations simultaneously continue to rise (Luoma-aho and Olkkonen, 2016). Improved transparency ensures democracy, yet stakeholders can and do have opposing needs that require balancing. As the focus is increasingly on the individual's service experience, the ideals of neutrality and equity may be challenged, and the choices made by public sector employees require ethical considerations. It is not enough to make a choice on justified grounds; in the current communication environment, choices also have to be perceived as fair. Similarly, better service often requires more resources, yet the global trend is toward a continuous decrease in resources.

3.3 Is There a Need for Intangible Assets?

We now elaborate more specifically on the trends in public sector management that, in our judgment, connect with both the notion and development of intangible assets.

3.3.1 From New Public Management to New Public Service

New public management is a set of assumptions and value statements about public management that incorporates guidelines from the private sector: a focus on performance and efficiency, quality criteria, greater autonomy, more deregulation, outsourced public services, private–public partnerships, fiscal-transparency mechanisms, increased use of competitive mechanisms, management based on objectives, reporting of results, and technological modernization. Despite criticism focused on its achievements (Diefenbach, 2009; Goldfinch and Wallis, 2010; Luke, Kearins, and Verreynne, 2011), new public management has important implications for public sector communication research and practice, and we agree with Garnett's assertion that public administration studies have not yet fully reviewed the implications of the proposals related to this area made in *Reinventing Government* (Osborne and Gaebler, 1992) in terms of communication theory and practice (2009, p. 245).

We would argue that with regard to the role of communication in building intangible assets, NPM (new public management) has several specific implications. First, its positions on organizational structures and processes imply a more strategic approach to the communication function, and they emphasize the pervasiveness of communication in public administrators' day-to-day work tasks. To the extent that NPM stands for more transparency, accountability, and responsiveness on the part of public sector organizations and seeks to tackle the needs of the community and citizens in a more effective manner, it requires communicators to participate in the strategic management of the organization (Valentini, 2013, p. 96). It is only with this strategic approach to communication that intangible assets can be built.

Second, this approach to public management also means conceptualizing outcomes of public management as services rather than as products, the result of which is to make measures of citizens' experiences and satisfaction a key focus of public management (Bouckaert and Van de Walle, 2003; James and Moseley, 2014). To the extent that NPM is a perspective based on results, it requires the use of control techniques to verify objective achievements in public performance, and intangible assets provide frameworks and tools for those measurements and indicators (Ramírez, 2010, p. 250). New public management stresses the importance of measuring certain values such as transparency, trust, accessibility, and responsiveness (Pandey and Garnett, 2006; Roosbroek, 2006; Spencer and McGrath, 2006; Fairbanks, Plowman, and Rawlins, 2007, pp. 23–37; Greiling and Spraul, 2010; Kim, Park, and Wertz, 2010, p. 215; Denhardt and Denhardt, 2015).

However, NPM has received criticism for being too customer oriented, and perhaps out of the recent decades' developing fads, of clearest value is the ideal of new public service (NPS) (Denhardt and Denhardt, 2000), as it is closest to the core purpose of public sector organizations with its focus on serving and empowering citizens. New public service suggests that administrations are merely one of the several actors in the public sector arena. NPS can be seen as being at the origins of citizen engagement, as public participation and citizen engagement will ensure greater commitment to public sector decisions and build the necessary intangible assets such as trust (Denhardt and Denhardt, 2000). However, as ideals are imported, it is vital to consider fully the differences between its original and the new context, as authentic public sector improvements seldom result from "massively borrowing the techniques and models used in private corporations" (Claver et al., 1999, p. 460).

3.3.2 From Management to Public Value

The notion of public value was coined by Mark H. Moore, who in 1995 published *Creating Public Value: Strategic Management in Government*, which he followed up with

Recognizing Public Value in 2013. Moore presents a public value account and a public value scorecard as aids for assessing the value that a public organization provides to society. A public value account is a summary term assessed and measured against the extent to which it achieves or realizes in practice more specific public values at reasonable cost. In more recent works, Moore has stressed the relation of his public value theory to democratic values, institutions, and processes (Moore, 2013, 2014, 2015). Scholars state that the public value approach derives from the trend toward a multisector public sector and collaborative governance (Bryson, Crosby, and Bloomberg, 2015a) and from the need for a new way of looking at the whole notion of value creation, which shifts the focus from a narrow financial and economic performance perspective to a broader concept that maintains and influences individual well-being as well as societal progress (Meynhardt, 2015).

Public value has been categorized as "the next 'Big Thing'" (Talbot, 2009, p. 167), "the next step in public service reform" (Coats and Passmore, 2008), and even the paradigm to eclipse and replace traditional approaches to public management (Stoker, 2006). Its evolution shows the need to combine the managerial values of efficacy and efficiency with social values (Bryson, Crosby, and Bloomberg, 2015b). "Public value" has to do with the idea of an organization and its behavior being good for society and its functioning (Meynhardt, Gomez, and Schweizer, 2014, p. 5), and when it is applied to the public sector, it is "a placeholder for what a society values and aims to create through its public institutions" (Moynihan and Kroll, 2015, p. 245).

To date, there has been no attempt to link the notion of "public value" to that of "intangible asset," and we would argue that progress made in the great challenge of finding the best formulas, methods, and techniques to measure intangible assets in the public sector would contribute to the development of the "public value" perspective, and hence to a better calibration of the value that public management provides. Moreover, the different responses to value-concern questions can complement and benefit approaches to measuring intangible assets and subsequently enhance the study and practice of public sector communication.

As a result of the introduction of discussion of public value, the role of intangible assets for public sector communication might become clearer. Studies of both public value and intangible assets deal with value-related concerns and with the intangibility dimension of an organization's value. Both sets of literature are concerned with putting into practice the democratic principle of public sector accountability, and their developments (concepts, frameworks, metrics, and so forth) aim to better capture the value that public sector organizations provide. In doing so, both pay attention to the managerial (and strategic) dimension of public management: the measures of both public value and intangible assets might inform decision making and help organizations to improve performance.

Both sets of literature also honor the centrality of relationship building as the basis for creating value. But while the literature on intangible assets looks at what intangibility adds to the organization as owner of a specific asset (the question that is asked is: How much value does this intangible asset have for this organization?), the public value perspective looks at society (the question asked here is: What makes an organization valuable to society?). Combining both approaches might help organizations face the challenge of putting stakeholders first and responding to organizational needs, and it nurtures this book's argument that an intangible asset exists to the extent that it provides value for both sides. Developing public value and intangible assets together is beneficial, but until public value thinking is fully integrated in intangible assets thinking, there are several challenges for public sector organizations to overcome. In fact, if public sector organizations preserve their current status quo with regard to communication, they risk becoming fragile in the face of the changing dynamics of contemporary global society. We will now take a closer look at the causes of such fragility for public sector organizations.

3.4 The Fragility of Public Sector Organizations

As we discussed in Chapter 2, different forms of change are currently taking place, and what matters is not the type of change, but the approach and attitude that the organization and its members take toward it. The most dangerous form of organizational fragility is Titanic syndrome – that is, the inability to see risks and change, as well as overconfidence in one's ability to overcome them. The areas of an organization that become stronger are precisely those which the organization chooses to focus on. As a result, public sector organizations' focus on efficiency and productivity in recent decades has made them increasingly dependent on the scientific management paradigm. This focus is not enough to survive in the new era of networked, empowered publics and real-time media. In fact, public sector organizations remain fragile as long as illusions that their operating environment is predictable, that change can be controlled, and that ex post adaptations are sufficient persist (Bourgon, 2009). Public sector organizations are unable to control the spread of either true or false information, and they can no longer place themselves at the center of their map of stakeholders (Luoma-aho and Vos, 2010). In organizations' attempts to survive in these uncontrollable networks in which interconnected individuals freely share information and experiences, intangible assets are one of the few available sources to stabilize their operations.

The *Merriam-Webster's Dictionary* defines the word *fragile* as the quality of being "easily broken or destroyed." Fragility, then, does not refer to breakage as a certainty, but rather to the likelihood of its occurring. Similarly, many public sector organizations today still function relatively well, but they are simultaneously becoming increasingly fragile due to the changing environment. In fact, for public sector organizations, constant change and unanticipated risks are becoming the norm. This means that the practices of high-reliability organizations are also becoming useful for other organizations that had not previously been associated with immediate threat or major risks (Lengnick-Hall, Beck, and Lengnick-Hall, 2011, p. 243).

3.4.1 Distrust

Perhaps the biggest cause of fragility to public sector organizations is a lack of the citizen or even employee trust required for democracy to operate. Certain sector-related traits (such as the various existing nondisclosure requirements, laws, and regulations that guide public sector organizations' operations) further cultivate distrust. What creates trust is an issue that will be fully addressed in Chapter 12, but we will mention that research shows that trust can be created by increased organizational transparency, which can be brought about through citizen engagement, provision of substantial information, and accountability (Rawlins, 2008). But if "trusted information makes the organization itself more resilient by increasing its capacity to learn" (Longstaff and Yang, 2008, p. 3), why are public sector organizations not simply communicating more openly to avoid such fragility?

The more complex a society becomes, the more complex the stakeholder and collaboration networks that public sector organizations depend on become. Complexity and interconnectedness make it difficult for organizations to assess their fragility and potential risks (Beck, 2000, p. 79). Nassim Taleb calls this a "Black Swan world," where unanticipated events occur and the consequences of choices and actions are increasingly difficult to assess in advance (Taleb, 2007). In a complex environment, communication becomes an analysis of cause-and-effect chains that are mostly established in hindsight. This is because in an environment characterized by surprises, even monitoring that environment is difficult, not least because even the target of monitoring may change in real time (Luoma-aho, 2014). As old institutions are questioned and traditional symbols and statuses diminish, organizations are increasingly dependent on their networks for information exchange (Castells, 2009). In fact, even the stakeholders that organizations once believed to be rather stable are today dynamic, as issues and problems may invite new and unplanned stakeholders to the conversation. Strategic communication for public sector organizations means "looking beyond obvious stakeholders into potential uncharted territory . . . Without this understanding, many important stakes as well as stakeholders may remain hidden" (Luoma-aho and Paloviita, 2010, p. 50), making public sector organizations vulnerable to potential harm.

3.4.2 Services and Experiences

The problems that create the greatest fragility in public sector organizations are often related to their services and actions. Negative citizen experiences produce individuals who are unwilling to cooperate: if bureaucracy, corruption, and inefficiencies are citizens' dominant experiences of the public sector, public sector organizations become fragile through a lack of support and threats to their legitimacy. But this organizational-level fragility is not the only kind of fragility that public sector organizations face. In fact, all changes that are unanticipated and not responded to pose potential vulnerabilities for public sector organizations, whether they occur on the individual, organizational, or societal level. Some changes may evolve into solutions, whereas others may mutate into crises. Recent examples of unanticipated risks that have turned into crises for public sector organizations include the 2015–2017 unplanned mass immigration of Syrian refugees into Europe, or the disclosure of classified information through leaks and websites such as the Panama Papers or Wikileaks.

Employees and citizens who feel a disconnect with the public sector and its services create fertile ground for distrust to grow in, making the public sector organizations that they work for vulnerable in the process. On the level of public sector employees, there is something of a tug of war between what traditionally has been required from public sector organizations (legal and democratic processes) and current citizen expectations (service and engagement). As long as public sector organizations fail to enable individual needs and expectations, this vulnerability remains.

However, fragility always starts on the individual level, even in organizations (Leng-nick-Hall et al., 2011, p. 243). In a society driven by communication, the most fundamental form of power lies "in the ability to shape the human mind . . . Because it is through communication that the human mind interacts with its social and natural environment" (Castells, 2009, p. 3).

3.4.3 Bureaucracy

There are often citizen complaints about public sector organizations being too bureaucratic. These can be partly explained by the history of the concept's origins in the public sector. Synonyms for bureaucratic culture include "conformity culture," "technical rationality culture," and "process culture" (Claver et al., 1999, p. 458). When public sector change is discussed, bureaucracy or a bureaucratic culture is often identified as a central problem to be addressed (Bourgon, 2011). As Claver et al. state (1999, p. 458), "The bureaucratic culture implies a stability that is usually detrimental to the needs of an innovative process and, therefore, to any kind of change." Bureaucracy has been linked with several ills, including greater calculation and control over citizens' lives, which contribute to what Max Weber described as an "iron cage of bureaucracy" that locks individuals inside the system. The most frequently raised ills of bureaucracy include stiffness, slowness, and a lack of adaptability, as well as an authoritarian, top-down control of management and minimal, and often only formal, communication (Claver et al., 1999, p. 459).

Although bureaucracy was created to ensure safety and equality in public services, it has changed from a modern concept to a curse word. Citizens often label public sector organizations as bureaucratic when their processes are slow. They accuse them of being irresponsible, reliant on a hierarchy, and mechanical in their operations. And they criticize them for their tendency to routinize operations and for their replacement of personal judgment with impersonal policies that often include filling in forms and excessive paperwork (Kotler, 1975). Bureaucracy was originally created for the benefit of individuals and organizations, as it enabled clear processes and stages to follow instead of irrational choices (see, for example, Weber, 1958). In fact, bureaucracy was assumed to be the most efficient mode of coordination owing to its standardization of and imposition of logic upon complex modern tasks. One could argue that the "problem is hence not in bureaucracy as such, but in its maladaptation to the changing dynamic environment in which the public organizations operate today" (Luoma-aho, 2005, p. 68).

3.4.4 The Political Dimension

This book is not only about serving an individual citizen but also about policy-making and implementation, which are subject to a political rationale. It has been extensively documented that in different countries and cultural settings, government communicators have to juggle what appear to be conflicting objectives set by political masters (Sanders and Canel, 2013); political control seems to be a variable that explains government performance outcomes (Andrews, Boyne, and Walker, 2011, p. i305)

There is an increasingly blurred distinction between politics and administration (Glenny, 2008; Skelley, 2008; Carpenter and Krause, 2012), which has important implications for communication management. Particularly problematic are communication goals related to persuasion, and for this reason, one of the most common approaches in addressing this issue is to analyze the propaganda aspect of public sector communication (Glenny, 2008; Bell, 2010; Bell, Hindmoor, and Mols, 2010; Gelders and Ihlen, 2010b) in an attempt to differentiate partisan communication from governmental communication as well as to identify the best institutional arrangements to save governmental messages from partisanship (Sanders and Canel, 2013).

A second focus in addressing this issue is that related to the identity, role, and tasks that ought to be attributed to public servants (Garnett and Kouzmin, 1997; Preston and Donaldson, 1999; Denhardt and Denhardt, 2015). Analysis has attempted to establish differences between professionals/bureaucrats and politicians (Carpenter and Krause, 2012), to identify information asymmetries that exist between them (Andrews et al., 2011), and to describe the pressures and dilemmas that civil servants face (Head, 2007) as a result of the fact that they "work in government public relations, but risk being identified with partisan political communication" (Gelders and Ihlen, 2010a, p. 59). Scholars have introduced the concept of communication ethics for civil servants and stressed the need for public administrators, in order to enhance democratic account-ability, both to keep people informed and to be provided with insights relating to how sectors of the public think and react to government decisions.

The entanglement of politics and public services has led authors to see the need for public relations in public administration (Gelders and Ihlen, 2010b), the practice of legitimacy as an intangible asset itself of public sector communication (Canel, 2014), the study of government communication outside the focus of elections (Young, 2007), and to argue about the tension civil servants have in developing strong dual identities as nonpartisan civil servants but also as professionals with a particular expertise within an area (Gelders and Ihlen, 2010a). In any case, public administrators need to develop policy while maintaining an ongoing dialogue with the actors involved in communication needs and standards (Gelders and Ihlen, 2010a, p. 61), and we believe that the intangible assets approach can help in meeting this need.

3.4.5 A Tactical Approach

We have mentioned several times so far that this book builds on a previous analysis of national, executive-level government communication in 16 sovereign states (including European and Anglo-American countries, newly emerging democracies, and countries that are regarded as nondemocratic according to Freedom House's indices). One of the findings of that cross-national analysis is that governments are being challenged to go beyond a tactical approach in their communication (that is, one more focused on formal presentation) to a strategic management function that allows successful interaction between governments and stakeholders and includes strategic communication planning, crisis communication, public opinion research, and intangible assets management.

A lack of the required strategic capacity has been corroborated by our review of existing teaching and training programs on public sector communication offered by universities and public administration schools, and it has been documented in different countries by other authors (Garnett, 1992; Valentini, 2013; Sanders and Canel, 2013). These studies reveal that although there are some countries (for example, the United States, Great Britain, and Australia) with more specialized organizational structures and processes, most of the countries analyzed (including European ones such as Sweden, France, Poland, Spain, and Germany, as well as ones on other continents, including Mexico, Chile, India, Singapore, China, South Africa, and Zimbabwe) exhibit improvised performance, scarce evaluation of communication performance, low knowledge of their stakeholders, and little strategic planning (Sanders and Canel, 2013).

Strategy is built on understanding the operating environment. Underneath much public sector change are the microlevel changes in citizens' attitudes and expectations. We will now address these.

3.5 Expectations as a Cause for Public Sector Fragility

Citizens' expectations are not fixed. Rather, they change as citizens and society change. As technology enables increased interaction and politics emphasize citizen activity, the myth of the passive citizen is giving way to citizens who ideally are "an active part of a common solution to social problems, bringing experiential expertise and local knowledge" (Durose, Justice, and Skelcher, 2015, p. 139). Although not all citizens are active, they all have expectations and experiences. In fact, citizens' experiences are formed when events reflect citizens' expectations, making the tacit, subconscious cues called expectations central for shaping the way in which individual citizens perceive public organizations' actions and communication (Dolan et al., 2010; Castelo et al., 2015). Expectations also contribute to citizens' perceptions about public service quality, and thus excessively high expectations may actually backfire through producing lower levels of satisfaction (Poister and Thomas, 2011; Font and Navarro, 2013) or even diminishing other intangible assets such as trust and a good organizational reputation (Luoma-aho, 2007, p. 124).

But what are expectations, and how do they work? According to Luoma-aho and Olkkonen (2016), "Expectations are mental models that affect the formation of relationships that individuals and stakeholders have with each other, organizations and brands." Based on both planned and unplanned cues (Coye, 2004), these mental models filter information about:

- whether events are desirable or undesirable from the citizen's point of view and
- the likeliness of the occurrence of the event (Van Ryzin, 2006; James, 2009; Poister and Thomas, 2011; Olkkonen and Luoma-aho, 2014; Olkkonen and Luoma-aho, 2015).

Expectations refer to the anticipated behavior of the organization (Coye, 2004), and they act as reference points for future assessments (Creyer, 1997, p. 421) guiding citizens' perceptions of the organization or its service (Luoma-aho, Olkkonen, and Lähteenmäki, 2013). Understanding expectations as mental models opens up the logic of expectations. Individuals search for logical and causal explanations of events and of organizations' and individuals' behavior. Based on their experiences, they aim to predict future events in a similar way to the practice of framing, highlighting certain aspects while diminishing others to provide a certain interpretation of events. Frames filter information and portray it in the context of a certain environment, and they help citizens to make sense of events and situations. Evaluations are made on whether the behavior or event meets both the broad general anticipations of societal norms – that is, whether it is considered typical or appropriate in the given culture and context – and detailed case-related individual experiences and previous knowledge (Luoma-aho and Olkkonen, 2016).

3.5.1 How Citizen Expectations Are Changing

Although there are several different reasons for public sector change, one clear factor is the changing logic according to which public sector organizations communicate. Three interrelated societal changes can be found to contribute to shaping citizens' expectations on the macrolevel of public services: promotional culture, mediatization, and social media logic.

1) *Promotional culture*: in *Promotional Culture*, Davis (2013) suggests that promotion and selling have been injected not only into citizens and their choices but also into organizations and society as a whole (Tufekci, 2013). Because promotional culture emphasizes individualism, in its best forms it can empower citizens, but at its worst it can tempt individuals to place individual needs and gains ahead of the common societal good. Promotionalism is also apparent in citizen expectations, in which services are thought of as trade-offs and the public sector is treated as a market that responds to rising citizen demand through promoting events and issues worthy of citizen attention.

2) *Mediatization:* building on agenda-setting theory, mediatization refers to the attempt to frame actions so that they best satisfy media interest (Fredriksson, Schillemans, and Pallas, 2015). In the case of public sector organizations, mediatization suggests that the public services or servants that are able to receive the most beneficial media coverage are the most valuable. For citizens, mediatization produces a self-enforcing loop of media attention. When citizens see media coverage of one service (for example, a new online tax-filing system with real-time chat), they consider that service to be more important and have rising expectations for it and ask for and demand it, whereas services that receive less media coverage (for instance, mobility assistance for disabled citizens) are not considered so important for society. In a mediatized environment, stronger legitimacy is granted to the public sector organizations that are capable of achieving greater visibility in the media (Davis, 2013; Fredriksson and Pallas, 2016).

3) *Social media logic*: the social media environment favors messages that are short, shareable, positive, and easily understood, such as visuals and videos. These shape not only how individuals both inside and outside organizations expect organizations to communicate but also what in general is desirable and what is not. Societal trends of all kinds often tacitly shape and change citizen expectations on the level of attitudes and salience (Dolan et al., 2012), though the origins of their expectations are seldom visible to individual citizens themselves. What becomes visible, however, is citizen dissatisfaction when some of these new expectations are not met by public sector organizations.

It has been suggested that we as a society are moving from an era of "media logic" to one of "social media logic." Social media logic is shaping user agency and affecting citizens' expectations, especially with regard to four areas related to services, namely programmability, popularity, connectivity, and datafication (Van Dijck and Poell, 2013). With regard to programmability, algorithms and online platform owners steer Internet traffic and attempt to trigger users' communicative contributions. Users, on the other hand, influence the flow that comes into their own social media "bubble" (Sloterdijk, 2011) through the various streams and feeds that they choose. Popularity refers to social media's ability to enable users to promote certain popular trends or topics, which creates the expectation that citizens' voices and opinions can and should carry more weight than they did before (Macnamara, 2015). Connectivity refers to the "platform apparatus" of mediating users' activities and changing "collective action" to "connective action," highlighting the individual above the group or society (Van Dijck and Poell, 2013). Finally, datafication refers to the capacity to build polling into a given medium, as each online citizen choice is traceable and quantified into massive data pools of user actions, raising citizens' expectations about the availability of big data based on their online journey and searches.

If Amazon and Google know what citizens should read next, why are public schools not able to recommend their services at the same pace? The major challenge with this new social media logic is that it is invisible to citizens, yet it strongly shapes their thoughts, emotions, attitudes, and behaviors and, as a consequence, their satisfaction with organizations. Moreover, these trends are leading citizens to expect public sector organizations to produce content that citizens can choose themselves and easily pull into their world when questions and needs arise.

3.5.2 Expectations through Experiences

There is consensus among researchers that citizens' expectations about public sector performance shape their overall satisfaction with the public sector and its services (Van Ryzin, 2004; Roch and Poister, 2006; Van Ryzin, 2006; Poister and Thomas, 2011; Luoma-aho et al., 2013). In fact, the level of satisfaction shapes not only the attitudes of citizens but also behaviors such as participating, volunteering, or voting (James and John, 2007; Thijs and Staes, 2008). Citizens' expectations in the public sector influence their actions in terms of whether, to use Hirschman's terminology, they remain loyal, exit the service situation, or voice their dissatisfaction (Hirschman, 1970), making expectations of strategic value.

Citizens' expectations stem from their experiences, which will often be at the local public service level, and from the prior performance of local government (James, 2011; Bowden et al., 2016). Experiences shape expectations: citizen expectation levels rise as previous expectations are met and experiences are good. Similarly, unmet expectations increase dissatisfaction with both overall public services and specific services. Where expectations are met, the predicted probability of dissatisfaction is very low compared to the predicted probability of satisfaction. Although researchers agree that fulfilled expectations reduce citizen dissatisfaction, meeting expectations does not necessarily increase citizen satisfaction (Van Ryzin, 2006).

There is a growing trend in the literature as well as in public sector organizations' practices to see the customer (Mickelsson, 2013) or citizen (Bourgon, 2009) at the center of such relationships, but research has also highlighted the role of public sector employees (Perry and Porter, 1982). These frontline bureaucrats are believed to shape citizens' experiences and expectations more than organizations do, as public sector employees often make the practical policy decisions that have the greatest effect on individual citizens and their lives (Lipsky, 2010).

3.5.3 Unmet Expectations

Expectations are most noticeable when they are not met. Such unmet expectations may be significant for the relationship between citizens and public sector organizations, as studies show that mismatched or unmet expectations appear to influence citizens' levels of satisfaction with public services (James, 2009). Moreover, emotions and frustration effects are reported to be strongly connected to prior levels of expectations (Font and Navarro, 2013).

Much of the research on satisfaction in relation to the private sector highlights the link between quality and satisfaction. Despite this connection, research suggests that public service quality does not necessarily lead to citizen satisfaction: there is an interplay of reality, perceptions, and expectations (Bouckaert et al., 2001; Van de Walle and Bouckaert, 2003, p. 892; Carmeli and Tishler, 2005). Gaps between what public managers think their performance is and what citizens (their stakeholders) think it is have been found (Sanders and Canel, 2015), as have gaps between citizens' perceptions and the perceptions of auditors and inspectors of services (James and Moseley, 2014).

These gaps demonstrate the role of expectations: managers, citizens, and auditors all have different expectations, and the same organizational performance is evaluated differently based on those mental models, resulting in satisfaction or dissatisfaction. Research findings suggest that extremes of both very satisfied and very dissatisfied citizens are more vulnerable to changing expectations than citizens in the middle ground are. The extremes, both positive and negative, seem to have a stronger association with positive expectations than midrange performance does (James, 2011). In fact, it appears that the higher the expectation, the higher the possibility of dissatisfaction (James, 2009), highlighting the need to maintain neutral levels of trust and reputation in the public sector (Luoma-aho, 2007, p. 124). Unmet expectations can shape the way in which citizens assess public managers and politicians (James, 2009). In fact, fulfilled expectations create trust, whereas unmet citizen expectations may even cause a gap in organizational legitimacy (Luoma-aho et al., 2013).

Communication is often listed as a source of dissatisfaction in the public sector. There are findings that allow the argument to be made that information provision on specific prior performance of public service influences citizens' expectations (James, 2011). Moreover, the communication standards that citizens expect from public sector organizations shape their satisfaction and assessment of factors such as reputation (Sanders and Canel, 2015). There are often discrepancies between what public sector organizations and local governments think about their reputation and what citizens think, but the cause-and-effect relations are complex because experiences are intangible and volatile.

With these points in mind, in the next chapter, we look at how to overcome this fragility.

References

Andrews, R., Boyne, G.A., and Walker, R.M. (2011). Dimensions of publicness and organizational performance: a review of the evidence. *Journal of Public Administration Research and Theory* **21** (suppl 3): i301–i319.

Beck, U. (2000). The cosmopolitan perspective: sociology of the second age of modernity. *British Journal of Sociology* **51** (1): 79–105.

Bell, S., Hindmoor, A., and Mols, F. (2010). Persuasion as governance: a state-centric relational perspective. *Public Administration* **88** (3): 851–870.

Bouckaert, G. and Van de Walle, S. (2003). Comparing measures of citizen trust and user satisfaction as indicators of 'good governance': difficulties in linking trust and satisfaction indicators. *International Review of Administrative Sciences* **69** (3): 329–343.

Bouckaert, G., Kampen, J.K., Maddens, B., and Van de Walle, S. (2001). *Klantentevredenheidsmetingen bij de overheid: eerste rapport burgergericht besturen: kwaliteit en vertrouwen in de overheid*. Leuven: *Instituut Voor de Overheid*.

Bourgon, J. (2009). New directions in public administration: serving beyond the predictable. *Public Policy and Administration* **24** (3): 309–330.

Bourgon, J. (2011). *A New Synthesis of Public Administration: Serving in the 21st Century*. Washington, DC: McGill Queen's Press.

Bowden, J.L.-H., Luoma-aho, V., and Naumann, K. (2016). Developing a spectrum of positive to negative citizen engagement. In: *Customer Engagement Contemporary Issues and Challenges*, 1st ed. (ed. R.J. Brodie, L. Hollebeek and J. Conduit), 257–277. London: Routledge.

Bryson, J.M., Crosby, B.C., and Bloomberg, L. (2015a). Introduction. In: *Public Value and Public Administration* (ed. J.M. Bryson, B.C. Crosby and L. Bloomberg), xvii–xxvi. Washington, DC: Georgetown University Press.

Bryson, J.M., Crosby, B.C., and Bloomberg, L. (2015b). Conclusions. In: *Public Value and Public Administration* (ed. J.M. Bryson, B.C. Crosby and L. Bloomberg), 239–284. Washington, DC: Georgetown University Press.

Canel, M.-J. (2014). Reflexiones sobre la reputación ideal de la administración pública. In: *Escribir En Las Almas. Estudios En Honor de Rafael Alvira* (ed. M. Herrero, A. Cruz, R. Lázaro and A. Martínez), 69–88. Pamplona: Eiunsa.

Canel, M.-J. and Sanders, K. (2015). Government communication. In: *The International Encyclopedia of Political Communication*, 3 Volume Set, vol. 1 (ed. G. Mazzoleni, K. Barnhurst, K. Ikeda et al.), 1–8. Boston: Wiley-Blackwell.

Carmeli, A. and Tishler, A. (2005). Perceived organizational reputation and organizational performance: an empirical investigation of industrial enterprises. *Corporate Reputation Review* **8** (1): 13–30.

Carpenter, D.P. and Krause, G.A. (2012). Reputation and public administration. *Public Administration Review* **72** (1): 26–32.

Castells, M. (2009). *Communication Power*. Oxford: Oxford University Press.

Castelo, N., Hardy, E., House, J. et al. (2015). Moving citizens online: salience and framing as motivators for behavioral change. *Journal of Behavioral Science and Policy* **1** (2): 57–68.

Cheung, A. (1996). Public sector reform and the re-legitimation of public bureaucratic power: the case of Hong Kong. *International Journal of Public Sector Management* **9** (5/6): 37–50.

Cinca, C.S., Molinero, C.M., and Queiroz, A.B. (2003). The measurement of intangible assets in public sector using scaling techniques. *Journal of Intellectual Capital* **4** (2): 249–275.

Claver, E., Llopis, J., Gascó, J.L. et al. (1999). Public administration: from bureaucratic culture to citizen-oriented culture. *International Journal of Public Sector Management* **12** (5): 455–464.

Coats, D. and Passmore, E. (2008). *Public Value: The Next Steps in Public Service Reform*. London: Work Foundation.

Cordella, A. and Willcocks, L. (2010). Outsourcing, bureaucracy and public value: reappraising the notion of the "contract state". *Government Information Quarterly* **27** (1): 82–88.

Coye, R.W. (2004). Managing customer expectations in the service encounter. *International Journal of Service Industry Management* **15** (1): 54–71.

Creyer, E. (1997). The influence of firm behavior on purchase intention: do consumers really care about business ethics? *Journal of Consumer Marketing* **14** (6): 421–432.

Davis, A. (2013). *Promotional Culture: The Rise and Spread of Advertising, Public Relations, Marketing and Branding*, 1st ed. London: Polity Press.

Denhardt, R.B. and Denhardt, J.V. (2000). The new public service: serving rather than steering. *Public Administration Review* **60** (6): 549–559.

Denhardt, J.V. and Denhardt, R.B. (2015). The new public service revisited. *Public Administration Review* **75** (5): 664–672.

Diefenbach, T. (2009). New public management in public sector organizations: the dark sides of managerialistic 'enlightenment'. *Public Administration* **87** (4): 892–909.

Dolan, P., Hallsworth, M., Halpern, D. et al. (2010). *MINDSPACE: Influencing Behaviour through Public Policy*. UK: Institute for Government, Cabinet Office.

Dolan, P., Hallsworth, M., Halpern, D. et al. (2012). Influencing behaviour: the mindspace way. *Journal of Economic Psychology* **33** (1): 264–277.

Durose, C., Justice, J., and Skelcher, C. (2015). Governing at an arm's length: eroding or enhancing democracy? *Policy & Politics* **43** (1): 137–153.

Fairbanks, J., Plowman, K.D., and Rawlins, B.L. (2007). Transparency in government communication. *Journal of Public Affairs* **7** (1): 23–37.

Font, J. and Navarro, C. (2013). Personal experience and the evaluation of participatory instruments in Spanish cities. *Public Administration* **91** (3): 616–631.

Fredriksson, M. and Pallas, J. (2016). Diverging principles for strategic communication in government agencies. *International Journal of Strategic Communication* **10** (3): 153–164.

Fredriksson, M., Schillemans, T., and Pallas, J. (2015). Determinants of organizational mediatization: an analysis of the adaptation of Swedish government agencies to news media. *Public Administration* **93** (4): 1049–1067.

Garnett, J.L. (1992). *Communicating for Results in Government: A Strategic Approach for Public Managers*. San Francisco: Jossey-Bass.

Garnett, J.L. and Kouzmin, A. ed. (1997). *Handbook of Administrative Communication*. New York: Marcel Dekker.

Gelders, D. and Ihlen, Ø. (2010a). Government communication about potential policies: public relations, propaganda or both? *Public Relations Review* **36** (1): 59–62.

Gelders, D. and Ihlen, Ø. (2010b). Minding the gap: Applying a service marketing model into government policy communications. *Government Information Quarterly* **27** (1): 34–40.

Glenny, L. (2008). Perspectives of communication in the Australian public sector. *Journal of Communication Management* **12** (2): 152–168.

Goldfinch, S. and Wallis, J. (2010). Two myths of convergence in public management reform. *Public Administration* **88** (4): 1099–1115.

Greiling, D. and Spraul, K. (2010). Accountability and the challenges of information disclosure. *Public Administration Quarterly* **34** (3): 338–377.

Head, B. (2007). The public service and government communication: pressures and dilemmas. In: *Government Communication in Australia* (ed. S. Young), 36–50. Melbourne: Cambridge University Press.

Hirschman, A.O. (1970). *Exit, Voice and Loyalty: Responses to Decline in Firms, Organizations, and States*, vol. 25. Cambridge, MA: Harvard University Press.

James, O. (2009). Evaluating the expectations disconfirmation and expectations anchoring approaches to citizen satisfaction with local public services. *Journal of Public Administration Research and Theory* **19** (1): 107–123.

James, O. (2011). Managing citizens' expectations of public service performance: evidence from observation and experimentation in local government. *Public Administration* **89** (4): 1419–1435.

James, O. and John, P. (2007). Public management at the ballot box: performance information and electoral support for incumbent English local governments. *Journal of Public Administration Research and Theory* **17** (4): 567–580.

James, O. and Moseley, A. (2014). Does performance information about public services affect citizens' perceptions, satisfaction and voice behaviour? Field experiments with absolute and relative performance information. *Public Administration* **92** (2): 493–511.

Jawahar, I.M. and McLaughlin, G.L. (2001). Toward a descriptive stakeholder theory: an organizational life cycle approach. *Academy of Management Review* **26** (3): 397–414.

Jørgensen, T.B., Hansen, H.F., Antonsen, M., and Melander, P. (1998). Public organizations, multiple constituencies, and governance. *Public Administration* **76** (Autumn): 499–518.

Kaplan, R.S. and Norton, D.P. (1996). *The Balanced Scorecard: Translating Strategy into Action*. Boston, MA: Harvard Business Press.

Kim, S., Park, J.-H., and Wertz, E.K. (2010). Expectation gaps between stakeholders and web-based corporate public relations efforts: focusing on fortune 500 corporate web sites. *Public Relations Review* **36** (3): 215–221.

Kotler, P. (1975). *Marketing for Nonprofit-Making Organisations*. Englewood Cliffs, NJ: Prentice-Hall.

Kreps, G.L. (1990). *Organizational Communication: Theory and Practice*, 2nd ed. New York: Addison-Wesley.

Lengnick-Hall, C., Beck, T., and Lengnick-Hall, M. (2011). Developing a capacity for organizational resilience through strategic human resource management. *Human Resource Management Review* **21** (3): 243.

Lipnack, J. and Stamps, J. (1994). *The Age of the Network: Organizing principles for the 21st century*. New York: Wiley.

Lipsky, M. (2010). *Street-Level Bureaucracy: Dilemmas of the Individual in Public Services*. New York, NY: Russell Sage Foundation.

Longstaff, P.H. and Yang, S. (2008). Communication management and trust: their role in building resilience to "surprises" such as natural disasters, pandemic flu, and terrorism. *Ecology and Society* **13** (1): 3 http://www.ecologyandsociety.org/vol13/iss1/art3/ (accessed 30 December 2017).

Luke, B., Kearins, K., and Verreynne, M.-L. (2011). The risks and returns of new public management: political business. *International Journal of Public Sector Management* **24** (4): 325–355.

Luoma-aho, V. (2005). *Faith-Holders as Social Capital of Finnish Public Sector Organizations*.". Doctoral dissertation, Jyväskylä Studies in Humanities 42. Jyväskylä University Press http://julkaisut.jyu.fi (accessed 2 January 2017).

Luoma-aho, V. (2007). Neutral reputation and public sector organizations. *Corporate Reputation Review* **10** (2): 124–143.

Luoma-aho, V. (2008). Sector reputation and public organisations. *International Journal of Public Sector Management* **21** (5): 446–467.

Luoma-aho, V. (2014). *Särkymätön Viestintä*. Helsinki: ProCom Ry.

Luoma-aho, V. and Canel, M.-J. (2016). Public sector reputation. In: *The SAGE Encyclopedia of Corporate Reputation* (ed. C. Carroll), 597, 600. Sage Publications.

Luoma-aho, V. and Olkkonen, L. (2016). Expectation management. In: *The SAGE Encyclopedia of Corporate Reputation* (ed. C. Carroll), 303–306. Sage Publications.

Luoma-aho, V. and Paloviita, A. (2010). Actor-networking stakeholder theory for today's corporate communications. *Corporate Communications: An International Journal* **15** (1): 49–67.

Luoma-aho, V. and Vos, M. (2010). Towards a more dynamic stakeholder model: acknowledging multiple issue arenas. *Corporate Communications* **15** (3): 315–331.

Luoma-aho, V., Olkkonen, L., and Lähteenmäki, M. (2013). Expectation management for public sector management. *Public Relations Review* **39** (3): 248–250.

Macnamara, J. (2015). *Creating an 'Architecture of Listening' in Organizations*. Sydney, NSW: University of Technology Sydney.

Meyer, J.W. and Rowan, B. (1977). Institutionalized organizations: formal structure as myth and ceremony. *American Journal of Sociology* **83** (2): 340–363.

Meynhardt, T. (2015). *Public Value: Turning a Conceptual Framework into a Scorecard*. Washington, DC: Georgetown University Press.

Meynhardt, T., Gomez, P., and Schweizer, M. (2014). The public value scorecard: what makes an organization valuable to society? *Performance* **6** (1): 1–8.

Mickelsson, K.-J. (2013). Customer activity in service. *Journal of Service Management* **24** (5): 534–552.

Moore, M.H. (1995). *Creating Public Value: Strategic Management in Government*. Cambridge, MA: Harvard University Press.

Moore, M.H. (2013). *Recognizing Public Value*. Cambridge, MA: Harvard University Press.

Moore, M.H. (2014). Public value accounting: establishing the philosophical basis. *Public Administration Review* **74** (4): 465–477.

Moore, M.H. (2015). Creating a public value account and scorecard. In: *Public Value and Public Administration* (ed. J.M. Bryson, B.C. Crosby and L. Bloomberg), 110–130. Georgetown: Georgetown University Press.

Moynihan, D.P. and Kroll, A. (2015). Performance management routines that work? An early assessment of the GPRA modernization act. *Public Administration Review* **76** (2): 314–323.

Nederhand, J., Bekkers, V., and Voorberg, W. (2016). Self-organization and the role of government: how and why does self-organization evolve in the shadow of hierarchy? *Public Management Review* **18** (7): 1063–1084.

North, D.C. (1990). *Institutions, Institutional Change and Economic Performance*. Cambridge, MA: Cambridge University Press.

Olkkonen, L. and Luoma-aho, V. (2014). Public relations as expectation management? *Journal of Communication Management* **18** (3): 222–239.

Olkkonen, L. and Luoma-aho, V. (2015). Broadening the concept of expectations in public relations. *Journal of Public Relations Research* **27** (1): 81–99.

Osborne, D. and Gaebler, T. (1992). *Reinventing Government: How the Entrepreneurial Spirit is Transforming the Public Sector*. New York: Adison-Wesle.

Pandey, S.K. and Garnett, J.L. (2006). Exploring public sector communication performance: testing a model and drawing implications. *Public Administration Review* **66** (1): 37–51.

Perry, J.L. and Porter, L.W. (1982). Factors affecting the context for motivation in public organizations. *Academy of Management Review* **7** (1): 89–98.

Poister, T.H. and Thomas, J.C. (2011). The effect of expectations and expectancy confirmation/disconfirmation on motorists' satisfaction with state highways. *Journal of Public Administration Research and Theory* **21** (4): 601–617.

Preston, L.E. and Donaldson, T. (1999). Stakeholder management and organizational wealth. *Academy of Management Review* **24** (4): 619–620.

Putnam, R.D. (1993). *Making Democracy Work: Civic Traditions in Modern Italy*. Princeton, NJ: Princeton University Press.

Ramírez, Y. (2010). Intellectual capital models in Spanish public sector. *Journal of Intellectual Capital* **11** (2): 248–264.

Rawlins, B. (2008). Give the emperor a mirror: toward developing a stakeholder measurement of organizational transparency. *Journal of Public Relations Research* **21** (1): 71–99.

Roch, C.H. and Poister, T.H. (2006). Citizens, accountability, and service satisfaction: the influence of expectations. *Urban Affairs Review* **41** (3): 292–308.

Roosbroek, S. (2006). *Comparing Trust in Government Across Countries: What Role for Public Administration?* Leuven, The Netherlands: Public Management Institute.

Sanders, K. and Canel, M.-J. ed. (2013). *Government Communication Cases and Challenges*. London: Bloomsbury Academic.

Sanders, K. and Canel, M.J. (2015). Mind the gap: local government communication strategies and Spanish citizens' perceptions of their cities. *Public Relations Review* **41** (5): 777–784.

Skelley, B.D. (2008). The persistence of the politics-administration dichotomy: an additional explanation. *Public Administration Quarterly* **32** (4): 549–570.

Sloterdijk, P. (2011). *Bubbles, Spheres I*. Cambridge, MA: MIT Press.

Spencer, T. and McGrath, C. ed. (2006). *Challenge and Response: Essays on Public Affairs and Transparency*. Brussels: Landmarks.

Staw, B.M. and Epstein, L.D. (2000). What bandwagons bring: effects of popular management techniques on corporate performance, reputation, and CEO pay. *Administrative Science Quarterly* **45** (3): 523–556.

Stoker, G. (2006). Public value management: a new narrative for networked governance? *The American Review of Public Administration* **36** (1): 41–57.

Talbot, C. (2009). Public value – the next "big thing" in public management? *International Journal of Public Administration* **32** (3–4): 167–170.

Taleb, N. (2007). *The Black Swan: The Impact of the Highly Improbable*. New York: Random House.

Thijs, N. (2011). *Measure to Improve: Improving Public Sector Performance by using Citizen-User Satisfaction Information*. Brussels: EUPAN/EIPA.

Thijs, N. and Staes, P. (2008). *European Primer on Customer Satisfaction Management*. Brussels: EUPAN/EIPA.

Tufekci, Z. (2013). "Not this one": social movements, the attention economy, and microcelebrity networked activism. *American Behavioral Scientist* **57** (7): 848–870.

Valentini, C. (2013). Public relations in the public sector: the role of strategic communication in the Italian public administration. *Sinergie Rivista Di Studi E Ricerche* **92**: 93–113.

Van de Walle, S. and Bouckaert, G. (2003). Public service performance and trust in government: the problem of causality. *International Journal of Public Administration* **26** (8–9): 891–913.

Van Dijck, J. and Poell, T. (2013). Understanding social media logic. *Media and Communication* **1** (1): 2–14.

Van Ryzin, G.G. (2004). Expectations, performance, and citizen satisfaction with urban services. *Journal of Policy Analysis and Management* **23** (3): 433–448.

Van Ryzin, G.G. (2006). Testing the expectancy disconfirmation model of citizen satisfaction with local government. *Journal of Public Administration Research and Theory* **16** (4): 599–611.

Wæraas, A. (2014). Beauty from within: what bureaucracies stand for. *American Review of Public Administration* **44** (6): 675–692.

Wæraas, A. and Maor, M. ed. (2015). *Organizational Reputation in the Public Sector*. London: Routledge.

Wæraas, A. and Sataøen, H. (2015). Being all things to all customers: building reputation in an institutionalized field. *British Journal of Management* **26** (2): 310–326.

Weber, M. (1958). *The Protestant Ethic and the Spirit of Capitalism*. New York: Scribners.

Whicher, A. and Cawood, G. (2013). *An Overview of Service Design for the Private and Public Sectors*. Cardiff, Wales: SEE Network.

Young, S. (2007). *Government Communication in Australia*. Cambridge, MA: Cambridge University Press.

4

Antifragile Communication: Closing the Gap through Intangible Assets

> *The most important things in life are intangible*
> (Thom Hartmann)

The core argument of this book is that intangible assets, both in terms of their study and practice, open fruitful avenues to close the described gaps that exist between citizens and public organizations. Public sector organizations need new ways of measuring their services and value, and intangible assets offer a productive view into both service and measurement. We propose that providing public value requires good management of intangible assets, which in turn will help public sector organizations to become "antifragile." In order to introduce the second part of this book, this chapter first looks at intangible assets in terms of their definition, specific requirements within the public sector for their construction, and their typologies. We then elaborate on how public sector organizations can survive and become more "antifragile" through five changes that strengthen the organization in advance through investing in intangible assets. Finally, we specify the classification of intangible assets used in this book.

4.1 Defining "Intangible Asset"

4.1.1 What Is an Intangible Asset About?

The *Merriam-Webster's Collegiate Dictionary* defines *intangible* as "not tangible," and *tangible* is defined as "capable of being perceived especially by the sense of touch." "Asset" is "an item of value owned." An intangible asset, then, has to do with nonphysical realities (as opposed to physical ones such as machinery, buildings, and land) that provide value.

The roots of intangible assets originate in the business world. Can something intangible provide value? Lev and Daum (2004, p. 6) concluded that it could. They describe the "intangible assets movement," which they locate at the beginning of the 1990s, when companies became aware of intangibility as a new source of corporate value and growth. During the 1980s, the book value of corporations constantly shrank in relation to their market value, and the difference was attributed to intangible assets: in only 10 years (from 1982 to 1992), the value of intangibles increased from 38% to 62% of market value, with book value decreasing from 62% to 38%.

Public Sector Communication: Closing Gaps Between Citizens and Public Organizations, First Edition. María-José Canel and Vilma Luoma-aho.
© 2019 John Wiley & Sons, Inc. Published 2019 by John Wiley & Sons, Inc.

Lev and Down provide data on the profit of intangibility. In the late 1990s, annual US investment in intangible assets (for example, research and development, brand enhancement, and employee training) was roughly $1.2 trillion, and this investment – particularly in the intangibles that enable enterprises to innovate – brought in returns that were significantly higher than capital costs and the returns of fixed-asset investments. The "intangible assets movement," these authors stated in 2004, had succeeded in what they deemed the first phase of its mission, namely, "creating awareness and active discourse about the economic role of intangible assets and their consequences" (p. 7).

At the beginning of the twenty-first century, organizations' productivity was deemed to be built on intangible assets (Sztompka, 2000). Intangibles are turning out to be the dominant means for creating value at companies, increasingly due to the urgent need to focus the company's business strategy on the creation of a competitive advantage. It is commonly agreed today in business that intangible assets are the key to gaining competitive advantage in the market. Despite this understanding and agreement, there are very few practical measures that have been found to demonstrate the true value of intangible assets, even in the business context.

4.1.2 Pinning Down Intangibility

Intangible things are by their very nature difficult to describe and explain. Intangible assets have been argued to be a contributor to the disparity between companies' value per their accounting records (book value) and companies' value per their market capitalization (market value). But how can this gray area that has been allocated for intangibility in accountancy terms be identified, understood, recognized, and assessed?

To understand what an intangible asset is, first it is important to understand that assets are to be understood in terms of value. Simply put, assets are things that have a value (that is, they are things or persons of use or value). Value is the monetary worth of an asset. Therefore, in order to be recognized as an asset, the thing in question has to have a value (a fair and realistic one) for its owner – that is, it has to be represented in the organizational balance sheet using a monetary term in a similar manner to what is required in representing a tangible asset such as a building (see Michael, 2016 for a clear explanation of this process).

Since putting a value on an intangible asset is open to disparities, the process of identifying the asset owned by a company, appraising its value, and disclosing it in the balance sheet is governed partly by regulatory accounting standards. Statement of Accounting Concepts number 4 (SAC 4), issued by the Australian Accounting Standards Board in 1995, was the first set of standards that provided that tangibility was not an essential characteristic of an asset. In 1998, the IASB issued Standard 38 (IAS 38), which defines an intangible asset as "an identifiable non-monetary asset without physical substance"; IAS 38 requires a *past event* that has given rise to a resource that the entity *controls* and from which *future economic benefits* are expected to flow. Thus, the extra provision for an intangible asset under IAS 38 is *identifiability*, a criterion that requires an intangible asset to be separable from the entity or something that arises from a contractual or legal right.

Therefore, one of the key features of an intangible asset, apart from its nonvisibility and profitability, is that it needs to be clearly distinguished. As we will discuss below, this characteristic, which is at the core of one of the critical issues in the world of intangibles, both in the public and private sectors, is their valuation.

4.1.3 The Features of an Intangible Asset

Building on these standards as well as the contributions of scholars and other sources such as documentation produced by international organizations, Table 4.1 systematizes the major features of an intangible asset.

An intangible asset is a nonphysical asset; it may be (though is not necessarily) knowledge based; it is identifiable and distinct from the company (and controlled by it); it acts as a source for an organization's competitive advantage; and future economic benefit is expected to flow from it, thereby enabling tangible assets. To acknowledge such a resource, standardized measurements and reporting are required, and the process of an intangible asset's generation has to be considered to contain two phases: research ("the original and planned investigation") and development ("the application of research findings to a plan or design for the production of" something that is new or improves what came before) (IAS 38). In terms of management, intangible assets transform the structures and procedural features of the organization.

However, several of these features do not seem to apply to the public sector, where one of the major contrasting characteristics is that there is seldom a measurable market value. For this reason, we will now explore different types of intangibles to identify which of them are transferrable to the public sector.

4.2 Types of Intangibles

But which intangible assets are transferable to the public sector? Which intangibles can be built through communication?

There is no clear typology of intangible assets that can be turned to. Rather, in the world of intangibles, a plethora of terms and noble-sounding words is found. The following is a list of things that have been described as intangible assets: fairness, dignity, equality, justice, quality of life, security, freedom, representation, participation, commitment, trust, creativity, communities of practice, innovation, social impact, and usefulness (Diefenbach, 2009, p. 900).

4.2.1 Accounting Categorizations

Based on contributions from different sources (Hall, 1992; Petty and Guthrie, 2000; Michael, 2016; Mard, Hyden, and Rigby, 2000), intangibles have been categorized according to their *origin*: they can be internally generated (as a result of the organic growth of the company) or externally acquired (for example, purchased). With regard to *life length*, there are intangible assets that have a limited life (for example, a patent) and others with an unlimited one (for example, a brand).

Submitted to regulatory accounting standards as they are, some intangible assets are identifiable, meaning that they are either separable (that is, capable of being separated from the entity and sold, transferred, or licensed) or arise from contractual or legal rights (irrespective of whether those rights are themselves separable). If they are identifiable, they are disclosed in the balance sheet. But other intangible assets such as staff competences or administrative systems, on the assumption that their value is not neatly measured, are nonidentifiable assets (and thus undisclosed: they do not appear in the balance sheet).

Table 4.1 Definitions and features of an intangible asset.

Source	Definition	Feature
IAS 38, 1995	Nonmonetary assets that have no physical substance and are identifiable (either by being separable or by arising from contractual or other legal rights). They account for the disparity that exists between a company's value per its accounting records and the value that it has per its market capitalization	*Nonphysical substance* *Explain disparities* between market value and book value (accounting records)
Hall, 1992	Resources (assets or skills) that act as "feedstock" of capability differentials and are the wellspring for an organization's competitive advantage	Source for an organization's *competitive advantage*
Cañibano, Garcia-Ayuso, and Sanchez, 2000	Developed at identifiable costs, purchased or internally developed, limited life (copyrights and patents), controlled by the entity Identifiable: an intangible asset is separable from the entity or arises from a contractual or legal right	*Identifiable* *Controlled* by the entity
OECD, 2008	Long-term investments, different from fixed assets, oriented toward increasing a company's future profits/outcomes	Nonphysical claim *to future benefits*; enablers of tangible assets; economic benefit is expected to flow *Future benefit* is expected to flow from them
Egginton, 1990 Belkaoui, 1992 Maher, Stickney, and Weil, 2012; Lev, 2001, 2002	A claim to future benefits that does not have a physical or financial (for example, a stock or a bond) embodiment; it enables tangible assets to emerge Intangibles represent capabilities and potential for future growth and income Future benefit is expected to flow from them	
Lev, 2002	The organizational infrastructure (the business processes and systems that help to create a competitive advantage and to generate sustaining cash flow) of a company becomes a critical "production factor" and thus becomes the major intangible of the enterprise	Managing intangibles requires appropriate support systems and *specific organizational recipes* Intangibles imply a *transformation in structural and procedural features of the organization*
Lev and Daum, 2004	Measurable	*Standardized measurements and reporting* are required
OECD, 1999	Defined merely as intellectual capital The economic value of organizational (structural) capital and of human capital	*Knowledge based*
Edvinsson and Malone, 1997	The possession of knowledge, expertise, technology, and customer relations that provide a competitive advantage	
IAS 38, 1995	Requires research development	Requires *research development*

Surprisingly, so far no category seems to embrace the long list of intangible assets with which we started this section. It seems that accounting standards don't quite know what to do with such a diffuse area of profitability. The ownership of relationships and goodwill has proven to be an especially great challenge for accounting.

Based on how ownership of intangibles is defined, there are intangibles that come from rights (for example, leases, distribution agreements, covenants, supply contracts, licenses, certifications, and franchises); others come from intellectual property, which includes patents, copyrights, trademarks, and proprietary technology (for example, recipes, marketing strategies, formulations, and customs lists); and finally, there is a group of intangibles that is classified under the label "relationships" and includes trained and assembled workforces as well as customer and distribution relationships (Brand Finance, 2016). In our understanding, this third categorization points to the idea that relationships might be the wellspring for the generation of intangibles, and it seems that it is out of well-managed relations among different actors that the intangibles mentioned above (such as representation, participation, commitment, and trust) can be engendered. To the extent that communication is a builder of relationships, it is not unreasonable to state that in accounting standards, the role of communication is implicitly acknowledged for a certain type of intangibles.

4.2.2 Relationships and Perceptions as the Basis for Intangible Assets that Aim to Build Competitive Advantage

"Goodwill" has been the label to which accounting has resorted in order to name the area of value that cannot be accounted for by all of the separable assets. It might derive from things that are highly intangible – for example, the perception that stakeholders have of an organization guided by high-quality standards. The *Business Dictionary* defines goodwill as the "assumed value of the attractive force that generates sales revenue in a business, and adds value to its assets." It is a broader term than reputation, and it could be said that goodwill is a sort of large label that embraces anything connoting the idea of being on good terms with another party in a way that produces some benefit for the organization.

However, because accountants took the view that goodwill was an overly broad (and vague) term, in 2001, the accounting standards IFRS 3 in Europe and FAS 141 in the United States attempted to escape from its catch-all nature and required companies to break down the value of the intangibles that they acquire into different categories. Leaving aside whether these categories refer to identifiable intangibles or not, the point we want to make here is that this typology opens new and larger categories for those intangibles that do not exist without communication. The IFRS3 categories of intangible assets include those which are marketing related (for example, trademarks and Internet domain names), customer related (for example, customer lists and customer relationships), contract based (for example, licensing, construction permits, and franchise agreements), technology based (for example, patented technology, databases, and recipes), and, finally, artistic related (for example, plays and advertising jingles).

The point of intangibles is that they enable the organization that owns them to be distinguished in the sector that it belongs to. This is the starting point that Hall takes for his typology (Hall, 1992), in which not only relations but also perceptions are shown to be relevant in the world of intangibles. Hall considers intangible assets to be feedstock for an organization's competitive advantage. Intangible resources act, he states, as the wellspring for four differentials: functional, cultural, positional, and regulatory ones (Hall, 1992, based on Coyne, 1986).

From these categorizations, three ideas emerge. First, the competitive advantage that an organization can build depends on the *knowledge* that it is capable of *sharing*. Second, to the extent that in relationship building mutual understanding is a key concept, intangible assets also depend on the *perceptions* that each side has of the other side of the relationship, which includes the extent to which the competitive advantage is *acknowledged*. Finally, and as a consequence, both in establishing relations in which knowledge is shared and acknowledged, as well as in managing perceptions, *communication* has a key role in the generation of intangible assets.

4.3 Why Are Intangibles Different in the Public Sector?

Importing the notion of intangible assets from the private sector to the public sector requires a new conceptualization. As concluded before, citizen needs, audience diversity, resource availability, and a need to work toward the common good are all aspects that are particular to the public sector (Luoma-aho, 2007; Wæraas and Byrkjeflot, 2012). Based on what has been discussed so far about the public sector in this book, Table 4.2 builds upon the different features of an intangible asset as these were identified above in order to profile the major factors that have led to the transfer of intangible assets to the public sector, as well as the threats and challenges that might be faced. We elaborate below on three specific issues that are critical for this transference.

Table 4.2 Transferring intangible assets to the public sector.

Feature of an intangible asset	Factors that have led to the transfer of intangible assets to the public sector	Threats and challenges of transfer
Nonphysical substance	Need to prove public value and efficiency of public sector organizations	Intangible nature of public services and benefits
Power to explain disparities between market value and book value (accounting records)	Debate on the need to measure public value	No market value apparent; mostly knowledge-based organizations; the complex aim of total social economic welfare
Source for the *competitive advantage* of an organization	Rising importance of citizen satisfaction and public sector reputation	The need to please all stakeholders and the multitude of constituencies equally
Role in distinguishing an organization from others	Challenged legitimacy	No requirement for uniqueness; the ideal for most public sector organizations is neutral rather than excellent reputation
Identifiability	The need to make tangible the contribution of the public sector	Complexities of legal frameworks of public sector organizations

Table 4.2 (Continued)

Feature of an intangible asset	Factors that have led to the transfer of intangible assets to the public sector	Threats and challenges of transfer
Control by the entity	Democratic ideals: controlled by all citizens equally; more diverse publics and stakeholders; multiplicity of roles	Democratic, participatory control remains a challenge in itself
Generates a *resource*	Diminishing resources	Resources that benefit are not economic in nature; examples include networking public support, rule following, and decision acceptance
Origin of economic benefits	Financial pressures	The challenge of processing the tension between economic value, social value, and public value
Nonphysical claim *to future benefits*	Need to increase revenues, reduce costs, and garner new resources	The problem of (long-term) outcomes
Managing intangibles requires appropriate support systems and *specific organizational recipes*	Citizen experiences of complexity and bureaucracy Debates about the public value of public management	Implies a modification in structural and procedural features of the organization Fewer incentives for efficacy and efficiency but greater public scrutiny and accountability
Standardized measurements and reporting are required	Rising need for accountability; cross-sector operating context of public sector organizations	Lack of standardized measures Short tradition of measuring despite urgent need of financial pressures The challenge of working at different amounts of publicness
Knowledge based	Need for innovation and knowledge transfer	Public sector organizations are involved in processes of research and development
It requires *research development*	Need to keep up with the changing environment	Lack of funding for extras such as research and development; slow processes and red tape
Communication has an implied role in its development	Public opinion and public sector legitimacy dependent on citizen relations and citizen perceptions and acknowledgement	Communication is treated as a cost center, not a revenue center; challenge of showing the key role communication has in increasing intangible assets

4.3.1 What Is the Value of Intangibility in the Public Sector?

The public sector faces the challenge of valuing intangible assets, though this challenge also exists in the private sector. As different finance papers show (see, for instance, Brand Finance, 2016), in 2016, the private sector continued to look for new forms of financial reporting, since a transaction is still required for an intangible asset to be recognized, and as a result many highly valued assets remain undisclosed (Haigh, 2016, p. 3; Tilley, 2016, p. 4). As Guthrie et al. stated years ago, the challenge of putting a value on intangibles is particularly problematic for knowledge-based organizations (Petty and Guthrie, 2000, p. 159), and the public sector is primarily composed of knowledge-based organizations.

The fact that public sector organizations are not all exposed to market value (meaning that there is a lack of easily accessible references as to valuation) and the multiplicity of instances (and thus also the multiplicity of criteria) against which an asset will be valued make evaluating intangibles a challenge in the public sector. Similarly, the obligation to combine different aspects of value at the moment of appraisal as a result of the multiple dimensions of public sector functions remains a challenge. Since, as Bond and Dent state, the specific role for public administrations is to contribute to an improvement in total social and economic welfare, "the contribution is not solely based on 'value for money' criteria but must also incorporate a 'quality of living' dimension" (Bond and Dent, 1998, p. 371). Therefore, discussion of efficiency must embrace different criteria, including (among others) money, social value, and quality of life.

When no profit is reported, other indicators are required, and the public sector needs to find ways to express satisfactorily the different dimensions in which public performance consists. This is challenging, as the value cannot be only based on quantitative measures but needs to include qualitative descriptions and statements (Bond and Dent, 1998). The methods currently available do not adequately reflect the service-based nature of assets in the public sector.

The public sector is composed of organizations with different degrees of publicness, and there is increasing competition among public sector organizations, albeit still less than that found in the private sector. But beyond helping with competition, intangible assets have proved to offer a management paradigm that increases efficiency and efficacy. First, they improve organizations' internal management, to the extent that they allow key strengths and a more efficient redistribution of resources to be identified. Second, they enable organizations to become known for those strengths, which will ultimately be to their benefit (Sánchez, 2008, p. 577). Third, in the new context of the knowledge-based economy (associated with the network society or innovation society), there is much support for the assertion that intangibles are instrumental in the determination of organizations' value. This is a point made by Petty and Guthrie (2000, p. 155) in relation to intellectual capital, but we regard it as applicable to all intangibles.

In our earlier consideration of the accounting systems used in the public sector, we suggested ways to look at the possible impact of different intangibles. It is reasonable to think that a well-reputed city council will attract tourism and international investment, that a legitimate government will save costs on systems of deterrence and coercion, and that a more engaged citizenry might reduce costs of social services thanks to coproduction of services and dialogue (Canel and Luoma-aho, 2015b). Some of these assumptions will be looked at in the specific cases of the second part of this book.

Regardless of whether their impact is economic or social, it is clear that the potential to provide a competitive advantage is not the only feature associated with intangible assets. Public sector organizations are required to fulfill certain standards that are socially constructed (by laws or by their stakeholders' expectations) and that determine the nature of the competition in which the public sector must engage.

The "intangible assets movement" in the public sector will not be without criticism. One such line of argument is that all investments that public sector organizations make are under scrutiny, and one could challenge why intangibles would matter more than the actual tasks of providing services (Wæraas and Byrkjeflot, 2012). Some have argued that there is no need to communicate when it comes to public services and that providers' reputations should be formed through actions alone. Similarly, it has also been argued that trust will be formed as a result of experiences and cannot be cultivated. Moreover, critics have also questioned whether it actually matters what kind of intangible assets public sector organizations have, as they are often monopolies in service provision and individual attitudes play a smaller role in guiding their operations.

4.3.2 Building Intangible Assets: Is It Possible?

But how can intangible assets be built? One could in fact argue that the present low levels of citizen trust in government and public service providers are due to both bad management and poor communication on the part of organizations. The logic behind this position is that public sector organizations with a better reputation would benefit society more: trusted public organizations maintain and attract business, increase legitimacy, guarantee fulfillment of public policies without the need to increase coactivity, enhance public participation, empower citizens, and increase engagement. The growing importance of intangible assets in public administration is now acknowledged in the literature, and their appropriate identification, valuation, and management contribute to the success of public entities by improving decision making and showing the quality of their management processes to the public (Ramírez, 2010, p. 252).

The challenges identified for building and managing public sector intangible assets are similar to those reported from the private sector: inputs are complex and difficult to define, and outputs are not easily measured. We propose communication to provide an answer, yet orienting public sector communication to the building of intangible assets implies important transformations in the way in which communication is managed, in terms of new quality criteria, public–private partnerships, management of objectives, communication of results, and assessment of the quality of relations (Garnett, Marlowe, and Pandey, 2008; Gelders and Ihlen, 2010; Pollit and Bouckaert, 2011; Wæraas and Byrkjeflot, 2012; Dahlberg and Holmberg, 2013; Sanders and Canel, 2013; Luoma-aho and Makikangas, 2014; Wæraas, 2014; Canel and Luoma-aho, 2015a).

We feel that despite the criticisms made in relation to intangible assets in the public sector context, public sector organizations need new ways of measuring their services. To this end, intangible assets offer a valuable possibility to understand public sector organizations' success in terms of both service and measurement of performance. Transferring intangible assets from the private sector will imply adjusting the concepts and practices to public sector settings, developing research on already "imported" assets, and opening lines of research to establish, coin, and build new intangible assets to respond better to the changing environments in which public sector communication operates today.

4.4 Different Intangible Assets in the Public Sector

The core point of building intangible assets in the public sector is to meet the changing expectations in citizens' and stakeholders' minds. In fact, what constitutes a good public service is a challenging question. The literature has attempted to establish different principles in this regard; they often include high quality of services, transparency, and efficiency, as well as rectification of errors. We would suggest that intangible assets play a critical role in determining the final outcome of all of these, though we are aware that these different intangibles (or their impact) might not be easily separated from each other.

Petty and Guthrie's comparative analysis of different models of intellectual capital (Petty and Guthrie, 2000) shows that Sveiby's (1997, 1998) intangible asset monitor and Kaplan and Norton's balanced scorecard (Kaplan and Norton, 1992) classify intangibles into three categories that differentiate internal capital (structural), external capital (customer related), and human capital (learning and growth). This differentiation is the basis upon which Bossi Queiroz, Fuertes Callén, and Serrano Cinca (2001) suggest public sector intellectual capital to consist of intangibles related to internal organization (like innovation and know-how), external relations (like image and quality of service), human capital (like employees' attitudes and skills), social and environmental capital (like social commitment), and transparency (like information release).

However, precisely because in our judgment it is a restriction to equate intangible assets with intellectual capital alone, we find that there are currently several intangible assets applicable to the public sector that do not fit the above typologies suggested, such as:

- Organizational culture (which ensures the efficiency of the organization); this is indicated through internal employee satisfaction and commitment measures.
- Legitimacy (which allows public acceptance of the organization and its functions); indicators of this include public opinion and a lack of questioning of the organization's role.
- Reputation (the record of past deeds, overall impression); this is indicated through reputation rankings.
- Satisfaction (the overall pleasantness of the public service experience); this can be described through quality performance indicators.
- Engagement (the capacity a public sector organization has to involve citizens in public administration processes); the number and extent of coproduction programs involving citizen participation is an indicator of this.
- Social capital (the capacity of an organization to generate social cohesion); this can be indicated by factors such as the development of dialogue processes.

We will return to the topic of typologies for intangibles later on, but in the next section, we will address the question of how intangibles help in addressing fragility.

4.5 Avoiding Fragility through Intangible Assets

Our proposition is that intangible assets help to balance the organization through increasing flexibility and generating goodwill that can be carried into uncertain times (Luoma-aho, 2005, p. 368). Investing in intangible assets is the only long-term builder of organizational resilience, particularly when the environment around public sector organizations becomes uncertain (Longstaff and Yang, 2008, p. 3). Intangible assets help organizations to become antifragile; we will now explain what this antifragility means.

As each chapter of the second part of the book will show, each specific intangible asset helps to address organizational fragility, and this is why many of the recent governance ideals build on the stabilizing role of intangible assets. For example, new public governance (NPG) emphasizes openness, active citizenship, and stakeholder networks and collaboration, principles that are close to ideals of public service cocreation (Ryan, 2012; Virtanen and Stenvall, 2014). Public value thinking notes that true value only results from perceptions and a mutual acknowledgement (Meynhardt, 2009). Similarly, another current trend, service design, has as its starting point the individual experiences and satisfaction of citizens, all of which are intangible in nature (Whicher and Cawood, 2013). All these government ideals refer to relations, and intangible assets in fact always reside in the context of a relationship between the organization, its employees, and citizens (Yang and Taylor, 2013; Bowden, Luoma-aho, and Naumann, 2016).

Changing from fragile to antifragile hence means changing the relationship between public sector organizations and citizens. Communication plays a central role in this changing relationship: open and transparent communication has been suggested as a central success factor in allowing organizations to survive in a turbulent environment (Longstaff and Yang, 2008, p. 3).

4.5.1 Antifragile Communication: Taking the Citizen Point of View

The notion of complexity relates to Nassim Taleb's concept of antifragile (2012) – that is, something that does not break but in fact improves in response to stress and shocks. Taleb writes of multiplicative chains of unanticipated effects that result from complexity, whether in organizations or in society. To survive in this challenging environment, antifragile communication has been suggested as a solution for organizations.

Antifragile communication is about making organizations strong enough to thrive in an unstable environment through strengthening their intangible assets (Luoma-aho, 2013). Although many of the needs and changes that public sector organizations will face in the future are to a degree unpredictable, the idea behind antifragile communication is to equip organizations to become more resilient, no matter what the change ahead may be (Luoma-aho, 2014). When relationships with citizens and stakeholders become stronger, unpredictable changes pose less of a threat to organizations.

The core principles of antifragile communication, stakeholder optimization and engagement, fit the public sector context well (Luoma-aho, 2014). The idea of stakeholder optimization stems from service design to always plan communication from the receiver's point of view. The focus of service design falls on making services that best meet citizen needs through understanding citizens' journeys before they come and use the service (customer journey) and the logic behind the choices made (Whicher and Cawood, 2013). Citizen experience is central: to enable the best possible experience for both public sector employees and citizens, the traditional model of discrete departments will need to be replaced by a common goal and cross-organizational sharing of data and information (McChrystal et al., 2015).

Optimization refers to making something fully functional and efficient, and for organizations, this means starting with actual citizen or stakeholder needs instead of organizational agendas or interests. In fact, if citizen needs are the driving force for communication, organizational messages can only be formed after hearing or studying citizen needs. This is a challenge for organizations that have been in charge for most of their existence (Bourgon, 2011), and sometimes even good attempts at ascertaining citizen needs are lost in surveys constructed according to the organization's ability to categorize and manage those needs.

Similarly, stakeholder engagement refers to a shared process of working together with stakeholders and citizens. Although engagement is now on the agenda of most public sector organizations across the world – as will be discussed in our chapter on engagement – it is still true that "whilst the rhetoric of policy makers emphasizes the importance of citizen 'participation' and interactivity, in practice the reality of this 'participation' is often basic one-way 'consultation'" (Bowden et al., 2016, p. 259). As the citizens and stakeholders of public sector organizations today are networked (Papacharissi, 2014), not all of their engagement efforts are recognized as such by public sector organizations. Authentic engagement and coproduction build on communication as the core of value creation (Prahalad and Ramaswamy, 2004).

4.5.2 The Steps toward Antifragility

Moving toward antifragility will take several changes in public sector organizations. The first steps here must take place inside the organization, and they will begin with focusing especially on public sector employees and internal culture, before then expanding to include outside stakeholders in listening, interaction, and expectation management.

Step 1: Moving from "humans as resources" to employee engagement.

Antifragility starts from the inside of the organization, and all stakeholder engagement is built on employee engagement, an area that is still often overlooked by public sector organizations. Only public servants who feel engaged are able to authentically engage others (Imandin, Bisschoff, and Botha, 2014).

Step 2: Moving from strategies to cultivating a strong internal culture.

Antifragile communication is based on establishing a strong organizational culture. A strong enough organizational culture acts as a script: it can guide actions to save time spent on dealing with specific procedures (Schein, 1985). Individual strategies are often useful, but if the organizational culture does not support them, the actions that stem from them do not bear fruit.

Step 3: Moving from messages to listening.

Public sector organizations are traditionally good at crafting messages to reach citizens, but the listening and receiving side of the interaction is often shallow. Even when public sector organizations attempt to "listen," they are often merely "hearing," as they simply ask citizens and stakeholders to answer surveys created according to organizational needs (Macnamara, 2016). To become antifragile, public sector organizations need to establish an infrastructure of listening that ensures authentic interaction with citizens (Macnamara, 2015).

Step 4: Moving from attention to interaction.

Attention alone does not guarantee that citizens engage or share their views, yet much of public sector organizations' and governments' communication today still relies on campaigns that mostly create attention (Canel and Sanders, 2015). Authentic interaction requires ongoing collaboration and meeting needs (Tirkkonen and Luoma-aho, 2014), which demands much more time and resources than most public sector organizations currently have to spare.

Step 5: Moving from reputation management to expectation management.

As all intangibles reside in relationships, managing reputation would mean managing citizens' and stakeholders' thoughts. Instead, public sector organizations should know their stakeholders' and citizens' needs to be able to anticipate their expectations. Managing expectations is a matter of ongoing interaction and monitoring (Luoma-aho and Olkkonen, 2016), and it signals a change from ongoing interaction and listening (Macnamara, 2016).

All these moves are ideals, and implementing them will not occur quickly. Some may take long periods of time and even be unrealistic for some public sector organizations. The order in which they are developed may not be linear, and the core argument of this book is that intangible assets play a key role in advancing all these movements.

4.6 Intangible Assets in this Book

We end this chapter by presenting the notion of intangible assets that will be used in this book, as well as the types of intangible assets that we will address. These derive from what has been discussed so far.

4.6.1 Definition of Intangible Asset in the Public Sector

For the purpose of this book, we define an intangible asset in the public sector as:

> *A nonmonetary asset (without physical substance) that enables and gives access to tangible assets, that is activated through communication, and that is built on past events (and linked to the behavior of the organization); therefore, it gives rise to a resource that is identifiable and from which a future (long-term) benefit/value (social, monetary, and so forth) is expected to flow, potentially, for both the organization and stakeholders/citizens.*

This conceptualization implies that an intangible asset:

- derives from good practices and experiences, and as such can be managed but not created from scratch;
- is a self-sustaining system that enforces itself over time by strengthening existing connections and accumulating other forms of assets (both tangible and intangible ones, including hybrid assets that mix tangibility and intangibility);
- is identifiable as belonging to the organization (attributed to it) and, therefore, depends on its being acknowledged. The intangible assets that we deal with in this book are perceptions-based assets;
- to the extent that it relies on being acknowledged, requires communication to be built;
- bridges the gap between citizens and public sector organizations by establishing common ground and understanding each other's points of view;
- has the ultimate end, in the context of the public sector, of building the public good – understood as those "needs and challenges we have in common" – and therefore, we argue, has the potential to benefit both the organization and the stakeholder.

Table 4.3 compares the features of intangible assets in the private and public sectors.

Table 4.3 Features of an intangible asset: From the private to the public sector.

Private sector	Public sector
Nonphysical substance	*Nonphysical substance*
Explains disparities between market value and book value (accounting records)	There is no need to explain disparities, since there is no market value; it explains the good performance of an organization relative to others
Source for *competitive advantage* for an organization	Source for *advantage* for the organization as it competes in a multipurpose public sector and for competing to meet socially construed standards of both excellence and integrity
Identifiable *Controlled* by the entity	*Identifiable* and *democratically controlled* by the organization
Nonphysical claim *to future benefits*; enablers of tangible assets *Future benefit* is expected to flow from them	With *monetary expression in accounting records*: an intangible asset reduces costs, garners resources, attracts investments; it enables both *economic growth and social values*, which are of *benefit for both the organization and stakeholders*
Managing intangibles requires appropriate support systems and *specific organizational recipes*	Since the public sector's audience is large (all citizens), intangible assets management is associated with visibility for and the acknowledgement of the asset by stakeholders
Intangibles imply a *transformation in structural and procedural features of the organization*	*Communication* has a role in its development to the extent that intangible assets depend on their being acknowledged
Standardized measurements and reporting are required	*Measured by both quantitative and qualitative methods*
Knowledge based	*Knowledge based*
Requires *research development*	Requires *research development*

4.6.2 Different Intangible Assets and the Relationships between Them

All intangible assets in this book reside in the relationship between the public sector organization and its stakeholders. All these intangibles assets require mutual acknowledgement to exist and hold the potential to benefit both sides. Therefore, they are all perceptions-based intangible assets. Communication is a key to building these assets, and the image below shows the dominant sources or bases for each intangible asset. Although the bases may overlap in practice, Figure 4.1 illustrates which is most important for each asset. Public sector communication should focus on these bases when building each intangible asset.

In the second part of the book, each chapter refers to one intangible asset. They have been selected according to existing needs and the prior existence of enough studies and practical cases in relation to them. All the presented intangible assets require

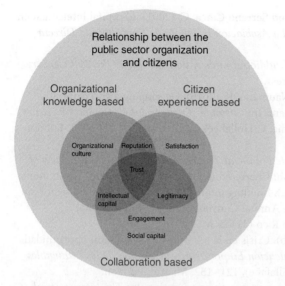

Figure 4.1 Typology of perceptions-based intangible assets in the public sector consisting of knowledge, experience, and mutual action based on the context of the relationship between the public sector organization and citizens.

communication to exist (that is, all of them are stakeholders' attributions regarding a public sector organization), and we have left out intangible assets that are not dependent on communication (for instance, patents).

The order of the chapters in the second part of the book is as follows. We start with intangible assets that are predominantly dependent on one of the actors: satisfaction (which is based on citizen experiences) and organizational culture (which is based on organizational knowledge). We then move on to intangible assets that are based on both an organization's knowledge and stakeholders' experience: reputation, legitimacy, and intellectual capital. There are two intangible assets that predominantly require mutual action (on the parts of both the organization and the citizen) if they are to emerge: engagement and social capital. Trust is an intangible asset that is based on both organizational knowledge and experience, and it requires actions on both sides. Indeed, all intangible assets ultimately involve trust. For this reason, trust is present in all chapters, and we also devote a final chapter to a systematic discussion of its meaning and role in the public sector. In each chapter, we first provide a full research map with an up-to-date literature review and research sources, and we then offer a specific practical case or best practices, or recommendations for building the asset in question.

References

Belkaoui, A.R. (1992). *Accounting Theory*. London: Academic Press.

Bond, S. and Dent, P. (1998). Efficient management of public sector assets the call for correct evaluation criteria and techniques. *Journal of Property Valuation and Investment* **16** (4): 369–385.

Bossi Queiroz, A., Fuertes Callén, Y., and Serrano Cinca, C. (2001). El capital intelectual en el sector público. *En II Congreso de La Asociación Española de Contabilidad Directa* 4–6.

Bourgon, J. (2011). *A New Synthesis of Public Administration: Serving in the 21st Century.* Washington, DC: McGill Queen's Press.

Bowden, J.L.-H., Luoma-aho, V., and Naumann, K. (2016). Developing a spectrum of positive to negative citizen engagement. In: *Customer Engagement Contemporary Issues and Challenges*, 1st ed. (ed. R.J. Brodie, L. Hollebeek and J. Conduit), 257–277. London: Routledge.

Brand Finance (2016). *Global Intangible Financial Tracker (GIFT): An Annual Review of the World's Intangible Value.* London: Chartered Institute of Management Accountants.

Canel, M.-J. and Luoma-aho, V. (2015a). Building intangible assets in the public sector: an introduction. Paper Presented at the Annual Convention of the International Communication Association, Puerto Rico (21–25 May 2015).

Canel, M.-J. and Luoma-aho, V. (2015b). Crisis en la administración pública, oportunidad para la intangibilidad. In: *La Comunicación Empresarial y la Gestión de los Intangibles en España y Latinoamérica* (ed. J. Villafañe), 121–132. Madrid: Pearson.

Canel, M.-J. and Sanders, K. (2015). Government communication. In: *The International Encyclopedia of Political Communication*, 3 Volume Set, vol. 1 (ed. G. Mazzoleni, K. Barnhurst, K. Ikeda et al.), 1–8. Boston: Wiley-Blackwell.

Cañibano, L., Garcia-Ayuso, M., and Sanchez, P. (2000). Accounting for intangibles: a literature review. *Journal of Accounting Literature* **19**: 102.

Coyne, K.P. (1986). Sustainable competitive advantage – what it is and what it isn't. *Business Horizons* **29** (1): 54–61.

Dahlberg, S. and Holmberg, S. (2013). Democracy and bureaucracy: how their quality matters for popular satisfaction. *West European Politics* **37** (3): 515–537.

Diefenbach, T. (2009). New public management in public sector organizations: the dark sides of managerialistic 'enlightenment'. *Public Administration* **87** (4): 892–909.

Edvinsson, L. and Malone, M.S. (1997). *Intellectual Capital: Realizing Your Company's True Value by Finding Its Hidden Brainpower.* New York: Harper Business.

Egginton, D.A. (1990). Towards some principles for intangible asset accounting. *Accounting and Business Research* **20** (79): 193–205.

Garnett, J.L., Marlowe, J., and Pandey, S.K. (2008). Penetrating the performance predicament: communication as a mediator or moderator of organizational culture's impact on public organizational performance. *Public Administration Review* **68** (2): 266–281.

Gelders, D. and Ihlen, Ø. (2010). Government communication about potential policies: public relations, propaganda or both? *Public Relations Review* **36** (1): 59–62.

Haigh, D. (2016). Foreword. In: *Brand Finance, Global Intangible Financial Tracker (GIFT) 2016: An Annual Review of the World's Intangible Value*, 3. London: Chartered Institute of Management Accountants.

Hall, R. (1992). The strategic analysis of intangible resources. *Strategic Management Journal* **13** (2): 135–144.

Hartmann, T. Azquotes. http://www.azquotes.com/quotes/topics/intangible.html (accessed 8 March 2018).

Imandin, L., Bisschoff, C., and Botha, C. (2014). A model to measure employee engagement. *Problems and Perspectives in Management* **12** (4): 520–532.

International Accounting Standards 38. (1995). http://dipifr.info/lib_files/standards/eng/eng_ifrs_010109/IAS38.pdf (15 September 2017).

Kaplan, R.S. and Norton, D.P. (1992). The balanced scorecard – measures that drive performance. *Harvard Business Review* **70** (1): 71–79.

Lev, B. (2001). *Intangibles: Management, Measurement and Reporting*. Bookings Institution Press.

Lev, B. (2002). Intangibles at a crossroads: what's next? *Financial Executive* **18** (2): 35–39.

Lev, B. and Daum, J.H. (2004). The dominance of intangible assets: consequences for enterprise management and corporate reporting. *Measuring Business Excellence* **8** (1): 6–17.

Longstaff, P.H. and Yang, S. (2008). Communication management and trust: their role in building resilience to "surprises" such as natural disasters, pandemic flu, and terrorism. *Ecology and Society* **13** (1): http://www.ecologyandsociety.org/vol13/iss1/art3/ (accessed 27 September 2017).

Luoma-aho, V. (2005). *Faith-holders as Social Capital of Finnish Public Organizations*, Studies in Humanities 42. Jyväskylä: University of Jyväskylä Press http://dissertations.jyu.fi/studhum/9513922626.pdf (accessed 2 January 2018).

Luoma-aho, V. (2007). Neutral reputation and public sector organizations. *Corporate Reputation Review* **10** (2): 124–143.

Luoma-aho, V. (2013). Antifragile communication. A keynote at "Why should I trust you? Challenges for Communication in Times of Crises, Regional Conference ICA/ACOP, Malaga (18–19 July 2013).

Luoma-aho, V. ed. (2014). *Särkymätön Viestintä [Antifragile Communication]*. Helsinki: ProCom Ry.

Luoma-aho, V.L. and Makikangas, M.E. (2014). Do public sector mergers (re)shape reputation? *International Journal of Public Sector Management* **27** (1): 39–52.

Luoma-aho, V. and Olkkonen, L. (2016). Expectation management. In: *The SAGE Encyclopedia of Corporate Reputation* (ed. C. Carroll), 303–306. Sage Publications.

Macnamara, J. (2015). *Creating an 'Architecture of Listening' in Organizations*. Sydney, NSW: University of Technology Sydney.

Macnamara, J. (2016). *Organizational Listening: The Missing Essential in Public Communication*. New York: Peter Lang.

Maher, M.W., Stickney, C.P., and Weil, R.L. (2012). *Managerial Accounting: An Introduction to Concepts, Methods and Uses*. San Diego, CA: Hatcourt Brace Jovanovich.

Mard, M.J., Hyden, S., and Rigby, J.S. (2000). *Intellectual Property Valuation*. Los Angeles: Financial Valuation Group.

McChrystal, S., Collins, T., Silverman, D., and Fussell, C. (2015). *Team of Teams: New Rules of Engagement for a Complex World*. New York: Portfolio.

Meynhardt, T. (2009). Public value inside: what is public value creation? *International Journal of Public Administration* **32** (3–4): 192–219.

Michael (2016). Intangible asset valuation. Article published in blog Michael's General Musings. https://blogs.harvard.edu/mparrington73/author/mparrington73/ (accessed 15 September 2017).

OECD (1999). Measuring and reporting intellectual capital. Amsterdam: OECD. www.oecd.org (accessed 15 September 2017).

OECD (2008). Intellectual assets and value creation. http://www.oecd.org/sti/inno/oecdworkonintellectualassetsandvaluecreation.htm (accessed 15 September 2017).

Papacharissi, Z. (2014). On networked publics and private spheres in social media. In: *The Social Media Handbook*, 1st ed. (ed. J. Hunsinger and T. Senft), 144–158. New York: Routledge.

Petty, R. and Guthrie, J. (2000). Intellectual capital literature review: measurement, reporting and management. *Journal of Intellectual Capital* **1** (2): 155–176.

Pollit, C. and Bouckaert, G. (2011). *Public Management Reform*. Oxford: Oxford University Press.

Prahalad, C.K. and Ramaswamy, V. (2004). Co-creation experiences: the next practice in value creation. *Journal of Interactive Marketing* **18** (3): 5–14.

Ramírez, Y. (2010). Intellectual capital models in Spanish public sector. *Journal of Intellectual Capital* **11** (2): 248–264.

Ryan, B. (2012). Co-production: option or obligation? *Australian Journal of Public Administration* **71** (3): 314–324.

Sánchez, M.P. (2008). Papel de los intangibles y el capital intelectual en la creación y difusión del conocimiento en las organizaciones. Situación actual y retos de futuro. *Arbor* CLXXXIV, **732**: 575–594.

Sanders, K. and Canel, M.-J. ed. (2013). *Government Communication Cases and Challenges*. London: Bloomsbury Academic.

Schein, E.H. (1985). *Organizational Culture and Leadership. The Jossey-Bass Management Series*. San Francisco, CA: Jossey-Bass Publishers.

Sveiby, K.E. (1997). The intangible assets monitor. *Journal of Human Resource Costing & Accounting* **2** (1): 73–97.

Sveiby, K.E. (1998). Intellectual capital: thinking ahead. *Australian Certified Practising Accountants* **68** (5): 18–23.

Sztompka, P. (2000). Cultural trauma: the other face of social change. *European Journal of Social Theory* **3** (4): 449–466.

Taleb, N. (2012). *Antifragile: Things that Gain from Disorder*. New York, NY: Random House.

Tilley, C. (2016). Foreword. In: *Brand Finance, Global Intangible Financial Tracker (GIFT) 2016: An Annual Review of the World's Intangible Value*, 4. London: Chartered Institute of Management Accountants.

Tirkkonen, P. and Luoma-aho, V. (2014). Authority crisis communication vs. discussion forums, swine flu. In: *Ethical Practice of Social Media in Public Relations*, 1st ed. (ed. M. DiStaso and D.S. Bortree), 192–204. Routledge.

Virtanen, P. and Stenvall, J. (2014). The evolution of public services from co-production to co-creation and beyond: new public management's unfinished trajectory? *International Journal of Leadership in Public Services* **10** (2): 91–107.

Wæraas, A. (2014). Beauty from within: what bureaucracies stand for. *American Review of Public Administration* **44** (6): 675–692.

Wæraas, A. and Byrkjeflot, H. (2012). Public sector organizations and reputation management: five problems. *International Public Management Journal* **15** (2): 186–206.

Whicher, A. and Cawood, G. (2013). *An Overview of Service Design for the Private and Public Sectors*. Cardiff, NSW: SEE Network.

Yang, A. and Taylor, M. (2013). The relationship between the professionalization of public relations, societal social capital and democracy: evidence from a cross-national study. *Public Relations Review* **39** (4): 257–270.

Part II

5

Satisfaction

> *In efforts to improve the responsiveness and quality of public services, more and*
> *more government organizations are proactively seeking and acting on feedback from*
> *citizens about their experiences*
> (OECD, 2013, p. 166)

This chapter addresses one of the most frequently studied intangible public sector assets: citizen satisfaction. Citizen satisfaction has been linked with several benefits for society, organizations, and individual citizens. Built on expectations, satisfaction is a volatile intangible asset. This chapter examines the different factors that contribute to citizens' satisfaction, which range from experiences to cognitive biases, and it summarizes previous findings on citizen satisfaction. The challenge with satisfaction as an asset is to find a balance between citizens' needs on the one hand and organizational goals in a dynamic environment that constantly introduces new expectations and demands on the other.

5.1   What Is Satisfaction?

Citizen satisfaction is believed to generate several benefits for the public sector and for society at large. In practice, citizen satisfaction may save money when unnecessary complaints and processes are cut, and overall citizen satisfaction has been linked with better democracy, better life outcomes, social tranquility, productivity, positive word of mouth, increased employee efficiency, lower costs for public administrations, and improved organizational operations (Thijs and Staes, 2008, p. 8; Morgeson, 2014; James and Moseley, 2014; James, 2011; Choy, Lam, and Lee, 2012; Oliver, 2010). More importantly, however, citizen satisfaction contributes to trust within society via an increased willingness to collaborate and contribute: satisfied citizens help to create an operating environment in which public sector organizations can function efficiently (Putnam, 1993). As Morgeson suggests, "For bureaucratic agencies in particular, satisfaction has been shown to be a strong determinant (or influencing factor) of citizen trust: as citizens become more satisfied with their interactions with a bureaucratic agency, they also tend to develop greater trust in both that particular agency and in the government as a whole" (2014).

Public Sector Communication: Closing Gaps Between Citizens and Public Organizations, First Edition.
María-José Canel and Vilma Luoma-aho.
© 2019 John Wiley & Sons, Inc. Published 2019 by John Wiley & Sons, Inc.

Citizen satisfaction is a general citizen response that reflects citizens' pleasure levels (Oludele, Emilie, and Mandisa, 2012). Citizen satisfaction is understood to be a positive attitude, a comfortable or affirmative feeling (Locke, 1976), or a simple positive or negative assessment by citizens with regard to the state of public services or public sector performance. A simple definition views it as a citizen's fulfillment response, the degree to which the level of fulfillment is pleasant or unpleasant. Contributing to service and organizational effectiveness, satisfaction reflects an individual's feelings toward the organization or service provided (Locke, 1976).

The concept has been further developed in marketing research, where satisfaction is seen to result from customers'(or citizens') comparison of their service-related expectations and their actual or mediated experiences of this service (Oliver, 1981, 2010). Researchers talk of a discrepancy between expectation and performance when citizens are dissatisfied.

Satisfaction and dissatisfaction can be seen as two extremes of citizens' evaluations. Satisfaction is often a more passive state than is dissatisfaction, which has been linked with certain citizen behaviors such as voicing complaints or attempting to terminate the relationship (Hirschman, 1970). It is a very popular intangible asset for public sector organizations to measure, as it is easy to quantify and mold into questions that citizens understand (Holzer and Yang, 2004). However, despite the popularity of citizen satisfaction surveys, it is still the case that "little is known about the processes citizens use to combine their various performance perceptions into an overall satisfaction judgment or sense of trust, as well as other behavioral consequences of inherent interest, such as complaining or leaving a jurisdiction" (Van Ryzin, 2007, p. 522).

As satisfaction is an intangible construct, there are several biases that shape it (Olsen, 2015). A common bias for all influence is the negativity bias. A negative reputation attributed to the public sector as a whole (sector reputation) may spill over into negative overtones toward individual public sector organizations (Luoma-aho, 2008). Moreover, negative information is considered more credible and reported more in the media than is positive information (Chen and Lurie, 2013). Hence, dissatisfied citizens make news more often than satisfied citizens.

5.2 Experiences and Satisfaction

If satisfaction is defined as a complex evaluation of overall satisfaction, or a multi-dimensional variable formed by different constituent elements identified by the various aspects of the service (Cappelli et al., 2010), then one central factor influencing it is the actual service/product experience. In fact, recent findings suggest that individual experiences are of critical importance when measuring satisfaction (Virmani and Dash, 2013).

There are two types of satisfaction: service specific and cumulative (Oliver, 2010). Most often, when research addresses citizen satisfaction, it refers to some overall collection of emotional experiences, not the individual citizen experiences as such. As it is an intangible evaluation, satisfaction can vary even between citizens of the same state or area, and as it is dynamic, satisfaction levels may change over time, even in the case of individual citizens (Thijs and Staes, 2008, p. 8). It is also possible for citizens to be satisfied with certain aspects of one service and dissatisfied with other aspects of the same service at the same time. For example, citizens may be satisfied with the overall operations of a local water delivery system but be dissatisfied with the prices of the distributed water. Citizen satisfaction is understood to arise from both service quality and the type of relationship between the citizen and the public servant.

Moreover, it is held to be built on previous experiences, both personal and mediated ones, as well as on confirmed or disconfirmed expectations (James, 2009). Negative opinions about the public sector in general may coincide with positive evaluations of specific services (Thijs and Staes, 2008, p. 8). Citizen expectations contribute to perceptions about public service quality, and thus excessively high expectations may actually backfire by leading to lower levels of satisfaction (Poister and Thomas, 2011; Font and Navarro, 2013) or at worst even loss of trust and reputation (Luoma-aho, 2007, p. 124). In turn, new experiences shape future expectations (Oludele et al., 2012; Poister and Thomas, 2011).

Ideally, satisfaction is coproduced by the service provider and citizens, though "whilst the rhetoric of policy makers emphasizes the importance of citizen 'participation' and interactivity, in practice the reality of this 'participation' is often basic and one-way 'consultation'" (Bowden, Luoma-aho, and Naumann, 2016, p. 259). Although citizen satisfaction itself cannot be managed, managing the expectations that contribute to citizen experiences is important for public sector organizations (Olkkonen and Luoma-aho, 2015; Luoma-aho and Olkkonen, 2016). Public sector communication plays a central role in this, as it sets the overall tone for citizen satisfaction through highlighting the most important factors for citizens to pay attention to and evaluate (Sanders and Canel, 2013). Communication sets the expectations against which services are then portrayed, resulting in either satisfaction or dissatisfaction.

Public sector satisfaction is a sum of many factors, as "quality of life issues are inextricably intertwined with consumers' (citizens') satisfaction with public agencies" (Oliver, 2010, p. 5). The way in which satisfaction reduces costs is simple: if the need to monitor is less pressing and if changes to inadequate functions are made more quickly, there will be savings to be had in both the direct and indirect costs of public sector organizations. Citizen satisfaction opens up ways to make resource and budget allocations as well as internal savings via employee morale and loyalty, and it matters for public sector organizations especially as it is related to the repeated nature that characterizes most public sector services (Oliver, 1981). In fact, most public services can be categorized under "constant experiences" (on the continuum from unique to constant) such as air quality, law, health, and well-being. Although citizens may find it challenging to evaluate public services, certain aspects remain easily approachable – for example, access to authorities and communication opportunities.

5.3 Why Should Public Organizations Care About Citizen Satisfaction?

> *Managing customer satisfaction is therefore indispensable for public organizations, to see if they are doing the right things and if they are doing things right*
> (Thijs and Staes, 2008, p. 8)

Satisfaction has been proven to improve societies and organizations. In the public sector, public service quality has been linked with citizen satisfaction, though they remain different constructs (James and Moseley, 2014). One challenge with regard to citizen satisfaction is the heterogeneity and preferences of the individuals: there is not one but several ways for citizens to behave, participate, expect, and engage, and hence for them to be either satisfied or dissatisfied. Moreover, even the same individual citizen may judge a service differently depending on the context.

Oliver argues that the value of satisfaction emerges from "comparison operators" that result in certain cognitive states – that is, expectations lead to either confirmation or disconfirmation; needs to fulfilment or a lack thereof; and quality, value, and fairness to their specific evaluations, to produce either satisfaction or dissatisfaction (Oliver, 2010).

Public service design has been suggested to offer a new way to enable authentic citizen engagement and coproduction of public services. Service design is believed to contribute to citizen satisfaction along with other benefits that accompany it, including better relations between service providers and citizens (Whicher and Cawood, 2013). Moreover,

> such information can help public managers identify which elements of service delivery drive satisfaction, as well as monitor the impact of reforms on end users. Measuring citizen satisfaction is also a means of allowing policy makers and managers to better understand their customer base, helping to identify subgroups of users and needs or gaps in accessibility. Moreover, citizen satisfaction can be an important outcome indicator of overall government performance.
>
> *(OECD, 2013, p. 166)*

Several gaps are bridged by satisfaction. Citizen satisfaction and citizen loyalty are believed to be influenced by citizens' expectations and their perceptions of public service quality (Morgeson, 2014). Satisfied citizens are more willing to cooperate, more prone to forgive, and more flexible in their demands and interaction (Oliver, 2010). An overall good, satisfaction can be understood to bridge not just one but several gaps, including those caused by distance, distrust, or bad service experiences.

However, focusing on citizen satisfaction alone is not enough. Public sector organizations need to simultaneously identify the causes and mechanisms that contribute to citizen satisfaction or dissatisfaction to ensure a wise utilization of public resources, and they must strategically consider the proportion of investments, effects, and costs of each improvement. For example, citizen satisfaction levels may result from a combination of factors, some of which will be very difficult to change (such as sector reputation or lifestyle choices), despite even heavy investments. Sometimes even a neutral level of satisfaction is beneficial – more so than overly high expectations, which can lead to dissatisfaction if they are not met (Luoma-aho, 2007, p. 124).

5.4 Communication and Satisfaction

Communication plays a central role in shaping citizen satisfaction (Riley et al., 2015, p. 201), with research showing that public sector organizations' communication (such as published absolute and relative performance measures) influence citizen satisfaction for better or worse (James and Moseley, 2014). Similarly, authority communication sets the expectations that guide satisfaction (Luoma-aho and Olkkonen, 2016). Moreover, communication is often understood to be a central determinant in the contribution that service quality makes to citizen satisfaction (Thijs, 2011).

Negativity bias shapes the way in which communication influences perceptions, as "information about low absolute performance, when provided on its own or with relative information, reduces satisfaction in the low performing area experiment but information about high performance in the high performing area experiment does not raise satisfaction" (James and Moseley, 2014, p. 505). In addition, cultural emphases, context, news criteria, and media polarization of opinions further emphasize the strength of negative information (Dixon et al., 2013).

Research suggests that citizens are often more satisfied with services close to their reach relative to those that are further away or less concrete (Thijs and Staes, 2008, p. 8). As a result, and also because citizens find it easier to assess their satisfaction through comparisons, a central way to improve citizen satisfaction is to make public services more tangible and comparable for citizens. Communication about available services may also be an important contribution to citizen satisfaction, as when information is lacking, judgments are made based on impressions.

Managing citizen satisfaction starts with the acknowledgement that no organization can fully manage satisfaction. There are ways to manage the individual service encounters that lead to transaction-specific citizen satisfaction, but often managing the cumulative overall satisfaction is very challenging (Boulding et al., 1993). Moreover, sector-specific reputation may contribute to certain stable expectations that shape satisfaction despite attempts to improve satisfaction (Luoma-aho, 2008; Luoma-aho and Makikangas, 2014). What public sector communication professionals can do is hence limited, but a central task remains setting the right expectations about services available, which contributes to citizen satisfaction over time (Luoma-aho and Olkkonen, 2016).

5.5 Measuring Citizen Satisfaction

Satisfaction is a very well-established concept, and most citizens and public administrators take it for granted. Evaluating satisfaction is suggested to involve consideration of a combination of a product's or service's perceived importance and the performance of it experienced (Oliver, 2010).

5.5.1 The Purpose of Measuring

Measurement of citizen satisfaction is believed to have several objectives, though much of the usefulness of satisfaction measures depends on the operationalization and the measurement system itself. The level on which satisfaction is measured may also shape the outcome, as citizens often find it easier to report on their personal experiences than on overall public sector performance. In fact, it is possible for citizens to be satisfied and dissatisfied at the same time with public sector organizations (Thijs and Staes, 2008, p. 8): they may be very satisfied with their local or municipal social services, but simultaneously very dissatisfied with certain government institutions, without always being able to distinguish these as separate levels and services. Hence, an overall satisfaction score of "public sector performance" remains an unrealistic and even misleading endeavor.

Morgeson lists seven purposes for citizen satisfaction measures and argues that although public sector satisfaction objectives may differ from private sector ones to some degree, citizen satisfaction is vital for public sector performance (Morgeson, 2014, p. 47):

1) Citizen satisfaction measurement provides a feedback loop about the work of the government and the public sector, highlighting successes and failures.
2) It increases the transparency and accountability of public sector organizations, as performance information is available and citizens are asked to assess it.
3) Measuring satisfaction improves citizens' trust in public sector performance, as citizens are able to contribute to the service via feedback.
4) Satisfaction measurement serves the purposes of improving quality and highlighting which aspects matter most for citizens.
5) Satisfaction measurement may enable benchmarking of successful organizations.
6) Satisfaction measures can help with budgetary allocations to those areas most in need of improvement.
7) Public service satisfaction measures can help motivate public sector employees with direct feedback from citizens and their experiences.

"Measuring users' satisfaction with public goods and services is at the heart of a citizen-centric approach to service delivery and an important component of organizational performance strategies for continual improvement. Perception data are commonly used to evaluate citizens' experiences with government organizations and obtain their views on the outputs received" (OECD, 2013, p. 166). Such measurement is useful for public sector development, but not all customer satisfaction tools transfer well from the field of marketing (Thijs and Staes, 2008, p. 8; Wæraas and Byrkjeflot, 2012), and not all citizens process satisfaction to the degree that they could report it (James, 2010). Measuring satisfaction always starts with understanding how citizens see satisfaction and whether they are able to report on it through the desired means.

Measuring satisfaction often builds on analysis of various citizen surveys, the questions of which the public sector entity will have structured to best meet their needs (Morgeson, 2014). In fact, the way in which citizen satisfaction surveys are constructed and the manner in which their results are reported can affect the scores and thereby shape citizen satisfaction levels (Olsen, 2015; Van de Walle and Van Ryzin, 2011).

Measurement is often based on certain established models that assume citizens to be honest and aim to show a causality between citizen satisfaction and public service quality in practice (Nigro and Gonzales Cisaro, 2014). There are different approaches to operationalizing satisfaction measures: the first is to see it as a general, overall comprehensive evaluation that citizens make based on their experiences, in which satisfaction is then measured as an overall score. The second is to see satisfaction as a "multidimensional variable formed by different constituent elements identified by the various aspects of the service," which can then be translated into various questions (Cappelli et al., 2010, p. 270).

Much of the academic literature on citizen satisfaction is focused on measuring the different factors affecting satisfaction. Although satisfaction is dependent on the cultural and contextual surroundings (Jilke, Meuleman, and Van de Walle, 2015), recent research has attempted to provide cross-national ways to measure citizen satisfaction. Common measurement frameworks such as the CAF (Common Assessment Framework), ECSI (European Customer Satisfaction Index), and some parts of Eurobarometer or the

Initiative for European Common Indicators all principally approach citizen satisfaction related to public services through comparing means of both overall reported satisfaction and that related to individual services.

In practice, citizen satisfaction is often measured by asking direct questions, whether through surveys or focus groups, or observing citizens' behavior online or in some specific setting (James, 2010). For example, the OECD (2013, p. 166) creates global comparative measures on citizen satisfaction through three questions related to safety, education, and health, reporting satisfaction scores in the form of the percentage of "yes" or "satisfied" answers to questions such as: "In the city or area where you live, do you have confidence in the local police force?"; "In the city or area where you live, are you satisfied or dissatisfied with the educational system or the schools?"; and "In the city or area where you live, are you satisfied or dissatisfied with the availability of quality health care?" Small western European and Nordic countries seem to dominate the global comparisons: in the 2012 data, the two leading countries in citizen satisfaction were Switzerland and Iceland in relation to trust in the police, Ireland and Finland in relation to satisfaction with education, and Switzerland and Austria in relation to satisfaction with health care.

5.5.2 Do Measurement Tools from the Private Sector Suit the Public Sector?

Building on total quality management, a central question with regard to the different measurement tools taken from business organizations is whether they fit the public sector context. The SERVQUAL has been suggested to be transferrable (Bennett and Barkensjo, 2005; James, 2011; Wisniewski, 1996), as its dimensions link mostly to generic dimensions and not to organization- or service-specific traits. A standardized framework in the realm of service quality, the SERVQUAL instrument, or GAP model (Parasuraman, Zeithaml, and Berry, 1988), originally consisted of 10 attributes. Most recent versions note five dimensions that contribute to satisfaction:

1) *Reliability*: ability to perform the promised service dependably and accurately.
2) *Assurance*: knowledge and courtesy of employees and their ability to inspire trust and confidence.
3) *Tangibility*: physical facilities, equipment, and appearance of personnel.
4) *Empathy*: caring individualized attention that the firm provides to its customers.
5) *Responsiveness*: willingness to help customers and provide prompt service.

Difficulties related to the use of SERVQUAL and its guiding logic have been noted (Van Ryzin, 2006, pp. 599–611). These include the diverse nature of different stakeholders involved, as well as the large size of the public sector and its services (Orwig, Pearson, and Cochran, 1997). Moreover, there is an ongoing discussion as to whether concepts taken from the business side can and should even be used by public sector organizations (Wæraas and Byrkjeflot, 2012). Building on the SERVQUAL, but going deeper into mere performances, the SERVPERF focuses exclusively on the perception of service, an approach that has been claimed to be more relevant than the SERVQUAL combination (Brady, Cronin, and Brand, 2002).

As much of public sector satisfaction measurement is survey based, ascertaining the real significance of and reasons for citizen satisfaction may be challenging. Moreover, not all citizens even have strong opinions about all services, and hence distinguishing the zone of indifference may help authorities understand where the citizen evaluation stems from. Whatever the chosen means to measure citizen satisfaction, it is always vital to ensure that the tool reflects actual citizen experiences. Before any measurement should occur, clear objectives and questions should be set, and choices should be made as to how the collected measurement information will be best put to use. Moreover, it is not realistic to assume that citizen satisfaction can be continuously improved, as citizens' expectations rise along with service improvements.

5.6 Summary of Citizen Satisfaction

Table 5.1 summarizes citizen satisfaction as an intangible asset that measures the extent to which an organization meets citizen expectations. Communication is needed to set the realistic expectations against which citizens are able to evaluate organizational performance. As focusing on citizen satisfaction appears to be a global need, there are several management transformations that this new focus may require, ranging from a different organizational culture to setting realistic goals.

As noted in Table 5.1, a focus on citizen satisfaction can help to move public sector organizations' focus from the administration process toward citizen needs, and it is thus

Table 5.1 Citizen satisfaction as an intangible asset in the public sector.

It is the intangible asset that measures the extent to which an organization meets citizen expectations	
Tangible asset satisfaction enables	Finances through savings and lower transaction costs, better life outcomes, social peace, and even organizational productivity
Resource satisfaction generates	Trust in the public sector, better democracy, better life outcomes, a good reputation through positive word of mouth, increased employee efficiency
Monetary expression	Costs savings, lower transaction costs, procedural time saving, efficiency
Value satisfaction provides the organization	Effective resource allocation, overall ease in operations, higher trust, easier collaboration, fewer complaints and exits, better employee commitment
Value satisfaction provides citizens and stakeholders	Improved overall well-being, trust, less stress
Gaps that satisfaction bridges	Misunderstanding, distance-related gaps, distrust-related gaps, gaps caused by bad experiences, lack of collaboration and engagement, the need for flexibility
Dependence on communication management	Communication sets the expectations that result in either satisfaction or dissatisfaction, and communication about the satisfaction of others contributes to individual assessments
Implied organization management transformations	Planning services that are citizen centered and not organization centered (service design), a shift from administrative logic to citizen-centered logic, an increase in transparency, management of expectations throughout the service process, and the setting up of measurable satisfaction goals and evaluation processes
Measures	Evaluations, surveys, and assessments reporting expectations about and experiences of services

a practical step toward citizen-centered services (Bourgon, 2009). Focusing on and measuring citizens' satisfaction with public sector organizations closes the gap of these two parties' failure to understand each other's needs and ignorance regarding what is expected. It is important for public sector organizations "to understand the issues, or key drivers, that cause satisfaction or dissatisfaction with a service experience. When an organization is able to understand how satisfied its customers are, and why, it can focus its time and resources more effectively" (Thijs, 2011, p. 15). Moreover, measuring satisfaction provides a reality check for current voiced and unvoiced expectations.

Although citizen satisfaction is by no means enough alone, it enables several other goods for public sector organizations and even society at large. Measuring satisfaction is often a good starting point for public sector organizations that are beginning to develop intangible assets. Satisfaction measurement should always be combined with expectation measurement, as these remain closely related, and changes in one result in changes in the other.

5.7 Case Study on Citizen Satisfaction

SMRT Corporation Ltd. (Singapore Mass Rapid Transit)

How can citizen satisfaction be achieved despite delays, renewals to the railway system, and management change?

Singapore is a city-state with a total population of 5.61 million people who live in high-density housing on a diamond-shaped island that is about 42 km long and 20 km wide. As Singapore is a hub for modern technology and is known for the efficiency of its transport – for example, the sea port and Changi Airport – its citizens' expectations in relation to this area of public service are high. However, the environment is challenging for rail operations and maintenance, and citizen complaints about noise and inconveniences are common. Citizens are very dependent on the rail system, increasing the urgency to maintain satisfaction.

In 2011, the North–South Line and the East–West Line, Singapore's oldest and longest metro lines, suffered two bad breakdowns on the last shopping weekend before Christmas. This event led to two major challenges: the infrastructural challenge of rebuilding the metro and the communication challenge of rebuilding public trust. As the engineering work would take multiple years and had several negative consequences for both staff and citizens (hectic workdays, travel disruptions, and noise), a campaign on sleeper replacement was launched to manage citizen expectations and prepare them for the inconveniences of the repairs and gain public support. The expectations of diverse stakeholders (for example, those of individuals wondering about the repairs, journalists writing about them, and the transport regulator overseeing the process) were also managed ahead of time.

Purpose

The main purpose of SMRT, the recently (2016) fully privatized company (in 2015 it was half-public, half-private; see Figure 5.1) that runs Singapore's largest rail network, is to provide satisfactory daily rail services for over two million people each day. During the engineering works, the communication strategy was to keep stakeholders engaged with two-way communication channels and convey to them that the works were crucial for rail

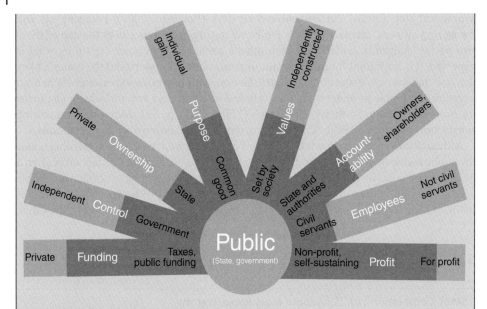

Figure 5.1 Publicness of the SMRT in Singapore (in 2015).

safety. Satisfaction resulted from realistic expectations, and to manage expectations, potential delays and inconveniences were explained in advance. SMRT was aware of the power of priming, and they adjusted and influenced citizen expectations through several modes – for example, through maintenance notices delivered to residential units near the construction area and the opening up of new feedback channels, both on site and online. To achieve satisfaction, expectations were approached on several levels, such as:

1) informing stakeholders of the process and its duration;
2) reassuring them of the quality of the engineering personnel's skills;
3) updating them on progress; and
4) educating them about the different skills and the work input needed for the entire process.

Messages were scripted to inform, educate, update, or reassure stakeholders with regard to what was being done, why it was necessary, how it would improve their travel experience, and where and when such work would be carried out. As Singapore's population is multiracial, the information was shared in four main languages: English, Chinese, Malay, and Tamil. To reach the young and the old, complex rail engineering projects were explained as simply as possible with the help of pictures, cartoons, and graphics.

Satisfaction was a means to an overall end of maintaining trust and a good reputation. The expectations of both internal stakeholders (staff and the transport union) and external stakeholders (commuting citizens, tourists, and the media) were managed to foster empathy and greater understanding in order to enable the success of the engineering works. The satisfaction levels of both groups were measured throughout the process, and messages were tailored according to the concerns raised.

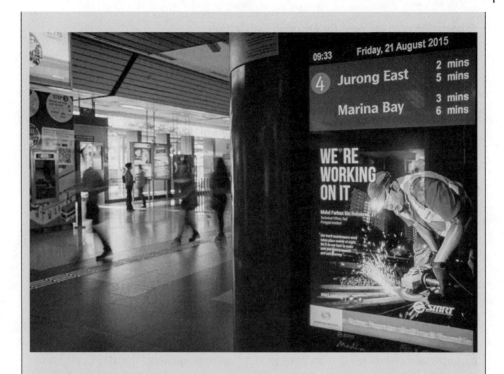

Source: Reproduced with permission of SMRT Limited.

Expectation management for ensuring satisfaction

Expectations were guided through public messages on posters, online messages, mailers to residents, infographics, and videos with memorable messages such as "Pardon the noise" and "We're working on it." The messages were made quite personal and relatable via portraying the real workers behind the project and explaining their input and work. In addition, to premanage emerging issues, focus groups were conducted with community leaders to gain a sense of local concerns. The results of the "Pardon the noise" campaign showed that during the major repairs, 60% fewer noise-related complaints were filed than before it. What is more, citizen engagement increased, and more feedback and suggestions from stakeholders were collected than before. Feedback was also encouraged through forms that were easily accessible (such as QR codes available in waiting areas of stations). Some small gifts (SMRT fridge magnets) as well as prizes (travel cards preloaded with $20) were also offered.

Why does satisfaction matter for this organization?

Citizen satisfaction is understood to be a condition for the functioning of modern societies. As expectations set the stage for satisfaction or dissatisfaction, ensuring citizen satisfaction must start with ensuring the right kind of expectations. If expectations are left unvoiced, they can cause potential damage for both citizens and the public authorities when disappointments occur. In fact, it could be argued that citizen dissatisfaction and customer complaints result from poor expectation management. The SMRT case shows this proposition to be true, as with properly managed expectations for the engineering project, the number of complaints went down and citizen engagement increased, thereby producing more feedback and suggestions, which in turn resulted in a better outcome and an improved system for all stakeholders involved.

Public sector organizations that are able to frame citizen expectations realistically avoid major dissatisfaction and disappointments that can harm their legitimacy. When citizen expectations are set and kept realistic, democracy is enabled and societies function well, as both citizens and public sector organizations can focus on their own call of duty and service instead of spending time on extensive contracts, agreements, and complaints that often in retrospect make for misaligned citizen expectations.

5.8 Route Guide to Building Citizen Satisfaction

Satisfaction rests on realistic expectations and transparent communication. For public sector organizations, several stages in building sustainable satisfaction are suggested:

1) **Measure and track expectations of both employees and citizens.**
   Questions to ask: What are the explicit and implicit expectations for this service? Are these expectations realistic/unrealistic? How are the expectations formed? How can we make them more realistic? Are there ways to actively manage the formation of these expectations? What are the elements of expectation formation that we can control?

Example: "Where do citizens share their experiences about local waste recycling online?"

2) **External satisfaction can only be built on internal satisfaction.**
   Questions to ask: How are our employees feeling? Are there any issues that they have requested to be fixed that have been overlooked? Is there a systematic way to include and better engage employees in future planning? How can we make employees feel valued?
   Example: "If we hope for a 10% increase in citizen satisfaction next year, how big an increase do we need in internal public sector employee satisfaction to achieve this?"

3) **Based on expectations, plan through the possible satisfaction scenarios and questions.**
   Questions to ask: What aspects are our employees/citizens likely to want to contribute to? What factors make the biggest difference to satisfaction? Are we covering both the perceived importance and experienced performance of our product or service?
   Example: "Which of these two services in the public school system would you prioritize when it comes to making improvements: after-school clubs or tutoring?"

4) **Select and tailor measurement tools to best suit your organization or service.**
   Questions to ask: Does this method provide material that we can directly use to assess our service? Does it provide results that are immediately applicable in improving services? Does this method match citizen expectations? Is this evaluation in line with how employees/citizens think? How can we encourage authentic participation? What do we report to the users afterward about the results and the utilization of their feedback?
   Example: "Is our senior management able to measure the value of investments in communication from these results?"

5) **Remember that a rise in satisfaction also includes a rise in expectations.**
   Questions to ask: How will the employee and citizen expectations change if their satisfaction increases? Will we have the resources to maintain the current target level of satisfaction in practice once it is achieved? How realistic is our target level of satisfaction? What would we lose if we stay at the current level of satisfaction?
   Example: "If citizens expect us to send their income tax information within five days after requests, do we have sufficient personnel to work during peak periods of requests?"

References

Bennett, R. and Barkensjo, A. (2005). Relationship quality, relationship marketing, and client perceptions of the levels of service quality of charitable organisations. *International Journal of Service Industry Management* **16** (1): 81–106.

Boulding, W., Kalra, A., Staelin, R., and Zeithaml, V.A. (1993). A dynamic process model of service quality: from expectations to behavioural intentions. *Journal of Marketing Research* **30** (1): 7–27.

Bourgon, J. (2009). New directions in public administration: serving beyond the predictable. *Public Policy and Administration* **24** (3): 309–330.

Bowden, J.L.-H., Luoma-aho, V., and Naumann, K. (2016). Developing a spectrum of positive to negative citizen engagement. In: *Customer Engagement Contemporary Issues and Challenges*, 1st ed. (ed. R.J. Brodie, L. Hollebeek and J. Conduit), 257–277. Routledge.

Brady, M., Cronin, J., and Brand, R. (2002). Performance-only measurement of service quality: a replication and extension. *Journal of Business Research* **55** (1): 17–31.

Cappelli, L., Guglielmetti, R., Mattia, G. et al. (2010). Statistical techniques for continuous improvement: a citizen's satisfaction survey. *The TQM Journal* **22** (3): 267–284.

Chen, Z. and Lurie, N. (2013). Temporal contiguity and negativity bias in the impact of online word of mouth. *Journal of Marketing Research* **50** (4): 463–476.

Choy, J.-Y., Lam, S.-Y., and Lee, T.-C. (2012). Service quality, customer satisfaction and behavioral intentions: review of literature and conceptual model development. *International Journal of Academic Research* **4** (3): 11–15.

Dixon, R., Arndt, C., Mullers, M. et al. (2013). A lever for improvement or a magnet for blame? press and political responses to international educational rankings in four EU countries. *Public Administration* **91** (2): 484–505.

Font, J. and Navarro, C. (2013). Personal experience and the evaluation of participatory instruments in Spanish cities. *Public Administration* **91** (3): 616–631.

Hirschman, A.O. (1970). *Exit, Voice and Loyalty: Responses to Decline in Firms, Organizations, and States*, vol. 25. Cambridge, MA: Harvard University Press.

Holzer, M. and Yang, K. (2004). Performance measurement and improvement: an assessment of the state of the art. *International Review of Administrative Sciences* **70** (1): 15–31.

James, O. (2009). Evaluating the expectations disconfirmation and expectations anchoring approaches to citizen satisfaction with local public services. *Journal of Public Administration Research and Theory* **19** (1): 107–123.

James, O. (2010). Performance measures and democracy: information effects on citizens in field and laboratory experiments. *Journal of Public Administration Research and Theory* **21** (3): 399–418.

James, O. (2011). Managing citizens' expectations of public service performance: evidence from observation and experimentation in local government. *Public Administration* **89** (4): 1419–1435.

James, O. and Moseley, A. (2014). Does performance information about public services affect citizens' perceptions, satisfaction and voice behaviour? Field experiments with absolute and relative performance information. *Public Administration* **92** (2): 493–511.

Jilke, S., Meuleman, B., and Van de Walle, S. (2015). We need to compare, but how? Measurement equivalence in comparative public administration. *Public Administration Review* **75** (1): 36–48.

Locke, E.A. (1976). The nature and causes of job satisfaction. In: *Handbook of Industrial and Organizational Psychology*, 1st ed. (ed. M.D. Dunnette), 1297–1349. Chicago, IL: Rand McNally.

Luoma-aho, V. (2007). Neutral reputation and public sector organizations. *Corporate Reputation Review* **10** (2): 124–143.

Luoma-aho, V. (2008). Sector reputation and public organisations. *International Journal of Public Sector Management* **21** (5): 446–467.

Luoma-aho, V. and Makikangas, M. (2014). Do public sector mergers (re)shape reputation? *International Journal of Public Sector Management* **27** (1): 39–52.

Luoma-aho, V. and Olkkonen, L. (2016). Expectation management. In: *The SAGE Encyclopedia of Corporate Reputation* (ed. C. Carroll), 303–306. Sage Publications.

Morgeson, F. (2014). *Citizen Satisfaction: Improving Government Performance, Efficiency, and Citizen Trust*. New York, NY: Palgrave MacMillan.

Nigro, H.O. and Gonzales Cisaro, S.E. (2014). Prediction of citizen satisfaction with local government based on perceptions of physical disorder. *Journal of Place Management and Development* 7 (2): 153–175.

OECD. (2013). "Citizen satisfaction with public services" In: *Government at a Glance 2013*, edited by OECD. http://dx.doi.org/10.1787/gov_glance-2013-56-en (accessed 29 September 2017).

Oliver, R. (1981). Measurement and evaluation of satisfaction processes in retail settings. *Journal of Retailing* 57 (3): 25–48.

Oliver, R. (2010). *Satisfaction A Behavioural Perspective on the Consumer*, 2nd ed. Armonk, NY: ME Sharpe.

Olkkonen, L. and Luoma-aho, V.L. (2015). Broadening the concept of expectations in public relations. *Journal of Public Relations Research* 27 (1): 81–99.

Olsen, A.L. (2015). Citizen (dis)satisfaction: an experimental equivalence framing study. *Public Administration Review* 75 (3): 469–478.

Oludele, A.A., Emilie, C.K., and Mandisa, P.M. (2012). An analysis of citizen satisfaction with public service delivery in the Sedibeng district municipality of South Africa. *International Journal of Social Economics* 39 (3): 182–199.

Orwig, R., Pearson, J., and Cochran, D. (1997). An empirical investigation into the validity of SERVQUAL in the public sector. *Public Administration Quarterly* 21 (1): 54–68.

Parasuraman, A., Zeithaml, V., and Berry, L. (1988). SERVQUAL: a multi-item scale for measuring consumer perceptions of the service quality. *Journal of Retailing* 64 (1): 12–40.

Poister, T.H. and Thomas, J.C. (2011). The effect of expectations and expectancy confirmation/disconfirmation on motorists' satisfaction with state highways. *Journal of Public Administration Research and Theory* 21 (4): 601–617.

Putnam, R.D. (1993). *Making Democracy Work: Civic Traditions in Modern Italy*. Princeton, NJ: Princeton University Press.

Riley, P., Thomas, G., Weintraub, R. et al. (2015). Good governance and strategic communication. In: *Handbook of Strategic Communication*, 1st ed. (ed. A. Zerfass and D. Holzhausen), 201–213. London, UK: Routledge.

Sanders, K. and Canel, M.-J. ed. (2013). *Government Communication Cases and Challenges*, 1st ed. London: Bloomsbury Academic.

Thijs, N. (2011). *Measure to Improve: Improving Public Sector Performance by using Citizen-User Satisfaction Information*. Brussels: EUPAN/EIPA.

Thijs, N. and Staes, P. (2008). *European Primer on Customer Satisfaction Management*. Brussels: EUPAN/EIPA.

Van Ryzin, G.G. (2006). Testing the expectancy disconfirmation model of citizen satisfaction with local government. *Journal of Public Administration Research and Theory* 16 (4): 599–611.

Van Ryzin, G.G. (2007). Pieces of a puzzle: linking government performance, citizen satisfaction, and trust. *Public Performance & Management Review* 30 (4): 521–535.

Van de Walle, S. and Van Ryzin, G. (2011). The order of questions in a survey on citizen satisfaction with public services: lessons from a split-ballot experiment. *Public Administration* 89 (4): 1436–1450.

Virmani, M. and Dash, M. (2013). Modelling customer satisfaction for business services. *Journal of Sociological Research* **4** (2): 51–60.

Wæraas, A. and Byrkjeflot, H. (2012). Public sector organizations and reputation management: five problems. *International Public Management Journal* **15** (2): 186–206.

Whicher, A. and Cawood, G. (2013). *An Overview of Service Design for the Private and Public Sectors*. Cardiff, Wales: SEE network.

Wisniewski, M. (1996). Measuring service quality in the public sector: the potential for SERVQUAL. *Total Quality Management* **7** (4): 357–366.

6

Organizational Culture

Culture eats strategy for breakfast
(Common saying)

This chapter addresses how organizational culture can strengthen organizations from the inside out. Organizations often introduce different procedures and projects to improve worker morale and satisfaction, yet studies show that the most effective way to improve employee welfare is through establishing a strong and supportive organizational culture. Public sector organizational culture has its unique traits, and this chapter addresses these as well. As public sector organizations attempt to move from a culture of controls to one of citizen engagement, the chapter also addresses changing organizational culture.

6.1 Organizations' Invisible Cultures

Why do some public sector organizations outperform others? Why is it that some organizations experience less turnover and higher employee satisfaction while others seem to struggle with these continuously? The answer has been suggested to lie in organizational culture – that is, the tacit principles that guide how people behave in organizations. Organizational culture is often difficult to identify, as it is a set of unspoken rules that encompass the memories, values, assumptions, and expectations that make the organization what it is (Cameron and Quinn, 2011).

Organizational culture has been linked with several benefits, including a positive communication climate and increases in organizational flexibility, organizational productivity, and the number of innovations produced (Hofstede, 2001; Martins and Terblanche, 2003; Døjbak Haakonsson et al., 2008; Naranjo-Valencia, Jiménez-Jiménez, and Sanz-Valle, 2011; Luoma-aho et al., 2012). In fact, research suggests that organizational culture may explain up to 28% of customer satisfaction where a good organizational culture contributes to more satisfied customers (Gillespie et al., 2008). Similarly, organizations with strong, positive internal cultures are understood to perform 20–30% better than those without a positive culture (Heskett, 2011).

Much of what happens in a given public sector organization (or conversely what does not happen) may to some degree be explained by a strong organizational culture that

Public Sector Communication: Closing Gaps Between Citizens and Public Organizations, First Edition.
María-José Canel and Vilma Luoma-aho.
© 2019 John Wiley & Sons, Inc. Published 2019 by John Wiley & Sons, Inc.

guides that organization's actions and development (Claver et al., 1999). Some have called for a complete change of the current public sector culture (Bourgon, 2011) in order to achieve the desired renewals in services and rid the public sector of its traditional bureaucratic processes. Organizational cultures are always embedded in their cultural surroundings, and hence no universal factors that make up "a good public sector culture" exist. However, despite the national and regional differences, there appear to be some traits and commonalities that enable organizations globally to function better, and this chapter addresses these.

Organizational culture is what makes an organization what it is, and it is commonly understood as the paradigm by which organizations operate. A culture is often so strong that despite the creation of innovative strategies to move the organization in the desired direction, progress only occurs to the extent allowed by the organizational culture. The saying "Culture eats strategy for breakfast" refers to how the existing organizational norms and practices that an organization has developed over time may in practice override attempts and ideas to change the organization. Despite organizational culture's strong role, however, organizations do not merely play host to one culture but instead combine several cultures that the individuals inside organizations represent.

The idea that organizations have cultures stems from organizational studies research from the 1970s, when researchers analyzed organizations with high performance levels and linked that performance to the strength of character of their founding individuals (Pettigrew, 1979). An organizational culture takes time to develop, as it is formed over time through joint practices and learned practices and attitudes (Schein, 1990). Scholars previously saw organizational culture as something that the organization *had*, whereas later theorizing has viewed organizational culture as something that the organization in itself *is*.

An abstract entity of meanings (Kargas and Varoutas, 2015), an organizational culture is understood to consist of both visible and invisible traits, ranging from organizations' buildings, languages, and employee uniforms and rites to the intangible values, norms, beliefs, and assumptions held by organization members (Schein, 1990). Although an organizational culture may develop on its own, the basic benefit of a strong organizational culture is that it enables the organization to fulfill its aims by helping it to adapt to its environment and supporting its employees and internal processes.

As an intangible asset, organizational culture is the software of the mind, the invisible rules that guide people's interpretations and behavior and that distinguish different organizations from one other (Schein, 2010). Organizational culture is a metaphor derived from national culture, which is understood to distinguish an entity from others. As organizations are looking for ways to be distinguished from the crowd, organizational culture has been introduced as a central building block for corporate character, the traits that distinguish organizations from others and make a distinct contribution to society (Arthur W. Page Society, 2016).

The terms "organizational culture" and "organizational climate" are often understood to refer to the same phenomenon of the intangible assets inside organizations (Denison, 1990). However, whereas organizational culture is a more encompassing concept that describes the state of the organization, organizational climate is understood to be a more temporary, more quantitatively measurable factor that affects the organization and its performance (Jung et al., 2009). In practice, however, the two may overlap, and it may be challenging for public sector managers to distinguish which behavior results from culture and which from the climate. Moreover, a positive organizational climate alone does not guarantee success, and by the same token "a strong culture does not guarantee performance" (2011, p. 61), though their coexistence has been proven.

6.2 Defining Organizational Culture

Cultures are sediments of collective experience (Sztompka, 1999). There are several different ways to understand culture rather than just one: there are scholars who like to quantify culture into measures, while others see it merely as a metaphor or a set of unique traits that cannot be replicated. Schein's classical definition views organizational culture as "the pattern of basic assumptions that a given group has invented, discovered, or developed in learning to cope with its problems of external adaptation and internal integration, and that have worked well enough to be considered valid, and therefore, to be taught to new members as the correct way to perceive, think and feel in relation to these problems" (Schein, 1985, p. 6). As a set of assumptions, culture has been linked with individuals' and groups of people's attitudes and actions: it shapes their perceptions, thoughts, and feelings, and through doing so, it also shapes their behavior.

Most of the benefits and resources that organizational culture shapes are formed over time. An organizational culture often develops through practices, and therefore it also shapes employees' attitudes and behavior (Flamholtz, 2001). An organizational culture is thus connected to the people working for the organization, though once it has been established, a strong organizational culture may remain despite changes in personnel.

Research on organizational culture has focused on the integration and differentiation perspectives on culture and change. According to the integration perspective, culture is seen as something to be shared and managed at the organizational level, whereas the differentiation perspective views culture in terms of its diversity and subcultures linked to professional cultures and demographics (Parker and Bradley, 2000).

Several different categorizations of organizational cultures have been established. Among these are the "clan culture" of long-term support and respect, the "adhocracy culture" of entrepreneurial thinking and risk taking, the results-driven "market culture" of efficiency and success, and the "hierarchical culture" of formal structures and rules (Kargas and Varoutas, 2015). Recent understanding of organizational culture refers to several overlapping cultures instead of merely one organizational culture. These sub-cultures play a role in public sector change and development, and there may even be great differences among subcultures in terms of how they guide employees even inside a single organization (Rondeaux, 2006). The complex interplay of organizational cultures, countercultures that go against the dominant view, and several competing subcultures may prove unpredictable (Zorn, Page, and Cheney, 2000).

Deal and Kennedy's early work on corporate culture suggests that it consists of six elements:

1) *History*: how managers and employees talk about the organization and its past.
2) *Values and beliefs*: what is really believed to be important in the organization and what it stands for.
3) *Rituals and ceremonies*: what brings employees together, and the small behaviors apparent in the organization.

4) *Stories*: what values that the organization stands for, and who personifies these values in practice.
5) *Heroic figures*: who is a role model and whose status is elevated in the organization because of his or her embodying of its organizational values.
6) *The cultural network*: the informal communication networks that informal players (such as gossips and spies) use to spread information (Deal and Kennedy, 1982).

Similarly, adding to these, the "cultural web" described by Johnson et al. (2014) includes stories, rituals, and symbols, and it also adds more organizing-related aspects:

7) The organizational structure of both official and unofficial power relations.
8) Financial, quality, and reward control systems.
9) Power structures that have the capacity to establish the organization's strategic direction.

The Denison model of organizational culture lists involvement, consistency, adaptability, and mission as factors that contribute to organizational culture (Denison, 1990, 2000). It places beliefs and assumptions at the center of organizational culture, and it divides culture into four quadrants on two continuums: external–internal and flexibility–stability. The flexible–external part includes issues such as adaptability (the bringing about of change, customer focus, and organizational learning), whereas the flexible–internal section features issues related to involvement (empowerment, team orientation, and capability development). The stability–external portion contains mission-related aspects (strategic direction and intent, goals and objectives, and vision), and the stability–internal segment accommodates consistency-related aspects (core values, agreement, and coordination and integration).

6.3 What Benefit Does Organizational Culture Bring?

"A resource must be rare if it is to sustain competitive advantage" (Kamaruddin and Abeysekera, 2013, p. 56), and organizational culture is one such unique resource that allows organizations to provide value through distinction. This distinction is especially important in the public sector, where operations are tightly guided by policies and laws, organizations are seldom able to compete for the best workforce based on salaries, and employees balance the public good against diminishing resources. Moreover, from a policy perspective, organizational culture provides a basis for explaining and assessing the match and success of organizational reforms (Parker and Bradley, 2000).

An organizational culture does not in itself bring any benefits to the organization or to the society around it – in fact, a negative organizational culture may even harm both the organization and the society. On the other hand, a positive organizational culture can benefit everyone, from the individuals in the organization to the society surrounding it, in the form of increased satisfaction, engagement, commitment, and flexibility. Some results from business organizations suggest that a good culture can add 20–30% to the value of an organization when compared to organizations with less distinct cultures (Heskett, 2011). As Habib et al. point out, "If the organizational culture is positive, it will enhance employees' commitment, job satisfaction and decrease employees' retention, automatically the performance will increase." (Habib et al., 2014, p. 220)

Although researchers still disagree on whether organizational success or a good organizational culture comes first, a good organizational culture is understood to provide organizations with several benefits. Starting from within the organization, a good culture enables employees to form an organizational identity, which in turn shapes commitment (Lee and Kamarul Zaman, 2009; Habib et al., 2014). As the organizational culture shapes individuals' behavior inside the organization, it also builds bonding social capital, which strengthens their commitment (Putnam, 1993). Identification with the organization is important, as it enables work satisfaction and commitment (McKinnon et al., 2003).

Organizational culture has been suggested to be a wheel-like self-feeding mechanism of goods that keeps producing benefits once it has been set in motion. In his "culture cycle," Heskett lists the outcomes of a positive culture, and within his list, he includes the formation of organizational policies, practices, and behaviors that benefit the organization – for example, transparency, an increased willingness to collaborate, and self-direction on the part of employees. Moreover, he suggests that a good culture enables continuous organizational learning and improvement, resulting in agility and flexibility as well as innovation, growth, and profitability for the organization (Heskett, 2011).

As the environment around public sector organizations is increasingly dynamic and unpredictable, organizational culture can be understood as a stabilizing force, since organizations with an adaptive organizational culture are more likely to survive despite changes in the surroundings (Costanza et al., 2015). In fact, organizations with an antifragile culture are even able to benefit from the change around them and gain competitive advantage from it, as they are seen as stronger in comparison to other organizations around them (Luoma-aho, 2014).

6.4 Public Sector Organizational Culture

Despite the trends of privatization and increasing business orientation in the public sector, public sector organizations' cultures are not exactly same as those of business organizations. As businesses and public sector organizations have fundamentally different reasons for their existence, there are clear differences in their respective organizational cultures as well (Wæraas, 2014, pp. 675–692). Public sector organizations have to serve the whole range of societal actors, not just mere customers, and their actions are to a significant degree set out in national legislation. There is greater accountability associated with public sector organizations on the basis that they serve the common good, and market mechanisms of demand and competition have less of an influence on them (Parker and Bradley, 2000). Instead, public sector organizations are subject to mechanisms of political control, which also restrict their communication (Sanders and Canel, 2013). Moreover, the values that public sector employees operate by seem to differ somewhat from those of business organizations' employees (Perry and Porter, 1982).

As an organization's culture describes "the way things are done around here" (O'Riordan, 2015, p. 8), a public sector organization's culture is a combination of the different factors that make up the environment within which the organization operates. In the public sector, strong, established institutions have a stabilizing effect on the norms and value systems of individual organizations, making organizational culture quite difficult to change (Scott, 1995).

Public sector organizations' cultures are often formed over long periods of time and are hence quite stable (Schein, 1990). Public sector organizations always exist in a national/ethnic cultural environment. On the macrolevel, regional cultures and religion shape an organization's culture, and on the mesolevel, the subgroup identities of industries or occupations play a role (Cameron and Quinn, 2011). Public sector organizations can thus only construct a culture that is to some degree congruent with their environment, and attempting to change beyond these limits may prove not only challenging but even harmful.

In fact, there are certain sector-based traits to organizational culture that are also visible in an organization's reputation – for example, the tendency to be more bureaucratic than flexible, or the tendency to remain distant from individual citizens rather than to closely relate to them (Luoma-aho, 2008; Luoma-aho and Makikangas, 2014; Kargas and Varoutas, 2015). Sector-based cultures may override individual attempts to bring about change, but they may also provide support and safety in times of uncertainty.

Most studies on public sector organizational culture focus on the problems of the existing culture and the pressing need to push bureaucratic culture toward superior citizen engagement and service provision (Bourgon, 2011; Brown et al., 2003b, p. 255). The old culture is often blamed for being too bureaucratic and inflexible, and serving citizens today is understood to need more flexibility. Change itself is understood to be dependent on culture, and some hold public sector culture and traditions responsible for causing resistance to development and change (Brown, Waterhouse, and Flynn, 2003a; Kumar, Kant, and Amburgey, 2007). In fact, public sector organizations are understood to have "lacked an orientation towards adaptability, change and risk taking (developmental culture) and they have lacked an orientation towards outcomes such as productivity and efficiency (rational culture)" (Parker and Bradley, 2000).

6.5 Subcultures

Members of organizations make their own interpretations of the existing organizational culture. It is often assumed that there is one strong main culture that overrides individual actions in public sector organizations. This thinking is somewhat outdated, as individuals today may come from diverse cultural backgrounds and combine several different professional cultures themselves. In fact, subcultures can be found in public sector organizations; these often form around teams or departments that have their own way of doing things. Such subcultures are often determined by their own, somewhat different values, or a mixture of the values of the main culture and those of the subcultures (Boisnier and Chatmann, 2003). The subcultures offer a unique identification point for employees, especially on the team level, and can hence be helpful for the organization.

The relative strength of these subcultures and their power are dependent on several different factors, including the physical environment, team dynamics, power relations, and the different communication practices that can be used to guide people in organizations. Borrowing from behavioral economics, norms, defaults, and priming can steer even the strongest culture (Dolan et al., 2010).

An organization's subcultures may become challenging for the organization to manage if their values do not align even with the most fundamental values of the whole organization (Hitt, Miller, and Colella, 2014). One example of this can be seen in the IT units of more traditional public sector organizations. These units tend to value freedom and autonomy as a result of their members' professional background, whereas the main organization values teamwork and prearranged processes. Although these two sets of values may coexist and ideally even complement each other, it is possible for conflicts to arise due to the different expectations caused by these cultures and their values. Public sector managers need to understand and engage with these subcultures to ensure their contribution to the whole organizational mission despite their differences.

6.6 Communication and Public Sector Culture

Communication and culture can be understood to coexist in a symbiotic relation-ship, as communication is what shapes the culture, while the culture dictates the communication style. Developing communication is always related to developing the culture of the organization itself, and hence "from a management perspective, a lack of understanding of organizational culture in the public sector is of concern because research on organizational culture indicates that culture is central to the change process and to the attainment of strategic objectives" (Parker and Bradley, 2000, p. 125).

Communication influences culture through making sense of events and changes, thereby framing them in a context that resonates with the organizational culture. Communication also sets the vision for the organization, and it thus sets the direction in which the organization should be moving. Expectations set by organizational culture are often verbalized through communication and only become conscious once dis-cussed. Communication is therefore a means for creating and changing organizational culture, and similarly, each organization's communication manifests the organization's culture to those outside.

6.6.1 Gaps that Public Sector Culture Can Fix

The type of organizational culture that an organization has determines the strengths and the weaknesses of the organization. To illustrate what specific gaps between citizens and public sector organizations can be fixed via organizational culture, we utilize the competing values framework (CVF) (Zammuto and Krakower, 1991). Built around two continuums – from internal demands to external demands on the one hand, and from control to flexibility on the other – it has been used to describe and measure the differences apparent in public sector organizations (Parker and Bradley, 2000). It is important to remember, though, that no culture is better than another, as they all result from the circumstances of the organization. The real value of organizations can be found in the way in which the culture enables the organization to best fulfill its mission in the changing environment (Deal and Kennedy, 1982).

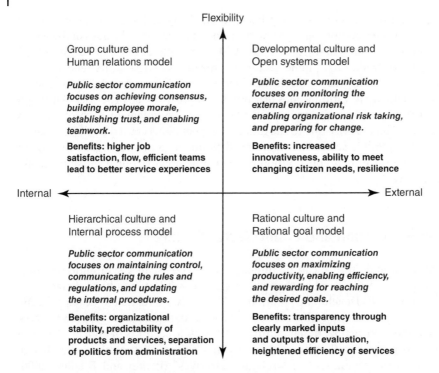

Flexibility

Group culture and
Human relations model

Public sector communication
focuses on achieving consensus,
building employee morale,
establishing trust, and enabling
teamwork.

Benefits: higher job
satisfaction, flow, efficient teams
lead to better service experiences

Developmental culture and
Open systems model

Public sector communication
focuses on monitoring the
external environment,
enabling organizational risk taking,
and preparing for change.

Benefits: increased
innovativeness, ability to meet
changing citizen needs, resilience

Internal ← → External

Hierarchical culture and
Internal process model

Public sector communication
focuses on maintaining control,
communicating the rules and
regulations, and updating
the internal procedures.

Benefits: organizational
stability, predictability of
products and services, separation
of politics from administration

Rational culture and
Rational goal model

Public sector communication
focuses on maximizing
productivity, enabling efficiency,
and rewarding for reaching
the desired goals.

Benefits: transparency through
clearly marked inputs
and outputs for evaluation,
heightened efficiency of services

Figure 6.1 How each public sector culture type shapes public sector communication foci and the benefits of each specific culture for the citizen–public sector organization relationship. Illustration based on the competing values framework. Source: Adapted from Zammuto and Krakower (1991) and Parker and Bradley (2000).

Based on their culture types, public sector organizations can be located between the four extremes of internal process model, rational goal model, human relations model, and open systems model. In practice, they often straddle and balance the four extremes. These four different cultures and their special communication foci are shown in Figure 6.1.

1) *Hierarchical culture (the internal process model)*: The internal process model remains the most common model in the public sector: "The internal process model most clearly reflects the traditional theoretical model of bureaucracy and public administration that relies on formal rules and procedures as control mechanisms" (Parker and Bradley, 2000, p. 129). The focus here is on the internal development of the organization, and the key principle is control. In the internal process model, management and communication are tools for gaining stability and control through formalized rules and procedures (Zammuto and Krakower, 1991). Measuring the degree to which an organization follows the internal process model involves employees' outputs and reports. This type of culture is especially geared toward fixing the gaps caused by an unpredictable environment, as it cultivates stability and predictability. In addition, this culture may best enable a separation between politics and administration, as hierarchical processes are well known in advance and strongly controlled by several layers of management.

2) *Group culture (the human relations model)*: The human relations model, also known as the group culture model, focuses on the internal side of organizational development while remaining flexible to changes. Its focus is on achieving cohesion and maintaining employee morale through trust and teamwork. Management and communication build on achieving consensus, and they are utilized to mentor and encourage employees and ensure the flow experience in work. Compliance is understood to automatically result from a strong, trust-filled culture within the organization (Luoma-aho, 2014), and measuring the degree to which an organization follows the human relations model is based on the levels of trust within the organization, as well as on team achievements and mentoring outcomes. Organizations of this kind typically have a low staff turnover, as employees experience a strong sense of allegiance and belonging to the organization. This type of culture is especially beneficial for improving public services through higher public sector job satisfaction and more efficient service teams.

3) *Rational culture (the rational goal model)*: The rational goal model produces a rational culture, which focuses on organizational productivity and efficiency. The focus is on outcomes and reaching the goals set, and management and communication are linked to maximizing the achievement of the goals set. In this model, rewards are linked to achieving preset goals, and the focus is on control, though there is an emphasis on understanding the external environment as well. This type of culture is especially beneficial for bringing about heightened transparency on the part of public sector organizations through the clearly marked inputs and outputs of public sector processes, and it also produces more efficient services through a strong focus on productivity.

4) *Developmental culture (the open systems model)*: The open systems model of developmental culture is able to ascertain changes in the external environment and utilize them to contribute to the organization's growth. This culture is the very opposite of the internal process model, as it emphasizes flexibility and networks. There is an entrepreneurial spirit in the organization: its leaders focus on innovation, and rewards are tied to individual initiative. Management and communication are utilized to prepare the organization to take risks and interact with the environment. This type of culture is especially beneficial for predicting and meeting rising and changing citizen needs and expectations due to its focus on monitoring. Other benefits include increased organizational innovativeness and resilience, which are achieved through a constant exchange of ideas and an overall proactive approach to public management (Figure 6.1).

Although some of these four cultures appear to be better suited to the present era and its communication environment, it is not always so clear what the disadvantages and benefits of each culture are. While the internal process model type of organizational culture may threaten the organization's survival through fragility caused by not sensing external developments (Luoma-aho, 2014), in some cases, this kind of internal focus may prove valuable. If, for example, the developments outside the organization are temporary or leading in an undesired direction, there is stability to be found in the internal focus. On the other hand, the open systems model may appear tempting for most public sector reformers, yet it may in fact prove ill suited for executive organizations whose main tasks include control or regulation of a sector or an industry. Ideally, a balanced public sector organization would be a combination of all four types of cultures, and failing to address one trait will result in performance and sustainability gaps.

6.6.2 What to Measure in Practice?

Several different measures and tools have been provided to gauge and develop public sector culture, but overall research has moved from measuring artifacts that are very organization dependent to measuring the more universal underlying values of organizations (Parker and Bradley, 2000). Access to values that individuals may be unaware of requires turning it to their behaviors, artifacts, and norms that they are familiar with. Measuring organizational culture is suggested to consist of four Rs: referrals, retention of employees, returns to labor, and relationships with customers (Heskett, 2011). Translated to the public sector, these would include in practice measuring:

1) *Referrals*: As public sector organizations can rarely compete for employees based on higher salaries, recommendations and referrals matter. One aspect of measuring a successful organizational culture is hence measuring the number and quality of referrals that existing and former employees give the organization.
2) *Retention*: There are several different costs associated with recruitment, hiring, training, and lost productivity due to employee changes and turnover. One aspect of measuring a successful organizational culture is measuring these, as a culture strengthened through employee loyalty will result in lower expenses.
3) *Returns to labor*: Employees who feel that they are appreciated and part of a greater cause in a good cultural environment are more productive. Measures of productivity can therefore be seen as measures of organizational culture.
4) *Relationships*: Satisfied public sector employees produce better relationships with citizens in service encounters and enable citizen engagement, fewer complaints, and higher satisfaction scores. Measuring these indicators of relationship quality would thus measure organizational culture.

Measuring simply one part of this combination will result in a skewed understanding of the organizational culture; all of them are needed for a balanced entity. Moreover, measuring organizational culture should always be done in accordance with the aims of the culture and the organization, as a culture can receive high praise but simultaneously move the organization in an unwanted direction.

6.7 Changing Organizational Culture

As Costanza et al. point out, "While culture can and does change, such changes generally occur very slowly and are difficult to effect" (2015, p. 362). As the society around public sector organizations changes, new expectations that require public organizations to change emerge.

Change and culture make for a complex pairing in the public sector. Whenever a management style or process changes in the public sector, it affects organizational culture over time (Schraeder, Tears, and Jordan, 2005). Despite this, research shows that not all managerial changes manage to touch the culture and that, despite renewals, some public sector organizations' culture remains more bureaucratic than flexible (Parker and Bradley, 2000). Moreover, some traits of public sector organizations are so strong that they endure despite major organizational restructurings such as mergers (Luoma-aho, 2008).

Organizational culture itself is a tool for dealing with organizational change, as it provides a framework for understanding the environment around the organization. Because of its heavy structure and its development over long periods of time, organizational culture often changes slowly (Schein, 2010). An organizational culture acts as a resource in times of change, as it provides individuals with clues about how to react to changes in the environment in which the organization operates. If successful, the culture may even predict organizational survival through its ability to adapt (Barney, 1986).

Especially in the public sector, where hierarchies still reign, the role of leaders during change and as actors capable of modeling the right behaviors is vital (Schraeder et al., 2005). This modeling should take place on the two levels of numbers and values, and if employees have been involved in shaping these aims, their involvement increases (Heskett, 2011). As change produces insecurity, there is often much resistance to it inside public sector organizations as questions arise regarding what will happen to individual employees and their competences.

Changing a culture can be achieved through new practices and behaviors (Zamanou and Glaser, 1994). Deal and Kennedy's early pioneering work on corporate culture (1982) views cultural change as something that occurs through employees' mere telling of new stories about their environment and explanation of what is going on around them. Such storytelling is also cost effective, as "a cultural change accomplished by changing large numbers of personnel is expensive in financial and human terms. One component of a less costly approach is to tell new and different stories within the corporation because stories establish the cultural DNA that gives organizations, families, and individuals their identities" (Wines and Hamilton, 2009, p. 433).

Adaptation is a central contributory factor to organizational change (Heskett, 2011). As a result, organizations with more adaptive cultures are better equipped for new environments. But what does adaptation entail? Costanza et al. (2015, p. 362) point to evidence that suggests that adaptive organizational cultures ensure long-term organizational survival. Both values- and action-related characteristics are necessary for a culture of adaptation. Adaptation stems from organizational beliefs: Is there enough confidence in the possibility of change and in the value of openness and flexibility to change? As the environment changes constantly around organizations, paying attention to changes in and needs of end users such as customers or citizens is crucial. However, mere attention and flexibility alone do not suffice; adaptive organizations also require actions to support these attributes – for example, anticipation and a proactive approach to solving emerging challenges. Collaboration both internally between units and externally with different stakeholders also contributes to adaptiveness (Costanza et al., 2015).

In cases where public sector organizational culture remains strong, some suggest that public managers should work with and within the current organizational culture rather than against it or with a view to escaping it. To this end, the Institute for Public Administration offers several practical suggestions for public sector organizations that wish to change their organizational culture (O'Riordan, 2015):

1) Matching the emerging strategies with the existing culture to ensure that they do not clash with one another, as it "has been well documented that culture trumps strategy every time" (O'Riordan, 2015, p. 25).
2) Focusing on a few critical behavior changes instead of the whole system: simple changes are easier for employees to adapt to and enforce.
3) Honoring the existing culture and its strengths instead of focusing on the problems in need of change in order to engage employees in the change.
4) Combining both formal (for example, rules, metrics, and reporting) and informal (for example, emotional links, networks, communities of interest, and ad hoc conversations) interventions through modeling and promoting new behaviors instead of relying on the formal routes for information provision.
5) Measuring the evolution to show progress and motivate employees and keep them engaged throughout the process.

6.8 Criticism of Organizational Culture

Although working on organizational culture seems to address many of the challenges faced by public sector organizations, it is by no means a universal cure, and nor is it easy to bring about in practice. Some have criticized the whole existence of organizational culture and prefer to speak merely of practices and habits occurring on the organizational level. There are also studies pointing to the impossibility of changing an organizational culture at will even in the long term: there are more reports of failures and lessons learned from instances of attempting to change cultures than there are success stories of changing organizational cultures (Wankhade and Brinkman, 2014), highlighting the challenge of changing an entity once its characteristics have been set.

Moreover, organizational culture alone can achieve nothing. It is only one part of the equation, and it must be combined with organizational strategy, an understanding of the context, and high-quality execution if it is to be fruitful (Heskett, 2011). Some also question the real power that organizational culture holds in guiding organizations. As with all development, the focus can shift too much onto the change process itself (Harris and Ogbonna, 2002), and efforts to manage a culture can cause disruption, lead to unexpected outcomes, and even prevent the desired change (Wankhade and Brinkman, 2014). Changing a culture for the sake of changing a culture is fruitless. Accordingly, culture in itself should rarely be an end; it will usually merely serve as a means for creating better public sector organizations.

6.9 Summary of Organizational Culture

Intangible assets are valuable to the degree that they are able to distinguish the organization from others and strengthen it (Kamaruddin and Abeysekera, 2013). The organizational cultures of public sector organizations appear to have some globally shared traits, but it is clear that the final differentiating powers result from the unique

Table 6.1 Organizational culture as an intangible asset in the public sector.

It is the intangible asset that measures the extent to which the organization is aligned with certain core principles

Tangible assets that organizational culture enables	Organizational effectiveness, increased productivity, and lower transaction costs resulting from trust and collaboration enabled by the organizational culture
Resources that organizational culture generates	Better-functioning public sector organizations thorough improved efficiency and work flow; citizen and employee satisfaction; increased engagement, commitment, and organizational flexibility
Monetary expression	Lower transaction, retention, and recruitment costs due to employees' greater engagement and loyalty
Types of value that organizational culture provides to the organization	Depending on the type of organizational culture, value can include greater organizational stability, work flow, innovativeness, employee satisfaction, or team efficiency
Types of value that organizational culture provides to citizens and stakeholders	Depending on the organizational culture, value can include better service experiences, increased transparency of organizational processes, easier evaluation of input–output ratio, or a superior ability to meet citizens' needs and expectations
Gaps that organizational culture bridges	Poor job satisfaction, low citizen satisfaction, poor service experiences, low efficiency, and a lack of understanding of citizens' needs and expectations
Dependence on communication management	Fully dependent: culture and communication form a symbiotic entity, and to change the organizational culture, communication needs to be changed
Implied organization management transformations	From bureaucratic culture to citizen optimized, culture of engagement achieved through rewards and modeling the desired behavior, and from internal, process-oriented culture to external, citizen-oriented culture via service design and monitoring
Measures	Organizational culture measurement through four Rs (Heskett, 2011): (1) referrals, (2) retention, (3) returns to labor, and (4) relationships

local combinations. Table 6.1 summarizes organizational culture and explains its functioning as an intangible asset for public sector organizations.

6.10 Case Study on Organizational Culture

Cultural research in the municipality of Zaanstad, the Netherlands

How can a public sector employee culture be turned into one of authentic service? Zaanstad is an industrial municipality of about 150 000 inhabitants in North Holland near Amsterdam in the Netherlands, famous for its traditional Dutch windmills. Like many similar municipalities, Zaanstad city officials realized the urgent need to change the public sector employee culture to better meet changing citizen expectations. Under the motto "Van zorgen voor, naar zorgen dat" (From taking care of, to ensuring that care is delivered), this Dutch municipality began to move away from the traditionally strong guidance of new public management thinking, to rewrite its own cultural story that employees could easily follow. The need was most urgent in the area of relating to and meeting citizens, as the latter felt that the public sector organizations existed in a world of their own and were unreachable. A public entity (as seen in Figure 6.2), Zaanstad faced similar challenges to those of most cities and municipalities in the Western world with regard to public sector culture.

Citizens walking around in Zaanstad, the Netherlands. (Reproduced with permission of Dreamstime LLC.)

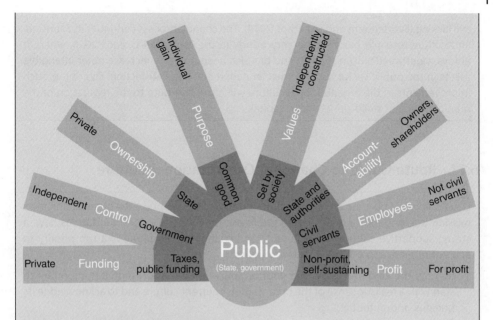

Figure 6.2 Publicness of the municipality of Zaanstad.

To achieve the change, in 2015, together with the Dutch Ministry of the Interior, a research group on management of cultural change from the Amsterdam University of Applied Sciences began a cultural study to help with the organizational culture change process in practice (Faddegonm and Straathof, 2014).

Culture research in Zaanstad

Before a culture can be changed, it needs to be fully understood. Culture research looks into the lifeworld of the public sector organization in detail and investigates whether the identified cultural patterns fit the current expectations, goals, and ambitions of the organization and its surrounding individuals, such as the citizens (Vos and Schoemaker, 2017). In Zaanstad, researchers applied the culture arena model (Straathof, 2009) to help the municipality change.

Three stages were applied in the research process:

1) First, the *mindset* of the municipality's employees was studied through their thoughts and motivations.
2) Second, the characteristics of the *arena* such as relationships inside the organization and management were studied.
3) Third, actual *behavior* apparent in the organization was mapped to see how employees acted in certain situations and whether they matched the desired state.

The results showed that the employees of the municipality of Zaanstad were aware of the urgent change needed in their culture, but that changing a mindset takes time and requires de-learning of old behaviors. The traditional models of New Public Management were very strongly embedded in their thinking and behavior, and collective thinking was still lacking (Faddegonm and Straathof, 2014). The change process continues in Zaanstad, and culture research has become very trendy in the Netherlands since 2015, where it enjoys widespread citizen support and has also been noted to increase other intangible assets in the public sector such as trust, engagement, and satisfaction. Over time, such improvements in the organizational culture will also contribute to the reputation of the municipality and build up its social capital.

6.11 Route Guide to Changing Organizational Culture

Developing and building an organizational culture to best support the organization in its mission is a long-term project. In the public sector, very rarely do organizations have a strong supportive culture to begin with, and changing the culture is a top priority to achieve resilience in a turbulent environment.

1) **Identify the kind of culture that your organization has at present**. It is important to start with a realistic sense of the organization's current culture and to acknowledge its benefits and potential.
   Questions to ask: What are the elements working positively inside the current organizational culture? What are the subcultures like, and are they aligned with the dominant organizational culture?

2) **Identify the strengths of the current organizational culture.** Change works best and occurs most easily when it is built on existing strengths and rewarded.
   Questions to ask: How engaged do employees feel with the organization? Do they understand its values and practice them, or do the organization's values remain mere statements on the wall?

3) **Enable the right stories.** Organizational culture is apparent in the stories told inside the organization and among employees and citizens. These stories also become a self-fulfilling prophecy.
   Questions to ask: What are new recruits first told about the organization? What are the stories that are told about the organization like in general? How could we influence these stories for the better? Who are the central opinion leaders contributing to the organizational culture, and how could they be invited along to bring about improvement?

4) **Lead by example.** Changing an organizational culture for the better comes about through changing one practice at a time, and leadership examples are central for potential change, especially in the more hierarchical public sector organizations.
   Questions to ask: Do the management actions support the desired culture? What are the unintentional messages that managers convey with their behavior? How are the current reward programs in place supporting the new desired culture?

5) **Recheck direction through measurement.** Though often treated as an end in itself, an organizational culture should be a means for achieving the greater end of the organization's mission, and as that mission changes, so should the organizational

culture. Continuous measurement enables an understanding of whether change is needed and in which direction.

Questions to ask: Have the four Rs of culture measurement yielded different results lately? Are the informal stories told of the organization changing? Is the current culture best optimized to take our organization where we need to go?

References

Arthur W. Page Society (2016). *The New CCO: Transforming Enterprises in a Changing World*. Arthur W. Page Society.

Barney, J. (1986). Organizational culture: can it be a source of sustained competitive advantage? *Academy of Management Review* **11** (3): 656–665.

Boisnier, A. and Chatmann, J. (2003). The role of subcultures in agile organizations. In: *Leading and Managing People in the Dynamic Organization*, Organization and Management Series (ed. R. Peterson and E. Mannix), 87–114. New York: Taylor and Francis.

Bourgon, J. (2011). *A New Synthesis of Public Administration: Serving in the 21st Century*. Washington, DC: McGill Queen's Press.

Brown, K., Waterhouse, J., and Flynn, C. (2003a). Change management practices: is a hybrid model a better alternative for public sector agencies? *International Journal of Public Sector Management* **16** (3): 230–241.

Brown, S.W., Boyer, M.A., Mayall, H.J. et al. (2003b). The GlobalEd project: gender differences in a problem-based learning environment of international negotiations. *Instructional Science* **31** (4): 255–276.

Cameron, K. and Quinn, R. (2011). *Diagnosing and Changing Organizational Culture: Based on the Competing Values Framework*. London: John Wiley.

Claver, E., Llopis, J., Gascó, J.L. et al. (1999). Public administration: from bureaucratic culture to citizen-oriented culture. *International Journal of Public Sector Management* **12** (5): 455–464.

Costanza, D., Blacksmith, N., Coats, M. et al. (2015). The effect of adaptive organizational culture on long-term survival. *Journal of Business and Psychology* **31** (3): 361–381.

Deal, T. and Kennedy, A. (1982). *Corporate Cultures, the Rites and Rituals of Corporate Life*. Reading, MA: Addison-Wesley Publishing.

Denison, D. (1990). *Corporate Culture and Organizational Effectiveness*. New York: Wiley.

Denison, D. (2000). Organizational culture: can it be a key lever for driving organizational change? In: *The Handbook of Organizational Culture* (ed. S. Carwright and C. Cooper), 347–372. London: Wiley.

Døjbak Haakonsson, D., Burton, R.M., Obel, B., and Lauridsen, J. (2008). How failure to align organizational climate and leadership style affects performance. *Management Decision* **46** (3): 406–432.

Dolan, P., Hallsworth, M., Halpern, D. et al. (2010). *MINDSPACE: Influencing Behaviour through Public Policy*. UK, Institute for Government, Cabinet Office.

Faddegonm, K. and Straathof, A. (2014). Zaanstad toont belang cultuuronderzoek voor verandering. http://www.binnenlandsbestuur.nl/cultuuronderzoek (accessed 24 September 2017).

Flamholtz, E. (2001). Corporation culture and the bottom line. *European Management Journal* **19** (3): 268–275.

Gillespie, M.A., Denison, D.R., Haaland, S. et al. (2008). Linking organizational culture and customer satisfaction: results from two companies in different industries. *European Journal of Work and Organizational Psychology* **17** (1): 112–132.

Habib, S., Aslam, S., Hussain, A. et al. (2014). The impact of organizational culture on job satisfaction, employees commitment and turn over intention. *Advances in Economics and Business* **2** (6): 215–222.

Harris, L. and Ogbonna, E. (2002). The unintended consequences of culture interventions: a study of unexpected outcomes. *British Journal of Management* **13** (1): 31–46.

Heskett, J. (2011). *The Culture Cycle: How to Shape the Unseen Force that Transforms Performance*. Upper Saddle River, NJ: FT Press.

Hitt, M., Miller, C., and Colella, A. (2014). *Organizational Behavior*, 4th ed. New York: Wiley.

Hofstede, G.H. (2001). *Culture's Consequences: Comparing Values, Behaviors, Institutions, and Organizations across Nations*, 2nd ed. Thousand Oaks, CA: Sage.

Johnson, G., Whittington, R., Scholes, K. et al. (2014). *Fundamentals of Strategy*, 3rd ed. London: Pearson.

Jung, T., Scott, T., Davies, H.T.O. et al. (2009). Instruments for exploring organizational culture: a review of the literature. *Public Administration Review* **69** (6): 1087–1096.

Kamaruddin, K. and Abeysekera, I. (2013). *Intellectual Capital and Public Sector Performance*. Bingley, UK: Emerald.

Kargas, A.D. and Varoutas, D. (2015). On the relation between organizational culture and leadership: an empirical analysis. *Cogent Business & Management* **2** (1): 1–18.

Kumar, S., Kant, S., and Amburgey, T. (2007). Public agencies and collaborative management approaches. *Administration & Society* **39** (5): 569–611.

Lee, H.Y. and Kamarul Zaman, B.A. (2009). The moderating effects of organizational culture on the relationships between leadership behaviour and organizational commitment and between organizational commitment and job satisfaction and performance. *Leadership & Organization Development Journal* **30** (1): 53–86.

Luoma-aho, V. (2008). Sector reputation and public organisations. *International Journal of Public Sector Management* **21** (5): 446–467.

Luoma-aho, V. and Makikangas, M. (2014). Do public sector mergers (re)shape reputation? *International Journal of Public Sector Management* **27** (1): 39–52.

Luoma-aho, V. ed. (2014). *Särkymätön Viestintä*. ProCom Ry: Helsinki.

Luoma-aho, V., Vos, M., Lappalainen, R. et al. (2012). Added value of intangibles for organizational innovation. *Human Technology: An Interdisciplinary Journal on Humans in ICT Environments* **8** (1): 7–23.

Martins, E.C. and Terblanche, F. (2003). Building organisational culture that stimulates creativity and innovation. *European Journal of Innovation Management* **6** (1): 64–74.

McKinnon, J., Harrison, G., Chow, C., and Wu, A. (2003). Organizational culture: association with commitment, job satisfaction, propensity to remain, and information sharing in Taiwan. *International Journal of Business Studies* **11** (1): 25–44.

Naranjo-Valencia, J.C., Jiménez-Jiménez, D., and Sanz-Valle, R. (2011). Innovation or imitation? the role of organizational culture. *Management Decision* **49** (1): 55–72.

O'Riordan, J. (2015). *Organizational Culture and the Public Service*. Dublin, Ireland: Institute of Public Administration.

Parker, R. and Bradley, L. (2000). Organisational culture in the public sector: evidence from six organisations. *International Journal of Public Sector Management* **13** (2): 125–141.

Perry, J.L. and Porter, L.W. (1982). Factors affecting the context for motivation in public organizations. *Academy of Management Review* **7** (1): 89–98.

Pettigrew, A. (1979). On studying organizational cultures. *Administrative Science Quarterly* **24** (4): 570–581.

Putnam, R.D. (1993). *Making Democracy Work: Civic Traditions in Modern Italy*. Princeton, NJ: Princeton University Press.

Rondeaux, G. (2006). Modernizing public administration: the impact on organisational identities. *The International Journal of Public Sector Management* **19** (6): 569–584.

Sanders, K. and Canel, M.-J. ed. (2013). *Government Communication Cases and Challenges*, 1st ed. London: Bloomsbury Academic.

Schein, E.H. (1985). *Organizational Culture and Leadership. The Jossey-Bass Management Series*. San Francisco, CA: Jossey-Bass Publishers.

Schein, E. (1990). Organizational culture. *American Psychologist* **45** (2): 109–119.

Schein, E. (2010). *Organizational Culture and Leadership*. San Francisco, CA: Wiley.

Schraeder, M., Tears, R.S., and Jordan, M.H. (2005). Organizational culture in public sector organizations: promoting change through training and leading by example. *Leadership & Organizational Development* **26** (6): 492–502.

Scott, R. (1995). *Institutions and Organizations*. Thousand Oaks, CA: Sage.

Straathof, A. (2009). *Zoeken Naar De Kern Van Cultuurverandering. Inzichtm Meten, Sturen*. Rotterdam: Erasmus Universiteit.

Sztompka, P. (1999). *Trust: A Sociological Theory (Cambridge Cultural Social Studies)*. Cambridge: Cambridge University Press.

Vos, M. and Schoemaker, H. (2017). *Geïntegreerde Communicatie (tiende druk): Concern-, Interne en Marketingcommunicatie [Integrated Communication: Concern, internal and marketing communication]*. Amsterdam: Boom.

Wæraas, A. (2014). Beauty from within: what bureaucracies stand for. *American Review of Public Administration* **44** (6): 675–692.

Wankhade, P. and Brinkman, J. (2014). The negative consequences of culture change management. *The International Journal of Public Sector Management* **27** (1): 2–25.

Wines, W. and Hamilton, J.B. (2009). On changing organizational cultures by injecting new ideologies. *Journal of Business Ethics* **89**: 433–447.

Zamanou, S. and Glaser, S.R. (1994). Moving toward participation and involvement: managing and measuring organizational culture. *Group & Organization Management* **19** (4): 475–502.

Zammuto, R. and Krakower, J. (1991). Quantitative and qualitative studies of organizational culture. In: *Research in Organizational Change and Development*, vol. 5 (ed. R.W. Woodman and W.A. Passmore), 83–114. Greenwich, CT: JAI Press.

Zorn, T., Page, D., and Cheney, G. (2000). Nuts about change: multiple perspectives on change-oriented communication in a public sector organization. *Management Communication Quarterly* **13** (4): 515–566.

7

Reputation

Reputation and trust might be a key part of the immune system of democracy – a set of technologies and practices that help power, influence, and legitimacy to flow toward those who are willing and able to tackle the challenges that affect us all
(Craig Newmark, Founder of Craigslist.com, Newmark, 2012, p. xi)

This chapter addresses the reputation of public sector organizations and its significance for closing the gap between citizens and public sector organizations. Reputation matters, as it sets citizens' expectations and the level of trust that they feel toward public sector organizations, and hence it guides the interaction process for better or worse. The reputation of public sector organizations is different from that of business organizations, and this places restrictions on reputation management. This chapter discusses how public sector reputation is constructed over time, and it provides some key insights into how reputation can be measured and how it can become a valuable intangible asset for public sector organizations.

7.1   What Is the Logic behind Organizational Reputation?

It has been suggested that as the volume of information in society increases, individuals make their choices based on impressions and experiences, which are often referred to as reputation. In fact, society today can be understood to be a "reputation society," where technology-enabled networks and relationships have taken over in providing us with impressions that help to determine whom to trust and collaborate with (Masum and Tovey, 2012).

Such a shift from relying on information to relying on impressions is challenging for public sector organizations, as their survival has ceased to depend on their performance alone; it now also increasingly rests upon how the organization itself is perceived by the diverse stakeholders around it (Luoma-aho, 2007, p. 124; Walker, 2010). The role of impressions is increasing owing to citizens' ability to use various online reputation systems to compare and rank their experiences with public sector organizations. Citizens and customers cannot be left unattended, even in the stages prior to their actual service

Public Sector Communication: Closing Gaps Between Citizens and Public Organizations, First Edition. María-José Canel and Vilma Luoma-aho.
© 2019 John Wiley & Sons, Inc. Published 2019 by John Wiley & Sons, Inc.

encounters, and this places new pressure on public sector organizations and their reputation management (Edelman and Singer, 2015). Moreover, reputations affect larger entities and sectors: "Globalization, standardization, and marketization of public sector services not only put the reputations of central and local government agencies at stake but also those of the entire public sector and the nation" (Sataøen and Wæraas, 2016, p. 165).

A good reputation creates several resources for public sector organizations, ranging from operational autonomy to increased trust and even organizational legitimacy (Carpenter and Krause, 2012). High scores from reputational rankings and positive feedback from stakeholder satisfaction surveys have been associated with budget increases and stronger citizen commitment (Sataøen and Wæraas, 2016). However, there are certain strongly negative reputational stereotypes that public sector organizations globally battle: many have a reputation for excess bureaucracy, inflexibility, nontransparency, and inefficiency (Wæraas and Byrkjeflot, 2012). Some of these appear to be difficult to shed as they are sector-based associations that are attributed to every public sector organization, regardless of their individual performance or functions (Luoma-aho, 2008). A bad reputation may even harm organizational legitimacy – that is, the organization's license to exist. If a bad reputation hinders citizens' acceptance of a particular organization, those citizens may miss life-saving messages about their own safety, such as warnings about instances of water contamination or other toxic hazards (O'Dwyer, 2015).

Public sector organizations are always tied to the political nature of the sector, and hence the challenges of political communication are also visible in public sector communication. In addition, the political choices of the leaders of public sector organizations may restrict public sector communication. An example of such an approach would be if a government minister arranged for his or her department to delay the release of positive results until the start of an election campaign in order to enhance his or her reputation at that politically important moment, rather than releasing the news immediately. In some states (for example, the Nordic countries), this is more strongly acknowledged and addressed by clearly separating politics and public administration, but in many parts of the world the two are inseparable. Moreover, public sector organizations serve several different stakeholders simultaneously, and prioritizing some over others is very challenging and potentially even unconstitutional. In fact, "satisfying some audience subset often means upsetting others" in the public sector context (Carpenter and Krause, 2012, p. 29).

Proving the value that public sector organizations provide remains a global challenge. Fundamentally, it is a challenge centered on the *legibility* of public sector organizations – that is, citizens' ability to read and understand public sector organizations' choices. As Picci comments (Picci, 2012, p. 142), "The situation generally imposes a heavy cognitive load on citizens and opens the door for strategies of obfuscation of various types – unwarranted attribution of credit or blame, spin, bureaucratic delays, and downright propaganda. The necessary information may be available – indeed, thanks to the Internet, lots of information is available – but making sense of it is challenging." Reputation offers a solution to the challenge of legibility through combining relevant factors into one clear entity to be assessed.

7.2 How the Digital Environment Shapes Reputation

The many effects that digitalization has had on the public sector are both good and bad. As the importance of digital technologies increases, both benefit and harm to reputation are becoming more pertinent issues for public sector organizations. Reputation systems available online mediate and facilitate information that is used to make value judgments through providing support and confirmation for choices made (Masum and Tovey, 2012). The logical argument made is that as organizations' and individuals' choices are made public and more transparent, citizens become less tolerant of the service and of any negative experiences that they have. Reputation hence resembles a brand promise that organizations are expected to live up to. Similarly, reputation systems may also make expectations more realistic, helping individuals to better deal with their experiences. On the other hand, verifying the authenticity of claims made online is a constant challenge, and reviews may be produced by entities whose identities are not what they appear to be. The most extreme examples appear to be statements praising the dictator on the official websites of North Korea, but more subtle forms include questions raised through conspiracy theories and fake news or false accusations of authorities' behavior written by individuals (Luoma-aho, 2015).

Borrowing from Cory Doctorow's *Down and Out in the Magic Kingdom*, the concept of "whuffie" (Hunt, 2009) has been introduced to describe the future importance of organizational reputation. In the future, citizens and customers will choose organizations and public services based on their level of this construct. Whuffie is the organization's reputation among its social networks. It consists of three factors: the organization's perceived niceness, the noteworthiness of its actions, and its position of value among social networks. The argument goes that these three aspects determine whether citizens will interact with the organization in the future, and an organization that wishes to succeed in its stakeholder relations should think in terms of all three factors. While the noteworthiness of actions and networks of collaboration are possible for public sector organizations to achieve, it is certain that niceness continues to be a challenge, as organizations balance bureaucratic order and a citizen-centered approach (Bourgon, 2009).

"Make America great again": Choosing change over a candidate's reputation

Source: https://twitter.com/DonaldTrump, accessed November 2, 2017

What matters more: the reputation of the entire public sector, or the reputation of the candidate? The poll-defying 2016 presidential elections in the United States brought in Donald Trump as the forty-fifth president of United States of America, even though he lacked a record of service in the public sector and was dogged by questions about aspects of his personal and business conduct. It seems that what mattered to voters more than his personal reputation were his claims about his ability to fix a broken system. The bad reputation of the public sector and political elites was strong enough to make a candidate who focused on changing them succeed. When compared to the reputation of his opponent, Hillary Clinton, Trump's reputation remains questionable, yet despite this he became the president. One could argue, however, that Hillary Clinton's reputation was too elitist for individuals to relate to, further contributing to Trump's win. Whichever of these two perspectives is most accurate, reputation and impressions played a much larger role than did facts and deeds, and this was exacerbated by the repetition of Trump's messages on social media and fake news sites. In fact, online reputation is becoming an important asset for the political communication of public sector organizations. When verification of news and the facts behind statements and stories is missing, overall impressions play a larger role, creating new challenges for public sector organizations.

7.3 Organizational Reputation Defined

Public sector reputation has been studied widely across disciplines, and contributions range from administrative and organizational studies to works focused on political communication, public relations, and marketing. Waeraas and Maor suggest three different perspectives for reputation research: (i) the "economics perspective" of reputation as an asset resulting from organizational actions; (ii) the "social constructionist perspective" of reputation as a collective aggregate product that is negotiated within society; and (iii) the "institutional perspective" of reputation as a positioning of the organization according to societal rankings by different institutional intermediaries (Wæraas and Maor, 2015).

Researchers debate whether reputation is mostly perceptual, mostly experiential, or a combination of the two (Gotsi and Wilson, 2001, p. 24). Those who refer to reputation as a sister concept of image note how reputation results from organizations' actions and behavior instead of from mere impression management (Luoma-aho, 2008). Overall, a reputation is based on what the organization does. It is a combination of perceptions and assessments; it is a record of the organization's past deeds (Sztompka, 1999); and it is an asset made up of the various perceptions held by all of its internal and external stakeholders (Fombrun and van Riel, 2004). As reputation is publicly held and resides in the opinions of stakeholders, it is vulnerable to external influences and subject to change (Walker, 2010).

Reputation is seen as a competitive asset that enables the organization to function, residing in the minds of the different stakeholders. Wæraas and Maor (2015) summarize that reputation is the aggregate perception of all stakeholders, that it can be compared with that of other organizations, and that it is stable and enduring. In practice, reputation can be understood as a continuous measure from worst to best. Moreover, it features an element of rivalry: when one organization's reputation increases, that of a competing organization usually decreases. Reputation serves to differentiate in the sense that it enables organizations to distinguish themselves from other similar organizations, and it is valuable because it is a strategic resource that contributes to organizational advantage (Wæraas and Maor, 2015, p. 3).

We define public sector reputation as

a collective assessment of the organization by both the mediated and personal experiences of stakeholders that results from the stakeholders' expectations and shapes their attitudes and trust toward and their collaboration with the organization and more broadly the sector in which that organization operates.

Reputation works in practice through several different mechanisms. For example, on the citizen side, balance theory explains how citizens handle conflicting information about an organization and attempt to reach a balance between their experiences and information (Deephouse, 2000). For instance, citizens balance their own experiences with media reports and stories from other citizens shared online (Luoma-aho, 2007, p. 124).

7.4 The Benefits of a Good Reputation

The benefits of a good reputation have been well documented for business organizations, and they include the ability to add a premium to prices, easier recruitment, greater customer loyalty, diminished employee churn, and higher trust in and overall satisfaction with the organization and its products and services (Fombrun and van Riel, 2004). For public sector organizations, reputation is of great value, as it can be "used to generate public support, to achieve delegated autonomy and discretion from politicians, to protect the agency from political attack, and to recruit and retain valued employees" (Carpenter, 2002, p. 491). For some public sector organizations, reputation can turn into financial advantage through their strengthened legitimacy and budget increases.

Reputation can serve as a proxy for other intangible assets such as organizational legitimacy (Staw and Epstein, 2000). A good reputation may provide the organization with more tangible forms of capital through word-of-mouth recommendations and referrals. Moreover, a good reputation increases positive word of mouth, because satisfied individuals share their good experiences. A positive reputation protects the organization from risks and crises through becoming a stabilizing force and increasing the likelihood that stakeholders will give the organization the benefit of the doubt.

Reputation becomes capital once it benefits the organization via stakeholder trust, commitment, and faith in the organization's future (Petrick et al., 1999). Reputational capital is understood to consist of the organization's credibility, reliability, responsibility, trustworthiness, and accountability as these elements are perceived by its stakeholders (Petrick et al., 1999). A good reputation is always formed in the context of a relationship or a network, and some define reputation as a resource embedded in a social network (Nahapiet and Ghoshal, 1998). Thus, although an organization may attempt to build a good reputation, a reputation is in fact property of the social network of individuals and groups that assess the organization, as reputation is a collective estimate (Carroll, 2016).

Reputation alone is valuable, yet it also enables and strengthens several other intangible assets. It may act as a proxy to organizational legitimacy, as organizations with a good reputation are considered more acceptable (Wæraas and Byrkjeflot, 2012). Social exchange theory explains how a good reputation builds citizens' trust and commitment, influencing their actions and contributing to higher citizen engagement (Carroll, 2015). A past reputation signals whether citizens should trust the organization, and in turn, citizens' trust becomes reputation in the same way that the present becomes history (Luoma-aho, 2007, p. 124). Similarly, however, a negative reputation diminishes trust, commitment, and engagement, resulting in disengagement or citizen passivity (Rothstein and Stolle, 2008).

7.5 Public Sector Organizations and Reputation

7.5.1 Reputation in a Context of Lower Competition

There appear to be certain reputational traits that are common to all public sector organizations regardless of their function – for example, bureaucracy and slowness (Luoma-aho, 2008). Such a shared sector reputation is a creator of safety as citizen expectations are met, yet it is simultaneously binding, as it shapes the impressions that citizens have. As reputation focuses on what citizens and stakeholders think, organizational reputation has been seen as a positive signal of a more customer-oriented approach in public sector organizations (Wallin Andreassen, 1994). In fact, reputation in the public sector is tightly linked to organizational actions. Citizens appear to be more concerned with what the organization does (such as service provision or policy formulation) than with who is leading it (Sanders and Canel, 2015). Moreover, the traits of the public sector system within which organizations are placed shape their reputation via enabling and restraining structures.

The strong institutional context of the public sector makes many public sector organizations conform to normative standards and hence build their reputation on similar traits to those of other public sector organizations around them (Carroll, 2015). Recent empirical findings suggest that some public sector organizations "face a trade-off between the contradictory demands of similarity and difference and hence legitimacy and reputation: They renounce the advantage of a unique reputation (i.e. competitive advantage) in order to retain the benefits of conformity (i.e. legitimacy)" (Wæraas and Sataøen, 2015, p. 310).

There is often less competition for public sector reputation, and there are certain sector traits that must be met for public sector organizations to remain credible. In democratic settings, for example, impartiality and equality are essential. In fact, to maintain citizens' and stakeholders' trust, there is a need for public sector organizations to be similar enough to existing legitimate public sector institutions and systems. Moreover, as many public services and products are guided by legislation, there are clear limits to uniqueness. A balance must be struck between isomorphism and different management reforms: "On the one hand there is the need to outshine other public organizations to create a reputational advantage, and on the other there is the need to maintain legitimacy via isomorphism" (Luoma-aho, 2007, pp. 124, 127).

In most cases, despite increased privatization and public sector reforms, public organizations are less open to market competition than are their private sector counterparts, and they are less concerned with citizen or end-user preferences. This is not to say that citizens' voices are not important. In fact, prioritizing citizen engagement is a global trend for public sector organizations (Bowden, Luoma-aho, and Naumann, 2016). Indeed, due to their publicness and principles of transparency, public sector organizations are often more subject to public scrutiny and required to have a high degree of accountability to constituencies (Canel and Sanders, 2015). In sum, "public sector organizations have to operate under different constrains, and to balance political guidelines, national guidelines, international cooperation, ideologies management, the bureaucratic culture of administration and current citizen and customer feedback" (Luoma-aho and Canel, 2016, p. 598).

Despite attempts to rebrand and restructure, sector reputation remains very stable in the public sector, and this creates challenges for any attempts at improvement (Luoma-aho and Makikangas, 2014). Moreover, the aspect of a good reputation that is based on eliciting positive emotions within service users represents a great challenge for public sector organizations, because they cannot choose their customers and often serve those unwilling to be served (such as criminals).

A good reputation is equal to a brand promise that must be kept if the risk of losing trust is to be avoided. However, public sector reputation differs from private sector reputation owing to the environmental characteristics of the public sector: there are more complexities in terms of goals, needs, audiences, definitions, and resources (Luoma-aho and Canel, 2016, p. 598). Moreover, there are challenges related to the political nature of public sector organizations, and these affect personnel, resources, and goals. As public sector organizations exist to serve the public, and since their mission is tied to public policy, they have less freedom in choosing the strategic direction to move in, and so standing out as unique is difficult (Wæraas and Byrkjeflot, 2012). In fact, public sector organizations must deal with a range of different needs and sometimes even conflicting values, challenging the consistency of their actions.

7.5.2 Neutral Reputation as Ideal for Public Sector Organizations

Due to the differences between the private and public sectors, the outcomes of public sector processes are less predictable, and a public sector organization's "brand promise" is renegotiated every time funding is altered, new political leadership is elected, or public policies change. In fact, a "high reputation adds to the visibility of actions, and invites more scrutiny and control by means of more demanding standards" (Sztompka, 1999, p. 76). An excellent reputation also brings with it a threat of easily being lost if expectations are not met. Moreover, as public funding does not allow extensive reputation cultivation, the optimal target reputation of public sector organizations should be neutral: to be trusted and taken seriously, but neutral enough to acquire the necessary distance to remain trusted even in times of crisis (Luoma-aho, 2007, p. 124). A neutral level is similar to "satisficing reputation": "Good enough to escape criticism from audiences but not so good as to generate opposition from those actors whose interests are at odds with the organization's mission" (Picci, 2012; Wæraas and Maor, 2015, p. 7).

Figure 7.1 shows this ideal zone for public sector reputation. It suggests that the ideal zone for public sector reputation to reside in is between the extremes of a strong and a vague reputation. In this zone, the expectations are ideally realistic, and reputation maintenance or management does not require excessive resources. Moreover, the ideal zone is somewhere between uniqueness and similarity, because the sector itself has some preset promises that may be difficult to shake off, and also because uniqueness is challenging to achieve. In the ideal zone, the public sector organization remains well regarded for its actions and not dependent on exhaustive reputation maintenance

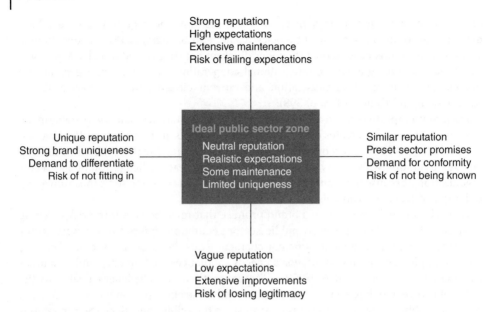

Figure 7.1 The ideal zone for public sector organizations' reputation is a balance between uniqueness, similarity, and vagueness.

programs. A neutral reputation, however, does not refer to passivity or a lack of engagement, but merely acknowledgement of the limits and resources with which the organization can make use of its intangible assets.

Both the concept of reputation and attempts to manage this intangible asset are understood to originate from the new public management paradigm (Wæraas and Maor, 2015). The idea is that for an asset to become useful, it has to be managed and utilized. Reputation management has been defined as "the deliberate actions by organizational leaders, spokespersons and agents to build, enhance, maintain, monitor, repair or defend their reputations" (Carroll, 2016, p. 644). As strategic communication is applied to build a good reputation, questions arise as to whether managing reputation by focusing on merely positive messages turns public organizations' serving of citizens and society at large into a pursuit of benefits exclusively for the organization (Wæraas and Byrkjeflot, 2012).

Instead of going down this path, public sector organizations could look to manage their stakeholders' expectations in order to maximize a good reputation (Luoma-aho, Olkkonen, and Lähteenmäki, 2013). This ideally creates a virtuous circle: a good reputation is the result of suitable stakeholder expectations regarding the organization (Luoma-aho and Olkkonen, 2016). Likewise, a good reputation creates the desired expectations. In fact, in the public sector, *reputation management* should be *expectation management*, as reputation itself cannot be managed, but expectations on which a reputation is formed can.

7.6 Measuring Public Sector Reputation

As many public sector organizations provide goods and services that are invisible to most citizens (such as monitoring the stability of banks or insurance companies, care for severely disabled individuals, or regulating nuclear power), reputation has been suggested as a direct measure for their otherwise invisible success. However, to provide valuable information, reputation needs to be measured among the stakeholders that the organization serves. For some public sector organizations, these stakeholders are simply citizens (as in the case of tax authorities, public transportation organizations, or the police), but for many public sector organizations, citizen interaction is minimal, and measuring their reputation should focus on the stakeholders that the organization actually serves, whether these are political decision makers, peer organizations, or ministries and municipalities (Luoma-aho, 2007, p. 124). Reputation should be measured among those who have actual experiences with the public organization and who are able to assess its performance.

Reputation measurement is always dependent on the organizational goals, values, and mission, as measurement is about seeing if the set aims have been reached. There is no one-size-fits-all reputation measurement, and the context should always be considered when planning to measure reputation. In fact, research suggests that reputation evaluation is affected by whether citizens perceive that the organization has competition or not, whether citizens have actual personal experiences with the organization, whether the media coverage of the organization is positive or negative, and whether the facts that are presented prior to posing questions about representation prime the respondent (Thijs and Staes, 2008; Dolan et al., 2010). Moreover, ethical questions related to measuring reputation require attention before any measurement efforts are undertaken.

In recent years, some public sector organizations have taken up the popular measure known as net promoter score (NPS; Reichheld, 2003, p. 46) which asks citizens or stakeholders: "On a scale of 1–10, how likely would you recommend this organization/ service to others?" NPS is based on the idea that only those who give the public sector organization a 9 or a 10 (the promotors) are valuable to the organization, whereas those who award a value of 6 or below (detractors) are actually harmful to the organization. Although the measure is simple enough for almost all public sector organizations to apply it, there are certain challenges to using the NPS in the public sector, as most services are not freely chosen, and some services (taxation and law enforcement, for example) may in fact go against the individual citizen's personal wishes, making reputation measurement inappropriate.

However, for most public sector organizations that produce knowledge or services, reputation measurement can provide a clear report on their performance. With regard to measuring reputation, public sector organizations are often assessed based on the quality of their outputs, which may range from policies and laws to goods and services. Most commonly, public sector organizations' reputation results from high quality, transparency, and the rectification of errors (Luoma-aho and Canel, 2016). To use a hypothetical example to demonstrate the importance of these elements, in the event of the construction of roads to rural areas, citizens may evaluate the actual quality and consistency of the road that they are driving on (quality), the process through which the construction project came about (transparency of political decision making and funding through taxes), and the speed and manner in which the roads are repaired (rectification of errors).

To measure reputation, researchers often divide the overall impression into various measurable factors and dimensions. As reputation resides among those assessing the organization, whether they are citizens or other kinds of stakeholders, measuring public sector reputation begins by asking whom the organization actually serves. Moreover,

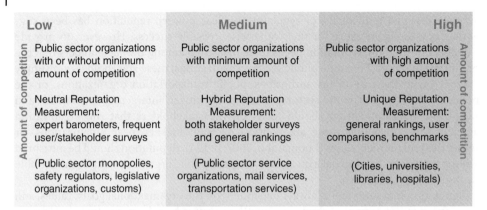

Figure 7.2 The different ways to measure reputation depending on the amount of competition that the organization faces, ranging from expert barometers to general rankings. Source: Adapted from Luoma-aho (2007).

formulation of the questions used to measure reputation makes a big difference, as research suggests that citizens find it easier to evaluate individual experiences than they do organizations and services in general (Thijs, 2011). In fact, the value and contribution that most public sector organizations make to society is difficult for citizens to assess, as not all public organizations have direct contact with them.

There are several ways to categorize reputation measurement. Experience with public sector organizations plays a central role, as does the service type (Van Der Hart, 1991). In our spectrum of judgment of public services' reputation, based on Laing's typology of public services (Laing, 2003), we distinguish two extremes of reputation evaluation. For public services that result in private benefits, reputation can be evaluated through citizens' and users' judgment and experiences. For public services that result in social benefit (and citizens often lack direct experiences), reputation is evaluated via the professional judgments of experts and the organization's stakeholders (Luoma-aho and Canel, 2016).

Figure 7.2 illustrates the continuum of reputation measurement in the public sector according to the degree of apparent competition for the services. In the case of low competition, the aim becomes to be acknowledged by the stakeholders that the organization serves. As there is less direct comparison, there is often also less direct citizen contact, making the success of the organization difficult to prove. Public sector organizations that fall into this category include ministries or agencies that have full responsibility for an entire sector, such as a ministry of internal affairs. As their field and challenges are unique and complex, their success is difficult to evaluate for those without sector expertise, and as a result measurement of their reputation is a matter of asking sector-specific questions directed at stakeholders with actual contact with the organization (Luoma-aho, 2007, p. 124).

When there is a high level of competition, the aim for the organization is to develop a unique reputation, for which measurements include more elements of comparison with similar organizations or services. Examples of such organizations include public universities that cannot rely merely on their local influence but must compete for talent on the levels of both faculty and students through rankings and comparisons. There are also as many opinions of these universities as there are faculty members, students, and alumni, making reputation management a challenge.

Most organizations, however, fall somewhere in between these two extremes. Mail services, for example, may hold a public monopoly in the nation but face some comparison beyond the public system, such as private mail services and global delivery companies. For these, reputation is a hybrid: it is partly compared with other public services, and partly with other competitors in the field. For measurement, both these aspects need to be acknowledged, and some comparative elements can be introduced to stakeholder and user surveys.

Though organizational differences are clearly categorized in Figure 7.2, in practice measuring reputation is always context and case dependent (Walker, 2010). There are aspects to public sector organizations that only locals and insiders know of, and hence global examples and barometers may deliver only superficial results. For organizations in the high competition segment, reputation surveys have been adapted directly from business organizations, with the simple addition of some statements that are specific to the public sector (Thijs, 2011). For organizations that experience less competition and less direct contact, surveys have to be tailored to measure their specific purpose and envisaged goals.

7.7 Two Examples of Measuring Reputation

Measurement example: What factors shape a city's reputation?

The Merco Ciudad city reputation barometer was created to compare cities' reputation in Spain in a collaborative effort between government, city officials, and university researchers. The starting point was the realization that there were gaps in terms of the reality of life in different cities, how and what the cities communicated about themselves, and how citizens perceived them. To begin the study, researchers combined in-depth interviews of public officials on their experiences and understanding of city reputation with desk research that combined actual performance records and previous satisfaction survey results.

Merco Ciudad divided the aspects that it measured into three categories: factors affecting reputation that are under city government control, factors that are not under city government control, and factors that are partially under city government control. For the survey, Spain's 78 largest cities were selected, and 9,000 citizens were polled. Merco Ciudad asked questions related to

Factors that are under government control:

1) Political management (how citizens assess political management of the city)
2) Government performance (how citizens rate the performance of their government)
3) Leadership (how citizens assess the city mayor)

Example of a question asked:
"On a 0–10 point scale, could you give an overall value to your local government's performance?"

Factors that are not under government control:

4) Physical reality of location and climate (whether citizens like the location and climate of the city)
5) People's civic manners and hospitality (how people from this city are perceived)

Example of a question asked:
"On a 0–10 point scale, to what extent do you think the city is welcoming, and to what extent are its people welcoming and hospitable?"
Factors that are under partial government control:

6) Manageability (whether citizens can walk easily to places, and whether the city is crowded)
7) Pleasantness (how beautiful citizens perceive the city to be)

Example of a question asked:
"On a 0–10 point scale, to what extent do you think you can walk to most places?"
The results varied across the 78 cities. Overall, the most decisive factors in determining city reputation in Spain appeared to be the city's perceived beauty, its pleasantness, and the manners and hospitability of the people. Pleasantness is partially under city government control, but people are not. The factors that city governments had most influence and control over appeared to be the least significant for city reputation (for example, leadership and performance). These findings would indicate that at the city level, reputation management is limited. In fact, reputation management should concentrate on factors that can be changed, emphasizing those factors in which the city can excel in comparison situations. Sources: Canel et al. (2015) and http://www.merco.info/es/ranking-merco-ciudad.

Measurement example: Stakeholder assessments of Finland's Ministry of Social Affairs and Health

The Finnish Reputation Rake ("Maineharava") was designed originally in 2003 by researchers to measure stakeholders' experiences and the reputation of the 16 organizations operating under the supervision of the Finnish Ministry of Social Affairs and Health (Luoma-aho, 2007, p. 124; Luoma-aho, 2008, pp. 446–467). The focus of the Reputation Rake was on frequent stakeholders that the organization served, and those who actually had personal experience of the organization (for example, employees, political decision makers, peer organizations, municipalities, public regulatory authorities, and customers), as most of the organizations had minimum contact with citizens directly.

To set the desired reputation attributes, desk research was conducted on the 16 organizations' values and mission-related materials, as well as on previous research results and stakeholder feedback. Interviews were also conducted at each of the 16 organizations' communication units to compare the organizations' missions and values in practice. Based on these, the Reputation Rake Questionnaire was constructed to measure top-of-mind impressions, stakeholder experiences shaping reputation, and future expectations (Luoma-aho, 2007, p. 124). The central idea behind the study was to determine how the reputation of such organizations serving multiple audiences is formed, and whether a sector reputation existed.

Analysis of the Reputation Rake following its application on 1,400 respondents yielded five factors that summarize what frequent stakeholders consider when they evaluate the overall reputation of the organizations that they collaborate with (for the detailed research process, see Luoma-aho, 2005). For each factor, semantically different statements were provided, and stakeholders had to evaluate them on a spectrum (negative wording at one end, and positive wording at the other):

1) The authority factor (examples of measures: "noncooperative–cooperative," "closed–open," "bureaucratic–flexible," "distant–humane," "dictatorial–engaged in conversation," "unable to listen–able to listen," "outdated-modern")

2) The esteem factor (for example, "not under constant development–under constant development," "not esteemed–esteemed," "lags behind in its field–trendsetter in its field," "poorly motivated employees–motivated employees," "poor employer–good employer")

3) The trust factor (for example, "for its own good–for the common good," "partial–neutral," "irresponsible–responsible," "unethical–ethical," "unfair–fair," "untrustworthy–trustworthy," "low expertise–high expertise")

4) The service factor (for example, "useless–useful," "does not meet expectations–meets expectations," "passive–active," "inaccessible–accessible," "does not find out customer needs–finds out customer needs")

5) The efficiency factor (for example, "inefficient–efficient," "poor leadership–good leadership," "slow–fast," "does not keep to schedule–keeps to schedule," "communicates its aims unclearly–communicates its aims clearly," "fractured–coherent")

Clear sector trends were found between all 16 organizations. The reputation of all these organizations was built to a large extent on trust, which received the highest rankings from all respondents across organizations. Despite the high trust levels that the stakeholders felt toward the public organizations, they simultaneously rated efficiency and customer service significantly lower. The factor of reputation that distinguished these organizations from private companies was the authority factor, as public sector organizations were perceived as bureaucratic, closed, and distant. The results were discussed in the organizations, and in some next steps were taken to evaluate whether the organization needed to change or whether the stakeholder assessment needed to change (for more on this fit-or-fix approach, see Chapter 13.2 on expectation management). Further communication guides were designed with the findings in mind to build on the strengths (trustworthiness and usefulness) and to attempt to address the challenges (bureaucracy, distance, closeness, and an inability to listen). The Reputation Rake continues to be run every three years at the ministry to yield comparative data on organizational development within the sector.

7.8 Summary of Public Sector Reputation

As the environment in which public sector organizations operate becomes increasingly complex and unpredictable, reputation is proving to be an asset that public sector organizations can draw on to stabilize their functions.

Table 7.1 Organizational reputation as an intangible asset in the public sector.

Reputation is a record of past deeds, an intangible asset that measures the overall impression of the organization among stakeholders

Tangible asset that organizational reputation enables	All physical capital through providing a record of trustworthy past deeds and building faith in potential good interactions and experiences Organizations need reputation to bridge the gap between citizen needs and organizational services: reputation lends the trust needed to the interaction when previous experiences are still missing Reputation shapes citizen expectations, enabling collaboration
Resource that organizational reputation generates	Other intangible assets: reputation engenders trust and shapes citizen expectations, enabling collaboration inside organizations Financial gains: a reputation for being a successful public sector organization or serving citizens well attracts more public investments, and it may even guard against cutbacks in competitive situations where public sector downsizing is aimed at some sectors
Monetary expression	Emotional attachment; "brand equity" as citizens believe the organization is better than others
Value that organizational reputation provides for the organization	A solution to the challenge of legibility, through combining relevant factors into one clear entity to be assessed; ease of interaction; speed; positive attitude toward the organization and its services
Value that organizational reputation provides to citizens and stakeholders	Positive experiences enforce general citizen welfare and diminish emotional or cognitive dissonance caused by negative experiences; employee and citizen engagement; confidence in the organization and its messages (warnings)
Gaps that organizational reputation bridges	Lack of information about the organization's character; gaps in attitude and engagement, where reputation helps to build a positive attitude
Dependence on communication management	Reputation results from doing good deeds and communicating about them. Reputation is formed based on expectations, hence expectation management is a direct way to shape organizational reputation
Implied organization management transformations	From merely focusing on good performance to ensuring that the good performance is also visible to the stakeholders; from impression management to expectation management, as expectations are what reputation is built on
Measures	Top-of-mind awareness, experiences, and expectations measured through various means, including surveys and barometers

Table 7.1 summarizes the chapter and explains the value of organizational reputation as an intangible asset in the public sector.

Focusing on reputation could increase the transparency of actions and make public sector organizations more legible to citizens through "reputation-based governance," through which citizens rate public sector organizations and decision makers (Picci, 2012). Ideally, this could incentivize governments to improve, make the feedback and satisfaction process more transparent, and enable citizens to choose between the types of investments that they prefer (Thijs, 2011). Direct citizen engagement via reputation systems could be the future of public sector reputation: "Imagine a scenario in which citizens assess policies online, these assessments form the basis for reputational measures of public officials and other actors of governance, and these measures in turn influence governance decisions – for example, by determining bureaucrats' promotions and the choice of policies" (Picci, 2012, p. 141).

7.9 Route Guide to Building Organizational Reputation

Organizational reputation flows from organizational actions, and a good reputation requires both action and communication.

1) **Start from the inside** Organizations' employees are the most credible source when it comes to stories told about the organization. Hence, all reputation management starts by asking how our employees feel about the organization and what they share about us among their own networks. Work satisfaction and a strong organizational culture feed into this by building a solid foundation for reputation. Forced guidelines may backfire, as employees may feel less involved and hence commit less to such orders from above. Ensuring that the organization has done its best to make employees feel well will be the strongest foundation that a reputation can have.
   Questions to ask: How do our own employees feel about our organization? Are they happy to work here, and do they feel heard and appreciated? How could we improve their experience? Are there certain complaints that keep resurfacing? Have we done our best to meet employee needs and requests? Are employees engaged, and do we have good ways to build and encourage employee engagement in our organization? Do they understand their own role's contribution to the organization's success? Does the leadership understand and value the employees? How is this demonstrated to employees in action?

2) **Manage expectations** Reputation is built on the different expectations that citizens and stakeholders have of the public organizations and the public sector at large. A good reputation often results from setting realistic expectations, whereas if citizen expectations are unrealistic, disappointments are likely to follow. Public sector communication should hence provide clear direction in terms of where the organization is headed and what should be expected from it in terms of service and development.
   Questions to ask: What kind of expectations do our current communications foster? Are these in line with our realities and resources? What is our current reputational brand promise? How do we follow what citizens and stakeholders think of us and our services? How do our services compare in importance to other aspects of their lives? How do our services resonate with their experiences, ideals, and personal interests?

3) **Measure to maintain** Reputation is subject to change every time funding is altered, new political leadership is elected, or public policies are changed. Monitoring citizen experiences as well as online discussions will ensure that organizations can follow what citizens feel about the organization.
   Questions to ask: Where and with which expressions do citizens discuss the issues that are related to our service? Where could we participate in discussions about rising

citizen concerns? In which cases is it better to not participate in citizen discussions? What are the weak signals that we should be looking for to see that our reputation is changing? What are the factors that end up shaping our reputation among citizens and stakeholders to the greatest extent?

References

Bourgon, J. (2009). New directions in public administration: serving beyond the predictable. *Public Policy and Administration* **24** (3): 309–330.

Bowden, J.L.-H., Luoma-aho, V., and Naumann, K. (2016). Developing a spectrum of positive to negative citizen engagement. In: *Customer Engagement Contemporary Issues and Challenges*, 1st ed. (ed. R.J. Brodie, L. Hollebeek and J. Conduit), 257–277. Routledge.

Canel, M.-J. and Sanders, K. (2015). Government communication. In: *The International Encyclopedia of Political Communication*, 3 Volume Set, vol. 1 (ed. G. Mazzoleni, K. Barnhurst, K. Ikeda et al.). Boston: Wiley-Blackwell.

Canel, M.-J., Sanders, K., Gurrionero, M., and Valle, M. S. (2010). Government reputation' as an intangible value for public institutions. Communicating Spanish local governments. Paper Presented at the Annual Convention of the International Communication Association, Singapore (22–26 June 2010).

Carpenter, D. (2002). Groups, the media, agency waiting costs, and FDA drug approval. *American Journal of Political Science* **46**: 490–505.

Carpenter, D. and Krause, G.A. (2012). Reputation and public administration. *Public Administration Review* **72** (1): 26–32.

Carroll, C. (2015). Theories of corporate reputation. In: *The Sage Encyclopedia of Corporate Reputation* (ed. C. Carroll), 835–856. Thousand Oaks, CA: Sage Publications.

Carroll, C. (2016). Reputation management. In: *The Sage Encyclopedia of Corporate Reputation* (ed. C. Carroll), 644–645. Thousand Oaks, CA: Sage Publications.

Deephouse, D. (2000). Media reputation as a strategic resource: an integration of mass communication and resource-based theories. *Journal of Management* **26** (6): 1091–1112.

Dolan, P., Hallsworth, M., Halpern, D. et al. (2010). *MINDSPACE: Influencing Behaviour through Public Policy*. UK: Institute for Government, Cabinet Office.

Edelman, D. and Singer, M. (2015). Competing on customer journeys. *Harvard Business Review* **93** (11): 88–100.

Fombrun, C.J. and van Riel (2004). *Fame and Fortune: How Successful Companies Build Winning Reputations*. New York: Prentice-Hall Financial Times.

Gotsi, M. and Wilson, A. (2001). Corporate reputation: seeking a definition. *Corporate Communications: An International Journal* **6** (1): 24–30.

Hunt, T. (2009). *The Whuffie Factor: Using the Power of Social Networks to Build Your Business*, 1st ed. New York: Crown Business.

Laing, A. (2003). Marketing in the public sector: towards a typology of public services. *Marketing Theory* **3** (4): 427–445.

Luoma-aho, V. (2005). *Faith-Holders as Social Capital of Finnish Public Organisations*, Jyväskylä Studies in Humanities 42. Jyväskylä: University of Jyväskylä.

Luoma-aho, V. (2007). Neutral reputation and public sector organizations. *Corporate Reputation Review* **10** (2): 124–143.

Luoma-aho, V. (2008). Sector reputation and public organisations. *International Journal of Public Sector Management* **21** (5): 446–467.

Luoma-aho, V. (2015). Understanding stakeholder engagement: faith-holders, hateholders and fakeholders. *RJ-IPR: Research Journal of the Institute for Public Relations* **2** (1): http://www.instituteforpr.org/understanding-stakeholder-engagement-faith-holders-hateholders-fakeholders/ (accessed 26 September 2017).

Luoma-aho, V. and Canel, M.J. (2016). Public sector reputation. In: *Sage Encyclopedia of Corporate Reputation* (ed. C. Carroll), 597–600. Sage Publications.

Luoma-aho, V.L. and Makikangas, M.E. (2014). Do public sector mergers (re)shape reputation? *International Journal of Public Sector Management* **27** (1): 39–52.

Luoma-aho, V. and Olkkonen, L. (2016). Expectation management. In: *The SAGE Encyclopedia of Corporate Reputation* (ed. C. Carroll), 303–306. Sage Publications.

Luoma-aho, V., Olkkonen, L., and Lähteenmäki, M. (2013). Expectation management for public sector management. *Public Relations Review* **39** (3): 248–250.

Masum, H. and Tovey, M. ed. (2012). *The Reputation Society: How Online Opinions are Reshaping the Offline World*. Cambridge, MA: MIT Press.

Nahapiet, J. and Ghoshal, S. (1998). Social capital, intellectual capital, and the organizational advantage. *The Academy of Management Review* **23** (2): 242–266.

Newmark, C. (2012). Foreword. In: *The Reputation Society: How Online Opinions are Reshaping the Offline World* (ed. H. Masum and M. Tovey), ix–xii. Cambridge, MA: MIT Press.

O'Dwyer, C. (2015). The relationship between an Irish government department and its newly established agency: a reputational perspective. In: *Organizational Reputation in the Public Sector* (ed. A. Wæraas and M. Moshe), 77–94. Routledge.

Petrick, J.A., Scherer, R.F., Brodzinski, J.D. et al. (1999). Global leadership skills and reputational capital: intangible resources for sustainable competitive advantage. *Academy of Management Executive* **13** (1): 58–69.

Picci, L. (2012). Reputation-Based Governance and Making States 'Legible' to their Citizens. In: *The Reputation Society* (ed. H. Masum and M. Tovey), 141–150. Cambridge, MA: The MIT Press.

Reichheld, F.F. (2003). The one number you need to grow. *Harvard Business Review* **81** (12): 46–55.

Rothstein, B. and Stolle, D. (2008). The state and social capital: an institutional theory of generalized trust. *Comparative Politics* **40** (4): 441–459.

Sanders, K. and Canel, M.J. (2015). Mind the gap: local government communication strategies and Spanish citizens' perceptions of their cities. *Public Relations Review* **41** (5): 777–784.

Sataøen, H.L. and Wæraas, A. (2016). Building a sector reputation: the strategic communication of national higher education. *International Journal of Strategic Communication* **10** (3): 165–176.

Staw, B. and Epstein, L. (2000). What bandwagons bring: effects of popular management techniques on corporate performance, reputation, and CEO pay. *Administrative Science Quarterly* **45** (3): 523–556.

Sztompka, P. (1999). *Trust: A Sociological Theory (Cambridge Cultural Social Studies)*. Cambridge: Cambridge University Press.

Thijs, N. (2011). *Measure to Improve: Improving Public Sector Performance by Using Citizen-User Satisfaction Information*. Brussels: EUPAN/EIPA.

Thijs, N. and Staes, P. (2008). *European Primer on Customer Satisfaction Management*. Brussels: EUPAN/EIPA.

Van Der Hart, H. (1991). Government organisations and their customers in the Netherlands: strategy, tactics and operations. *European Journal of Marketing* **24** (7): 31–42.

Wæraas, A. and Byrkjeflot, H. (2012). Public sector organizations and reputation management: five problems. *International Public Management Journal* **15** (2): 186–206.

Wæraas, A. and Maor, M. ed. (2015). *Organizational Reputation in the Public Sector*. London: Routledge.

Wæraas, A. and Sataøen, H. (2015). Being all things to all customers: building reputation in an institutionalized field. *British Journal of Management* **26** (2): 310–326.

Walker, K. (2010). A systematic review of the corporate reputation literature: definition, measurement, and theory. *Corporate Reputation Review* **12** (4): 357–387.

Wallin Andreassen, T. (1994). Satisfaction, loyalty and reputation as indicators of customer orientation in the public sector. *International Journal of Public Sector Management* **7** (2): 16–34.

8

Legitimacy

> *Government loses its claim to legitimacy when it fails to fulfill its obligations*
> (Martin L. Gross, cited in Arora, 2010)

Are public sector organizations entitled to exist and operate? This chapter deals with a very basic and preliminary aspect of public sector organizations' operations: the justification of their role in the social system, and the ways in which antifragile communication can contribute to building the intangible asset of legitimacy. The chapter first discusses legitimacy as a concept and its application to the public sector as an intangible asset. Second, it explores the process of conferring legitimacy upon a public sector organization. Third, it elaborates on how communication shapes and is shaped by legitimacy. Finally, the chapter provides some best practices and strategies to suggest a route guide for building legitimacy in public sector organizations.

8.1 Conferring Legitimacy upon Public Sector Organizations: What Does It Mean?

Merriam-Webster's Collegiate Dictionary offers three different meanings for *legitimate*, and these may serve as a starting point for introducing the concept. According to the dictionary, this concept has to do with the fulfillment of rules ("allowed according to rules or laws"), as well as approval ("real, accepted, or official") and logic ("fair or reasonable") (Merriam-Webster's Collegiate Dictionary, 2004). The question remains: Is legitimacy attributable to organizations?

There are works within the literature that consider "(i)legitimate" a plausible attribute for organizations, but there is nevertheless no unanimously agreed definition of "organizational legitimacy," and further integrative efforts in this area are required (Suchman, 1995, p. 572; Díez Martín, Blanco González, and Prado Román, 2010, p. 128). However, there are certain elements that are common to the definitions provided by different scholars: legitimacy is a *judgment* about an *organization's actions*, made *by its strategic audiences*, according to *cultural norms and standards* (Maurer, 1971; Scott, 1995; Deephouse, 1996; Ruef and Scott, 1998; Johnson, Dowd, and Ridgeway, 2006; Tyler, 2006; Díez Martín et al., 2010; Bitektine, 2011). We will now elaborate on these elements.

Public Sector Communication: Closing Gaps Between Citizens and Public Organizations, First Edition. María-José Canel and Vilma Luoma-aho.

The legitimacy of an organization has to do with a judgment, assessment, or evaluation made by its publics: it is a perception or assumption that "represents a reaction of observers to the organization as they see it; thus, it is possessed objectively, yet created subjectively" (Suchman, 1995, p. 574). What stakeholders judge is whether the organization's actions follow certain norms and standards so as to confer upon it a "right to exist" (Maurer, 1971, p. 361). Organizational legitimacy refers to the "extent to which the array of established cultural accounts provide explanations for [an organization's] existence" (Meyer and Scott, 1983, p. 201), and thus legitimacy is the intangible asset that focuses on the acceptability of an organization's values and actions. It allows the organization and its functions to be accepted, and for now it suffices to say that it is the minimum required for an organization to be entitled to operate and undertake actions.

A legitimacy judgment entails a process of construal that takes into account social factors. Legitimacy is the "generalized perception or assumption that the actions of an entity are desirable, proper, or appropriate within some socially constructed system of norms, values, beliefs, and definitions" (Suchman, 1995, p. 574). Legitimacy connotes "congruence" between the social values associated with or implied by organizational activities and the norms of acceptable behavior in the larger social system (DiMaggio and Powell, 1991; Suchman, 1995; Deephouse, 1999; Johnson et al., 2006; Bitektine, 2011). A legitimate organization is in "cultural conformity" with its external environment (Suchman, 1995, p. 573; Deephouse, 1996; Ruef and Scott, 1998) and is perceived to be pursuing socially acceptable goals in a socially acceptable manner (Ashforth and Gibbs, 1990, p. 177).

The roots of the modern approach to legitimacy lie in the writings of Weber (1978) (Johnson et al., 2006; Gordon, Kornberger, and Clegg, 2009; Gustavsen, Røiseland, and Pierre, 2014). He took the view that the rule of law is only one of the ways in which social arrangements might be potentially justified. Moreover, he argued that social norms and values can operate upon individuals, who internalize them and act in accordance with the prevailing order, even if they privately disagree with it. The efficacy of authority is not simply based on formally sanctioned rules and positional power but also on socially constituted norms (Gordon et al., 2009). Thus,

> the Weberian formulation offers the central insight that legitimation occurs through a collective construction of social reality in which the elements of a social order are seen as consonant with norms, values, and beliefs that individuals presume are widely shared . . . Consequently, legitimacy is indicated by actors' compliance with a social order as either (i) a set of social obligations, or as (ii) a desirable model of action.
>
> *(Johnson et al., 2006, p. 55)*

Therefore, although organizational legitimacy is mediated by the perceptions and behaviors of individuals, it is derived from a socially and collectively focused process of construal (Johnson et al., 2006, p. 57).

Legitimacy stems, then, from an internalized disposition to willingly obey authority or rules without any actual coercion from the authorities, and it seems logical that the type of public sector organization that receives the most attention in legitimacy research is the police (see, for instance, the following studies: Chermak and Weiss, 2005; Gordon et al., 2009; Grimmelikhuijsen and Meijer, 2015). Organizations that are fortunate enough to be considered legitimate find it easier to implement their decisions.

8.2 The Legitimacy Judgment: What Confers Organizational Legitimacy in the Public Sector?

How a framework of beliefs, values, and norms is established through a social and collective interpretative process to define what is right, and how the congruence and compliance of organizations' actions with that framework are examined are interesting research questions. What norms, values, and beliefs held by citizens might the idea of legitimacy be contrasted with? And how are an organization's perceived features processed by the person who judges?

8.2.1 Achievements versus Procedures

In exploring legitimacy, a basic distinction has been suggested by scholars to differentiate what confers legitimacy in relation to origin (a concept known as "legitimacy of origin": a government is legitimized if its authority derives from the established democratic system – for example, elections) from what confers legitimacy during the exercise of authority (which is known as "legitimacy of exercise": legitimacy depends on how the government performs once elected) (Canel, 2014). Political systems generate legitimacy by both democratic procedures and performance in service production.

This distinction is parallel to that of "procedure-based legitimacy" (a decision is legitimate if it follows the correct procedures) and "performance-based legitimacy" (legitimacy is based on service delivery, outcomes, achievements, and so forth) (Gustavsen et al., 2014). Maccarthaigh, Painter, and Yee (2016) talk of "input legitimacy" (a system in which the chain of democratic control runs from the citizenry by way of elections and the national legislature) versus "output legitimacy" (the "end products" delivered by the bureaucracy), and have applied them in a comparative study to conclude that in governing their agencies, the elected government of Ireland's parliamentary democracy pays more attention to input legitimacy, while the executive governance of Hong Kong's administrative state favors output legitimacy.

But if regarded as an intangible asset, legitimacy is approached in organizational communication as the result of the attribution of stakeholders, and thus typologies are needed to explore the mental process that is behind the legitimacy judgment.

8.2.2 Typologies of Legitimacy

Works within the literature distinguish types of legitimacy in order to ascertain the analytical processing that yields the different types of judgment that can be rendered with respect to the organization based on the same set of observed characteristics (Scott and Meyer, 1991; Scott, 1995; Deephouse and Carter, 2005; Golant and Sillince, 2007; Díez Martín et al., 2010; Bitektine, 2011). Typologies are helpful conceptual tools to explore the dynamics of legitimacy and thus to identify the different aspects, angles, and objects that are focused on by the person who judges.

Scott (1995) suggests a "regulative legitimacy" that flows from actors who have some sort of sovereignty over organizations and who thus define the range of what is legally or procedurally acceptable via requirements and sanctions. "Normative legitimacy" stems from actors (for example, professionals) who define what is morally desirable (rather than legally required), thereby stipulating standards and values. Finally, "cognitive legitimacy" flows from the prevalence of comparable organizational actions.

Suchman (1995) builds on Scott's typology to differentiate "pragmatic legitimacy" from "cognitive legitimacy" and "moral legitimacy." (The examples of these that we provide are our own.) Pragmatic legitimacy rests on a self-interested calculation of what an organization provides. Subtypes of this legitimacy include "exchange legitimacy" (support is based on an audience's scrutiny of the organizational behavior to determine the practical consequences for them – for example, "I accept this Ministry of Education because it grants me funds for my university studies"), "influential legitimacy" (support depends not on favorable exchanges and immediate results but on organizational responsiveness to larger interests – for instance, "I accept this parliamentary group because it allows me to participate in public hearings for law making"), and "dispositional legitimacy" (support rests on shared values such as trustworthiness, honesty, decency, and wisdom – for example, "I accept this university program because I feel it is intellectually worthwhile").

Cognitive legitimacy is based more on cognition than on interest or evaluation (Aldrich and Fiol, 1994), and it refers to the "taken-for-grantedness" and comprehensibility of an organization's behavior. Subtypes of cognitive legitimacy include legitimacy based on comprehensibility and legitimacy based on taken-for-grantedness. The first of these stems from the availability of cultural models that furnish plausible explanations for the organization and its endeavors; a cognitively legitimate organization is predictable and meaningful. The second represents the most subtle and powerful source of legitimacy: with it, the organization not only makes disorder manageable but even transforms it into "a set of intersubjective 'givens' that submerge the possibility of dissent" (Suchman, 1995, p. 583). For an organization whose legitimacy is based on taken-for-grantedness, alternatives become unthinkable and challenges impossible, "and the organization itself becomes unassailable by construction. On the whole, the cognitive dimension of legitimacy refers to the way in which collective action is an outcome based on common understanding rather than on an assessment of means and ends" (Suchman, 1995, p. 583). The taken-for-granted element is highly applicable to public sector organizations, many of which have to be accepted for the mere reason that they are necessary since there is no alternative (for instance, somebody has to be in charge of distributing resources for public needs).

Finally, moral legitimacy reflects a positive normative evaluation: the judge questions whether "this is the right thing to do," and since this typology has proven useful in analyzing legitimacy as an intangible asset of national central governments (Canel, Oliveira, and Luoma-aho, 2017), we elaborate more on it in the next section.

8.2.3 Moral Legitimacy

The typology for moral legitimacy includes (Suchman, 1995; see also Deephouse and Carter, 2005; Bitektine, 2011 [the examples given below are our own]):

- "Consequential legitimacy," which is based on evaluations of the outcomes of an organization's activity. The judgment examines what the organization accomplishes (outcomes, results, and achievements; for example, mortality rates at public hospitals), for which measures of achievements and organizational effectiveness are applied (Scott, 1977, p. 75; see also Suchman, 1995, p. 580).
- "Procedural legitimacy," which is based on favorable evaluations of the soundness of procedures, processes, and means (Berger, Berger, and Kellner, 1973). Applied to the public sector, procedural legitimacy refers to the process followed in public

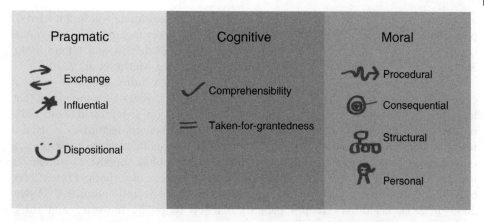

Figure 8.1 Major foci of types of legitimacy. Source: Adapted from Suchman (1995).

management (such as dialogue, consensus seeking, or following procedural requirements – for example, "This regulation on hospitals has been passed through consensus between all political parties").

- "Structural legitimacy" refers to organizational structures: audiences "see the organization as valuable and worthy of support because its structural characteristics locate it within a morally favored taxonomical category" (Suchman, 1995, p. 581). This judgment focuses on general organizational features, including buildings, resources, quality control, working policies, and so forth – for example, "This Ministry of Health provides empowering labor programs to its employees."
- Finally, "personal legitimacy" refers to the person who represents the organization, either in relation to his or her professional capacity or in relation to personality features such as empathy, communication, integrity, and so forth – for example, "This minister of health pays her taxes and solves problems."

Figure 8.1 represents the major foci of each type of legitimacy.

We will return to these typologies, since exploring them will provide clues about how audiences formulate their legitimacy judgments. First, however, we need to elaborate on the benefits that legitimacy produces.

8.3 Resources Generated by Legitimacy

There is an extensive body of literature that considers legitimacy as an intangible asset that is conferred upon or granted to organizations by organizational stakeholders (Suchman, 1995; Hamilton, 2006; Tyler, 2006; Díez Martín et al., 2010). A review of the literature reveals that legitimacy fits the features that we attributed to intangible assets in the public sector in Chapter 4 in the following ways.

First, legitimacy enables and gives access to tangible assets. It affects an organization's ability to garner resources such as capital and personnel, and organizations with a higher level of legitimacy will produce and increase resources more easily (Baum and Oliver, 1991; Díez Martín et al., 2010). The opposite also holds true: a loss of legitimacy damages external ties and taints reputation (Hamilton, 2006, p. 333). A legitimate mayor will attract investment for the city, whereas a mayor seen as illegitimate will find it hard to participate in international networks. Legitimacy is thus a key factor for the survival of organizations as well as for their growth and success (Ashforth and Gibbs, 1990; Suchman, 1995; Zyglidopoulos, 2003; Hamilton, 2006; Díez Martín et al., 2010).

Second, legitimacy gives rise to a resource from which a future benefit or value is expected to flow for both the organization and stakeholders/citizens. To the extent that legitimacy is "the degree of cultural support of an organization" (Meyer and Scott, 1983, p. 201) and justifies the organization's role in the social system, legitimacy is itself a resource (Ashforth and Gibbs, 1990, p. 177). In the case of public sector organizations, a crucial resource generated by legitimacy is political and public support. Legitimacy is loyalty (Gibson, 2004, p. 289); it facilitates the personal exercise of authority (Tyler, 2006, p. 379) and "provides a 'reservoir of support' for institutions and authorities" (Tyler, 2006, p. 381). Legitimacy shapes people's reaction to public measures and rules, facilitating the ability to bring about acceptance of decisions and to encourage rules to be followed: it is the perception that one ought to obey another (Hurd, 1999, p. 381), thus saving resources required by systems of deterrence strategies and incentives.

Authority is therefore one of the most important resources generated by legitimacy, and from a psychological perspective, it has been argued to be a social influence induced by feelings of "should," "ought to," or "has a right to." People allow legitimate authorities to define the appropriate behavior in a given situation, and hence legitimacy is an additional form of power distinct from control over incentives or sanctions (Tyler, 2006, p. 377). Legitimacy is thus "an endorphin of the democratic body politic; it is the substance that oils the machinery of democracy, reducing the friction that inevitably arises when people are not able to get everything they want from politics" (Gibson, 2004, p. 289).

The value of being perceived as legitimate might be becoming a crucial resource for the survival of public organizations in contexts of conflict, crises of trust, and resource scarcity: "When the public views government as legitimate, it has an alternative basis for support during difficult times" (Tyler, 2006, p. 377). In increasingly fragmented societies, legitimacy is a resource that helps to address the problem of an absence of a unified popular will (Bevir, 2013, p. 536). Legitimacy can also become a reservoir of goodwill that "allows the institutions of government to go against what people may want at the moment without suffering debilitating consequences" (Gibson, 2004, p. 289). Illegitimate governments will find it more difficult to ask citizens to accept demanding and tough measures.

Finally, legitimacy is also associated with trust to the extent that legitimate organizations are perceived not only as more worthy but also as more meaningful, predictable, and credible (Hamilton, 2006; Tyler, 2006). In this sense, apart from the benefit that it provides to the organization (for legitimacy promotes acceptance of the decisions and the rules that organizations promulgate), legitimacy also provides a benefit for society in the respect that the more a public organization is supported, the more stability and institutional effectiveness there will be; the latter "are virtues that benefit all members of society" (Tyler, 2006, p. 391).

8.4 Communication and Legitimacy Building

To what extent does legitimacy depend on the degree to which it is acknowledged by the organization's stakeholders? How does management of this intangible asset modify and transform public sector management? In this section, we attempt to explore how communication both shapes legitimacy and is shaped by legitimacy building.

8.4.1 Being Acknowledged as Legitimate

Communication might play a role in generating legitimacy to the extent that the latter results from the attribution made by somebody with regard to the organization. As already discussed, legitimacy represents a reaction from observers, and it is therefore created subjectively in the minds of the organization's stakeholders. Suchman states that, as is the case with regard to most cultural processes, legitimacy management rests heavily on communication between an organization and its various audiences (Suchman, 1995, p. 586). For legitimacy to exist, there has to be somebody to acknowledge something about the organization. Organizational legitimacy is thus the result of people's making attributions with regard to an organization (Hegtvedt, Clay-Warner, and Johnson, 2003).

This acknowledgement aspect of legitimacy is associated with a relational one: legitimacy represents a relationship with audiences rather than a possession of the organization (Hamilton, 2006). Organizations continuously interact with relevant stakeholders to sustain their legitimacy, and Grimmelikhuijsen and Meijer (2015) highlight this idea in relation to perceived procedural fairness: legitimacy entails various dimensions of government–citizen interaction, among which these authors stress being treated with respect and being given a voice. Communication is needed in generating impressions in people's minds about what the organization is and does, as well as in establishing relations with them that entail their participation.

8.4.2 Legitimacy Building as Sense Making

But the role of communication in building legitimacy moves at a deeper level than that of impressions management: "No matter how lofty the aims of a government program, it usually won't make a difference if people can't understand it" (Leonhardt, 2007, cited in Lee, 2009, p. 519). Communication plays a crucial function to the extent that legitimacy is related to collective accounts and rational explanations about what an organization is doing and why. Building legitimacy means helping to make sense of why a specific organization has a right to exist, and what its functions are.

Legitimacy has been defined as sense making (Gordon et al., 2009), and the process of legitimation as a collective making of meaning (Neilsen and Rao, 1987, p. 524, cited in Ashforth and Gibbs, 1990). Therefore, what legitimacy has an effect on is not only people's actions toward organizations but also how they understand them. Part of the cultural congruence captured by the term "legitimacy" involves the existence of a credible collective account or rationale that explains what an organization is doing and why (Jepperson, 1991). Organizations that "lack acceptable legitimated accounts of their activities are more vulnerable to claims that they are negligent, irrational or unnecessary" (Meyer and Rowan, 1991, p. 50).

In fact, organizational crises result from a collective breakdown in sense making among organizational stakeholders. A lack of organizational sensibility, reasonable explanations, shared understandings, rationalization, or meaning creation may be the basis of organizational crises (Pfeffer, 1981; Suchman, 1995; Pearson and Clair, 1998;

Gordon et al., 2009). Therefore, legitimation strategies related to organizational activities have to do with elaborating narratives that help this sense making.

8.5 How Legitimacy Typologies Help Legitimacy Builders

The different categories of legitimacy can provide information about the different dimensions that citizens take into account when assessing public organizations, and thus exploring these types of legitimacy will help in identifying which concerns are stressed by a specific audience. For instance, research shows that efficiency and performance alone are not sufficient to allow organizations the right to exist (Epstein and Votaw, 1978). Rather, audiences require organizations to be pursuing socially acceptable goals in a socially acceptable manner, and in this sense, Ashforth and Gibbs's distinction between the performance dimension (constituents assess whether goals have been achieved) and the value dimension (what is assessed is whether the organization has fulfilled its mission) (Ashforth and Gibbs, 1990, p. 177) is useful for understanding how legitimacy might be built and maintained.

Exploring types of legitimacy can give organizations clues about strategies that can help to bridge gaps between them and citizens, and it can contribute to the design of public policies and to the management by public institutions of legitimacy in order to meet citizens' expectations and needs. Two important distinctions drawn by Suchman (1995) are relevant here. First, while pragmatic legitimacy rests on audience self-interest, moral and cognitive legitimacies do not (p. 584). Therefore, organizations can purchase pragmatic legitimacy by directing tangible rewards to specific constituents. But moral and cognitive legitimation implicates broader cultural rules, and thus it is more difficult to manage this legitimacy in relation to a specific constituent without contravening the organization's coherence. Second, whereas pragmatic and moral legitimacy rest on discursive evaluation, cognitive legitimacy does not. Therefore, organizations could earn pragmatic and moral legitimacy by actively participating in public discussions about cost–benefit appraisals and ethical judgments, but since cognitive legitimation implicates unspoken orienting assumptions, explicit advocacies of organizational endeavors could imperil the objectivity of such taken-for-granted schemata. These observations suggest, Suchman concludes, that "as an organization moves from pragmatic legitimacy to moral legitimacy and then to cognitive legitimacy, legitimacy becomes more elusive to obtain and more difficult to manipulate, but it also becomes subtler, more profound, and more self-sustaining once established" (p. 585).

In managing legitimacy, therefore, organizations should craft strategies that combine different aspects and angles, and they should take into account that, as Bitektine states, the process by which people render these social judgments is "complex and non-deterministic" (Bitektine, 2011, p. 151). There is an underlying similarity in the validation processes (Golant and Sillince, 2007, p. 1149) and although different types of legitimacy often reinforce one another, they can occasionally come into conflict as well (Suchman, 1995; Hegtvedt et al., 2003); they might interact with each other in stakeholders' minds, or even pull in different directions. Gustavsen et al. (2014) found evidence that among citizens in Norway and Sweden, perceptions of legitimacy rooted in local government procedure and performance exist in a synergetic and mutually reinforcing relationship.

But they also found differences according to the type of policy: performance-based legitimacy appears to be regarded as more important for respondents in the case of care for the elderly, while procedural legitimacy is valued as more important in the case of building and planning policies.

In elaborating legitimacy strategies, public managers should start out from different assumptions: although it may be expected that legitimate outcomes as well as legitimate processes are required by citizens to confer legitimacy upon institutions, it might also be the case that higher-quality outcomes are the product of illegitimate processes, or that an illegitimate process might ruin high-quality achievements. Moreover, legitimacy strategies should take into account that when people formulate a legitimacy judgment, they make use of a number of cognitive shortcuts, heuristic methods, and incomplete stakeholder assessments (Bitektine, 2011, p. 164). In circumstances of uncertainty (that is, when people do not have enough knowledge or information with regard to a given matter), legitimacy judgments will draw on familiar organizational forms that most closely resemble the entity under judgment (for example, "This is a governmental-type organization"). It is plausible to think that certain public organizations might be categorized as legitimate unless there is evidence to the contrary (for example, "If this is a ministry-type organization, it might be legitimate"). Bitektine also suggests that when the costs of searching for and processing information are high, legitimacy judgments are also influenced by others' judgments of the organization (Bitektine, 2011, pp. 165–166).

8.6 Building Legitimacy

Legitimacy "takes time to develop and extend" (Grimmelikhuijsen and Meijer 2015, p. 600). It has been stated that the purpose of legitimacy management is "to foster the belief among constituents that the organization's activities and ends are congruent with the expectations, values and norms of constituents" (Ashforth and Gibbs, 1990, p. 182). But what capability does an organization have in achieving positive outcomes in this endeavor? Based on the approaches to legitimacy research identified by Suchman (1995), there are two different responses to this question. On the one hand, strategic-legitimacy researchers assume that there is a high level of managerial control over the legitimation process, and that a lot is in the organization's hands. On the other, institutional-legitimacy researchers see organizational legitimacy as a "byproduct" of external institutionalization processes, meaning that the environment determines an organization's legitimacy, and thus the latter is beyond the control of the organization's management. A major assumption that we make in this book is that intangible assets can be built through communication. Accordingly, we take the strategic approach and suppose that an organization can build, maintain, and improve its legitimacy with proper legitimacy strategies. However, we are also aware of the contingencies that intangibles building is subject to, and hence our intention here is to provide certain guidelines that help to identify what falls within the margin of maneuver and what is outside of legitimacy builders' control.

The type of communication that legitimacy building requires "extends well beyond traditional discourse to include a wide range of meaning-laden actions and nonverbal displays. Thus, skillful legitimacy management requires a diverse arsenal of techniques and a discriminating awareness of which situations merit which responses" (Suchman, 1995, p. 586).

Based on literature review, we identify four areas that public sector organizations need to clarify when elaborating legitimacy strategies.

First, in crafting their strategy, legitimacy builders need to clarify whether what they need is to gain, maintain, or repair legitimacy (see the different strategies in Suchman, 1995; see also Ashforth and Gibbs, 1990; Díez Martín et al., 2010). The first of these options corresponds to when new organizations are created, something that only occurs in the public sector when units merge or when special units for emerging social needs are established (for example, bodies that focus on gender issues). Legitimacy narratives have to account for the new organization and its function in such a way that it resonates with people's needs and expectations so that they accept the new costs that it entails. The most common need for public sector organizations is to maintain legitimacy, for which a watchful attitude is suggested in order to monitor people's reactions and to anticipate new changes in the sector. Unlike legitimacy creation, legitimacy repair generally represents a reactive response to an unforeseen crisis of meaning. This situation requires strategies that pair well with crisis communication strategies.

Second, legitimacy builders have to define the sort of support that they need to garner. The distinction suggested by Suchman (1995) between passive and active support might be helpful here. If organizations need to avoid being questioned, the goal has to be to "make sense." But if organizations need to mobilize affirmative commitments, they must also "have value," "either substantively, or as a crucial safeguard against impending *non-sense*" (p. 575). Whether the organization seeks active support or merely passive acquiescence is something that has to be discerned in each specific situation. Public sector organizations might count on a taken-for-granted cultural assumption, since people assume there *must* be a ministry for distributing resources, organizing a health care service, or looking after infrastructure such as roads and railways. Thus, mere acceptance of the organization as necessary or inevitable might be an appropriate goal. However, if the objective is to promote a new health care system, a strategy that looks for affirmative backing might be needed.

Third, and subsequently, public leaders also need to determine what source of legitimacy they need to refer to in their legitimacy narratives: What is being challenged? Is it what supports the origins of their authority – that is, factors such as election results or having been legally appointed, which allow them to make binding decisions? Or is the exercise of power throughout the mandate what is at stake?

Finally, public leaders have to select the type of legitimacy that best suits their legitimacy needs. It has been already mentioned that pragmatic legitimacy operates at the level of immediate and circumstantial exchanges driven by self-interest, whereas moral and cognitive legitimacies involve broader cultural rules. While organizations can "purchase" pragmatic legitimacy by directing tangible rewards to specific constituents, to gain cognitive and moral legitimacy they should actively participate in public debate and become involved in the social process that establishes the criteria against which the legitimacy judgment will be formulated. And as already mentioned, time investment requirements vary according to the type of legitimacy.

Figure 8.2 indicates the different levels that legitimacy builders need to take into account when elaborating legitimacy strategies. The focus of communication is indicated.

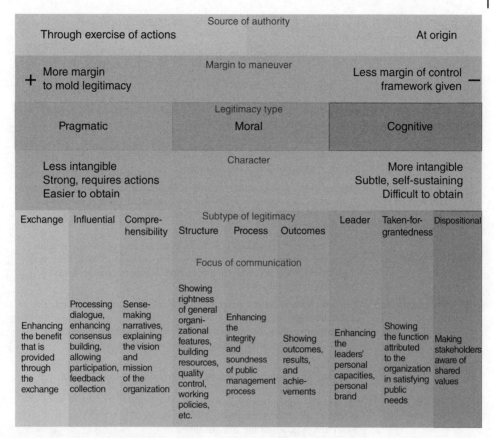

Figure 8.2 The focus of communication in legitimacy strategies. Source: Adapted from Suchman (1995).

8.7 Critical Issues and Further Research

There are still areas of legitimacy that researchers have not explored, and among these we focus here on the ways in which legitimacy can be measured. Measuring legitimacy is problematic: social values and expectations are often contradictory and difficult to operationalize, and they also evolve over time (Ashforth and Gibbs, 1990, p. 177). As is the case with regard to other intangible assets, what the best measures are is also a critical issue in relation to legitimacy.

Zelditch (2001) points out that in measuring legitimacy it should be taken into account that it is a ubiquitous phenomenon that is always auxiliary to certain other processes. Therefore, its dependent variable is always the extent to which it increases the acceptance of, or reduces the resistance to, something else, but what is accepted or resisted always seems to be observable only in the dependent variable of other processes.

The strategic public value account suggested by Moore (2013) includes specific measures that reveal potential sources of legitimacy and support that might be tapped or strengthened (p. 116). Research that combines literature on intangible assets with that on public value might help in advancing the endeavor of finding appropriate measures of legitimacy to capture all angles of the value that public management provides to society (Canel and Luoma-aho, in press).

The relationship between legitimacy and the measurement of other intangible assets such as trust and transparency and how this relationship should be analyzed is another critical issue (see for instance French's research [French, 2011] on the legitimacy of local

Table 8.1 Legitimacy as an intangible asset in the public sector.

Legitimacy is the intangible asset that generates the perception that an organization has the right to exist: it allows acceptance for the organization and its functions

Tangible asset that legitimacy enables	Organizations need legitimacy to undertake actions It affects an organization's ability to garner capital and recruit personnel It is a key factor for the survival of organizations as well as for its growth and success
Resource that legitimacy generates	To the extent that legitimacy is the cultural support of an organization and justifies its role in the social system, legitimacy is in itself a resource Legitimacy generates loyalty, support, and decision acceptance, and it promotes rule following
Monetary expression	Legitimacy saves resources required by systems of deterrence strategies and incentives A legitimate public sector organization/authority attracts investment; an illegitimate one requires additional costs to motivate and coerce acceptance of rules
Value that legitimacy provides to the organization	Authority: it is an additional form of power distinct from control over incentives and sanctions Legitimacy reduces frictions and conflict Decision acceptance, stability Reservoir of goodwill for difficult times Legitimate organizations are perceived as worthier and more meaningful, predictable, and credible
Value that legitimacy provides to stakeholders	Legitimacy helps to unify popular will Stability, certainty, institutional effectiveness, trust
Gaps that legitimacy bridges	Lack of meaning, lack of understanding, lack of shared standards and criteria to judge, lack of collective accounts and rational explanations, lack of trust
Dependence on communication management	Legitimacy management rests heavily on communication: it results from the attribution of stakeholders Communication is required for sense making, relations establishment, and continuous interaction with stakeholders
Implied organization management transformations	Organizational charts, distribution of functions, professional profiles, and working dynamics are required to combine organizational behavior with persuasive communication, substantive legitimacy management with symbolic legitimacy management, and actions with messages Ongoing monitoring of what people think and expect from the organization and to identify what reduces diversity in the legitimacy judgment
Measures	Message content analysis, social network analysis, surveys, focus groups, indicators of authorization and support

government planning for influenza pandemics in the United States through examining transparency and engagement). Finally, how legitimacy measures vary according to cultural contexts has been addressed by scholars (Maccarthaigh et al., 2016), though more cross-national comparative research is needed.

8.8 Summary of Legitimacy

Table 8.1 shows the different features of legitimacy as an intangible asset in the public sector.

8.9 Case Study on Legitimacy

Strategies to build legitimacy among employees in order to implement new public management in a public library

The context

Since the end of the 1980s, public sector organizations have gone through a series of reforms to implement the new public management (NPM) approach. For a Danish public library (the Danish State and University Library), this entailed new organizational practices – for example, digitalization, broader incorporation of information technology, online access, and more navigation facilities.

   The case shows what strategies the head of the library undertook to build legitimacy in order to gain employees' support for the implementation of the changes that NPM entailed. The information used in presenting this case is taken from Aggerholm and Thomsen (2016).

   Figure 8.3 shows that the Danish State and University Library scores the highest degree of publicness for all the variables of the fan.

Why was legitimacy needed?

In order to convince the library's employees to change their daily practices and traditional ways of thinking, the head of the library needed to gain legitimacy. When an organization goes through changes that affect dominant values, the intangible asset of legitimacy is needed so that stakeholders modify the standards against which they will judge an organization in a specific situation. In this case, the director needed his employees to undertake new organizational practices, and so he also needed them to accept the new policy and to confer legitimacy to lead the required change upon him.

Actions undertaken

In 2010, the Danish Ministry of Culture (the governmental institution to which the Danish State and University Library belongs) shifted its approach to the implementation of NPM practices. Although previously it had left it up to the individual bodies to identify their mission and vision, it decided to go for a more centralized strategy formulation: "The new

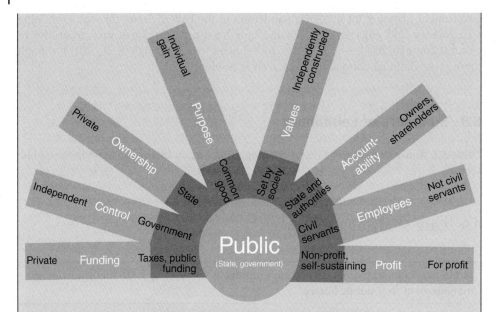

Figure 8.3 Publicness of the State and University Library in Denmark (2010).

and more radical NPM rhetoric constituted a clear breach with old practices and organizational self-understandings at the library, and the legitimation of alternative practices (e.g., the practice of strategizing) and novel ways of thinking constituted a major challenge for the locally situated management team" (Aggerholm and Thomsen 2016, p. 199).

From June 2010 until January 2011, the head of the library held several meetings with employees to respond to the ministry's requirement to formulate a strategy to implement NPM in the library in a way that fitted the ministry's overall strategy. There were initial organization-wide meetings followed by discussions in smaller groups led by frontline managers. The analysis focuses on the legitimation strategies deployed by the head of the library in the organization-wide meetings.

Legitimacy strategies deployed

According to Aggerholm and Thomsen's analysis (2016), the legitimation strategies were the following:

1) *Authorization*, which is "legitimation by reference to the authority of tradition, custom, law, and persons in whom institutional authority of some kind is vested" (p. 200). Two resources were utilized by the director of the library in order to legitimize the process for defining the strategy at the local level. First, the ministry, a political power whose authority is based on tradition, was mentioned by the director to explain the process that he wanted to undertake. He announced that over the course of several meetings, they would analyze their environment, vision, mission, priorities, and achievements, and they would analyze how all of these fitted the ministry's overall strategy. The director presented in the meetings the issues that needed to be analyzed as follows:
    "Does the ministry think that we have made the right observations when we look around? What is it that affects the State Library? What are we going to do? That's what we

are facing – some kind of exam!" (Excerpts from the director's talk in the meetings, taken from Aggerholm and Thomsen 2016, p. 200).

The ministry was therefore mentioned as the voice from which the director sought support for his legitimacy.

2) Second, references to the law (in terms of the library budget) were included as an economic power to authorize legitimacy. This was a rhetorical strategy to legitimize the need for a centrally formulated and controlled strategic plan. As an indication of how to elaborate the strategy of the library, the director stated, "You can have just as many professional goals as you wish, but if you do not meet the budget, then you fail" (p. 200).

The examples show how semantic references to the ministry and the law – and thereby the incorporation of political and legal voices – were used with the intention of legitimizing the contentious new strategic development that would lead to new organizational practices.

3) *Rationalization*, which is "legitimation by reference to the utility of specific actions based on knowledge claims that are accepted in a given context as relevant" (p. 202). The director referred to external and environmental transformations in order to frame the changes that the Danish State and University Library needed to undertake within the context of the Danish public library sector: what we have to do is what everybody is doing. Therefore, the need for changes was shown as self-evident, accepted by others, and common in the everyday operation of Danish public libraries.

4) *Moral evaluation*, which is "legitimation by reference to specific value systems that provide the moral basis for legitimation" (p. 202).

The head of the library said, "There is only one thing the ministry is concerned about. It is basically the boundary between us and the Agency for Libraries and Media" (p. 203). By reminding the audience of the boundaries between the library and the Agency for Libraries and Media, the head established the core value of the library: it is a *state* library, and hence particular to it are the values of free access to information, reading, and learning – values that are part of Danish culture. By connecting the required changes to Danish culture, the director of the library tried to establish a moral basis for legitimizing the transformations that NPM entails.

Lessons learned with regard to building legitimacy

1) The fact that public sector organizations are constantly exposed to changes implies an ongoing challenge for their taken-for-granted legitimacy.

2) In incorporating changes, particularly when the latter are contentious, public managers need to work on legitimacy strategies. Legitimacy is an intangible asset that helps public managers to lead transformations.

3) The focus of legitimacy strategies on incorporating changes in public management should respond to the questions of what changes are needed and why. Stakeholders will adopt changes only if the latter make sense for them.

4) Public sector organizations need first of all to build their legitimacy in the eyes of stakeholders within the organization.

5) Change agents have to navigate between different legitimation strategies: those of the individuals who make decisions (politicians) and those of the people who implement them (civil servants).

6) In building legitimacy, managers have to seek out additional voices that could enhance their authority, and they must incorporate these voices into their message.

7) Only if the manager is seen as legitimate in the eyes of the receivers will he or she be trusted to lead others through the uncertainty that is implied by changes.

8.10 Route Guide to Building Legitimacy

1) **Define your current legitimacy situation.** Determine whether you need to gain, maintain, or repair your legitimacy.
   Questions to ask: Do we have data about how our publics assess our legitimacy? What is being challenged? Is it our mere existence, our functions, or specific policies?

2) **Categorize the support that you need to garner from your audiences.**
   Questions to ask: Do we need specific affirmative commitments to be mobilized? Is passive support enough? Can we count on taken-for-granted legitimacy, or does our existence in fact not make sense to our publics?

3) **Determine what aspect of your legitimacy is at stake.**
   Questions to ask: What are the narratives about the origin of our authority? Do they make sense to my publics? How well is the origin of our authority portrayed in every specific action that we take in exercising our power? Are they consistent narratives?

4) **Subsequently, map your under-control area versus your out-of-control area in legitimacy intervention.**
   Questions to ask: What change is possible? What is the margin for maneuver I have?

5) **Identify the core elements of the message that make sense of your existence and functions sufficiently well so as to gain acceptance.** Identify and prioritize the major attributes that best portray your authority, in terms of both its origin and your exercise of functions.
   Questions to ask: What are the major predominant attributes in our communication products (website, speeches, tweets, profiles on social networks, and so forth)? Do they resonate with the goals of our legitimacy strategy? Are we focused on those attributes?

6) **Associate the goals of your legitimacy strategy with the corresponding typology.** Define whether you want to aim for a pragmatic, moral, or cognitive legitimacy.
   Questions to ask: How much time do we have to craft and implement our legitimacy strategy? Do we have time to invest in cognitive and moral legitimacy? Is it preferable to aim for the immediate goals of pragmatic legitimacy?

7) **Ensure that the focus of your communication corresponds to the type of legitimacy that you are aiming for.**
   Questions to ask: What do I need to show? The benefit of an exchange, of our being responsive, of our rightfulness, or of the common grounds that we share with our stakeholders?

8) **Seek out the voices that might help to build and support your legitimacy and incorporate them into your messages.**
   Questions to ask: Who or what are the major actors in relation to this issue? Which of them has pragmatic, moral, or cognitive authority for my stakeholders? Are they congruent with my organization's message? Are they available to be incorporated?

9) **Look for the channels through which you are going to implement your legitimacy strategy.** Associate the type of legitimacy with which you wish to operate with the type of actions.
   Questions to ask: Are there specific opportunities on which we could focus for an exchange with my publics to happen? What are the issue arenas in which we should be involved in order to take part in the elaboration of the legitimacy criteria related to our organization and its policies? Are we present in those arenas? If not, what should we do to be present and active in them?

10) **Be vigilant about your legitimacy.** Establish an ongoing unit to monitor your legitimacy, in both discourse arenas and your publics' perceptions.
    Questions to ask: What do our publics care about most in assessing our legitimacy? What changes in the environment might challenge our legitimacy? Which actors present in our issue arenas can foster or challenge our legitimacy? What are the attributes in the public discourse about us that might compete with our desired legitimacy attributes?

References

Aggerholm, H.K. and Thomsen, C. (2016). Legitimation as a particular mode of strategic communication in the public sector. *International Journal of Strategic Communication* **10** (3): 195–206.

Aldrich, H.E. and Fiol, C.M. (1994). Fools rush in? The institutional context of industry creation. *The Academy of Management Review* **19** (4): 645–670.

Arora, N.D. (2010). *Political Science*. New York: Tata McGraw Publishers.

Ashforth, B.E. and Gibbs, B.W. (1990). The double-edge of organizational legitimation. *Organization Science* **1** (2): 177–194.

Baum, J.A.C. and Oliver, C. (1991). Institutional linkages and organizational mortality. *Administrative Science Quarterly* **36** (2): 187–219.

Berger, P.L., Berger, B., and Kellner, H. (1973). *The Homeless Mind: Modernization and Consciousness*. New York: Random House.

Bevir, M. (2013). Legitimacy and the administrative state: ontology, history, and democracy. *Public Administration Quarterly* **37** (4): 535–549.

Bitektine, A. (2011). Toward a theory of social judgments of organizations: the case of legitimacy, reputation, and status. *Academy of Management Review* **36** (1): 151–179.

Canel, M.-J. (2014). Reflexiones sobre la reputación ideal de la administración pública. In: *Escribir en las almas. Estudios en honor de Rafael Alvira* (ed. A.M. Herrero Cruz, R. Lázaro and A. Martínez), 69–88. Pamplona: Eiunsa.

Canel, M.J. and Luoma-aho, V. (In press). Public sector communication and public-valued intangible assets. In: *Handbook of Public Sector Communication* (ed. V.L. Luoma-aho and M.J. Canel). Boston: Wiley-Blackwell.

Canel, M.J., Oliveira, E., and Luoma-aho, V. (2017). Exploring citizens' judgments about the legitimacy of public policies on refugees: In search of clues for governments' communication and public diplomacy strategies. *Journal of Communication Management* **21** (4): 355–369.

Chermak, S. and Weiss, A. (2005). Maintaining legitimacy using external communication strategies: an analysis of police-media relations. *Journal of Criminal Justice* **33** (5): 501–512.

Deephouse, D.L. (1996). Does isomorphism legitimate? *Academy of Management Journal* **39** (4): 1024–1039.

Deephouse, D.L. (1999). To be different, or to be the same? It's a question (and theory) of strategic balance. *Strategic Management Journal* **20** (2): 147–166.

Deephouse, D.L. and Carter, S.M. (2005). An examination of differences between organizational legitimacy and organizational reputation. *Journal of Management Studies* **42** (2): 329–360.

Díez Martín, F., Blanco González, A., and Prado Román, C. (2010). Legitimidad como factor clave del éxito organizativo. *Investigaciones Europeas de Dirección y Economía de La Empresa* **16** (3): 127–143.

DiMaggio, P.J. and Powell, W.W. (1991). *The New Institutionalism in Organizational Analysis*, vol. 17. Chicago, IL: University of Chicago Press.

Epstein, E.M. and Votaw, D. (1978). *Rationality, Legitimacy, Responsibility: Search for New Directions in Business and Society*. Santa Monica, CA: Goodyear Publishing Company.

French, P.E. (2011). Enhancing the legitimacy of local government pandemic influenza planning through transparency and public engagement. *Public Administration Review* **71** (2): 253–264.

Gibson, J.L. (2004). Overcoming apartheid: can truth reconcile a divided nation? *The Annals of the American Academy of Political and Social Science* **603** (1): 82–110.

Golant, B.D. and Sillince, J.A.A. (2007). The constitution of organizational legitimacy: a narrative perspective. *Organization Studies* **28** (8): 1149–1167.

Gordon, R., Kornberger, M., and Clegg, S.R. (2009). Power, rationality and legitimacy in public organizations. *Public Administration* **87** (1): 15–34.

Grimmelikhuijsen, S.G. and Meijer, A.J. (2015). Does twitter increase perceived police legitimacy? *Public Relations Review* **75** (4): 598–607.

Gustavsen, A., Røiseland, A., and Pierre, J. (2014). Procedure or performance? Assessing citizen's attitudes toward legitimacy in Swedish and Norwegian local government. *Urban Research & Practice* **7** (2): 200–212.

Hamilton, E.A. (2006). An exploration of the relationship between loss of legitimacy and the sudden death of organizations. *Group & Organization Management* **31** (3): 327–358.

Hegtvedt, K.A., Clay-Warner, J., and Johnson, C. (2003). The social context of responses to injustice: considering the indirect and direct effects of group-level factors. *Social Justice Research* **16** (4): 343–366.

Hurd, I. (1999). Legitimacy and authority in international politics. *International Organization* **53** (2): 379–408.

Jepperson, R. (1991). Institutions, institutional effects, and institutionalism. In: *The New Institutionalism in Organizational Analysis* (ed. W.W. Power and P.J. DiMaggio), 143–163. Chicago, IL: University of Chicago Press.

Johnson, C., Dowd, T.J., and Ridgeway, C.L. (2006). Legitimacy as a social process. *Annual Review of Sociology* **32**: 53–78.

Lee, M. (2009). The return of public relations to the public administration curriculum? *Journal of Public Affairs Education* **15** (4): 515–533.

Leonhardt, D. (2007). Sometimes, what's needed is a nudge. *New York Times*, C1, C9.

Maccarthaigh, M., Painter, M., and Yee, W.H. (2016). Managing for legitimacy: agency governance in its 'deep' constitutional context. *Public Administration Review* **76** (3): 496–506.

Maurer, J.G. (1971). *Readings in Organizational Theory: Open System Approaches*. New York: Random House.

Merriam-Webster (2004). *Merriam-Webster's Collegiate Dictionary*. Merriam-Webster.

Meyer, J.W. and Rowan, B. (1991). Institutionalized organizations: formal structure as myth and ceremony. In: *The New Institutionalism in Organizational Analysis* (ed. W.W. Powell and P.J. DiMaggio), 41–62. Chicago, IL: University of Chicago Press.

Meyer, J.W. and Scott, W.R. (1983). Centralization and the legitimacy problems of local government. In: *Organizational Environments: Ritual and Rationality* (ed. J.W. Meyer and W. Richard Scott), 199–215. Beverly Hills, CA: Sage.

Moore, M.H. (2013). *Recognizing Public Value*. Boston: Harvard University Press.

Neilsen, E.H. and Rao, M.H. (1987). The strategy-legitimacy nexus: a thick description. *Academy of Management Review* **12** (3): 523–533.

Pearson, C.M. and Clair, J.A. (1998). Reframing crisis management. *Academy of Management Review* **23** (1): 59–76.

Pfeffer, J. (1981). Management as symbolic action: the creation and maintenance of organizational paradigms. In: *Research in Organizational Behavior* (ed. L.L. Cummings and B.M. Staw), 1–52. Greenwich, CT: JAI Press.

Ruef, M. and Scott, W.R. (1998). A multidimensional model of organizational legitimacy: hospital survival in changing institutional environments. *Administrative Science Quarterly* **43** (4): 877–904.

Scott, W.R. (1977). Effectiveness of organizational effectiveness studies. In: *New Perspectives on Organizational Effectiveness* (ed. P.S. Goodman and J.M. Pennings), 63–95. San Francisco: Jossey-Bass.

Scott, W.R. (1995). *Institutions and Organizations. Institutions and Organizations: Ideas and Interests*. Thousand Oaks, CA: Sage.

Scott, R.W. and Meyer, J.W. (1991). The organization of societal sectors: propositions and early evidence. In: *The New Institutionalism in Organizational Analysis* (ed. W.W. Powell and P.J. Di Maggio), 108–140. Chicago, IL: University of Chicago Press.

Suchman, M.C. (1995). Managing legitimacy: strategic and institutional approaches. *Academy of Management Review* **20** (3): 571–610.

Tyler, T.R. (2006). Psychological perspectives on legitimacy and legitimation. *Annual Review of Psychology* **57**: 375–400.

Weber, M. (1978). *Economy and Society. An Outline of Interpretive Sociology*, vol. 1. Berkeley, CA: University of California Press.

Zelditch, M. (2001). Processes of legitimation: recent developments and new directions. *Social Psychology Quarterly* **64** (1): 4–17.

Zyglidopoulos, S.C. (2003). The issue life-cycle: implications for reputation for social performance and organizational legitimacy. *Corporate Reputation Review* **6** (1): 70–81.

9

Intellectual Capital

> *Knowledge is like money: to be of value it must circulate, and in circulating it can increase in quantity and, hopefully, in value*
> (L'Amour, 1908–1988, American author, https://km.nasa.gov/km-quotes/)

Intellectual capital is an intangible asset that involves the knowledge required to address the challenges faced by the public sector. The core argument of this chapter is that different ways of managing knowledge can affect the success of public policies. We begin by defining intellectual capital, and we then consider how it is measured and communicated.

9.1 What Intellectual Capital Is About

9.1.1 Definition

Because intangible assets as a research area are still emerging, there is still no clear consensus or solid foundations with regard to the definitions of intangible assets. Intellectual capital is no exception in this regard (Grasenick and Low, 2004; Ferenhof et al., 2015; Dumay, 2016). Nevertheless, a recent reflection on the future of intellectual capital by Dumay (2016) is helpful in identifying its core idea as an intangible asset. He refers back to Steward's (1997) understanding of intellectual capital as the sum of every immateriality (such as knowledge and information) that can be put to use to create wealth, and he updates it in the light of the most recent debates on intangible assets by replacing the word "wealth" with "value." Intellectual capital is therefore knowledge that can be applied to yield value, something that Edvinsson and Sullivan had already stated in 1996 (Edvinsson and Sullivan, 1996).

Intellectual capital has been viewed by some authors as synonymous with intangible assets (Lev and Daum, 2004; Sánchez, 2008). However, others take the position that there are items of an intangible nature that do not logically form part of a company's intellectual capital but are instead, as is the case of reputation, the result of the judicious use of it (Petty and Guthrie, 2000, p. 158). Intellectual capital is also closely associated with knowledge management, though we agree with the distinction that Petty and Guthrie (2000, p. 159) draw between the two: knowledge management, as a function, describes the act of managing intellectual capital (the object). Our understanding is that

Public Sector Communication: Closing Gaps Between Citizens and Public Organizations, First Edition. María-José Canel and Vilma Luoma-aho.
© 2019 John Wiley & Sons, Inc. Published 2019 by John Wiley & Sons, Inc.

intellectual capital is a subset of a given organization's intangible value, and hence as an intangible asset it is different from others (for instance, social legitimacy or engagement): it is the intangible asset that measures the extent to which an organization manages knowledge well.

As we discussed in Chapter 4, intangibles have been vaguely referred to under the label "goodwill," and intellectual capital has been taken as part of this goodwill. But contemporary classification schemas (OECD, 1999) have refined the distinction by specifically dividing intellectual capital into the categories of external (customer-related) capital, internal (structural) capital, and human capital. This delineation has been useful when it has come to the task of drawing up reports on an organization's intellectual capital. This classification also makes the link between tangible and intangible factors clear in relation to intangible assets: intellectual capital resources include intangible capital resources (for example, knowledge) and tangible assets (for instance, software), both of which are part of an organization's property (Canibano et al., 1999)

We can infer from these considerations that there is value in the knowledge that an organization "controls," but for this knowledge to have a value, organizations have to undertake certain actions to acquire, improve, assess, and control knowledge. Two features characterize an effective and timely use of knowledge in an organization. The first of these is the extent to which knowledge is shared: the greater the sharing of knowledge, the higher the quality of the knowledge that the organization manages. The second is the systematization and codification of knowledge creation: there are decisions made by the organization that, once routinized, contribute to the achievement of the organization's goals (Sánchez, 2008, p. 576). Intellectual capital is therefore an intangible asset that both fosters and measures the sharing and systematizing of knowledge in an organization.

9.1.2 What Has Been Done So Far on Intellectual Capital in the Public Sector?

The findings of the most recent reviews of research on intellectual capital in the public sector (Guthrie, Ricceri, and Dumay, 2012; Dumay, Guthrie, and Puntillo, 2015; Guthrie and Dumay, 2015) could be summarized as follows: despite the fact that the public sector contributes significantly to GDP in most economies and is strongly reliant on the generation, use, and management of knowledge, there is still little in the way of literature on intellectual capital. However, developing intellectual capital as an asset in the public sector is becoming a more common practice since it is proving to be helpful in responding to the challenges that public sector organizations face today in their attempts to legitimize themselves.

Two factors help to explain this increase in the use of intellectual capital as a management tool in the public sector. First, intellectual capital has been shown to be helpful in responding to the demands of the so-called "knowledge-based economy," in which wealth generation is associated with the development and management of factors of an intangible nature (Ramirez, 2010, p. 248). Second, public services are nowadays to a significant extent managed, delivered, and governed by private and third-sector organizations, which has blurred the boundaries between the public and private sectors (Guthrie and Dumay, 2015, p. 259). In this context, the new public management stream (already discussed in Chapter 3) has developed as a perspective that is oriented toward improving services based on results and focused on the use and implementation of knowledge to modernize administration. Intellectual capital is an intangible asset that provides specific measures to account for outcomes (Ramirez, 2010, p. 250).

Wall's description (Wall, 2005) of the increase in efforts to measure intellectual capital in the United Kingdom demonstrates the emphasis placed by public administrations on improving and reporting performance. From the early 1990s, public agencies were expected to publish commercial-style accounts that contained details of how an organization had performed against preset targets. At the local level, public authorities started to both use and disclose prescribed performance indicators that covered the three aspects of intellectual capital mentioned above. For instance, in the case of water services, local authorities nowadays measure items such as the percentage of total waste water received that is recycled (organizational), the percentage of citizens satisfied with council services (customer relations), and the proportion of working days lost to sickness or unauthorized absence (human).

From an academic research perspective, Syed-Ikhsan and Rowland state that few studies examine knowledge management in the public sector. The foci of those which do include benchmarking of knowledge management, knowledge sharing, knowledge management initiatives, and knowledge management practices (2004, p. 96). In a more recent review, Guthrie et al. found that the public sector is one of the least addressed areas within research on intellectual capital, and existing studies cover a wide spread of public organization types, including universities, local governments, hospitals, government departments, research organizations, police departments, and regional clusters (Guthrie et al., 2012, p. 74).

Building upon this finding, Dumay et al. (2015) present a structured review of the literature on intellectual capital in the public sector. They conclude that the primary research focus with regard to public sector intellectual capital is central government and central government agencies. In terms of the area of public service addressed, they found that education (which accounted for almost 40% of the analyzed dataset) was the area that received the most attention, and within this area universities featured with particular prominence. The next two most commonly researched areas – though these have received far less attention than education – are health and infrastructure. The primary location that has been focused on is Europe (with a clear predominance of studies on Italy and Spain within this region) followed by Australia. Unlike research on intellectual capital in the private sector, which is grounded in the seminal works of practitioners such as Sveiby and Edvinsson, few practitioners from the public sector have become involved in research on intellectual capital in their field. Finally, and again unlike the private sector, researchers who focus on intellectual capital in the public sector are firmly entrenched in what these authors call "performative third-stage research," which investigates how intellectual capital works in organizations rather than offering normative solutions.

9.2 Why is Intellectual Capital Needed?

Intellectual capital is required for different reasons, all of which are related to the fact that intellectual capital involves making use of knowledge when addressing the challenges that the public sector faces, on the basis that the quality and amount of knowledge available has a strong influence on public sector management. In the context of safety policies, Guthrie and Dumay (2015) express the need for intellectual capital in radical terms. Recent concerns about increases in terrorism and the resulting call for enhanced security measures, they say, highlight "the need to understand how organizations tasked with protecting society operate," and "a failure to utilize knowledge on police and emergency services in a timely and effective way could be the difference between life and death" (Jones and Mahon, 2012, p. 774, cited in Guthrie and Dumay, 2015, p. 259). A more detailed exploration of intellectual capital reveals further ways in which it provides a benefit to both the organization and its stakeholders.

In terms of organizational management, the effective and timely use of knowledge helps public sector organizations to contend more effectively in an increasingly competitive public sector. As Guthrie and Dumay highlight (2015, p. 259), the public sector will continue to experience change in terms of the way in which it delivers services, and the trend toward the privatization of services and partnerships between the public and private sectors will further increase competition within the sector. A clear example of this dynamic can be found in the world of education, where universities and schools must compete to a greater extent to attract potential students. This environment of increased competition perhaps explains why education, as already mentioned, has received the greatest amount of attention within research on intellectual capital in the public sector. Moreover, the success of universities nowadays is tied to their capacity to demonstrate the extent to which they are able to generate, employ, and share knowledge.

Intellectual capital indicators are also needed to refine the measurement of public policy outcomes. Better measures of these outcomes facilitate the task of gauging the gaps that exist between real achievements (deeds) and people's perceptions. If public sector organizations have data on these gaps, they will be better equipped to devise strategic plans for their policies and communication, and hence they will be in a better position to attune their messages in relation to both their behaviors and citizens' expectations. Intellectual capital has an important role to play in shedding light on the inner workings of public services and in contributing to the measurement and management of resources in order to communicate realistic expectations.

Within the scope of this book, however, perhaps the strongest reason for emphasizing intellectual capital as an intangible asset is the impact that it has on making the value that an organization provides visible for its stakeholders. As already discussed, for value to exist, it has to be acknowledged by somebody, and intellectual capital plays an important role in relation to the two stakeholder groups of employees and citizens. Intellectual capital helps employees to visualize the collective knowledge that is being developed. An intellectual capital perspective, Laskari et al. argue, helps public managers to better envision their targets and principles and to better develop the organization's orientation and culture (Laskari, Kostagiolas, and Kefis, 2016, p. 156). The more visible the nature and extent of an organization's learning, the higher the collective awareness, and therefore, the better the organization responds to questions of identity such as "Who we are?" and "What are we for?"

As we have already mentioned, a component of this collective knowledge derives from the organization's capacity to share knowledge, and in this respect Syed-Ikhsan and Rowland's work (2004) explores the relationship between organizational elements and the performance of knowledge sharing. The ability to share knowledge is shaped by organizational culture, organizational structure, technology, human resources, and political directives. Knowledge transfer requires the willingness of a group or individual to work with others and share knowledge to their mutual benefit, and Syed-Ikhsan and

Rowland show that it will not occur in an organization unless its employees and work groups display a high level of cooperative behavior. Through empirical observation, they found that government agencies are typically hierarchical and bureaucratic and thus less open to sharing knowledge. They suggest that in employing measures of intellectual capital, these organizations will become more aware of the need for it; measures will also boost processes of knowledge sharing, which might ultimately enhance the workforce's capabilities to manage knowledge well.

Intellectual capital also helps real achievements to be visualized in the eyes of citizens (Laskari et al., 2016, p. 152) and allows the latter to evaluate the activities that the administration carries out, a process that improves citizens' satisfaction with these activities and increases their well-being (Ramirez, 2010).

9.3 What Resources Does Intellectual Capital Generate? Measuring Intellectual Capital

The previous section makes it clear that intellectual capital may generate the following resources: quality and strategic management, a well-built and consistent organizational culture, knowledge visibility, knowledge sharing, accountability, and good governance. But to better respond to the question of what resources this intangible asset yields, we now deal in detail with the issue of measuring intellectual capital.

9.3.1 What Does Intellectual Capital Tell Us About? The Dimensions of IC

There is consensus both in research and in practice that intellectual capital comprises three dimensions (Kaplan and Norton, 1992; Sveiby, 1997, 1998; Petty and Guthrie, 2000; Bossi Queiroz, Fuertes Callén, and Serrano Cinca, 2005; Bueno Campos, Salmador, and Merino, 2006; European Commission, 2006). First, there is *human capital*, which entails the knowledge, either tacit or explicit, that the individuals and groups in an organization have and that is useful for the organization's mission. It includes skills, experiences, and capabilities. This knowledge resides in individuals, and it goes with them when they leave the organization. Second, there is *structural capital*, which, unlike human capital, resides in the organization (it is the organization's property). It includes supply chains, software, distribution networks, procedures, codes of conduct, and organizational routines. Finally, there is *relational capital*, which comprises the value of the relationships established between the organization and the major agents involved in the organization's basic processes. It includes customers, providers, and research and development partners.

In a recent review of the state of the art of intellectual capital research (one not confined to research related to the public sector), Ferenhof et al. (2015) found that in peer-reviewed articles in English, French, Spanish, Portuguese, and German that appeared in major publications between 2004 and 2014, up to 83 additional models were suggested for measuring this intangible asset. These authors analyze all these models and elaborate a metamodel to synthesize research activities in the field and highlight the main dimensions and subdimensions of intellectual capital (see image in Ferenhof et al., 2015, p. 91). Intellectual capital consists of the following second-order constructs: structural capital, human capital, relational capital, and social capital. *Structural capital* is what keeps the organization running. It covers tangible and intangible assets, and it rests upon third-order constructs – that is, innovation capital, process capital, technological capital, and organizational capital. *Human capital*, considered by scholars to be the most important asset, is responsible for executing the other forms of capital, and it is established through the following third-order constructs: motivation, knowledge, skills, and attitudes. *Relational capital* embodies all the organization's relationships with customers, suppliers, and other critical stakeholders, and it comprises the third-order constructs of customer capital and business capital. *Social capital* also concerns relationships, but in contrast to relational capital, it relates to society as a whole, and it is determined by the third-order constructs of social activities and social interactions.

In our judgment, this metamodel demonstrates that intellectual capital research is evolving so that it includes approaches in which organizations' relations with society carry greater weight. What intellectual capital provides, therefore, is not only the capacity to produce knowledge but also the extent to which that knowledge is valued by society. The level of value created and the criteria according to which value is measured are both critical issues, and different models have been suggested for measuring intellectual capital in the public sector.

9.3.2 Measuring Intellectual Capital in the Public Sector

We have already mentioned that different reviews of the state of the art show that unlike the private sector, where over the course of 10 years a total of 83 additional models for measuring intellectual capital were suggested (Ferenhof et al., 2015), public sector research has been focused on applying already existing models and on adjusting them to the specificities of the public sector (Dumay et al., 2015; Guthrie and Dumay, 2015).

There are different approaches to assessing intellectual capital in the private sector (that is, direct intellectual capital, market capitalization, return on investment, and the balanced scorecard), but the major difficulty in importing them to the public sector is its lack of a market value. To overcome this problem, research on intellectual capital in the public sector has built upon the following models: the balanced scorecard (Kaplan and Norton, 1992; Kaplan and Norton, 2000), the capital assets monitor (Sveiby, 1997), and the Skandia Navigator (Edvinsson and Malone, 1997; for comparisons, see Petty and Guthrie, 2000; Ramírez, Manzaneque, and Priego, 2017). All of these models have been regarded as applicable to the public sector (Bossi Queiroz et al., 2005).

One of the most thorough and up-to-date reviews of different models for measuring intellectual capital in the public sector is that by Ramirez (2010). This author argues that the specificities of the public sector require models to provide information on the capability of the public administration to generate sustainable results and on the possibility of constant improvement, going beyond the short-term view of financial-accounting models (p. 260). Therefore, what is crucial for well-adjusted models is that they capture not only growth and efficiency but also innovation and sustainability. Moreover, as we have argued, the public sector needs to include measures that combine the different value criteria against which it is assessed and, more specifically, economic and social values. Finally, since the public sector has a multisectorial nature, models should be able to embrace the diverse legal and financial frameworks that coexist within it (Sarmiento and Roman, 2011, p. 5).

There are several proposals for readjusting classical intellectual capital models to the public sector, including those by Garcia Arrieta (2001); Caba and Sierra (2003); Serrano Cinca, Molinero, and Queiroz (2003); and Bueno Campos et al. (2006).

The model suggested by Bueno Campos et al. (2006) aims to identify and measure intangible resources that are potential sources of value creation and help to improve efficacy and efficiency in public services. The model's structure identifies the three main components of intellectual capital already mentioned, but owing to the complexities of public administration entities, structural capital is divided into three subcomponents here: public organizational capital (explicit or implicit and formal or informal knowledge that structures and develops organizational activity in efficient and effective ways), public social capital (related to the value that a public service represents to the organization based on trust, fidelity, and ethics), and public technological capital (which derives from technological knowledge and comprises activities and functions with either internal or external scope related to products and services that characterize the different operations of the organization). The model deems intellectual capital to comprise five factors, and for each one the authors suggest a set of variables with indicators and specific measures. For instance, public human capital has the following factors and variables: attitudes and values (commitment, feeling, motivation, satisfaction, sociability, flexibility and adaptability, and creativity), technical knowledge (formal education, specialized training, professional experience, and personal development), and capacities and competencies (learning, collaboration, communication, and leadership). Interestingly, public social capital includes social cohesion (service philosophy, social services and resources, social innovation, and social welfare), social stability (transparency, ethics, and citizen participation), and social connection (citizens' relationships and employees' relationships). Therefore, this model captures what the intangible asset provides for both organizational management and society.

The model suggested by Caba and Sierra (2003) is based on that of the European Foundation for Quality Management and integrates its different elements in the three blocks that comprise intellectual capital (human capital, structural capital, and relational capital), but it considers there to be a direct relationship between them. Another characteristic of this proposal is that it focuses on both present and potential future value. For instance, the human capital block refers not only to present competences but also to people's and working teams' capability to learn and create. Other factors in this block are personnel's ethics, responsibility, and satisfaction. The structural capital block reflects the know-how of the organization, including the process for defining strategies, management resources, operative processes, and innovation processes. Finally, the relational capital block consists of the value created as a consequence of the external relationships of the entity, the success of which can be detected in users' loyalty and satisfaction; information mechanisms for the service user; the organization's reputation; and the ability to anticipate social needs. At the level of human capital (the commitment of personnel in public entities to achieving value), the indicator included in this model is "human quality." For the structural dimension, the indicators are efficiency and efficacy in policies and strategies, resource management, and the operative process. And for relational capital, the indicators are excellence, equity, environment, sustainability, and demand.

Also worth mentioning here is the model suggested by García Arrieta (2001) because, based on Ramírez's (2010) review of it, we see it as a good example of how an intellectual capital model can bring strategic capacity to public sector organizations. García builds on Sveiby's (1997) monitor and the intellect model (Euroforum, 1998) to suggest what he calls the "intangible assets statement," which is a nonfinancial section that refers to intangible investments that do not comply with any requirements that allow them to be counted as an asset. García applied it to the local council of Pozuelo (Madrid, Spain). Twelve strategic goals were set; these were to be achieved through 15 intangible factors and 90 intangible-focused activities (for example, establishing conditions for staff composition and competences, changes in working procedures, and actions to collect citizens' feedback). This model, Ramírez argues, provides information both on strategic investments (and, therefore, on efficiency and efficacy) and on citizens' assessments (and, therefore, on the impact on citizens' satisfaction and well-being). Based on this proposal, a route guide for public managers to focus on building intellectual capital can be drawn up.

In our judgment, the most thorough model for the public sector is that proposed by Bossi Queiroz and coworkers (2001; 2003; 2005). They put forward five perspectives that affect intellectual capital: the three traditional variables – which are labeled human resources, internal processes (which is structural capital), and external relations (which is relational capital) – and another two elements, namely transparency and quality. The transparency element is very particular to the public sector, and it allows a higher control of public management. Its values provide insight into the extent to which an administration is available for public service users and is free of corruption (Bossi Queiroz et al., 2001). Several features of this model are of additional value to other models that have been proposed for the public sector. First (though this feature is not exclusive to this model), the amount of intellectual capital is measured here not only in terms of efficiency and efficacy but also in terms of the commitment of the organization to adopt practices to collect data on citizens' and users' satisfaction. Second, the model also captures a possible negative form of intellectual capital. This is measured by what is called "intellectual liability," which represents the space between ideal management and real management (Ramírez, 2010, p. 259). Finally, in providing a visual representation of what intellectual capital management means within the whole process of an organization's operations, the model also captures the relation between what is tangible and what is intangible. The model is represented via a matrix in which the X axis goes from the most tactical operative level (for instance, elaborating budgets) to the most strategic one (for instance, building and measuring intellectual capital). The Y axis goes from the most tangible to the most intangible. The metaphor of a staircase is used to convey that in their journey toward excellence (the step at the top-right of the matrix), organizations need to start with tactical-tangible operational actions and cumulatively take further steps toward more intangible strategic work.

9.4 Communicating Intellectual Capital

9.4.1 Does Communication Play a Role in the Acknowledgement of Intellectual Capital?

We have already pointed out that intellectual capital helps employees to visualize the collective knowledge that is being developed within their organization: the more visible the content and depth of what an organization is learning, the higher the collective awareness of value. In this respect, the study by Vagnoni and Oppi (2015) describes a case in which the visualization of intellectual capital made a difference in the strategic management of an Italian university hospital in which academic, clinical, and research functions are performed. Starting out from the assumption that university hospitals' managerial reports often lack information about the drivers of their performance, they demonstrate that intellectual capital had been the main driver of performance, and showing that this was the case helped the organization to realign its two dimensions (those of university and hospital) in a more integrated management. When intellectual capital is visualized, the organization becomes more collectively aware of its goals and more focused on knowledge creation. Vagnoni and Oppi's study therefore documents not only the role of communication in helping a given asset to be acknowledged but also the impact of this acknowledgement for strategic management purposes and for the success of the organization. In today's knowledge economy, the collective knowledge of an organization is of utmost importance (Kong and Thomson, 2009, p. 359), and intellectual capital represents the collective knowledge that is embedded in the organization's personnel, organizational routines, and network relationships (Ramirez, 2010, p. 251). Intellectual capital "forces public managers to investigate what they know (know-what) and the ability to deliver what they know (know-how)" (Ramírez, 2010, p. 252), and we would argue that communication is crucial in advancing and consolidating these endeavors.

Intellectual capital also helps citizens to visualize real achievements (Laskari et al., 2016, p. 152). One would expect that the higher the values of public sector intellectual capital, the higher the awareness that people will have of the quality of knowledge use and management. This relationship is expressed in particular in the National Intellectual Capital Index (NICI), which includes the hidden values of individuals, enterprises, institutions, communities, and regions that are the current and potential sources for wealth creation. Public sector intellectual capital is an important component of the NICI, and to the extent that it seeks to improve the efficiency of the public sector, public sector intellectual capital will lead to benefits for society as a whole. The higher the value of a specific country's NICI, the more its citizens will acknowledge what the public sector provides (Mačerinskienė and Aleknavičiūtė, 2015).

It has been argued that intellectual capital is a hidden treasure that needs to be discovered (Laskari et al., 2016), and we argue that it is the role of communication to bring this treasure to the attention of the public sector's stakeholders. This section therefore concludes by asserting that communication itself is what builds intellectual capital.

9.4.2 Intellectual Capital Management and Communication Management

How does management of this intangible asset modify and transform the communication management undertaken by public organizations? Dumay's (2016) reflection on the future of intellectual capital challenges today's communication practices. The core of his argument is that intellectual capital reports should focus on value instead of wealth, and he defines value in four ways: monetary (which is still needed to make organizations work), utility (the usefulness of the goods and services an organization produces), sustainable (meeting the needs of the present without compromising the ability of future generations to meet their own needs), and social (which relates to the benefits that an organization provides to society in general). He argues that more attention should be paid nowadays to social value, and this implies a change in communication practices.

Rather than being concerned with reporting, intellectual capital communication should focus more on disclosing information in a timely manner, so that all stakeholders understand how an organization takes into consideration its ethical, social, and environmental impacts. Through doing so, organizations do not focus solely on wealth creation but instead on providing monetary, utility, sustainable, and social value.

Based on the models described above, we can infer that building intellectual capital requires several steps – we deal with these at the end of this chapter – and to go through them, it is necessary for communication managers to be located in strategic positions (next to professionals); their job role should no longer be seen as a "post hoc" (postdecision) intervention. Allowing a public sector organization to focus on intellectual capital entails an organization of communication that differs from the traditional model.

9.5   Critical Issues, Unanswered Questions, and Future Research

Having considered different reviews of intellectual capital research (Petty and Guthrie, 2000; Dumay et al., 2015; Ferenhof et al., 2015; Guthrie and Dumay, 2015), we end this chapter with the following list of critical issues of relevance to the public sector.

First, the question of models and measures is always open. Research has shown that models need an ongoing readjustment to the public sector's new needs and challenges, as well as to different specific cultural contexts. We believe that what Ferenhof et al. (2015) state with regard to the private sector is applicable to this endeavor: the major dimensions of intellectual capital have been identified, but it is necessary to develop the way in which they should and could be measured. The public sector needs to come up with ways and approaches that make the contribution of intellectual capital to real value creation in organizations more visible; these measures should better explore the link between the tangible and the intangible.

A second area that needs further research is the effects that reporting practices have. The questions that Petty and Guthrie suggested in relation to the private sector several years ago (Petty and Guthrie, 2000, p. 169) are applicable to the public sector today: Is reporting intellectual capital likely to favorably impact productivity and efficiency? To what extent do reporting indicators actually enhance public sector organizational culture? How can intellectual capital reporting be transferred to the strategic building of institutional identity?

Third, there are questions regarding intellectual capital management that remain unanswered with regard to the public sector. These concern whether it is feasible (in terms not only of costs but also of the appropriate mindsets in public authorities) to measure and manage intellectual capital, and also who – what department and with which functional dependence – is best positioned to do this.

Regarding specific practices, the issue about where information on intellectual capital should be presented (for example, annual reports, press releases, or promotional material) is also an open one. The question of disclosing rather than reporting (Dumay, 2016) introduces new challenges, because disclosing demands more transparent, robust, reliable, timely, and verifiable intellectual capital indicators. With a disclosure-based approach, annual reports lose relevance, and thus organizations will no longer rely on these "protective barriers" or "window displays" and will instead be exposed to a greater level of accountability.

Finally, with regard to research areas, future studies of intellectual capital in the public sector need to go beyond education and expand to areas such as security, health, and energy, in which well-managed knowledge is of the utmost importance. Scholars also face the challenge of involving practitioners (public managers) in their research to provide both academia and public administrations with high-quality case studies, which today are still lacking (Dumay et al., 2015).

9.6 Summary of Intellectual Capital

Table 9.1 summarizes intellectual capital as an intangible asset that measures the extent to which an organization manages knowledge well.

Table 9.1 Intellectual capital as an intangible asset in the public sector.

Intellectual capital is the intangible asset that measures the extent to which an organization manages knowledge well	
Tangible asset intellectual capital enables	All physical capital through providing well-managed (timely, efficient, shared, and systematized) knowledge The quality and amount of knowledge makes a difference in public sector management
Resource intellectual capital generates	Quality and strategic management, good governance, well-built and consistent organizational culture, knowledge visibility, knowledge sharing, knowledge systematization, accountability, transparency
Monetary expression	Costs savings, higher investments, procedural time saving
Value intellectual capital provides the organization with	Strategic capacity, systematization of processes, improvement of procedures, efficiency, increased networking
Value social capital provides citizens and stakeholders with	Satisfaction, wellbeing, access to information
Gaps that intellectual capital bridges	The gap between real achievements and people's perceptions: intellectual capital provides insights from public services and ways to measure and manage resources to meet citizens' expectations
Dependence on communication management	The more visible the content and extent of what an organization is learning, the higher the collective awareness of intellectual capital The higher the values of public sector intellectual capital, the higher the awareness that people will have of the quality of knowledge use and management
Implied organization management transformations	Building intellectual capital implies that communicators work together with those generating knowledge to strategically build and measure the asset
Measures	Self-reported values and externally provided values regarding structural capital, human capital, relational capital, and social capital

9.7 Case Study on Intellectual Capital

A strategic approach to intellectual capital management in European universities

The context

In the late 1980s, several European countries started to build what is now the European Higher Education Area. At present, 50 countries follow what is called the Bologna Process, the aim of which is to ensure comparability in the standards and quality of higher-education qualifications. It challenges universities to be more competitive, dynamic, and transparent. The subsequent reforms "have increased the autonomy of universities, providing a central role to performance measurement and efficiency, leading to the creation of national accreditation agencies and promoting the use of new managerial tools" (Secundo et al., 2015, pp. 18–19).

This case shows that the intangible asset of intellectual capital is a managerial tool that helps universities (both public and private ones) to address this challenge. Information for the metaanalysis of this case has been taken from Leitner et al. (2014) and Secundo et al. (2015).

Why was intellectual capital needed?

The structural transformations driven by the Bologna Process oblige universities to raise new financial resources and to find new ways of accounting for their investments and expenditures. In pursuing these aims, producing knowledge has proved not to be sufficient; universities also have to position themselves strategically and identify which aspects of their knowledge production differentiate them from other universalities or similar institutions. Intellectual capital is an asset that can help in the challenge of

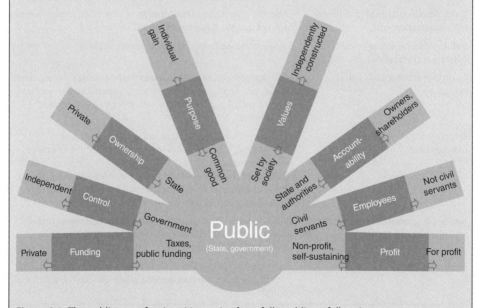

Figure 9.1 The publicness of universities varies from fully public to fully private.

identifying, measuring, and evaluating the quality of knowledge management as part of an overall management perspective.

Why is there a need for an intellectual capital model?

Within an increasingly competitive context, universities are becoming more active in the task of measuring their capacity to produce and manage knowledge distinctively. But the European High Education Area is characterized by diversity: universities differ in terms of missions, forms of governance, levels of autonomy, strategic capacities, and management processes. And in terms of intellectual capital management and report systems, a wide range of individual experiences has developed, mostly as standalone practices that lack temporal continuity (Secundo et al., 2015, p. 19). A research team supported by several public and private institutions undertook the task of exploring the similarities and differences of IC management and reporting systems developed in eight countries (Spain, Austria, Greece, Italy, Romania, Lithuania, Poland, and Latvia) to propose an IC model that allows both comparisons and flexibility with regard to individual needs and capabilities.

The IC Maturity Model (ICMM) for universities

Three principles guide the model (Secundo et al., 2015, p. 12). First, IC management systems should be introduced by considering the mission, objectives, and unique features of a specific university. Hence, universities start at different levels and proceed to the next stage at varying speeds; they may also exit the process at different stages. Second, the process is iterative rather than linear: IC measurements should be systematically integrated into decision-making processes and periodically reviewed in line with shifting strategic and operational objectives. Finally, IC management should be at the heart of strategic and operational decisions taken by the university. Therefore, adopting an IC approach transforms the whole organization.

The process consists of seven successive levels (Leitner et al., 2014; Secundo et al., 2015):

1) *Data collection*: this is the standard measurement that most universities use for accounting, management, and/or external accountability purposes (for example, number of degrees or number of staff members).
2) *Awareness of IC*: at this stage, the university becomes aware of the intangible factors that make it unique and that are difficult to imitate. These factors differ according to the university's mission, its engagement in the regional community, and its ranking at the national and international levels.
3) *Adjustment of monitoring systems*: once the objectives and scope of IC monitoring are defined, indicators and routines for data collection are reviewed so as to explicitly incorporate relevant dimensions of organizational IC.
4) *Measurement of IC*: at this level, the university will be able to propose a set of indicators to measure its intellectual capital. Measurement involves systemic collection of data in line with ex ante defined indicators.
5) *Reporting of IC*: the specific information needs of different stakeholder groups are taken into consideration when IC measures are reported. Reporting fulfills two functions: (i) to inform decision making and management and (ii) to be accountable to external stakeholders and taxpayers at large.

6) *Interpretation*: IC indicators are analyzed, interpreted, and controlled alongside other indicators for use in everyday decision making: they become an integral part of recruitment policies as well as of curricula, research agendas, and investment decisions.

7) *Strategy and planning*: the last level involves the use of information to review universities' internal processes and to redefine missions, values, objectives, and strategic plans. Universities determine their core strengths and how these should be monitored and managed to improve the institution's mission and performance.

Methods and tools used

From those suggested by Leitner et al. (2014), the following are just some examples of methods and tools used to advance the IC model:

Deviation analysis: comparison between target (planned) values and actual values; comparison between different time periods, organizational units, disciplines, or universities (benchmarking).

IC checklist: based on the assumption that the mere existence of a certain IC attribute is an indicator of high performance, when the university possesses one, it receives a positive score.

Core competencies analysis: the process of identifying strengths that are specific (and resistant to imitation) and that give a university a competitive advantage. These strengths are mostly related to the capabilities of research staff, but they also may derive from the institution's tradition (for example, universities founded in the medieval era), or they may be related to the environment (for example, location).

Process auditing: to audit is to compare gathered evidence to established requirements. From auditing, good and bad observations emerge, and these are analyzed in order to establish conclusions that can be a guide during decision making.

Examples of IC indicators

The following are just some examples of the different indicators (see Leitner et al., 2014 for the full list):

- *Input*: number of faculty members; student-to-faculty ratios (human capital); number of courses/modules taught; capital investment in research equipment (structural capital); levels of foreign students; faculty members who are graduates of other institutions (relational capital).
- *Process*: student satisfaction levels in relation to teachers, classrooms, laboratories, and libraries; average number of library visits per student (education); occupancy of laboratories; mobility of academic staff (research); university–business collaborative research projects (what the authors call "third mission").
- *Outcomes*: completion rate; average time to graduation for PhD students (education); number of peer-reviewed publications per faculty member; average number of citations per publication (research); patents granted; license and patent revenues ("third mission").

What benefits has intellectual capital provided?

Experiences collected for the elaboration of the model show that for knowledge-based organizations such as universities, intellectual capital is a helpful managerial tool that provides benefits to members of the organization and external stakeholders alike (see Leitner et al., 2014, p. 46):

For the organization

- IC helps in profiling the competitive advantage of the university: it forces the university to define and update its mission statement and to identify priorities.
- IC enhances organizational culture, as it communicates strategy throughout the organization and enables discussion of intangible value drivers and success factors; it also allows individual goals to be aligned with institutional objectives.
- IC promotes an internal process of learning about the institution's structure and performance: What is this university good at?
- IC increases strategic capacity: it links objectives to long-term targets and annual budgets.

For citizens (and other external stakeholders)

- IC reporting increases communication with funding bodies, businesses, and the public in general.
- Transparency levels are improved.
- Students, teachers, businesses, and society in general are provided with better information about the university's developments and achievements.
- Policy makers are provided with information for their decisions regarding the formulation of research programs and the evaluation of research proposals, as well as for the strategic development of the research sector as a whole.
- IC facilitates the presentation of results, thereby allowing all stakeholders to attract funding and be more competitive.
- People become aware of the extent to which universities are using, managing, sharing, and producing knowledge.

Lessons learned with regard to building intellectual capital

1) Strategic leadership is essential in tackling inertia in routines and practices, and in taking tough decisions for reallocating resources according to IC measures.

2) Since continuous efforts from the academic community are required for building IC, all university stakeholders should be aware of the benefits that this intangible asset offers.

3) Strategic planning of IC management might require the introduction of additional analytical and managerial systems.

4) The impact of IC management on universities' performance depends on the specific managerial capacities, resources, and legal and administrative frameworks. In universities with low managerial capacities, IC programs could lead to higher administrative burdens without having actual effects on performance.

5) IC builders should be aware of the dangers involved in IC programs: the possible use of IC reporting as "window dressing" for funders rather than as a facilitator of learning processes; reluctance from universities based on an unwillingness to make their weaknesses visible; possible use of IC programs for internal politics.

6) Universities have to be selective in defining their goals and not attempt to be distinctive by boasting many strengths.

7) Universities have to define the most relevant measures that express their specific goals and strategies.

8) In choosing indicators, universities have to be guided by the impact that IC has on output. This implies taking into account the cost of their production, their lifetime, and their impact on learning and leadership.

9) As is the case for all organizations, the success of universities depends on how visible their knowledge production is.

9.8 Route Guide to Building Intellectual Capital

1) **Identify the sources of your intellectual capital in all areas**
   Questions to ask: Where, who, and what are the sources for knowledge production in this organization? What parts of our structure produce knowledge (systems, software, policies, and so forth)? To what extent do our employees have/produce knowledge? What is the relational capacity of our organization?

2) **Assess the capacity of your organization to share knowledge:** Explore the relationship between your organizational elements and the performance of knowledge sharing.
   Questions to ask: Are our managers sensitive to sharing knowledge? Do we have the required technology to undertake knowledge-sharing processes? Are people trained in sharing knowledge?

3) **Identify obstructions to knowledge sharing and eliminate them**
   Questions to ask: Who or what is impeding knowledge to be shared? Is it a matter of structures, skills, or culture? What can be done to eliminate these barriers, or at least to reduce their harm?

4) **Assess your capacity to systematize knowledge**
   Questions to ask: Are our routines codified? Is information about our processes clear to all the employees who have a stake in them?

5) **Decide whether to enter the league**
   Questions to ask: Do we want to be part of the rankings of intellectual capital in our sector? If so, undertake the subsequent steps.

6) **Ensure you have the data**
   Questions to ask: Do we collect and process the data that will be needed to elaborate IC indicators?

7) **Choose the distinctive attributes of your intellectual capital**
   Questions to ask: What is our knowledge useful for? What are we strong at? What do we do well?

8) **Choose the indicators to measure your intellectual capital**
   Questions to ask: What are the indicators that best measure our distinctiveness? Which indicators from those in the sector are helpful?

9) **Analyze IC measures for strategic planning**
   Questions to ask: What have we achieved? How far are we from our goals? How do we behave in comparison to others? What subsequent measures should we adopt?

10) **Report your IC measure and make sure your IC is visible**
    Questions to ask: Do our stakeholders know what makes our knowledge distinctive? Are our IC values displayed? Do we use our IC values to tell people who we are and what our purpose is?

References

Bossi Queiroz, A., Fuertes Callén, Y., and Serrano Cinca, C. (2001). El capital intelectual en el sector público. In: II Congreso de la Asociación Española de Contabilidad Directa 4-6 July. León, Spain.

Bossi Queiroz, A., Fuertes Callén, Y., and Serrano Cinca, C. (2005). Reflexiones en torno a la aplicación del capital intelectual en el sector público. *Spanish Journal of Finance and Accounting/Revista Española de Financiación y Contabilidad* **34** (124): 211–245.

Bueno Campos, E., Salmador, M.P., and Merino, C. (2006). Towards a model of intellectual capital in public administrations. *International Journal of Learning and Intellectual Capital* **3** (3): 214–232.

Caba, C. and Sierra, M. (2003). La evaluación del capital intelectual en la administración local. *Auditoría Pública: Revista de Los Organos Autónomos de Control Externo* **29** (abril): 32–41.

Canibano, L., Garcia-Ayuso, M., Sanchez, P.M., and Olea, M. (1999). Measuring intangibles to understand and improve innovation management. In: *OECD Symposium on Measuring and Reporting of Intellectual Capital: Experience, Issues and Prospects*, 1–24.

Dumay, J., Guthrie, J., and Puntillo, P. (2015). Intellectual capital and public sector: a structured literature review. *Journal of Intellectual Capital* **16** (2): 267–284.

Dumay, J. (2016). A critical reflection on the future of intellectual capital: from reporting to disclosure. *Journal of Intellectual Capital* **17** (1): 168–184.

Edvinsson, L. and Sullivan, P. (1996). Developing a model for managing intellectual capital. *European Management Journal* **14** (4): 356–364.

Edvinsson, L. and Malone, M.S. (1997). *Intellectual Capital: Realizing your Company's True Value by Finding its Hidden Brainpower*. New York: Harper Business.

Sveiby, K.E. (1997). The intangible assets monitor. *Journal of Human Resource Costing and Accounting* **2** (1): 73–97.

Euroforum (1998). *Medición del Capital Intelectual: Modelo Intelect*. San Lorenzo del Escorial: Instituto Unviersitario Euroforum Escorial.

European Commission. (2006). "RICARDIS: reporting intellectual capital to augment research, development and innovation in SMEs." http://ec.europa.eu/invest-in-research/policy/capital_report_en.htm (accessed 26 September 2017).

Ferenhof, H.A., Durst, S., Zaniboni Bialecki, M., and Selig, P.M. (2015). Intellectual capital dimensions: state of the art in 2014. *Journal of Intellectual Capital* **16** (1): 58–100.

Garcia Arrieta, M. (2001). La información contable de los activos intangibles. Unpublished Ph.D. thesis. Madrid: University of San Pablo CEU Madrid.

Grasenick, K. and Low, J. (2004). Shaken, not stirred: defining and connecting indicators for the measurement and valuation of intangibles. *Journal of Intellectual Capital* **5** (2): 268–281.

Guthrie, J. and Dumay, J. (2015). New frontiers in the use of intellectual capital in the public sector. *Journal of Intellectual Capital* **16** (2): 258–266.

Guthrie, J., Ricceri, F., and Dumay, J. (2012). Reflections and projections: a decade of intellectual capital accounting research. *The British Accounting Review* **44** (2): 68–82.

Jones, N.B. and Mahon, J.F. (2012). Nimble knowledge transfer in high velocity/turbulent environments. *Journal of Knowledge Management* **16** (5): 774–788.

Kaplan, R.S. and Norton, D.P. (1992). The balanced scorecard: measures that drive performance. *Harvard Business Review* **70** (1): 71–79.

Kaplan, R.S. and Norton, D.P. (2000). Having trouble with your strategy? Then map it. *Harvard Business Review* **78** (5): 167–176.

Kong, E. and Thomson, S.B. (2009). An intellectual capital perspective of human resource strategies and practices. *Knowledge Management Research and Practice* **7** (4): 356–364.

Laskari, T., Kostagiolas, P., and Kefis, V. (2016). *An Intellectual Capital Perspective for Good Governance of the Public Sector*. In C. Bagnoli, C. Mio, A. Garlatti, and M. Massaro (Eds.), ECIC 2016 8th European Conference on Intellectual Capital. Venice: ACPI.

Leitner, K.H., Elena-Perez, S., Fazlagic, J., and Kalemis, K. (2014). *A Strategic Approach for Intellectual Capital Management in European Universities: Guidelines for Implementation*. Bucharest: UEFISCDI.

Lev, B. and Daum, J.H. (2004). The dominance of intangible assets: consequences for enterprise management and corporate reporting. *Measuring Business Excellence* **8** (1): 6–17.

Mačerinskienė, I. and Aleknavičiūtė, R. (2015). Comparative evaluation of national intellectual capital measurement models. *Business: Theory and Practice/Verslas: Teorija Ir Praktika* **16** (1): 1–14.

OECD (1999). Measuring and reporting intellectual capital, OECD, Amsterdam. www.oecd.org (accessed 15 September 2017).

Petty, R. and Guthrie, J. (2000). Intellectual capital literature review: measurement, reporting and management. *Journal of Intellectual Capital* **1** (2): 155–176.

Ramírez, Y., Manzaneque, M., and Priego, A.M. (2017). Formulating and elaborating a model for the measurement of intellectual capital in Spanish public universities. *International Review of Administrative Sciences* **83** (1): 149–176.

Ramirez, Y. (2010). Intellectual capital models in Spanish public sector. *Journal of Intellectual Capital* **11** (2): 248–264.

Sánchez, M.P. (2008). Papel de los intangibles y el capital intelectual en la creación y difusión del conocimiento en las organizaciones. Situación actual y retos de futuro. *Arbor* **184** (732): 575–594.

Sarmiento, G. and Roman, I. (2011). Propuesta de un modelo de capital intelectual para medir y gestionar los intangibles de las entidades públicas. In: Proceeding of XVI Conference AECA, Granada, 21, 22 y 23 de septiembre de 2011. Retrieved from http://www.aeca1.org/pub/on_line/comunicaciones_xvicongresoaeca/cd/77f.pdf.

Secundo, G., Elena, S., Martinaitis, Z., and Leitner, K.-H. (2015). An intellectual capital maturity model (ICMM) to improve strategic management in European universities: a dynamic approach. *Journal of Intellectual Capital* **16** (2): 419–442.

Serrano Cinca, C., Molinero, C.M., and Bossi Queiroz, A. (2003). The measurement of intangible assets in public sector using scaling techniques. *Journal of Intellectual Capital* **4** (2): 249–275.

Stewart, T.A. (1997). *Intellectual Capital: The New Wealth of Organisations*. London: Doubleday-Currency.

Sveiby, K.E. (1998). Intellectual capital: thinking ahead. *Australian Certified Practising Accountants* **68** (5): 18–23.

Syed-Ikhsan, S.O.S. and Rowland, F. (2004). Knowledge management in a public organization: a study on the relationship between organizational elements and the performance of knowledge transfer. *Journal of Knowledge Management* **8** (2): 95–111.

Vagnoni, E. and Oppi, C. (2015). Investigating factors of intellectual capital to enhance achievement of strategic goals in a university hospital setting. *Journal of Intellectual Capital* **16** (2): 331–363.

Wall, A. (2005). The measurement and management of intellectual capital in the public sector. *Public Management Review* **7** (2): 289–303.

10

Engagement

> *Not to engage in the pursuit of ideas is to live like ants instead of like men*
> (Mortimer Adler, American Philosopher,
> https://www.brainyquote.com/quotes/quotes/m/mortimerad110442.html)

Globally, citizen engagement has become a central aim for public administration policy and practice, on the assumption that involving those who are served is vital for a blooming society (Tam, 1998; Carpini, 2004; Fung, 2015). "Engagement" has emerged as a mechanism for public sector organizations to better understand their citizens' wants, needs, and expectations and, therefore, to connect with them in a more collaborative manner (Holmes, 2011; Bowden et al., 2016).

The body of literature on engagement and related terms is huge, and in order to narrow the focus of this chapter, we set out from a simple classification: there is literature that focuses on the citizen side, analyzing what it is and what it means to be engaged (for example, in terms of mental process, expressions, causes, and effects); and there is literature that focuses on the organizational side, describing and analyzing the specific actions that public authorities undertake in order to engage citizens. Since this book is focused on intangible assets built by public sector organizations, this chapter is based on this second group of studies. Nevertheless, the first group is briefly reviewed in order to establish some basic conceptual boundaries.

10.1 What Citizen Engagement Is About

Engagement is the act of engaging or the state of being engaged; definitions from different dictionaries refer to the idea of agreement, obligation, interlocking, and mutuality. Imported to the organizational world, the idea of involvement is the one that has predominated. Roughly speaking, to say that organizations engage means that they manage to get others involved in something.

10.1.1 Looking at Engagement from the Citizen Side

The roots of citizen engagement in the public sector context lie in civic and political engagement. The term "civic" implies that engagement occurs in the public sphere

Public Sector Communication: Closing Gaps Between Citizens and Public Organizations, First Edition.
María-José Canel and Vilma Luoma-aho.

instead of in the private lives of citizens (Dahlgren, 2009, p. 58). The term also signifies the public good and conveys a sense of the altruistic and of services for the good of others. Political and policy engagement, on the other hand, is reserved for activities oriented toward influencing governmental action in some way (Theiss-Morse and Hibbing, 2005; Dahlgren, 2009; Halpin and Thomas, 2012). Civic engagement is a broader construct consisting of forms of voluntary activities aimed at solving problems in the community and helping others. These two types of engagement are interrelated, as civic engagement can be seen as a precondition for political engagement to occur. In fact, some describe democratic engagement as consisting of both political engagement and civic engagement (Carpini, 2004).

One of the major debates about defining civic engagement relates to the scope of the content and terms of the relationship that the act of engagement entails. A definition grounded in the notions of the individual and the community is provided by Adler and Goggin: "Civic engagement describes how an active citizen participates in the life of a community in order to improve conditions for others or to help shape the community's future" (Adler and Goggin, 2005, p. 241). Amnå states that this definition may excessively narrow down the focus so that it primarily concerns local issues and, also, that it places too much weight on measurable activities (Amnå, 2012, p. 613).

Bole and Gordon (2009) elaborate on a broader conceptualization of civic engagement, relying on Levine's (2007) consideration that community participation, political engagement, and political voice are overlapping themes in civic engagement. The intersection of these three elements, they suggest, goes well beyond commonly held conceptions of participating solely in electoral cycles. Civic engagement, Levine states, consists of "any action that legitimately influences public matters in ways that benefit the underlying political structure" (pp. 7–8). But "public matters," Bole and Gordon argue, refer to what is not privately owned, including the distribution of goods and resources in society as well as laws and norms prohibiting particular behaviors. This definition, therefore, challenges the tendency to equate civic life with voting behavior (Bole and Gordon, 2009, p. 276).

Definitions of civic engagement also relate to deliberative actions and how they might affect political actions. According to Cooper, civic engagement entails "people participating together for deliberation and collective action within an array of interests, institutions and networks, developing civic identity, and involving people in governance processes" (Cooper, 2005, p. 534).

Whether they focus on voting behavior, helping others, or influencing public matters, all the definitions reviewed here so far describe engagement in terms of what a citizen does.

10.1.2 Engagement from the Organization Side: The Role of Public Administrations in Engaging Citizens

Public administrations have undertaken different actions to engage citizens and make them participate in different organizational forms. Such initiatives have been based on a wide range of topics and problem areas.

To address the study and analysis of these actions, it is of use to turn to the distinction made by Wang and Wart (2007) between "political participation" and "public participation." Political participation, they say, is public involvement in expressing preferences on a broad spectrum of policies at national, regional, or local levels, though mainly during the process of selecting political representatives. These actions refer not only to the central executive level but also extend to the parliamentary and judicial spheres. Participation in administration is public involvement in administrative processes and decision-making; actions take many different formats and occur on a continual basis, and they mainly take place at the executive level (for example, public services). Public participation is thus defined as "direct or indirect public involvement in articulation or evaluation of administrative objectives, service levels, administrative guidelines, and overall results" (p. 268). It is this second type of participation which opens up wider areas for building engagement as an intangible asset in the public sector.

Somewhat similar to Wang and Wart's definition is the distinction made by Yang and Pandey (2011), who, turning to other authors, differentiate public participation (the role of the public in the process of administrative decision making) from citizen participation (efforts to influence the administrative decisions of policy-implementing agencies).

These distinctions are useful to stress the idea that as an intangible asset in the public sector, the aspect of engagement that is of interest is that related to how public sector organizations can have an impact in encouraging citizens to participate in administrative decision-making processes.

Several terms are used in the literature to refer to what public authorities do to engage citizens (this is not an exhaustive list): "collaborative citizenship" (Smith, 2010), "community engagement"(Head, 2008), "collaborative governance" (Sirianni, 2010), "citizen-centered collaborative public management" (Cooper, 2005), "coproduction" (Bovaird, 2007; Bovaird and Loeffler, 2009, 2012; Brandsen and Honingh, 2015; Bovaird, Van Ryzin, and Loeffler, 2015), and "citizen involvement efforts" (Yang and Callahan, 2005, 2007; Heikkila and Isett, 2007; Yang and Pandey, 2011).

The literature also considers the different formats that governmental actions can adopt, as well as the different purposes (Thomas, 1995; Roberts, 2004; Marlowe Jr. and Arrington-Marlowe, 2005; Glaser, Yeager, and Parker, 2006; Head, 2007). Open public meetings and hearings have been the predominant format that legislation has required, but other forms without a statutory basis are the use of citizen advisory committees or special task forces to identify community needs and interests and to solicit recommendations to meet those needs. Surveys, group interviews, and panels are other formal methods for collecting information from citizens. More informal methods include calling up key contacts or community leaders to assess community needs and opinions or sending agency representatives to attend meetings of community groups.

Undertakings by public authorities can have different aims and goals, and the typology provided by the International Association for Public Participation (IAPP) includes a list of purposes that are graded based on the extent to which decision making is left to citizens: public organizations might aim to inform, consult, involve, collaborate with, or empower citizens (see IAPP's table reproduced in Head, 2007, p. 445).

10.2 Going Deeper into Public Sector Engagement

In this section, we deal in detail with the labels most commonly used in addressing the actions undertaken by public sector organizations: "citizen involvement efforts" and "coproduction." These labels are not mutually exclusive; they overlap and refer to similar phenomena with different nuances. They have been created to embrace new developments and variants of governmental actions aimed at engaging citizens.

10.2.1 Governmental Efforts to Involve Citizens

The literature on public administration pays great attention to engagement from the perspective of the efforts made by public authorities to involve citizens (Yang and Callahan, 2005, 2007; Heikkila and Isett, 2007; Yang and Pandey, 2011). But there is an important distinction in terms of the actions that they attempt to involve citizens in. The term "citizen involvement efforts" refers to "activities initiated by government to encourage citizen participation in administrative decision making and managerial processes" (Yang and Callahan, 2007, p. 249). Actions occur primarily at the interface of administrators and citizens; they differ from political participation such as voting in elections, contacting elected officials, and campaigning for political candidates; and they also differ from civic engagement, which can take many forms, from individual volunteerism to organizational involvement and electoral participation. Public managers have discretion over decisions regarding when and how citizen involvement is initiated and structured, and they influence the structure and meaning of citizen–government interactions by the decisions that they make.

The framework that Yang and Callahan (2005) use to analyze citizen involvement efforts gives a thorough overview of the purposes, activities, and formats that these efforts can involve and a list of subjects who can undertake them. The purposes are the objectives and outcomes to be accomplished, and they include determining community priorities, planning on a strategic level, clarifying programs' goals and objectives, developing strategies to achieve goals, developing programs and policy alternatives, negotiating budgets, making personnel recommendations, measuring performance, and evaluating program achievement. The range of activities or formats that can be undertaken includes public hearings, citizen advisory boards/committees, community/neighborhood committees, citizen surveys, citizen focus groups, and issue-oriented committees. Finally, the list of subjects (units of government and functional areas) to which the actions can refer includes budgeting, personnel, purchasing, zoning and planning, parks and recreation, policing and public safety, code enforcement, street maintenance, and garbage collection/recycling, among others.

10.2.2 Deepening Engagement: The Coproduction Perspective

Coproduction has become a vibrant area of research and practice (Bovaird, 2007; Alford, 2009; Bovaird and Loeffler, 2009, 2012; Brandsen and Honingh, 2015; Bovaird et al., 2015), and it has proved to be a fruitful development in engaging citizens in relation to different areas such as health, urban services, and education, to mention just a few. Roughly defined, it is a practice in the delivery of public services in which citizens are involved in both the creation (design) and the implementation of public policies and services.

The major assumption of coproduction is that public services' users can provide good (or even the best) input for public services. For instance, in a neighborhood, nobody is better than its residents at providing information to the police for the purposes of crime prevention. Coproduction implies a reinterpretation of the role of policy-making and service delivery in the public domain, such that they are no longer one-way processes – the preserve of policy planners, professional managers, and top decision makers – but are rather the negotiated outcome of many interacting policy systems, decisions, and outcomes that are also shaped by the community (Bovaird, 2007, p. 847).

According to Bovaird and Loeffler (2012, p. 1122), the genesis of coproduction of public services goes back to the 1980s. It was a reaction to the limitations of traditional "provider-centric" models, and it sought to afford a larger role to customer service, user research, quality assurance, and competition among providers. Today, it has become widely accepted that services operate in multisector contexts and generally require inputs from both professionals and users to be fully effective (Bovaird et al., 2015). In parallel to the academic debate, coproduction has increasingly come onto the agenda of policy-makers (Brandsen and Honingh, 2015, p. 427).

However, since the seminal formulation provided by Ostrom ("The process through which inputs used to produce a good or service are contributed by individuals who are not 'in' the same organization"; Ostrom, 1996, p. 1073), the definition of coproduction has evolved in a way that shows relevant outcomes for its consideration as an intangible asset. In 2007, Bovaird defined user and community coproduction of public services as "the provision of services through regular, long-term relationships between professionalized service providers (in any sector) and service users or other members of the community, where all parties make substantial resource contributions" (p. 847). Together with other colleagues (Bovaird and Loeffler, 2012; Bovaird et al., 2015), Bovaird builds on the definition provided by Governance International ("The public sector and citizens making better use of each other's assets and resources to achieve better outcomes or improved efficiency"; Governance International 2011, cited in Bovaird and Loeffler, 2012, p. 1121) to stress the relational aspect of coproduction. Based on two criteria (whether the outcomes are collectively enjoyed and whether the inputs are collectively supplied), they define *collective coproduction* as the *joint* action of citizens to support services and achieve outcomes, while *individual coproduction* covers those actions *not jointly* undertaken. Collective coproduction can arise from individual self-interest (for example, that of service clients, volunteers, or other involved citizens), other motives such as general altruism, or specific concerns for particular groups or social causes.

In 2015, Brandsen and Honingh (2015) attempted to establish a definitional consensus by trying to clarify different types of coproduction, and they provide a revised definition that reads as follows:

> "Coproduction is a relationship between a paid employee of an organization and (groups of) individual citizens that requires a direct and active contribution from these citizens to the work of the organization" (p. 431).

With this proposal, they seek to make explicit that (i) coproduction is a relation between the employees of an organization and individual citizens; (ii) coproduction requires direct and active inputs from these citizens in relation to the work of the organization (passive receipt of services is thus not coproduction); and (iii) the professional is a paid employee of the organization, whereas the citizen receives compensation below market value or no compensation at all.

Coproduction can take a variety of forms, depending on the criteria based on which coproduction activities are classified. According to Brudney and England, there are *individual, group* and *collective* forms of coproduction (Brudney and England, 1983, pp. 63–64). Depending on the phase at which it occurs, coproduction may be termed *complementary coproduction in service design and implementation*, in which citizens are engaged in coproduction related to tasks that are complementary to the core process rather than part of it. *Complementary coproduction in implementation* occurs when citizens are actively engaged in the implementation, but not the design, of a complementary task. Examples of it include students who assist their university in organizing welcome days and parents who help to prepare school plays. *Coproduction in the design and implementation of core services* is a situation in which citizens are directly involved in producing the core services of an organization and in both the design and implementation of the individual service provided to them. An example of this type of coproduction is postgraduate training modules in which participants, together with instructors, define their own learning objectives and learning activities. *Coproduction in the implementation of core services* occurs when citizens are actively engaged in the implementation, but not the design, of an individual service that is at the core of the organization. Examples are children's education in which students follow strictly defined lessons but, nevertheless, provide input that is crucial to effective learning, and enforced services such as mandatory employment reintegration.

The typology of formats suggested by Bovaird (2007) is useful because it indicates a wide variety of coproduction types and specifies the role of different actors (for example, professionals, service users, and the nonprofessional community), the relationships that coproduction establishes among them, and the different stages at which the coproduction takes place (for example, service planning and service delivery). This typology contains the following kinds of coproduction:

- Traditional professional service provision with user and community consultation on service planning and design issues: services are delivered by professionals, but the planning and design stages closely involve users and community members. Examples: participatory budgeting (in which community members can influence the annual budget cycle of a public service or agency); parent governors of schools with power over strategy.
- User codelivery of professionally designed services: professionals dictate the design and planning of the service, and users and community members deliver the service. Example: direct payments to users in care services who can then purchase professional care.
- Full user-professional coproduction: users and professionals fully share the task of planning and designing the service, and they then deliver it. Examples: neighborhood watch schemes in which local residents work with police and local authorities to raise vigilance against crime and tackle antisocial behavior.
- User-community codelivery of services with professionals, without formal planning or design processes: users and community groups take responsibility for undertaking activities but call on professional service expertise when needed. Example: local associations that specialize in leisure activities such as music, sports, and cultural trips and call on professional help only when organizing special events.
- User-community sole delivery of professionally planned services: users and other community members take responsibility for delivering services planned by professionals. Example: volunteers who are trained to deliver professionally designed counseling services on an anonymous basis to individuals who are considering suicide.
- User-community sole delivery of coplanned or codesigned services: users or other community members deliver services that they also partly plan and design. Examples: contract services undertaken by local community groups that are under contract to

public agencies (for instance, for the maintenance of housing estates or cleaning of community centers).
- Traditional self-organized community provision. Examples: children's playgroups, school breakfast clubs, and local festivals.

The idea of coproduction points to many different ways of fostering citizen involvement that are applicable to ongoing citizen needs, go beyond voting in elections and other political expressions, and permeate citizens' daily life more broadly. Since the improvement of the service is the result of joint efforts and only happens if both sides get something out of it, coproduction implies a benefit for both sides.

10.3 Why Is Engagement Needed?

Before examining the outcomes of engagement, a prior description of its context is required to explain why engagement has become a topic of interest in the public sector.

10.3.1   The Context for an Increasing Concern with and Practice of Citizen Engagement

The origin of the term described above highlights a decrease in rates in participation as the trigger for debates on engagement. Leaving aside the debate on whether people, particularly the young, are opting for other ways to become involved in politics (Prentice, 2007; Bole and Gordon, 2009; Dahlgren, 2009; Milner, 2010; Ekman and Amnå, 2012; Denhardt and Denhardt, 2015), there seems to be a consensus in the literature about a decrease in all measures that gauge relations between citizens and public organizations and, in particular, in those focused on citizen trust. The decline of trust in government is frequently considered one of the most important problems faced by the public sector today (Wang and Wart, 2007, p. 265), and it is not unreasonable to argue that a more engaged citizen would have greater trust in public sector organizations.

Recent changes with regard to citizen expectations, which were discussed in the first part of this book, have necessitated a reconceptualization of citizen engagement. These include changing citizen communication needs, motivations, and expectations; preferred types of participation; and cynicism toward public organizations. These societal changes have provided an opportunity to reconsider the specific implications of the implementation of citizen engagement programs and actions in the public sector.

The literature also confirms a worldwide trend toward increased governmental actions to engage citizens (Head, 2007; Coursey, Yang, and Pandey, 2012; Denhardt and Denhardt, 2015). Reasons for this increase vary and include international trends in governance and political economy; the availability of improved communications technologies; the need to share responsibility for resolving complex issues; and the local politics of managing social, economic, and environmental projects (Head, 2008, p. 441).

10.3.2   What Specific Gaps Does Engagement Help to Bridge?

Engagement has been proposed as one way in which to close the gap between the one-directional and static nature of traditional public sector communication, on the one hand,

and the need to more effectively meet citizens' needs and changing expectations, on the other. Engagement is viewed as an important objective for public administrations, since the ultimate goal of democracy is to have engaged citizens (Carpini, 2004; Head, 2007; Smith, 2010; Amnå, 2012). In fact, the value of engagement lies in its understanding of dialogue dynamics and enabled participation.

Engagement as a construct actually brings the relationship between citizens and public organizations to a more equal level. Instead of a setting in which officials and authorities dictate their will, in the current highly networked and citizen-empowered environment, modern public administrations and public sector organizations have to interact with citizens in various and diverse forums of citizen interest. They are also required to deal with issue arenas both within and outside of their control (Luoma-aho and Vos, 2009).

10.4 Outcomes of Engagement: Calibrating Its Value as an Intangible Asset

As we have argued throughout this book, an intangible asset enables access to tangible assets, giving rise to a resource from which a future (long-term) benefit (social, monetary, and so forth) is expected to flow for the organization as well as for stakeholders and citizens.

But what resources are generated by engagement, what value do they have, and for which stakeholders do they have value? Responding to this question is a complex endeavor, because it entails an overall assessment of the huge volume of literature that looks at the different variety of actions and formats related to public sector organizations. Complexity is also created by the fact that research has associated engagement with different types of resources such as dialogue, participation, capacity, and citizen empowerment, as well with other intangibles such as social capital, legitimacy, and trust. Calibrating each of these resources entails different angles, frameworks, methods, and indicators. Finally, it has to be taken into account that measuring the impact of engagement requires the caveats that stem from the fact that different studies and analyses come from different contexts, time frames, and cultural settings and that their findings are not always transferrable.

Therefore, what follows is a synthesis of major ideas regarding what is known so far about what engagement provides. We limit our description to the type of engagement actions that we have described above, namely those related to the participation and involvement of citizens in administrative processes, and hence we disregard citizens' political involvement and participation. The focus of this section is on the resource (and the associated benefit) that engagement provides and whether it is for one side (and which one) or for both sides – that is, for citizens and the organization.

10.4.1 A General Positive Assessment of the Impact of Engagement

As a starting point, we should mention that it has been stated that engagement has positive effects. Denhardt and Denhardt (2015) answer with a "resounding yes" the question of the effect of engagement (a question that they word as follows: "Have citizen engagement strategies been used and resulted in benefits to citizens and communities?"). An increase in engagement programs and actions led these authors to state that the argument for increased citizen involvement continues to gain ground and to support

Roberts's statement that "citizen engagement is no longer hypothetical: it is very real, and public administrators are central to its evolution" (cited in Denhardt and Denhardt, 2015, p. 666). Many countries have seen an increase in engagement programs and governmental attempts to develop dialogue and to interact with citizens, to such an extent that the question is no longer how citizen involvement can be made to work but rather what its results are (Coursey et al., 2012, p. 572).

If taken in terms of citizen participation in administrative processes, an increasing proportion of the literature documents the positive outcomes arising from the direct involvement of citizens in the assessment of needs and in deliberation about practical solutions (Adams and Hess, 2001; Head, 2008, p. 449). Based on a literature review, Yang and Pandey (2011) argue that citizen involvement has great value. In their view, it fosters citizenship values, enhances accountability, improves trust in government, maintains legitimacy, and helps to achieve better decisions and to build consensus (see also Coursey, Yang, and Pandey, 2012). Support has also been mentioned as a resource that stems from citizen involvement, as have social capital and an increased capacity to resolve problems (Heikkila and Isett, 2007).

Therefore, based on this review of literature, it can be said first of all that the following resources have been shown to be associated with engagement in its various forms: capacity, support, dialogue, consensus, social cohesion, accountability, and legitimacy.

10.4.2 More Mixed Evidence that Cannot Be Disregarded

However, the picture would be incomplete without an acknowledgment of the more mixed evidence contained in the literature. Most of the studies and analyses of practical cases reveal some sort of deficiency: sometimes no benefit is evidenced, sometimes the benefit gained is not the one expected, and sometimes there is a benefit, but it is accompanied by an associated negative boomerang effect. Therefore, a second conclusion of a review of the literature is that there is room for doubt about the impact that engagement has.

Appearing most frequently on the list of negative effects is the cost of engagement actions (to be more precise, of coproduction actions). Such initiatives can be costly (Thomas, 1995), and although major improvements in outcomes (for instance, enhanced service quality or significant cost savings) can be achieved, they require resources. Coproduction, for example, may offer "'value for money,' but it usually cannot produce value without money" (Bovaird and Loeffler, 2012, p. 1137). High costs have made professionals reluctant to consider coproduction based on the view that they will have to bear all of them (Bovaird, 2007).

A second problem is the clash of values that coproduction actions may entail: some stakeholders have conflicting values and differential levels of power, so outcomes of self-organizing processes around coproduction are not always socially desirable (Bovaird, 2007, p. 857). Moreover, it seems to be the case that coproduction involves greater risks than professionalized service provision (though this issue has not yet been properly explored), and it is not yet fully understood how the quality of services can be assured more successfully through involving users (Bovaird and Loeffler, 2012).

In terms of distribution of power, there has been some skepticism as to whether these actions result in actual involvement of citizens or whether they are in fact the result of state-directed outsourcing and state-controlled devolution (Rhodes, 2003; Head, 2007; Head, 2008).

10.4.3 Engagement Effects for the Organization: The Managerial Side

Engagement has been shown to produce benefits for the organization. Citizen involvement, including the collaboration of groups across a spectrum of interests, has been revealed to be vital for resolving community-based issues such as the micropolitics of conflict related to service provision, land-use planning, and infrastructure projects (Hemmati, 2002; Innes and Booher, 2004).

With regard to coproduction, evidence shows that it provides an important integrating mechanism that brings together a wide variety of stakeholders in the public domain (Bovaird, 2007). Engagement is also of value for the organization when addressing deep and complex problems, for which broader civic participation in deliberative processes that consider important social issues have been highly recommended (Dryzek, 2000; Fung, 2003, cited in Head, 2008, p. 449).

10.4.4 Benefit for Both Sides: The Cobenefit of Coproduction

Coproduction is probably the engagement action that best fits the idea that an intangible asset entails benefits for both sides. Coproduction has been found to be "a key driver for improving publicly valued outcomes" (Bovaird and Loeffler, 2012, p. 1136), and not only value for the organizations.

In this respect, the contributions of Bovaird and his colleagues are particularly relevant. After reviewing a long and thematically broad list of cases, Bovaird (2007) concludes that to the extent that coproduction goes beyond the "services performed on users" approach, it opens wider choices up to users by exploring mechanisms for active experience of service; that in the respect that both parties contribute resources and have a legitimate voice, coproduction may transfer some power from professionals to users; and that it may even mobilize community resources that would not otherwise be available. (Bovaird uses as examples the word-of-mouth pressure by citizens to encourage reluctant fellow parents to participate in immunization campaigns and the peer pressure that residents exert on one another to cooperate and comply with regulations such as land-use planning controls.) There is also a benefit for both parties in terms of the division of risk that mutual relationships between service users and professionals entail. In a later article that reviews more recent cases, Bovaird and Loeffler (2012) argue that coproduction produces not only user value but also social and environmental value as well as value to wider groups; it is also likely to be particularly valuable where there is a need to trigger behavior change focused on prevention of future problems (Bovaird and Loeffler, 2012).

Finally, coproduction has been shown to produce benefit for both sides to the extent that it enhances relationships, but research shows that these relationships might need the intervention of communication to go in the right direction. Exploring the extent of collective coproduction as compared to individual coproduction, Bovaird et al. (2015) found that citizens generally show high levels of engagement when they can undertake activities that do not need much effort or interaction with third parties (for example, locking doors and windows in their home before going out, recycling household rubbish, and saving water and electricity). They conclude that more imaginative and attractive methods will need to be found to convince citizens to reorient their coproduction activities toward more collective action. Finally, given that individual coproduction is likely to rise when government performance is perceived as poor, communication is needed to guide citizens who have become engaged out of anger and frustration so that they feel greater support for the state.

10.5   Building and Communicating Engagement

What role does communication play in enhancing engagement? Since coproduction and citizen involvement stem from relationships between citizens and professionals (civil servants) who make reciprocal use of each other's strengths, communication is a prerequisite for bringing about engagement: it is only by communication that the required mutual understanding can be advanced.

This implies profound transformations in communication and public policy management, insofar as the whole idea of fostering citizen involvement goes hand in hand with a certain, specific, segmented, and accurate knowledge of what citizens need and look for. Different types of coproduction can be implemented by public managers if there is an in-depth knowledge of the degree to which citizens are involved in the design of services that they individually receive (Brandsen and Honingh, 2015). With little information on what most citizens are interested in, public organizations will find it hard to make attractive targeted offers. Public managers need to work on ways to obtain information from the public and make them feel confident about the role that they can play in public administration processes (Bovaird and Loeffler, 2012).

Building engagement requires the whole organization to be focused and motivated, and this not only profoundly transforms the style and approach, but even requires a new public service ethos, in which the central role of public managers is to support, encourage, and coordinate citizens' capabilities. Bovaird (2007) goes as far as to advocate a new type of public service professional, whom he calls the "coproduction development officer" and who "can help to overcome the reluctance of many professionals to share power with users and their communities and can act internally in organizations (and partnerships) to broker new roles for coproduction between traditional service professionals, service managers, and the political decision makers who shape the strategic direction of the service system" (p. 858).

Engagement, therefore, entails new changes in organizational structures so that they include officers who are equipped and qualified to undertake these practices. In this sense, Ramsey (2015) provides a revealing case in his analysis of how an engagement office transformed central government communication in the United Kingdom under Tony Blair's New Labour government. Engagement action, he explains, involves gaining profound insights into what motivates people, and thus government communication must undertake a new mission: to help the government understand and respond to what people want and need, and to help people find what they want and need from government. Therefore, Ramsey argues, government communication must be adapted so that its agenda is set by societal trends. Engagement-focused communication demands more attention, and approached in this way, government communication should be attributed a significance that is similar to that for other areas of government expenditure.

Finally, there are also important transformations at the level of qualification and practices. To be focused on building engagement, public managers need to revisit the conceptualization of the roles that they and the public should play in public services and assume the three principal roles relative to government: as customers, as citizens, and as partners. Understanding how to work with the public in all three roles, Thomas argues, should be within the abilities of most public managers (Thomas, 2013). Yang and Callahan (2007) suggest certain strategies and practices to improve citizen involvement efforts. These include treating citizen involvement as a policy issue and involving elected officials in it, adopting a network mode of participation that includes long-term commitment from community stakeholders such as nonprofit organizations and the business community, emphasizing professionalism and cultural norms that value citizen involvement, providing training for public managers on group processes and network management skills, marketing participation opportunities to citizens, and educating citizens to become effective participants.

10.6 Summary of Engagement

Table 10.1 summarizes engagement as an intangible asset that measures the capacity of an organization to get citizens involved in public administration processes.

Table 10.1 Engagement as an intangible asset in the public sector.

Engagement is the intangible asset that measures the capacity of an organization to get citizens involved in public administration processes	
Tangible asset that engagement enables	All physical capital through providing citizen involvement
Resource that engagement generates	Capacity, support, dialogue, consensus, social cohesion, accountability, legitimacy, and trust
Monetary expression	Costs savings and procedural time savings
Value engagement provides to the organization	Conflict reduction, integration of a wide variety of stakeholders, wider support, social capital, and better distribution of resources
Value engagement provides to citizens and stakeholders	Wider choices, active experience of service, shared authority in decision-making for service users, prevention of future problems, enhanced relationships, self-efficacy, and networking
Gaps engagement bridges	The gap between the one-directional and static nature of traditional public sector communication and the need to more effectively meet citizens' needs and changing expectations; the gap between professionals and civil servants and ordinary citizens
Dependence on communication management	Since coproduction and citizen involvement stem from relationships between citizens and civil servants who make reciprocal use of each other's strengths, communication is a prerequisite for engagement to take place; it is only by communication that the required mutual understanding can be advanced
Implied organization management transformations	For an organization to be focused on engagement building, a new public service ethos is required, as are a new type of public service professional and changes to organizational structures so that they include officers and positions equipped and qualified to gain certain, specific, segmented, and accurate knowledge of what citizens need and expect and of what they are capable of
Measures	Self-reported values on engagement programs (scope, participants, outcomes, and so forth); qualitative and quantitative analysis of citizens' involvement

10.7 Case Study on Public Sector Engagement

The Public Engagement Division of US Citizenship and Immigration Services (USCIS), an agency of the US government

In 2008, President Obama's administration established the Office of Public Engagement to give citizens "a way to engage with [their] government on the issues that matter the most," thereby "making the government inclusive, transparent, accountable and responsible." The Office of Public Engagement attempted to open a two-way dialogue between the Obama administration and the American public in order ultimately to help people's concerns be translated into action by the appropriate bodies of the federal government (https://www.whitehouse.gov/engage).

To achieve this aim, the various departments of the executive branch of the federal government established an engagement unit. This case study focuses on one unit within the Department of Homeland Security: the Customer Service and Public Engagement Directorate (CSPED) within US Citizenship and Immigration Services (USCIS). Data for this case study comes from an interview with Mariela Melero, who served as the first head of USCIS's Office of Public Engagement (established in 2009) and later as the associate director of CSPED (from May 2012), and with Carlos Munoz-Acevedo, deputy chief of CSPED's Public Engagement Division.

USCIS is one of 22 agencies within the Department of Homeland Security. Among its goals is to "secure America's promise as a nation of immigrants by strengthening the security and integrity of the immigration system, providing effective customer-oriented immigration benefit and information services, granting immigration benefits, promoting awareness of U.S. citizenship" (https://www.uscis.gov/aboutus).

USCIS has 19,000 government employees and contractors working at 223 offices across the world. The head of the agency is a political appointee who is chosen by the president. The agency's funding, which was about $3.8 billion in the 2016 fiscal year, comes primarily from fees that immigrants and customers pay to have their cases processed and decided. A small percentage of the agency's funding comes from appropriated funds (tax revenue) from Congress, which are directed toward certain programs (Figure 10.1).

Building an engagement program within the immigration service

Within the context of the agency's mission to administer immigration benefits, the Public Engagement Division (PED) aims to create platforms for customers and stakeholders to voice opinions about operations and policies. To this end, it strives to create relationships with intergovernmental agencies, stakeholders, advocacy groups, and customers and "to provide clear, accurate, and timely responses to customer concerns and questions, and engage the public through transparent dialogue that promotes participation and feedback."

PED coordinates agency-wide dialogue with external stakeholders and seeks feedback from stakeholders to inform USCIS policies, priorities, and organizational performance reviews. It accomplishes this by sharing feedback with agency leadership, coordinating follow-up, and reporting back to stakeholders.

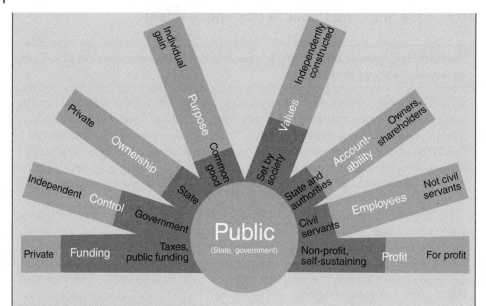

Figure 10.1 Publicness of USCIS.

Specific actions for engagement building

Working with a network of community relations officers in the field, PED undertakes daily interaction with community-based organizations; faith-based and advocacy groups; employer and employee associations; ESL/civics instructors; and international, business, and legal organizations. It also conducts regular liaison with state and local agencies, including governors; legislatures; mayoral offices; other elected and appointed officials; benefit-granting agencies; and federal, state, and local law enforcement agencies.

PED's communication with its broad base of stakeholders includes the proactive dissemination of information, updates, and invitations (pushing out) and the soliciting and gathering of feedback and opinions (pulling in). PED, as well as CSPED as a whole, uses a variety of two-way channels to accomplish this, including:

- Leveraging an email subscription management system that proactively delivers policy and program updates to subscribers through email and wireless alerts. Currently, over 35,000 people are subscribed for USCIS's GovDelivery service.
- Email and website invitations soliciting public comment on draft or proposed regulations before they are finalized.
- In-person meetings at the headquarters, regional, and district levels.
- Surveys and focus groups conducted monthly by independent contractors.
- Monthly analyses of website and social media traffic as well as of user patterns and pathways.
- Strategic use of crowdsourcing tools to gather feedback on proposed ideas.
- Conducting in-depth usability testing with real customers to refine tools, work flows, and processes to ensure customers can navigate the tools easily and get what they want from them.
- Analyzing Web metrics and customer behavior to better understand customers' needs.

Examples of engagement tools

In engagement building, designing tools hand in hand with citizens is key. In 2015, CSPED shifted gears and began using agile development, which allows for design improvements through an iterative process. This approach flips the traditional design model by seeking customer input throughout the process and basing design decisions on real user feedback and needs instead of on perceptions and assumptions. This approach helps to ensure that the tools that USCIS releases meet or surpass customer needs and expectations.

The latest suite of USCIS's customer self-help tools is housed in an online customer portal called myUSCIS. The site includes the following:

- A set of tools called Explore My Options, which allows customers to explore the immigration options that they may be eligible for, including a work permit, Green Card renewal or replacement, sponsorship of a relative, and so forth.
- A feature called Find a Class, which uses a zip-code-based locator to help people find a citizenship or English class near them.
- A service called Find a Doctor, which uses a zip-code-based locator to find designated physicians to perform the Green Card medical exam.
- An interactive set of practice civics tests, which helps naturalization applicants prepare for their interview and feel more confident.
- A tool that assesses citizenship eligibility, which helps applicants determine if they are ready and eligible to submit their application for naturalization.

The newest tool is Emma, the department's first Intelligent virtual assistant. Customers can ask Emma a question in their own words, and she will provide the answer in plain language and refer users to relevant websites where they can research the topic further. If she does not know the answer, CSPED analysts work behind the scenes to create answers to questions. Emma is the result of a cocreation process through which the agency and customers collaborate to develop content. External customers and the entire department are invited to contribute questions in their own words to form the basis for Emma's content and structure.

To develop the new online version of N-400, Application for Naturalization, CSPED collaborated with PED, community relations officers, and community-based organizations around the country to identify students in citizenship classes to test the customer experience and understand the English and technical proficiencies needed to file the prototype N-400 online. The new online N-400 resonates with users because naturalization applicants in multiple cities shared their reactions to a myriad of touchpoints, including their understanding of the English instructions and their technical proficiency in completing the online form successfully.

Based on user feedback, CSPED greatly simplified the InfoPass user interface and added Google Maps. The online civics practice test was improved by seeking customer input on ease of use, functionality, and design. Finally, to better understand the Family-Based Adjustment of Status process, the myUSCIS team applied an innovative "story harvesting" technique: after numerous interviews with potential and current applicants and their relatives, a set of design principles, assumptions, and requirements were generated to guide the development of future online tools and policies.

Impact of engagement: Achievements

USCIS interacts with hundreds of stakeholders across the country on a daily basis. In the 2016 fiscal year, USCIS held 3,973 engagements for about 185,000 people. Many participants in these engagements include attorneys, law firms, faith-based groups, advocacy organizations, and community-based organizations that represent larger audiences, and thus are considered "force multipliers."

Regarding Emma, in all, more than 135,000 people asked her questions. The result is that Emma "speaks" like an average person, and the more she is used, the smarter she gets. In fact, Emma's "I don't know" rate is less than 10% in both English and Spanish.

Overall, the daring shift to cocreate tools with customers exemplifies USCIS's core value of ingenuity, and it has earned USCIS a reputation as a public sector innovator. For instance, in 2016, several media outlets (Nextgov, Telemundo, Univision) gave Emma very positive coverage (see links to the stories below).

How has engagement proven to be important? What benefits does engagement provide?

According to the officials interviewed, "Engagement builds a freeway for policy making. It creates multiple channels for constant interaction with different publics, through which you can consult and also involve people in the decision-making process. The generated synergies are an intangible value that improves decisions for better government."

For the organization:

- In advancing a better understanding of an executive action, USCIS can anticipate how customers calibrate policy decisions before full implementation.
- Audiences' feedback helps in setting and validating agency priorities.
- Ongoing interaction allows the organization to anticipate the impact of failures or problems (for example, delays in processing applications) on customers (for example, losing jobs or opportunities to enroll in schools), and hence, it can adjust course or design interventions.
- Engagement creates better decisions by recognizing the needs of the publics and decision makers.
- With customers' feedback, USCIS can assess the performance of the organization.

"To have a better-informed customer is priceless. Engagement allows customers to know more about the process and have a better experience and complete paperwork that makes it easier for the agency to process their cases. Better completed applications lead to more timely decisions" (interview).

For citizens:

- They benefit from transparency and timely information about their processes.
- They are better equipped to understand what the end of the process could be for them.
- They can contribute to and influence the decision-making process.
- Therefore, they will be able to respond better to personal concerns (for example, "Will I be able to bring my family over? Will I be able to support my family? Will I be able to send money to the family members I left behind?").

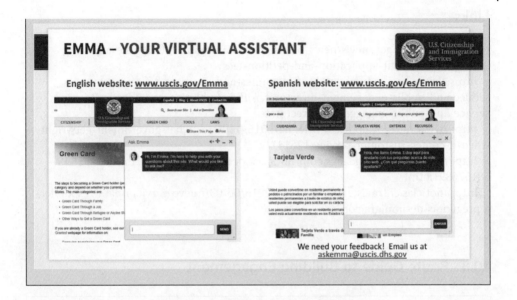

Lessons learned with regard to building engagement efforts

1) A champion is critical: the leader at the top has to believe in engagement and care deeply about it.

2) A sense of common purpose should be established: the whole organization needs to be aligned with the purpose of engaging.

3) Engagement changes the communication approach radically: it is not about pushing information out, but about soliciting input and actively engaging throughout the year, regardless of what happens in the organization. When the organization is oriented to engage, there is constant communication back and forth.

4) Strategic planning is critical. Systemic feedback collection and analytical tools help create better engagement opportunities. Being flexible is important, but engagement should not be left to chance or circumstances.

5) The organization's personnel should be trained in communication skills, listening skills, and resilience: they are going to hear things they don't like.

6) It is important to create channels for the public to have some role in the decision making in the agency and for decisions and how the public affected a decision to be communicated.

7) Connections should be established with technology departments to elaborate the technical tools that best fit the needs for two-way communication.

8) There ought to be an attempt to systematize procedures to better process and interpret feedback from the organization's stakeholders.

9) It is necessary to demonstrate that the costs of engagement efforts (especially time) are balanced by the benefits they render.

Links

https://www.uscis.gov/news/news-releases/uscis-announces-final-rule-adjusting-immigration-benefit-application-and-petition-fees

https://www.uscis.gov/about-us/directorates-and-program-offices/customer-service-and-public-engagement-directorate/office-public-engagement-customer-service-and-public-engagement-directorate

http://www.nextgov.com/cio-briefing/2016/02/heres-what-government-gets-right-when-it-comes-customer-service/126141/

http://www.telemundodallas.com/noticias/local/La-asistente-virtual-de-USCIS--381576891.html

http://noticias.entravision.com/laredo/2016/06/03/nuevo-servicio-para-responder-a-preguntas-de-inmigracion/

10.8   Route Guide to Building Engagement

As has been discussed, the variety of the actions that a public sector organization can undertake to engage stakeholders in public administration processes is huge. The route varies according to purposes, targets, issues, geographical distribution, channels, and so forth. It is beyond the scope of this chapter to provide a route guide that covers all varieties. The following are general indications.

1) **Build an engagement-focused organization**
   Questions to ask: Is everybody aware of this organization's focus on engagement? Is this organization willing to engage? Are the employees motivated?

2) **Define your aims**
   Questions to ask: What is my target? Who do I want to engage, and what for? What is the purpose of this engagement effort? Is it to inform, consult, involve, collaborate, or empower?

3) **Define the scope**
   Questions to ask: What are the benefits of this action? What are the available resources? How much time do we have available?

4) **Ensure your people have got the skills to engage**
   Questions to ask: Do people know how to address the specific targets? Do they know how to interact? Do they want to listen? Should we train? Do we need to hire independent facilitators? Do we need external consultants?

5) **Plan the action**
   Questions to ask: What are the objectives? What are possible drawbacks? Who are the stakeholders? What is the budget? What is the schedule?

6) **Identify and address barriers**
   Questions to ask: Why are people not getting engaged? Why is participation so low? Who are the major opponents, and what can we do about them?

7) **Communicate engagement**
   Questions to ask: What can people expect of this action? Are people aware of the limitations and constraints of this action? Do people know what their participation will be used for? What are the channels in which I should be interacting with my target?

8) **Evaluate outcomes**
   Questions to ask: What have we done well? Has the feedback that we have provided met expectations? What mistakes have been made? Possible indicators include the number of participants, feedback from participants, costs, and acceptance of outcomes (versus complaints).

9) **Provide feedback to the people whom you have engaged or attempted to engage**
   Questions to ask: Does our target know the engagement outcomes? Have we communicated what their opinions will be used for? Are they aware of what the benefit of their participation was?

10) **Build a system for ongoing listening**
    Questions to ask: Where can we get feedback from our stakeholders? Is it systematic enough? Do we process feedback adequately?

References

Adams, D. and Hess, M. (2001). Community in public policy: fad or foundation? *Australian Journal of Public Administration* **60** (2): 13–23.

Adler, R.P. and Goggin, J. (2005). What do we mean by 'civic engagement'? *Journal of Transformative Education* **3** (3): 236–253.

Alford, J. (2009). The multiple facets of co-production: building on the work of Elinor Ostrom. *Public Management Review* **16** (3): 299–316.

Amnå, E. (2012). How is civic engagement developed over time? Emerging answers from a multidisciplinary field. *Journal of Adolescence* **35** (3): 611–627.

Bole, B.E. and Gordon, M. (2009). E Pluribus Unum: fostering a new era of citizenship by teaching civic engagement and healthy civic discourse. *Journal of Public Affairs* **9** (4): 273–287.

Bovaird, T. (2007). Beyond engagement and participation: user and community coproduction of public services. *Public Administration Review* **67** (5): 856–860.

Bovaird, T. and Loeffler, E. (2009). User and community co-production of public services and public policies through collective decision-making: the role of emerging technologies. In: *The Future of Governance* (ed. T. Brandsen and M. Holzer), 231–251. Newark, NJ: National Center for Public Performance.

Bovaird, T. and Loeffler, E. (2012). From engagement to co-production: the contribution of users and communities to outcomes and public value. *VOLUNTAS: International Journal of Voluntary and Nonprofit Organizations* **23** (4): 1119–1138.

Bovaird, T., Van Ryzin, G.G., and Loeffler, E. (2015). Activating citizens to participate in collective co-production of public services. *Journal of Social Policy* **44** (1): 1–23.

Bowden, J.L.H., Vilma, L.-A., Naumann, K. et al. (2016). Developing a spectrum of positive to negative citizen engagement. In: *Customer Engagement: Contemporary Issues and Challenges* (ed. R.J. Brodie, L. Hollebeek and J. Conduit), 257–277. New York, NY: Routledge.

Brandsen, T. and Honingh, M. (2015). Distinguishing different types of coproduction: a conceptual analysis based on the classical definitions. *Public Administration Review* **76** (39): 427–435.

Brudney, J.L. and England, R.E. (1983). Toward a definition of the coproduction concept. *Public Administration Review* **43** (1): 59–65.

Carpini, M.D. (2004). Mediating democratic engagement: the impact of communications on citizens' involvement in political and civic life. In: *Handbook of Political Communication Research* (ed. L. Lee Kaid), 395–434. London: LEA.

Cooper, T.L. (2005). Civic engagement in the twenty-first century: toward a scholarly and practical agenda. *Public Administration Review* **65** (5): 534–535.

Coursey, D., Yang, K., and Pandey, S.K. (2012). Public service motivation (PSM) and support for citizen participation: a test of Perry and Vandenabeele's reformulation of PSM theory. *Public Administration Review* **72** (4): 572–582.

Dahlgren, P. (2009). *Media and Political Engagement*. Cambridge: Cambridge University Press.

Denhardt, J.V. and Denhardt, R.B. (2015). The new public service revisited. *Public Administration Review* **75** (5): 664–672.

Dryzek, J.S. (2000). *Deliberative Democracy and beyond: Liberals, Critics, Contestations*. Oxford: Oxford University Press.

Ekman, J. and Amnå, E. (2012). Political participation and civic engagement: towards a new typology. *Human Affairs* **22** (3): 283–300.

Fung, A. (2003). Associations and democracy: between theories, hopes, and realities. *Annual Review of Sociology* **29** (1): 515–539.

Fung, A. (2015). Putting the public back into governance: the challenges of citizen participation and its future. *Public Administration Review* **75** (4): 513–522.

Glaser, M.A., Yeager, S.J., and Parker, L.E. (2006). Involving citizens in the decisions of government and community: neighborhood-based vs. government-based citizen engagement. *Public Administration Quarterly* **30** (2): 218–262.

Halpin, D.R. and Thomas, H.F. (2012). Evaluating the breadth of policy engagement by organized interests. *Public Administration* **90** (3): 582–599.

Head, B. (2007). The public service and government communication: pressures and dilemmas. In: *Government Communication in Australia* (ed. S. Young), 36–50. Melbourne: Cambridge University Press.

Head, B.W. (2008). Community engagement: participation on whose terms? *Australian Journal of Political Science* **42** (3): 441–454.

Heikkila, T. and Isett, K.R. (2007). Citizen involvement and performance management in special-purpose governments. *Public Administration Review* **67** (2): 238–248.

Hemmati, M. (2002). *Multi-Stakeholder Processes for Governance and Sustainability: Beyond Deadlock and Conflict*. Routledge.

Holmes, B. (2011). *Citizens' Engagement in Policymaking and the Design of Public Services*. Canberra: Australian Parliamentary Library.

Innes, J.E. and Booher, D.E. (2004). Reframing public participation: strategies for the 21st century. *Planning Theory & Practice* **5** (4): 419–436.

Levine, P. (2007). *The Future of Democracy: Developing the next Generation of American Citizens*. Lebanon, NH: Tufts University Press.

Luoma-aho, V. and Vos, M. (2009). Monitoring the complexities: nuclear power and public opinion. *Public Relations Review* **35** (2): 120–122.

Marlowe Jr., H.A. and Arrington-Marlowe, L.L.C. (2005). Public engagement: theory and practice, working paper.

Milner, H. (2010). *The Internet Generation: Engaged Citizens or Political Dropouts*. Medford, MA: Tufts University Press.

Ostrom, E. (1996). Crossing the great divide: coproduction, synergy, and development. *World Development* **24** (6): 1073–1087.

Prentice, M. (2007). Service learning and civic engagement. *Academic Questions* **20** (2): 135–145.

Ramsey, P. (2015). The engage programme and the government communication network in the UK, 2006–2010. *Journal of Public Affairs* **15** (4): 377–386.

Rhodes, R.A.W. (2003). What is new about governance and why does it matter. In: *Governing Europe* (ed. J. Hayward and A. Menon), 61–73. Oxford: Oxford University Press.

Roberts, N. (2004). Public deliberation in an age of direct citizen participation. *The American Review of Public Administration* **34** (4): 315–353.

Sirianni, C. (2010). *Investing in Democracy: Engaging Citizens in Collaborative Governance*. Washington, DC: Brookings Institution Press.

Smith, N. (2010). The public administrator as collaborative citizen: three conceptions. *Public Administration Quarterly* **34**: 238–262.

Tam, H. (1998). *Communitarianism: A New Agenda for Politics and Citizenship*. New York: New York University Press.

Theiss-Morse, E. and Hibbing, J.R. (2005). Citizenship and civic engagement. *Annual Review of Political Science* **8**: 227–249.

Thomas, J.C. (1995). *Public Participation in Public Decisions: New Skills and Strategies for Public Managers*. San Francisco, CA: Jossey-Bass.

Thomas, J.C. (2013). Citizen, customer, partner: rethinking the place of the public in public management. *Public Administration Review* **73** (6): 786–796.

Wang, X.H. and Wart, M.W. (2007). When public participation in administration leads to trust: an empirical assessment of managers' perceptions. *Public Administration Review* **67** (2): 265–278.

Yang, K. and Callahan, K. (2005). Assessing citizen involvement efforts by local governments. *Public Performance & Management Review* **29** (2): 191–216.

Yang, K. and Callahan, K. (2007). Citizen involvement efforts and bureaucratic responsiveness: participatory values, stakeholder pressures, and administrative practicality. *Public Administration Review* **67** (2): 249–264.

Yang, K. and Pandey, S.K. (2011). Further dissecting the black box of citizen participation: when does citizen involvement lead to good outcomes? *Public Administration Review* **71** (6): 880–892.

11

Social Capital

> *The most valuable of all capital is that invested in human beings*
> (Economist Alfred Marshall)

This chapter addresses situations in which the main cause for a gap between the public sector and citizens is a lack of participation and representativeness in the public sector. What suffers as a consequence of this gap is dialogue and citizens' commitment and willingness to collaborate with the public sector. This chapter addresses how antifragile communication helps to build organizational social capital resulting from good relations, and it also discusses the fake forms of social influence that are sometimes applied via astroturfing and fake grassroots movements. The chapter closes with an example of building social capital in practice in the form of national defense courses in Finland.

11.1 Theory of Social Capital

Given that public sector organizations aim to produce common societal goods, the theory of social capital is useful. Social capital theory examines how once social relationships have been formed they can benefit individuals and organizations beyond their original context of creation, while social capital itself enables people to collaborate, socialize, establish communities, and live together in harmony (Coleman, 1990; Putnam, 1995; Portes, 1998; Lin, 2001). Social capital enables collaboration and engagement, as it facilitates the flow of information, and through a sense of belonging and social obligations, it may exert influence on others (Saffer, 2016). Two types of motives have been suggested in relation to social capital actions: expressive actions that aim to maintain societal and organizational resources and instrumental actions that aim to obtain new and desired resources (Lin, 2001). Both of these are needed by public sector organizations.

Social capital explains how relationships enable access to goods and resources that are otherwise unattainable for individuals (Bourdieu, 1980; Coleman, 1988). Although it has only received significant attention in recent decades, the ideas behind social capital are not new. Scholars have considered them previously when talking about a sense of community (Chicago School); customer capital (Bontis, 1998, pp. 63–76); social connectedness (Putnam, 1996); and generalized reciprocity, social trust, and tolerance (Putnam, Leonardi, and Nanetti, 1993; Fukuyama, 1995).

Public Sector Communication: Closing Gaps Between Citizens and Public Organizations, First Edition.
María-José Canel and Vilma Luoma-aho.
© 2019 John Wiley & Sons, Inc. Published 2019 by John Wiley & Sons, Inc.

Social capital is intangible in nature and hence difficult to define. A useful explanation comes from the political scientist Robert Putnam:

> Whereas physical capital refers to physical objects and human capital refers to the properties of individuals, social capital refers to connections among individuals – social networks and the norms of reciprocity and trustworthiness that arise from them. In that sense social capital is closely related to what some have called "civic virtue." The difference is that "social capital" calls attention to the fact that civic virtue is most powerful when embedded in a dense network of reciprocal social relations. A society of many virtuous but isolated individuals is not necessarily rich in social capital.
>
> *(Putnam, 2000, p. 19)*

Social capital is a metaphor that builds on other more tangible types of capital. It is often defined as networks of trust, and it is useful because it provides access to resources via social connections. Social capital is only beneficial once it is mobilized, and as a system it feeds on itself: trusting relationships help build other trusting relationships. However, social capital cannot be built directly. In fact, like reputation, social capital is a byproduct of long-term social relationships resulting from citizens' positive experiences of exchange and communication.

Social capital for public sector organizations is connected to collaboration and citizen behavior. If social capital is "features of social organization, such as trust, norms, and networks that can improve the efficiency of society by facilitating coordinated actions" (Putnam et al., 1993, p. 167), it not only benefits those involved but also society at large.

Social capital is about "making connections among people, establishing bonds of trust and understanding, building community" (Putnam, Feldstein, and Cohen, 2003, p. 9). The idea is related to what public sector organizations were originally created for: achieving goals that would be difficult for individual citizens alone. But achievements are not the sole function of social capital, as networks and groups provide citizens with the satisfaction of belonging to something and a sense of community that motivates actions.

The public relations model of civil society notes that the quality of relationships matters with regard to generation of social capital, as only trusting relationships produce intangible assets. Moreover, building social capital in practice is about nurturing networks, and to achieve this, "important civil society organizations should occupy positions that bridge structural holes" – for example, by connecting actors who are otherwise unconnected (Sommerfeldt, 2013a, p. 8). Vital to the public sector, social capital enables citizens to collaborate, socialize, establish communities, and live better together, in relation to both other citizens and public sector organizations. Moreover, social capital has been linked with a decrease in societal ills such as tribal conflict, poor voter turnout, and citizen alienation and dissatisfaction. In short, social capital builds and maintains a thriving community, and it is social capital that decreases as a sense of society is lost.

For public sector organizations, communication with stakeholders has both instrumental value and eigenvalue: not only do stakeholder networks enable organizational survival via culture creation and information exchange, but having established channels of communication and being heard in today's communication-entrenched society are of value by themselves (Luoma-aho, 2005, p. 368). Public sector organizations with reciprocal, trusting networks of citizens and stakeholders can be understood as having high amounts of social capital. In a fragile environment, this trust provides a safety zone, and increasing social capital is becoming an aim in itself for many public sector organizations.

11.2 What Kind of Value Does Social Capital Produce?

The value of social capital for public sector organizations lies in the benefits that it produces for both individuals and society at large. Among the fruits claimed by societies that enjoy high social capital are increased trust among citizens, higher levels of health and happiness, lower crime rates, an improved sense of community, and better reciprocity practices. Networks of civil engagement appear to be mutually enforcing, and once established they feed on themselves: the more trust there is within a network of individuals and organizations, the more they are able to share and collaborate in ways that benefit everyone in the network. Not only do individuals benefit, but some researchers have also linked social capital to increased investments and economic prosperity (Fukuyama, 1995).

One central way in which social capital provides value for society is through trust and trustworthiness (Coleman, 1990; Fukuyama, 1995). Trustworthiness as a form of social capital increases "the capacity to form new associations" (Fukuyama, 1995, p. 27). Trust is "an expectation that individuals will exhibit behavior that is consistent with expectations" (Fussell et al., 2006, p. 151). To develop, such strong connections between people or organizations and people require time, emotional intensity, intimacy, and reciprocity.

With regard to communication, social capital in organizations has been linked with decreasing transaction costs as well as improved organizational outcomes (Fussell et al., 2006). However, the real value of social capital is often evident only in the long term. Typical measures of social capital include analysis of networks and different measures of trust and welfare in society. Although most countries and societies feature a mixture of both trust and distrust depending on the settings, two extreme forms of trust in society have been established. In societies where generalized trust in other people is low, collaboration is difficult, and scholars speak of the "social trap" (Rothstein and Stolle, 2003; Kumlin and Rothstein, 2005; Luoma-aho, 2009). In such settings, individuals' willingness to collaborate is minimum, as they do not trust others to collaborate within society and they do not wish to be taken for fools.

Although a society with an active social trap is a difficult setting for public sector organizations to function in, it is possible to build trust even in societies lacking in social capital and collaboration (Putnam et al., 2003). In a similar manner to a positive culture, social capital is built one experience at a time. The key is to get people involved with each other on a smaller scale – for example, through clubs, societies, hobbies, and associations. These grassroots-level experiences of working together are the building blocks of trust in society at large, as they form the basis for learning democracy (Putnam et al., 1993).

But if one asks the old question of whether structure or agency matters more for a prosperous society, it is clear that for social capital, agency is the creator of structure. A civic community is characterized by civic engagement, political equality, solidarity, trust, and tolerance, as well as by a strong associational life (Putnam et al., 1993). On the level of society, social capital eases tensions between groups and individuals and enables collaboration among diverse citizen groups. Social capital cannot, however, exist or be built starting with or based only on the societal level or without the lower levels, as society consists of individuals, groups, and organizations. Likewise, social capital must be built through individuals, groups, and organizations. The value of social capital can be understood on the following three levels, as Figure 11.1 shows: (1) individual; (2) groups; and (3) organizations.

1) On the level of individuals such as public sector employees or citizens, social capital fosters a sense of community that contributes to their health and happiness, and social capital is apparent in trust between individuals and their willingness to collaborate with and tolerate each other. This level is the most common focus of research on social capital, and examples include personal access to different resources such as power (Brass et al., 1992), professional status and occupational gains (Lin, 2001), societal and individual welfare (Putnam et al., 1993), individual health (Hyyppä and Mäki, 2003), and the psychological flexibility of individuals to be open to new ideas (Luoma-aho et al., 2012). The value of social capital for an individual in network terms depends on that individual's location within the network, and individuals who are well connected have better access to desired resources or valuable actors with status.

2) On the level of groups and interpersonal relationships, social capital produced through trust enables transactions and even career advancement, as networks and connections enable individuals to borrow the trust established elsewhere (Oh, Labianca, and Chung, 2006). Scholars who take the network view highlight how a central position in the network enables better cooperation and quality of information (Sommerfeldt, 2013b): public sector organizations that are able to facilitate between stakeholders or organizations are better equipped for their operations. Groups that are high in social capital are reported to be more effective, and Ihlen (2005, p. 495) suggests that social capital may even be more important for organizations than it is for individuals: "The vast number of connections gathered by most organizations points to how they are socially embedded in a much stronger sense than individuals." Although group social capital is mostly approached as a merely positive force, it can also at times be exclusive, leaving others outside the group.

3) On the level of organizations, social capital both enables individuals to collaborate inside the organization and builds bridges to individuals and resources outside the organization's reach. Organizations can be seen as markets in which people trade goods and ideas, and good networks improve success in this trade (Henttonen, 2009). Nahapiet and Ghoshal (1998) distinguish between several different types of value – structural, relational, and cognitive – that social capital has for organizations. Similarly, Burke, Martin, and Cooper (2011) see social capital (resulting from harmonious culture and investments) as central for organizational practices such as human resources, in which employee engagement and identification are central. Organizational social capital results in a positive organizational reputation (Preston, 2004; Luoma-aho, 2013), whereas a lack of social capital on the organizational level could signify inherent liabilities. Interorganizational studies have suggested that prior relationships shape future relationships (Gulati, 1995), and organizational units that are centrally located in a network are often highly visible entities and sharers of

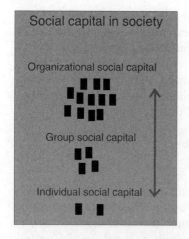

Figure 11.1 The levels of social capital in society.

information with others, making them attractive collaborative partners to others (Tsai, 2000). In fact, social capital turns stakeholders into organizational "faith-holders" – that is, individuals with positive experiences and high trust levels toward the organization (Luoma-aho, 2015). Faith-holders are beneficial both inside the organization (where they take the form of public sector employees) and outside of it (where they take the form of citizens and other groups or organizations), as they are the ones whose support the organization can rely on in both good and bad times.

The lines between these levels are arbitrary and dynamic, and different levels of social capital can and do lead to other levels when needed. Similarly, if social capital is decreased on one level, this will affect the other levels. A society's measure of social capital overall is, therefore, the sum of its individual social capital, its group social capital, and its organizational social capital.

11.3 What Kind of Gaps Does Social Capital Help to Bridge?

The gaps that social capital bridges are those related to exclusion, distrust, and a lack of collaboration. These gaps are mostly of a mental nature, as they manifest themselves in the form of citizens' prejudices and behaviors, but through these mental barriers physical restrictions are also established. These are often formed individually but quickly become collective in the sense that particularly negative emotions and affects are contagious and can become commonly shared (Bougie, Pieters, and Zeelenberg, 2003).

There are two types of social capital that serve different functions (Burt, 1992; Putnam, 2000): they can be bridging or inclusive and bonding or exclusive social networks (Coleman, 1990). Bonding social capital furthers in-group cohesion, which is much needed within public sector organizations and among collaborative networks, whereas bridging social capital is understood as relationships with those outside the individual citizen's core group.

Previous studies have found that both types of social capital are valuable for individuals and society. For example, there is a relationship between job satisfaction and bonding relationships (Lucius and Kuhnert, 1997), as well as between bridging social capital and group effectiveness (Wong, 2008). Moreover, both types of social capital contribute to organizing and efficiency of teams – for example, in research and development (Raegans and Zuckerman, 2001), in which both collective action inside the team and external information transfer are needed.

On the level of individual citizens and groups, bonding social capital is especially important because it adds to individual citizens' or public sector employees' satisfaction and happiness. Bonding social capital has been likened to a glue that makes individuals and groups stick together. There are, however, threats to excess amounts of bonding social capital, and several negative byproducts have been associated with it, such as groupthink (in which novel ideas fail to emerge due to group cohesion) or exclusivity (in which individuals who are not in-group members feel left out).

Fewer dangers have been found in relation to bridging social capital. Bridging social capital identifies networks that bridge social divides and promote heterogeneity in groups and societies. It reinforces inclusive identities and thus runs less risk of excess. In fact, for public sector organizations serving diverse citizen needs, bridging social capital is central, because it describes how resources and goods such as valuable information or access to desired positions are received through looser social relations and networks beyond the bonding in-group. Bridging social capital has been likened to an oil that lubricates relations between groups and individuals. Bridging social capital is close to what Granowetter (1973) calls "weak ties," and it is related to what Burt (1992) calls "structural holes." The theory of structural holes in a network suggests that distant or infrequent relationships can sometimes be beneficial, as they provide access to new thinking and information. For public sector organizations aiming to understand the citizen's point of view, bridging social capital, especially between public sector employees and citizens, can offer insights that help to make public sector services better and more effective.

11.4 Communicating Social Capital

Recent research on social capital in the organizational public relations context has noted that social capital provides a framework for measuring both "the value of intangible (e.g., relationships, reputations, trust) and tangible (e.g., financial profitability) outcomes of public relations activities" (Dodd, Brummette, and Hazleton, 2015). Coleman (1990, p. 321) asserts that "like human capital and physical capital, social capital depreciates if it is not renewed. Social relationships die out if not maintained; expectations and obligations wither over time: and norms depend on regular communication." As communication depends on the relationship and attributes between citizens and public sector employees, past experiences and organizational reputation may shape the amount of social capital available to a public sector organization or its representatives. Social capital sets the stage for public sector communication, either in a positive manner in settings in which plenty of social capital is available, or in a negative manner in those which lack social capital.

Social capital and reputation are related, as social capital via communication enforces the virtuous circle of good experiences and collaboration (Luoma-aho, 2013). As social and real-time media make organizational social capital visible through citizens' feedback, recommendations, and stories, communication shapes the social capital available for organizations. In the online environment, reputation is "an integral part of an organization's social-cognitive capital" (Aula, 2011, p. 30). Moreover, research focusing on communication professionals' roles has shown that professionals are more active in producing social capital through Putnam's "vigorous civic connections" than average citizens are (Dodd et al., 2015).

As we have stated elsewhere (Coleman, 1990; Luoma-aho, 2013, p. 282), "Communication is central for social capital as human messaging and symbolic activity are the basis on which social relationships are formed." In fact, relationships between public sector employees and citizens are shaped via the structures of interpersonal interaction and communication (Henttonen, 2009; Van Emmerik and Brenninkmeijer, 2009). As such, communication can be understood as the mechanism through which social capital is in practice accessed, whether on the individual, group, or organizational level. Moreover, "communication characteristics influence the potential for social capital formation, maintenance, and expenditure" (Fussell et al., 2006).

But how does communication in practice allow access to social capital? Below we build on Hazelton and Kennan (2000) and Luoma-aho (2013) to suggest six communication functions that provide the mechanism for accessing social capital in organizations:

1) *Information exchange*: the ability of the public sector organization to deal with relevant information and symbols through the level of trust available.
2) *Problem/solution identification*: the public sector organization's ability to interpret changes and potential problems relevant to it and its operating environment.
3) *Behavior regulation*: the possibility of aligning individual public sector employees' behavior and organizational image to match organizational goals and aims.
4) *Conflict management*: handling normal organizational disagreements that may provide valuable insights if the organizational environment is safe enough for employee feedback.
5) *Relationship maintenance*: the ability to maintain positive interactions and work with diverse individuals toward a common goal, while creating positive experiences of collaboration.
6) *Enabling innovation*: the amount of trust sufficient for necessary risk taking, and processing and cross-pollination of ideas across organizational division and teams.

11.5 What Does This Mean for Public Sector Organizations' Communication Management?

The inherent function of public sector organizations is to maintain a robust society, and social capital has been linked with maintaining networks that enable this (Sommerfeldt, 2013b, pp. 1–12). In practice, daily communication between public sector organizations and citizens is what fosters the social capital that makes society function (Saffer, 2016, pp. 1–23).

Borrowing from Luoma-aho (2009, p. 243), Figure 11.2 illustrates how social capital is created on the societal level in the daily works of public sector organizations. Individual citizens' encouraging experiences of collaborating with public sector organizations create a positive reputation and foster trust, which in turn creates new social capital for the organization. Similarly, negative experiences of corruption or frustration cause a bad reputation and foster distrust. Social capital is also helpful for understanding the

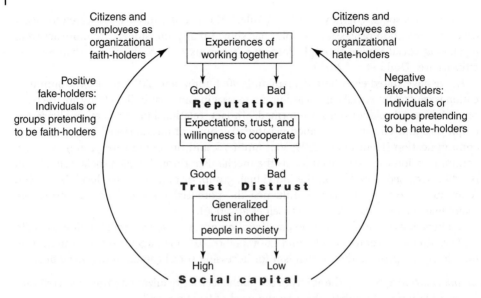

Figure 11.2 Model of the extremes of social capital creation and the different forms of citizen engagement, faith-holding, hate-holding, and fake-holding. Source: Adapted from Luoma-aho (2015).

emergence and functions of networks. These not only foster reciprocity but also facilitate coordination and communication and amplify information about the trustworthiness of individuals or organizations – that is, their reputation.

Citizen participation and citizen engagement are becoming universal values of public sector organizations, and understanding the role of individual experiences and interactions is central. The model has both instrumental and theoretical value, as it demonstrates how experiences become expectations, which contribute to reality (Putnam et al., 1993).

As we suggest in Figure 11.2, stakeholders with positive experiences that they are willing to share can be understood as "faith-holders" or "social capitalists" for organizations: they spread goodwill and uphold a positive reputation (Luoma-aho, 2015). Stakeholders as social capitalists are also a credible source, as they often have personal experiences of the corporation. Similarly, stakeholders with negative experiences that they are willing to share are seen as "hate-holders" who destroy organizational social capital. Organizational legitimacy can only be maintained if there are more faith-holders than hate-holders (Luoma-aho, 2015), as the total amount of social capital created is what shapes individuals' impressions and assessments.

The process of social capital creation is cyclical, and it starts with the experiences of an individual, group, or organization. The model is based on communication on both the intrapersonal and interpersonal levels, as individuals make sense and share their experiences. Whether they are good or bad, these experiences of working together (which can be mediated or personal) contribute to forming a reputation. This reputation is communicated to others consciously or unconsciously, and it carries with it certain expectations and facilitates willingness to trust (Putnam et al., 1993; Misztal, 1996; Luoma-aho, 2006). The level of trust results in high or low amounts of social capital, which in turn shapes experiences and expectations and thus the possibilities for working together.

The idea behind many communication departments in public sector organizations is to address citizens' queries or provide them with information on organizational or government decisions. When social capital becomes important, there will be a twist to these basic functions: instead of focusing on providing information to and engaging as many new citizens as possible, public sector employees may understand how existing networks and structures could be applied for communication purposes. Moreover, there are several different citizen groups that are willing to work as faith-holders for public sector organizations but that merely lack engagement and empowerment from the public sector.

11.6 Measuring Social Capital

As the gains of social capital are only apparent over time, its real-time measurement is challenging. So far, most common measures of social capital are self-reported measures of the good that social capital is suggested to produce, such as increases in citizens' health, happiness, welfare, and democracy, as well as decreases in tribal and cultural clashes, racism, and discrimination (Putnam et al., 2003). Societal measures deployed in the political sciences have included voter turnout, citizen participation in associations, and trust in political institutions (Putnam et al., 1993; Coleman, 1988, pp. 95–120; Hyyppä and Mäki, 2003). In communication studies, suggestions have been made to measure social capital via network analysis (Ihlen, van Ruler, and Fredriksson, 2009; Yang and Taylor, 2015; Yang, Taylor, and Saffer, 2016), communication networks (Sommerfeldt, 2013b; Sommerfeldt and Kent, 2015), and shared meanings (Saffer, 2016).

Measurement for the bonding type of social capital has focused on networks and their reach. Network density has been studied, as have in-group cohesion and changing of identity toward a sense of community, belonging, norms, and reciprocity (Coleman, 1988; Putnam et al., 1993; Jonson, Smith, and Gambill, 2000), whereas for bridging social capital researchers have paid attention to network location, access to information, control, boundary-spanning relationships, and individual gains (Leana and Van Buren, 1999, pp. 538–555; Burt, 1992). Career advancement (Lin, 2001) and the roles of communication professionals (Dodd et al., 2015) have also been studied via the concept of social capital.

Several other intangible assets are strongly associated with social capital, including trust, reputation, expectations, and engagement. Whereas the link with engagement is obvious due to the engaging nature of social capital, especially in its bonding form, expectations come into play when social capital shapes the way in which people assume organizations or individuals will behave in the future. Trust is a leap to future behavior, and either social capital sets the stage for trust to be formed or a lack of it prohibits the formation of trust. As for reputation, Lin (2001) and Bourdieu (1980) explain how individual reputation acts as a status builder and hence could be understood as a form of social capital. Luoma-aho (2007, p. 124) concludes that trust and reputation make up the social capital that organizations can have and suggests that both trust and reputation help to balance the organization in turbulent settings.

Several scholars of social capital have discussed these neighboring concepts. Bourdieu writes of "the capital of trust that stems from a reputation for honor as well as wealth" and notes the facilitating role of trust: "Because of trust they enjoy the capital of social relations they have accumulated" (Bourdieu, 1980, p. 119). Putnam et al. (1993, p. 170) use the concept in a similar way: "For example, my reputation for trustworthiness benefits you as well as me, since it enables us both to engage in mutually rewarding cooperation." In a similar manner, Putnam et al. cite Ostrom and conclude that "norms are reinforced by the network of relationships that depend on the establishment of a reputation for keeping promises and accepting the norms of the local community regarding behavior" (Putnam et al., 1993, p. 173).

11.7 Are All Networks Real?

Communication for public sector organizations means looking beyond obvious faith-holders and hate-holders and acknowledging that not all influences and networks are real. When issues of common interest and public affairs are discussed, the stakes are high to influence others and policymakers. Especially in the online environment, not all influences are real. Behind the rise of fake-holders is the rising trust in "people like me" (Edelman, 2017, Edelman Trust Barometer). Research suggests many online reviews are fake, despite their trustworthy reputation and consumers' heavy reliance on them (Kolivos and Kuperman, 2012, pp. 38–41). As the value of customer reviews increases, so does the pressure to produce favorable content. Fake-holders are increasingly eroding trust and diminishing social capital levels (Luoma-aho, 2015).

Fake-holder support is related to the often-applied concept of astroturfing. As a concept, astroturfing takes its name from the installation of real-looking fake grass on sports fields (Tigner, 2010). The term was made famous by Senator Bentsen's 1986 comment on how he could tell the difference between real support and "astroturf," referring to the letters that he was receiving that had in fact been generated by the insurance industry (Malbon, 2013). Fake-holders may be the product of astroturfing, but they also emerge on a smaller scale. Astroturfing refers to fake stakeholders' artificial grassroots campaigns that are created by unethical public relations practitioners or by lobbyists via fake personalities or persona management software. Astroturfing aims to influence or support via "synthetic advocacy efforts" (McNutt and Boland, 2007, p. 165). Examples of fake-holders can be seen on the level of individuals and organizations or nations.

Examples of such influence include fake grassroots movements that appear to be a combining of forces by citizens to address some emerging issue or to lobby for or protest against a decision. Some examples of fake-holders on the side of faith-holders in the public sector include the Chinese government's unofficial 50 Cent Party, whose recruits are paid to promote progovernment messages. Public sector organizations and authorities hoping to distinguish between their real stakeholders and those responses created automatically or through algorithms and robots find themselves in novel situations: Can certain stakeholders be ignored?

Fake-holders are opinions, sociobots, and stakeholders artificially generated by either individuals or persona-creating software and algorithms to either oppose or support an issue. These unauthentic faith-holders or fake-holders do not exist in reality, and their influence appears larger than it is in practice. If important stakes as well as stakeholders remain hidden or fake-holders are given the freedom to reign, public sector organizations may be exposed to potential harm. Fake-holders are stakeholders that appear to be real citizens and interest groups but that in reality may turn out to be unauthentic or fake

(Luoma-aho, 2015). Fake-holders are an emerging trend that encompasses ghostwriters, meatpuppets, and sockpuppets (Kolivos and Kuperman, 2012).

Though often not included in the meaning, the source behind the fake-holders and astroturfing is of central importance, but like propaganda, the actual sources attempt to hide. Fake-holders are artificially created products that encourage some aim or issue. Fake-holders are individuals or organizations that appear to be more powerful than they are in reality and lobby for or hinder individuals', governments', or organizations' interests. Fake-holding in practice is carried out via sockpuppets or meatpuppets, controlled by sophisticated persona management software. On the larger scale, astro-turfing has been used by governments such as that of China, which reportedly paid five yuan for each progovernment message online. The role of fake-holders increases in times when legitimacy is questioned or challenged, and stakeholders look for confirmation about their engagement, whether it is positive or negative. In addition, sometimes fake-holders can also be the cause of a questioning of legitimacy.

11.8 Closing the Gap through Social Capital

Recent communication research on social capital suggests that in practice, it works via networks and meanings that are shared via communication (Saffer, 2016, pp. 1–23; Yang and Taylor, 2015, pp. 91–115). In a practice book on social capital entitled *Better Together*, Putnam et al. (2003) describe how social capital might be constructed in the public sector setting. They explain how the Experience Corps in Philadelphia was built out of elderly citizens who acted as school volunteers and gave up 15 hours of their time per week to tutor and engage with elementary school students from diverse backgrounds. The benefits of the Experience Corps program were shared by all involved: the students, the elderly, the schools, and society at large. The benefits arising from the initiative that have been suggested include authentic relationships, a feeling of belonging, and commitment to the school and to the organizations involved, which range from public schools to the National Senior Service and the American Association of Retired Persons, the NGO involved in the project. The results of the scheme were exceptional, with 75% of the students involved in the Experience Corps experiencing an increase of one grade band in their school results. Investment in both individual and group social capital produced reciprocal benefits.

However, "Building social capital depends both on the actions of protagonists and on key enabling structural conditions in the broader environment" (Putnam et al., 2003, p. 271), and the history of the public sector organization in question plays a role in its formation. In addition, public sector organizations may have a reputation that hinders their level of social capital (Luoma-aho, 2008; Luoma-aho and Makikangas, 2014). Despite these factors, fostering social capital in the public sector is possible, though its nature as a byproduct must be considered. A good example of how social capital works in practice and how it requires an active response from the public sector as well is provided in the book *Better Together* (Putnam et al., 2003, p. 248), which describes civic activity and engagement in a city context in Portland, Oregon. Despite the diversity of population patterns and other challenges, the government managed to genuinely begin a virtuous circle where response to citizens' calls for participation encouraged further participation and collaboration.

11.9 Future Research on Social Capital

Some researchers have suggested that the differences between public sector organizations and business organizations are diminishing, as businesses are expected to be more transparent and public sector organizations are increasingly concerned with efficiency and finances. Moreover, as sustainability and responsibility remain societal values, both types of organization are moving from one-time interactions to building lasting relationships with different stakeholders. This can be seen as an increase in social capital through individual faith-holder relationships. There is also a clear trend toward reporting the intangible side of organizations (see, for example, the integrated reporting initiative), and investments in social capital are becoming more tangible (Lev, 2001). For such reporting

Table 11.1 Social capital as an intangible asset in the public sector.

Social capital is the intangible asset that reveals the quality of relationships that an organization has been able to build with stakeholders and citizens	
Tangible asset that social capital enables	All physical capital through providing connections for sharing and reciprocity Organizations need social capital to enable collaboration, both inside organizations and among citizens Social capital builds trust and reciprocity and through doing so improves democracy
Resource that social capital generates	Goodwill for purposes of collaboration: it creates bridges between people beyond their initial core groups It diminishes racism, discrimination, and hate crimes It increases health, sense of security, and belonging Internal communication: glues diverse authority teams and collaboration networks together, improving their efficiency and reach (bonding social capital) Citizen collaboration: establishes a sense of community among strangers and neighborhoods, improving their resilience (bonding social capital) Group/organizational social capital: builds trust to diminish transaction costs such as extra regulations and limitations
Monetary expression	Easing transactions and diminishing processing time and bureaucracy to mobilize needed resources
Value that social capital provides to the organization	Satisfaction, welfare, and a sense of belonging for citizens, employees, and society as a whole
Value that social capital provides to citizens and stakeholders	Networks to utilize for their needs; a sense of community; improvements in societies in terms of safety, happiness, health, and feelings of empowerment
Gaps that social capital bridges	Lack of trust and lack of collaboration between strangers; lack of facilitation between individuals, groups, and organizations
Dependence on communication management	Social capital is built as a byproduct of communication and collaboration; social capital via communication helps to enforce the virtuous circle of collaboration
Implied organization management transformations	From controlling individuals toward inclusion, cocreation, and enabling of networks and sharing
Measures	Self-reported values, network analysis, empowerment, and efficacy

to be accurately conducted, the nature and logic behind social capital and communication need to be better understood, and the long time span of the development of social capital must be considered.

What future research should continue to focus on is the connection between social capital and citizen behavioral outcomes. Future studies have to clarify the role of group social capital (Oh et al., 2006), and whether social capital is actually needed or not. In fact, a certain degree of commonality among organizations with regard to their knowledge is enough for successful alliances (Cowan and Jonard, 2009), and social capital may not be needed. Future studies should also focus on whether social capital can be created on the organizational level as opposed to those of teams, groups, and individuals inside organizations.

11.10 Summary of Social Capital

Table 11.1 summarizes the chapter and explains the value of social capital as an intangible asset in the public sector.

11.11 Case Study on Social Capital in the Public Sector

National Defense Courses, Finland

How can a small nation survive next to one of the Cold-War-era giants?

Finland is located in northern Europe between Russia, Sweden, and Norway, and due to its history of war with Russia, the closeness of the border remains a concern. A small army alone is not sufficient; all the key individuals in society need to be engaged, networked, and willing to help out if necessary. Voluntary defense and its role in comprehensive security were well understood by Finnish Defense Force officials as early as 1961, when they established the National Defense Course, a unique combination of networking, elite training, and information. Unique key-citizen engagement programs of this kind operate in only a few other countries at present, including Norway, Sweden, and France (Institut des hautes études de défense nationale; IHEDN).

Purpose of the course
The course operates under the Public National Defense University (Figure 11.3), and it was established to strengthen key citizens' national defense abilities and mentalities in the fragile Cold War era. As such, the course's aim was to engage and build goodwill and trust among the key entrepreneurs, politicians, academics, and opinion leaders in relation to the armed forces in advance of a potential new war. By 2016, more than 8,000 Finnish leaders had completed the course since its beginning in 1961, and they continue to highly recommend this invitation-only training despite its long duration and large information load.

The course is focused on providing an informational overview of Finnish foreign, security, and defense policy; fostering cooperation in society; and enhancing the networking of the individuals who work in Finland's security sector. The National Defense

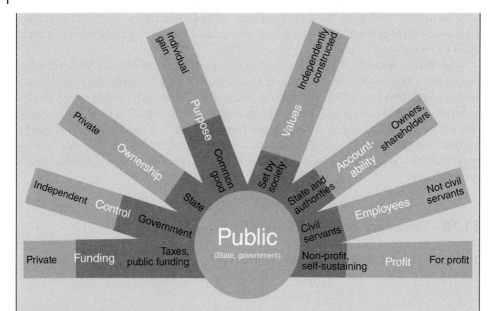

Figure 11.3 Publicness of the National Defense Course in Finland. The organization is mostly public, but its activities are partly run by donations from course participants, and its operations and control remain partly independent. Moreover, its purpose appears to be not just the common good but also the individual gain to the invitation-only participants and members of the association.

Courses are meant for civil officials and military officers working in executive positions and also leaders of major corporations and nongovernmental organizations. The aim is to build trust and networks between key individuals in society across diverse fields and services. As the program involves a major commitment (four weeks away from the office at the C-suite level is a challenge), it also makes those willing to invest in it feel a special connection and value the time and effort that they have put in.

Organization of the courses

On an administrative level, the National Defense Courses are part of the National Defense University. However, the content and the selection of the participants is governed by the Delegation of National Defense Education, whose chairman is the chief of staff (COS), Defense Command, and the members are heads or permanent secretaries of different ministries and organizations. The invitations for the National Defense Courses are sent by the commander of the Finnish Defense Forces.

The National Defense Course lasts three-and-a-half weeks at a time and is held four times per year. In addition, National Defense Courses include other minor courses and events. As the selection criteria are demanding and not all who are willing to participate receive an invitation, the organization has extended to also hold shorter, regional defense courses around the country. The course consists of lectures, visits to organizations of restricted access, and a boarding week at an actual army, navy, or air force base somewhere in Finland. During these diverse events, the participants take part in organizing group events for their course, making a publication to remember, collecting sponsors, arranging parties, and planning ahead for new meetings.

Why is this intangible asset valuable for this organization and the participants?

Source: MPK212/Vilma Luoma-aho

The course's aim is to build trust and networks between key individuals in society who represent leadership across the diverse fields that have been established as central for national security and sustainability. The secret of the course is that it builds social capital not only for the armed forces as its initiator and issuer of invites, but also among the participants of each group. Following the logic of social capital, once established it feeds on itself, and those who have attended the course come back feeling valued and appreciated by the armed forces, and hence they represent a reservoir of reciprocity and social capital that could be built on by the armed forces if needed.

The all-expenses-paid exclusive course establishes both bonding and bridging social capital in the order, in that it first bridges individuals across society to other key individuals from different sectors that they would normally not interact with. During the exercises and simulations, all participants are divided into a government consisting of ministries, heads, and ministers who have to deal with, budget for, decide upon, and communicate imagined upcoming global and local crises and challenges. During these challenging exercises, bonding occurs, and the participants not only come to understand the choices that authorities have to make and learn to weigh up their options, but they also continue to bond and build bridges with their classmates decades beyond their original course date.

Still in operation today and viewed as increasingly important in view of Russian forces' entry into Ukraine, the National Defense Course won the 2015 Communication Act of the Year award from Finnish communication practitioners ProCom. In their reasons for giving the award to the course, they mentioned the successful engagement of key individuals via communication, the course's ability to engage key individuals in society, and its "building real faith-holders whose social capital is on especially strong ground despite the constant savings and legitimacy challenges of the armed forces."

A public sector organization able to identify well in advance what kind of social capital it needs in the future ensures that its challenges and risks are assessed by individuals who are informed of its needs.

11.12   Route Guide to Building Social Capital

In *Better Together*, Putnam et al. (2003) emphasize the role of individual experiences and meeting citizen needs and empowering them to act. For public sector organizations, the starting point of building social capital is, hence, understanding the key experiences and points of interaction that affect citizens' experiences most significantly. Several stages are suggested to building social capital in public sector organizations:

1) **Establish key experiences** of both employees and citizens or other end users. A good starting point for building social capital will be to establish the experiences that employees from the public sector and citizens actually have. An excellent starting point is to ask employees and citizens to describe where their impressions come from and to establish a list of central experiences and their duration.
   Questions to ask: Where do they talk to us? When do they meet us for the first time? What kind of circumstances are they usually coming from? What are their basic needs and expectations? What do they wish for? What would an ideal key experience look like?

2) **Enable a positive experience** on both sides of the key experience. It could be that red tape stops the public sector employee from doing all he or she would like to do, or that citizens do not know their rights, and simple expectation management could help enable a positive experience.
   Questions to ask: What would employees like to do but cannot? What factors of the experience matter the most? What are people likely to remember? What emotions are present, and what do they require to be accepted?

3) **Find and empower the faith-holders** who matter most for your organization or service.
   Questions to ask: Who are the faith-holders? What would they like to tell everyone? Are there ways in which they feel appreciated? Are they empowered and encouraged to share their experiences? Are they motivated and appreciated? What ways could they be encouraged to continue?

4) **Look out for fake-holders** or fake forms of social capital that attempt to influence public opinion and citizens' views in a particular direction.
   Questions to ask: What are the real individuals and organizations behind these attempts at influencing? How could we invite them to a real conversation? How can fake influence be revealed?

References

Aula, P. (2011). Meshworked reputation: publicists' views on the reputational impacts of online communication. *Public Relations Review* **37** (1): 28–36.

Bontis, N. (1998). Intellectual capital: an exploratory study that develops measures and models. *Management Decision* **36** (2): 63–76.

Bougie, R., Pieters, R., and Zeelenberg, M. (2003). Angry customers don't come back, they get back: the experience and behavioral implications of anger and dissatisfaction in services. *Journal of the Academy of Marketing Science* **31** (4): 377–393.

Bourdieu, P. (1980). *The Logic of Practice.* Cambridge: Cambridge University Press.

Brass, D.J., Burkhardt, M.E., Nohria, N., and Eccles, R.G. (1992). *Networks and Organizations: Structure, Form and Action.* Boston: Harvard Business School Press.

Burke, R., Martin, G., and Cooper, C. (2011). *Corporate Reputation, Managing Opportunities and Threats.* London: Ashgate Publishing.

Burt, R.S. (1992). *Structural Holes: The Social Structure of Competition.* Cambridge, MA: Harvard University Press.

Coleman, J. (1988). Social capital in the creation of human capital. *American Journal of Sociology* **94**: 95–120.

Coleman, S. (1990). *Foundations of Social Theory.* Cambridge, MA: Harvard University Press.

Cowan, R. and Jonard, N. (2009). Knowledge portfolios and the organization of innovation networks. *Academy of Management Review* **34** (2): 320–342.

Dodd, M.D., Brummette, J., and Hazleton, V. (2015). A social capital approach: an examination of Putnam's civic engagement and public relations roles. *Public Relations Review* **41** (4): 472–479.

Edelman (2017). *The Edelman Trust Barometer.* New York: Edelman.

Fukuyama, F. (1995). *Trust: The Social Virtues and the Creation of Prosperity.* New York: Free Press.

Fussell, H., Harrison-Rexrode, J., Kennan, W.R., and Hazleton, V. (2006). The relationship between social capital, transaction costs, and organizational outcomes: a case study. *Corporate Communications: An International Journal* **11** (2): 148–161.

Granowetter, M. (1973). The strength of weak ties. *American Journal of Sociology* **78** (6): 1360–1379.

Gulati, R. (1995). Social structure and alliance formation patterns: a longitudinal analysis. *Administrative Science Quarterly* **40** (4): 619–652.

Hazelton, V. and Kennan, W.I. (2000). Social capital: reconceptualizing the bottom line. *Corporate Communications: An International Journal* **5** (2): 81–86.

Henttonen, K. (2009). The effects of social networks on work-team effectiveness. Doctoral dissertation. Lappeenranta University of Technology.

Hyyppä, M. and Mäki, J. (2003). Social participation and health in a community rich in stock of social capital. *Heath Education Research* **18** (6): 770–779.

Ihlen, Ø. (2005). The power of social capital: adapting Bourdieu to the study of public relations. *Public Relations Review* **31** (4): 492–496.

Ihlen, Ø., van Ruler, B., and Fredriksson, M. (2009). *Public Relations and Social Theory,* 1st ed. (ed. Ø. Ihlen, B. van Ruler and M. Fredriksson), 1–20. London: Routledge.

Jonson, O., Smith, M., and Gambill, D. (2000). Reconstructing "we": organizational identification in dynamic environment. In: *Relational Wealth: The Advantages of Stability in Changing Economy* (ed. C. Leana and D.M. Rousseau), 153–168. New York: Oxford University Press.

Kolivos, E. and Kuperman, A. (2012). Web of lies – legal implications of astroturfing. *Keeping Good Companies* **64** (1): 38–41.

Kumlin, S. and Rothstein, B. (2005). Making and breaking social capital: the impact of welfare-state institutions. *Comparative Political Studies* **38** (4): 339–365.

Leana, C.R. and Van Buren, H.J. (1999). Organizational social capital and employment practices. *Academy of Management Review* **24** (3): 538–555.

Lev, B. (2001). *Intangibles: Management, Measurement and Reporting.* Washington, DC: Brookings Institution Press.

Lin, N. (2001). *Social Capital: A Theory of Social Structure and Action*, Structural Analysis in the Social Sciences. Cambridge: Cambridge University Press.

Lucius, R. and Kuhnert, K. (1997). Using sociometry to predict team performance in the work place. *Journal of Psychology* **131** (1): 21–32.

Luoma-aho, V. (2005). Faith-Holders as Social Capital of Finnish Public Organisations. University of Jyväskylä, Studies in Humanities, No. 308, Jyväskylä, Finland.

Luoma-aho, V. (2006). Intangible of public organizations: trust and reputation. In: *Public Organizations in the Communication Society* (ed. V. Luoma-aho and S.-M. Peltola), 11–58. Jyväskylä: University of Jyväskylä.

Luoma-aho, V. (2007). Neutral reputation and public sector organizations. *Corporate Reputation Review* **10** (2): 124–143.

Luoma-aho, V. (2008). Sector reputation and public organisations. *International Journal of Public Sector Management* **21** (5): 446–467.

Luoma-aho, V. (2009). On Putnam: bowling together-applying Putnam's theories of community and social capital to public relations. In: *Ihlen, O., & Fredrikson (Eds.), Public Relations and Social Theory: Key Figures and Concepts*, 231–251. London: Routledge.

Luoma-aho, V. (2013). Corporate reputation and the theory of social capital. In: *The Handbook of Communication and Corporate Reputation* (ed. C.E. Carroll), 279–290. Wiley-Blackwell: Malden, MA.

Luoma-aho, V. (2015). Understanding stakeholder engagement: faith-holders, hateholders and fakeholders. *Research Journal of the Institute for Public Relations* **2** (1): http://www.instituteforpr.org/understanding-stakeholder-engagement-faith-holders-hateholders-fakeholders/ (accessed 26 September 2017).

Luoma-aho, V. and Makikangas, M. (2014). Do public sector mergers (re)shape reputation? *International Journal of Public Sector Management* **27** (1): 39–52.

Luoma-aho, V., Vos, M., Lappalainen, R. et al. (2012). Added value of intangibles for organizational innovation. *Human Technology: An Interdisciplinary Journal on Humans in ICT Environments* **8** (1): 7–23.

Malbon, J. (2013). Taking fake online consumer reviews seriously. *Journal of Consumer Policy* **36** (2): 139–157.

McNutt, J. and Boland, K. (2007). Astroturf, technology and the future of community mobilization: implications for nonprofit theory. *Journal of Accounting and Public Policy* **34** (3): 165–178.

Misztal, B. (1996). *Trust in Modern Societies.* Padstow: Polity Press.

Nahapiet, J. and Ghoshal, S. (1998). Social capital, intellectual capital, and the organizational advantage. *The Academy of Management Review* **23** (2): 242–266.

Oh, H., Labianca, G.(.J.)., and Chung, M.-H. (2006). A multilevel model of group social capital. *Academy of Management Review* **31** (3): 569–582.

Portes, A. (1998). Social capital: its origins and applications in modern sociology. *Annual Review of Sociology* **24** (1): 1–24.

Preston, L. (2004). Reputation as a source of corporate social capital. *Journal of General Management* **30** (2): 43–49.

Putnam, R. (1995). Bowling alone: America's declining social capital. *Journal of Democracy* **6** (1): 65–78.

Putnam, R. (1996). The strange disappearance of civic America. *The American Prospect* **7** (24): 34–48.

Putnam, R. (2000). *Bowling Alone: The Collapse and Revival of American Community*. New York: Simon & Schuster.

Putnam, R., Leonardi, R., and Nanetti, R. (1993). *Making Democracy Work; Civic Traditions in Modern Italy*. Princeton, NJ: Princeton University Press.

Putnam, R., Feldstein, L., and Cohen, D. (2003). *Better Together: Restoring the American Community*. New York: Simon & Schuster.

Raegans, R. and Zuckerman, E. (2001). Networks, diversity, and productivity: the social capital of corporate R&D teams. *Organization Science* **12** (4): 502–517.

Rothstein, B. and Stolle, D. (2003). Introduction: social capital in Scandinavia. *Scandinavian Political Studies* **26** (1): 1–26.

Saffer, A.J. (2016). A message-focused measurement of the communication dimension of social capital: revealing shared meaning in a network of relationships. *Journal of Public Relations Research* **28** (3-4): 170–192.

Sommerfeldt, E.J. (2013a). The civility of social capital: public relations in the public sphere, civil society, and democracy. *Public Relations Review* **39** (4): 280–289.

Sommerfeldt, E.J. (2013b). Networks of social capital: extending a public relations model of civil society in Peru. *Public Relations Review* **39** (1): 1–12.

Sommerfeldt, E.J. and Kent, M.L. (2015). Civil society, networks, and relationship management: beyond the organization–public dyad. *International Journal of Strategic Communication* **9** (3): 235–252.

Tigner, R. (2010). Online Astroturfing and the European Union's Unfair Commercial Practices Directive. European Union. http://www.droit-ecoulb.be/fileadmin/fichiers/Ronan_Tigner_-_Online_astroturfing.pdf (accessed 26 September 2017).

Tsai, W. (2000). Social capital, strategic relatedness and the formation of intraorganizational linkages. *Strategic Management Journal* **21** (9): 925–939.

Van Emmerik, I.J.H. and Brenninkmeijer, V. (2009). Deep-level similarity and group social capital: associations with team functioning. *Small Group Research* **40** (6): 650–669.

Wong, S.-S. (2008). Task knowledge overlap and knowledge variety: the role of advice network structures and impact on group effectiveness. *Journal of Organizational Behaviour* **29** (5): 591–614.

Yang, A. and Taylor, M. (2015). Looking over, looking out, and moving forward: positioning public relations in theorizing organizational network ecologies. *Communication Theory* **25** (1): 91–115.

Yang, A., Taylor, M., and Saffer, A.J. (2016). Ethical convergence, divergence or communitas? An examination of public relations and journalism codes of ethics. *Public Relations Review* **42** (1): 146–160.

12

Trust

Trust is the glue of life. It's the most essential ingredient in effective communication.
It's the foundational principle that holds all relationships
(Covey et al., 1995, p. 203)

This chapter is almost the last stop on a journey whose departure point was two assumptions. The first of these is that public sector organizations need to recover from a crisis of distrust that might be due to several gaps between organizations and citizens. The second is that communication can help in bridging these gaps by building intangible assets. In each of the chapters of the second part of the book, it has been argued that a specific intangible asset provides and gives access to tangible assets. We conclude here by exploring whether intangible assets actually build trust by bridging gaps.

The chapter starts by elaborating on the idea that trust provides intangible value that enables tangible value. The meaning of trust is then explored, and the causes of trust are analyzed in order to make the case for a causal relationship between intangible assets and trust. We then discuss what trust is built upon and how to build it, and we end by suggesting critical issues for further research.

12.1 Why Does Trust Matter? The Intangible and Tangible Value of Trust

The assertion that trust is needed in today's society has been made in the literature at different levels. First, it has been agreed that trust in public institutions is an important part of democracy in general. Fukuyama (1995) claims that "a nation's well-being, as well as its ability to compete, is conditioned by a single, pervasive cultural characteristic: the level of trust inherent in a society" (1995, p. 7). Sztompka (1999) adds that democracy itself is a means of establishing a culture of trust. A lack of political trust may affect the stability of democratic regimes or increase the willingness of citizens to engage in illegal behavior (Poppo and Schepker, 2010; Kestilä-Kekkonen and Söderlund, 2016).

At a mesolevel, the argument is that trust enables the interaction and cooperation necessary for everyday life. Putnam comments that "honesty and trust lubricate the inevitable frictions of social life" (Putnam, 2000, p. 135). Trust is a form of calm

Public Sector Communication: Closing Gaps Between Citizens and Public Organizations, First Edition.
María-José Canel and Vilma Luoma-aho.
© 2019 John Wiley & Sons, Inc. Published 2019 by John Wiley & Sons, Inc.

interaction, and an ideal model for communal life (Seligman, 1997). Luhmann (1988) associates trust with a certain unselfishness that is traditional in small communities, where trust is formed over long-term interactions and networks of friendships based on the traditional values and backgrounds of the actors involved. Although small communities have evolved into large societies, Luhmann argues that long-term trust networks still function in modern society. In fact, Rawls defines a good society as one where members willingly cooperate for the ultimate benefit of all (Hosmer, 1995, p. 394).

The literature provides a forceful description of the relationship between trust and public organizations. First, organizations require trust to survive. Governments need to be trusted to gain the public support that they need for the implementation of policy programs (Ruscio, 1997; Kim, 2005); and society needs trustworthy public organizations, as these spread trust throughout society and even produce social capital (Harisalo and Stenvall, 2003; Kumlin and Rothstein, 2005). Without trust or some form of agreement, opportunism prevails, all social exchange becomes risky, and there is no way of establishing a cooperative equilibrium (Gambetta, 1996).

What is the resource that trust generates? Trustworthy public organizations bring benefits to different areas of society: they maintain and attract business, enhance public participation, empower citizens, and increase engagement (Andreassen, 1994; Da Silva and Batista, 2007; Luoma-aho, 2008). Trust generates compliance (Van de Walle and Lahat, 2016) and legitimates the public bureaucracy's performance (Van der Meer, Steen, and Wille, 2015). Trustworthy public organizations are in a better position to make binding decisions, attract public resources, fulfill aims, increase legitimacy, and guarantee the fulfillment of public policies, and these elements reduce the costs of coercive systems (Easton, 1975; Levi, 1997; Scholz and Lubell, 1998). Furthermore, the intra-organizational components of trust affect efficiency and professional pride, factors that play essential roles in providing social services. Collaboration and trust appear to be essential elements for the operation of public services (Van de Walle and Lahat, 2016). Trust's opposite, distrust, "tends to evoke resistance, evasion, and dishonesty" (Cook, Hardin, and Levi, 2005, p. 161), and low levels of public trust harm the retention and recruitment of public employees, as well as their morale (Houston, Aitalieva, and Morelock, 2016).

Recent literature reviews have brought together different sources that support the benefits that trustworthiness brings public organizations today. Citizens' trust in public officials facilitates citizen participation, and trust in public administration has a positive effect on political efficacy. Public organizations enjoy higher levels of support for public policies when the public has greater trust in government. Trust is associated with satisfaction with services (Hamm, Hoffman, and Tomkins, 2016), and trust in government encourages individual citizens to disclose important personal information which is relevant for government performance (for example, during the collection of census data) (Kim, 2005, p. 628). In a distrustful relationship, by contrast, citizens might fear that the government would abuse their rights and that its programs would be harmful rather than helpful. As a result, citizens might refuse to participate in policy-implementation processes (Kim, 2010). Research evidence has also supported the idea that citizen trust in government increases compliance with tax laws, participation in vaccination programs, and acquiescence with evacuation orders during natural disasters, whereas a lack of trust is associated with the limited delegation of administrative authority, excessive oversight, and an overreliance on formal rules and procedures (Houston et al., 2016, p. 1204).

There is therefore an extensive body of literature that allows the argument to be made that trust enables cooperation, reduces harmful conflict, and decreases the costs of transactional and coercive systems.

12.2 What Is Trust?

Since the 1980s, the concept of trust has received special interest in research fields such as communication, sociology, psychology, and economics. Despite the vast literature on the matter, scholars continue to state that there is lack of consensus about the definition of trust (García and Fernández-Alfaro, 2014; Van de Walle and Six, 2014; Hamm et al., 2016; Robbins, 2016; Houston et al., 2016; Poppo et al., 2016). No universally accepted definition of "trust in public sector" has been produced, and the literature provides little consistency about what elements of research on trust are applicable to the public sector. Here, we first explore the definitions of trust and related terms that have been attempted, and we then propose a definition of "trust in public sector."

12.2.1 What is Trust About?

Trust is "a bet about the future contingent actions of others" (Sztompka, 1999, p. 25). It has been defined as a kind of deep sentiment that is more fundamental than mere acceptance, satisfaction, or legitimacy (Harisalo and Stenvall, 2003). Trust is "the expectation that arises within a community of regular, honest and cooperative behavior, based on commonly shared norms on the part of other members of that community" (Fukuyama, 1995, p. 26).

Trust has cognitive, emotional, and behavioral dimensions (Lewis and Weigert, 1985). It is a psychological state "comprising the intention to accept vulnerability based upon positive expectations of the intentions or behavior of another" (Rousseau, Sitkin, and Burt, 1998, p. 395), and it has behavioral consequences (Kim, 2005).

Different definitions of and approaches to trust contain a common feature: to trust entails vulnerability. Trust is placed in actors on the basis of expectations of certain beneficial actions. These expectations are primarily based on past experience with similar actors and situations (Quandt, 2012, pp. 8–9). But expecting means giving up control, since there is never a full guarantee in terms of outcomes – if there was, no trust would be needed. Therefore, trust inevitably requires a "leap of faith" in which the irreducible uncertainty and vulnerability are suspended (Van de Walle and Six, 2014). There is no trust without the willingness of the person who offers his or her trust to somehow be defenseless, since the decision to trust is based on the belief that the party in which trust is placed will meet one's own expectations, even in situations where the trusted party cannot be monitored or controlled (Kim, 2005, p. 621). For someone to be trustworthy, the individuals who might place their trust in that person must be willing to be vulnerable under conditions of uncertainty and interdependence.

Trust is especially important for repeated interaction; it is a prerequisite for a relationship (Lahno, 1995; Sydow, 1998). Long-term relationships are not formed without trust, honesty, and reliability. Trust is thus a willingness to open oneself up and a faith in the other party's refusal to exploit one's goodwill (Grunig and Huang, 1999, p. 44).

The difficulty in defining trust comes from the complex and multidimensional nature of this construct, which permeates both interpersonal and institutional levels (Kim, 2005). To analyze trust effectively, it has proved useful to view it as a three-part relationship involving the properties and attributes of the party that trusts, the party that is trusted, and possible trust intermediaries (Hardin, 1993; Bentele, 1994). In a recent work, Robbins (2016) suggests conceiving of trust as a single concept built around four essential properties: actor A's beliefs (*how* one trusts), actor B's trustworthiness (*who* one trusts), the matter(s) at hand (*what* one trusts another person to do), and unknown outcomes.

12.2.2 Can There Be Trust in Public Sector Organizations?

Can the process of trusting go beyond the individual personal level and affect the organizational level? Different concepts have been provided to answer to this question. Easton's (1975) differentiation between "specific" and "diffuse" support has been followed by discussion of "generalized trust" – that is, the trust that is evident among all members of society. While particularized trust indicates trust in one's immediate social circles (for example, family members, relatives, friends, and neighbors), generalized trust reflects trust in those beyond one's immediate circle, including strangers (Hu, Sun, and Wu, 2015). Generalized trust thus refers to the general will to cooperate with people even if one does not know them personally (Luoma-aho, 2005; Kääriäinen and Sirén, 2012).

Although some have argued against the possible existence of such confidence or generalized trust (see Granovetter, 1985), Rothstein and Stolle (2002) have developed what they call an "institutional theory of generalized trust." They claim that trust in society becomes generalized through institutions: the structure of contemporary institutions generates generalized trust, especially in societies where institutions are trustworthy. The process of generalized trust is similar to the imitation process of trust formation in early childhood (Erikson, 1963); the influence of the "care givers" is crucial. In the case of society, the care givers would be the institutions and organizations. Rothstein and Stolle note that especially significant requirements for the formation of generalized trust are organizations and institutions that provide order and implementation, as many public organizations do. They state that "the impartiality and efficiency of these institutions influences basically citizens' institutional trust and more specifically (i) how they experience feelings of safety and protection, (ii) how citizens make inferences from the system and public officials to other citizens, (iii) how citizens observe the behavior of fellow citizens, and (iv) how they experience discrimination against themselves or close others" (Rothstein and Stolle, 2002, p. 27). Therefore, it can be stated that trust is something that can occur in the interactions between public sector organizations and different publics.

12.3 Trust in the Public Sector

Van de Walle states that "citizens' confidence in the public sector features high on the political agenda," based on an entrenched conviction that confidence in the civil service, public administration, or public services is low and declining (Van de Walle, 2007, p. 6). An impetus for a wider variety of institutional efforts to increase trust has also been detected (Hamm et al., 2016). There are many government initiatives that include the word *trust* in their names (for example, the US Department of Justice's National Initiative for Building Community Trust and Justice; Department of Justice 2014), as well as others that have trust as their ultimate goal, even if they do not include the word in their title (for example, the central government of Colombia's Urna de Cristal project, which aims to allow citizens to monitor government initiatives and have a say in policy making).

From a conceptual perspective, no definition of "trust in the public sector" specifically has been produced. The attention paid to this area in the scholarly literature is somewhat fragmented, and it centers on different concepts such as "political trust," "trust in government," "trust in public administration," "trust in public services," and "trust in civil servants." There is little research dealing with public services or the civil service. A small amount of empirical research on trust refers to public administration, and many studies only focus on specific services such as schools, health care, fire departments, or local government (Van de Walle, 2007). There are some studies on citizens' attitudes toward the public administration in a single country (Harisalo and Stenvall, 2003; Van de Walle, 2004).

12.3.1 Political Trust, Public Trust, and Trust in Government

Several concepts that are close to the study of trust in the public sector can be found in the literature: "public and political trust" (Hu et al., 2015), "relational trust" (Poppo et al., 2016), "public trust" (Kim, 2005), and "trust in government" (Bouckaert and Van de Walle, 2001).

Political trust has been defined by scholars as "a basic evaluative orientation of how governmental institutions, political parties, and actors operate against the backdrop of one's normative expectations" (Kestilä-Kekkonen and Söderlund, 2016, p. 138). For example, Seyd comments that "political trust represents a judgment that, even in the absence of ongoing scrutiny or enforcement by citizens, a political institution will act in a way that is broadly consistent with those citizens' interests" (Seyd, 2015, p. 74). In these definitions, the notion of one's own vulnerability and lack of control is, once again, associated with trust, and this idea is specifically mentioned in Kim's statement that "public trust derives from the citizens' willingness to be vulnerable based on a belief that government and public employees will meet the expectations of credible commitment, benevolence, honesty, competency, and fairness without regular monitoring" (2005, p. 621).

Kim (2005, 2010) clarifies our understanding of the concept of trust in government by elaborating on the cognitive, affective, and behavioral aspects of trust. Trust is, first, a cognitive decision by individuals who are willing to grant discretion based on their evaluative beliefs in government. Second, trust is an affective notion that demonstrates an emotional attachment by those who are in the trust relationship; this affective foundation implies a willingness to be vulnerable to another's behavior and forsakes or significantly reduces the desire for a controlling mechanism to check government decisions. Finally, trust involves a behavioral dimension: citizens' attitudes vary depending on the ways in which the government approaches trust relationships, and thus, from trustworthy governments, citizens' voluntary compliance with policies can emerge. However, measuring these different aspects is complex. Bouckaert and Van de Walle (2001) provide a thorough and helpful discussion of the dependence of the meaning of trust on the methods used to assess it. "Trust in government" as an attitude, these authors state, refers to "government" in general, more in political terms (and thus "trust in government" is a contextual phenomenon mixed with other attitudes such as trust in incumbents or in the political system) rather than in terms of its role as a service provider. Therefore, this attitude might say little about trust in public services, public administration, or the public sector.

12.3.2 Trust in Public Administration

One of the domains of trust research is trust in "public administration." This is understood broadly by some researchers as the administration of government in general, while others focus on specific governmental entities. In their cross-domain comparison, Hamm et al. (2016) state that in public administration trust, the trustors are usually the general public; the *target* of trust varies in that it can be a legislative, executive, or general governmental agency.

Trust in public administration has been defined as the confidence and faith placed in the latter in accordance with normative expectations held by the public (Wang and Wart, 2007). This concept has a normative component: it is the belief that the public administration is "doing the right things," and it includes the assumption that the intentions and actions of officials are ethical, fair, and competent, meaning that the public administration "operates in the best interests of society and its constituents" (Kim, 2010, p. 803). Hamm et al. (2016) mention that scholars also incorporate the notion of *vulnerability* by defining trust as "a psychological state that is willing to take a risk by accepting vulnerability, even in situations where the trustor cannot recognize, monitor or control the target" (p. 4). Drawing on Ruscio (1999), Kim states that trust in public administrations is an institutional construct that involves "weaving together judgments of the integrity and capability of public officials with confidence in the institutional structures in which they operate" (Kim, 2005, p. 613).

Different aspects can be taken as an object of trust in the realm of public administration: there can be trust in the public service, civil service, public officials, public policies, and public bureaucracy (Van de Walle, 2007). In assessing the state of the art of research on trust in public administration, Bouckaert (2012) points out the need to go beyond traditional studies that see citizens as customers of public services and to focus on their individual trust. Bouckaert suggests three clusters of studies: society's trust in the public sector, the public sector's trust in society, and trust within the public sector. In this regard, Bouckaert understands that trust is a feature of the relationships of individuals, of organizations, and of institutions, and he adds that "to better understand how trust regimes in policy fields or countries have an impact on relations and interactions, it is necessary to broaden the concept, the data and the context" (Bouckaert, 2012, p. 94).

12.3.3 Going Beyond the Public Administration: Trust in the Public Sector

From the above literature review, it can be ascertained that the following components should appear in a definition of trust in the public sector: uncertainty, vulnerability, interdependence, ongoing interaction, and willingness to grant a discretional margin to do something.

In accordance with the definition of public sector communication that we provided in Chapter 2 (which embraces a varied amount of publicness for the different variables according to which organizations can be classified), we propose a definition of trust in the public sector that goes beyond fully public organizations to include the relations between all organizations and entities that provide a specific public service. Trust in the public sector includes trust involving all the types of organizations that belong to it, and there are organizations that are at different levels of publicness in terms of funding, control, ownership, and purpose.

Our definition assumes that the public sector always operates in a *context of a lack of certainty* about outcomes – and hence there is a certain level of *vulnerability* – and that the components of the public sector – both organizations and individuals – play an interdependent role in addressing that uncertainty.

Trust in the public sector is:

> *The willingness, within the context of uncertainty, to grant discretion to the other party (an organization, a leader, a citizen, and so forth) in the use of public resources for the provision of public services, from which a certain compliance, or at least a reduction in the desire to control, emerges.*

A key question that follows on from this definition is what trust is built upon – that is, what creates trust? We explore this issue in the following sections.

12.4 Sources of Trust: What Generates Trust in the Public Sector?

What can increase (or decrease) this willingness to grant discretion to the other side? As research has shown, trust in public institutions is multicausal, contingent, and contextual (Citrin and Green, 1986; Nye, Zelikow, and King, 1997; Bouckaert et al., 2002; Karens, Eshuis, and Klijn, 2015; Hamm et al., 2016). Variables that explain (dis)trust vary, and they include party affiliation, personal experiences, and satisfaction with government performance and public services. In an analysis of a public brand, Karens et al. (2015) classify the sources of citizen trust in the brand into three categories: benevolence, honesty, and competence. Referring specifically to trust in public administration, Hamm et al. (2016, p. 4) classify the possible sources into five broad categories:

1) performance (understood as the target's previous output as assessed/perceived by the party that offers trust);
2) institutional design (features such as citizens' participation mechanisms, a parliamentary structure, and electoral systems);
3) attributes of the public officials (ethical behavior/integrity, competence, and benevolence);
4) environment (political stability, economic prosperity, generalized social trust, and trust in government);
5) the actor that offers trust (individual characteristics such as demographics, party affiliation, and political ideology).

Based on these categories and a review of the literature, we will now elaborate on the four blocks of variables that cover the major research developments on trust in the public sector: demographics, political variables, events management, and performance.

12.4.1 Demographics

Gender, age, education, social class, and income are variables that are frequently found in research designs to explain different levels of trust. However, evidence of these variables is mixed and tied to specific contexts (Van de Walle, 2007; Houston et al., 2016; Kestilä-Kekkonen and Söderlund, 2016). Studies show that sociodemographic factors are not terribly helpful in explaining trust, and variables referring to these factors are often excluded from explanatory models (Van de Walle, 2007). This has been corroborated by recent studies that attempt to explain attitudes toward public administrations in different countries (Houston et al., 2016; Van de Walle and Lahat, 2016).

12.4.2 Political Attitudes as Explainers of Trust

Political variables (such as party alignment, perception of personal ideology on a left/right-wing spectrum, and voting intention) have been found to explain different levels of trust. Those who voted for the government tend to trust it and the public services that the latter delivers, regardless of their actual experiences (Citrin and Green, 1986; Ostrom Jr. and Simon, 1988; Lanoue and Headrick, 1994; Gronke and Newman, 2003). In fact, political variables have been shown to have an important role in explaining trust. Party identification conditions attitudes and support for the government and its institutions (Houston et al., 2016), something that has been proved in recent analyses (Söderlund and Kestilä-Kekkonen, 2009).

However, there are studies that show that the partisan commitment of citizens who are close to the party in government may decrease when the economy slows down, in which case, the government's economic performance is subsequently assessed less favorably (Fiorina, 1981; Kinder and Kiewiet, 1981). Moreover, some studies have shown that this loss of political variables' power to explain trust is associated with contexts of economic crisis (Canel, 2009; Canel and Echart, 2011; Canel and García-Molero, 2013).

12.4.3 The Influence of Events Management

Both ideology and "what happens" influence citizens when they assess trust in government. The way in which public sector authorities manage events such as terrorist attacks, strikes, demonstrations, war, and scandals has an impact on how citizens trust those authorities. Studies consistently conclude that assessments of the ways in which heads of government have handled significant international and domestic crises have had a powerful effect on government approval and, indirectly, on trust (Edwards III and Swenson, 1997; Chanley, Rudolph, and Rahn, 2000; Nicholson, Segura, and Woods, 2002). Governments are held responsible for problems and conflicts, and specific events might boost or depress trust in government and subsequently shape citizens' assessments of specific public services.

12.4.4 Performance as a Source of Trust

One of the variables that has been most explored as a cause of trust is performance (of public policies) and, more specifically, economic performance (which includes macroeconomic indicators such as the employment rate and inflation as well as perceptions at the individual level such as views on the state of one's personal finances). The classical theory on voting based on economic factors (according to which citizens respond to both past and upcoming economic events) assumes that people hold the government responsible for the evolution of the economic situation. A high number of empirical studies confirm this theory: economic conditions and perceptions of them powerfully affect public evaluations of government performance (Citrin and Green, 1986; Brace and Hinckley, 1992; Nadeau, Niemi, and Fan, 1999; Chanley et al., 2000; Nicholson et al., 2002; Gronke and Newman, 2003).

In public administration literature, the prevalent performance-trust hypothesis posits that trust results from a positive assessment of governmental performance (Houston et al., 2016). A brief review of recent scholarly articles suggests that organizational effectiveness, satisfactory public services/service quality, policy consistency, transparency/corruption, responsiveness and accessibility, and economic development/growth/stability are some of the important specific evaluations within this broader performance category (Hamm et al., 2016, pp. 4–5). In general, trust in public administration is expected to increase when a public administration performs better, and "poor bureaucratic performance most commonly takes the blame for a decline in trust" (Houston et al., 2016, p. 1203).

However, there is also a set of literature that challenges this predominance of the performance-trust hypothesis. First, there is research evidence that points out angles aside from performance outcomes that are becoming relevant for citizens when they form their views on the trustworthiness of the public sector. People seem not to be merely interested in the outcome of public official processes; the process itself has to be fair (Gustavsen, Røiseland, and Pierre, 2014; Aggerholm and Thomsen, 2016; Whiteley, Clarke, and Sanders, 2016). And sometimes the process becomes even more important in determining public trust than are results (Van Ryzin, 2011). It might be the case that focusing trust strategies on making visible the outcomes of public policies and in so doing neglecting the process behind them is ultimately detrimental to trust.

Second, studies have found that perceptions of the political and economic environment, as opposed to objective indicators alone, drive approval, and that perceptions do not always perfectly follow objective indicators. In fact, there seems to be consensus among researchers about a complex dynamic that involves no direct causal relationships between public organizations' achievements, public policy results, communication performance, citizen satisfaction, and citizen trust. The subtle interplay of reality, perceptions, and expectations means that the performance of a public administration, the satisfaction of its users, and trust are not necessarily related (Bouckaert et al., 2002; Bouckaert and Van de Walle, 2003; Van de Walle and Bouckaert, 2003; Carmeli and Tishler, 2005; James, 2009; Van De Walle, 2011; James and Moseley, 2014).

Research is needed to elaborate models that capture possible causes of trust other than constant contextual changes. The next section discusses other intangible assets as possible causes of increased trust.

12.5 Other Intangible Assets as Causes of Trust

Besides studies that suggest that other intangible assets can act as sources of trust in the public sector, there is literature that identifies sources of trust that are derivations of intangible assets. For instance, Hosmer mentions that characteristics such as integrity, competence, consistency, loyalty, and openness contribute to a trusting relationship (Hosmer, 1995). We would argue that when these characteristics exist, it is because the organization owns the intangible asset of legitimacy. Bentele (1994, p. 145) lists eight trust factors that either increase or diminish the level of trust: expertise, the ability to solve problems, adequacy of communication, communicative consistency, transparency, publicity, social responsibility, and responsible ethics. Should these factors be highly rated, trust is won, but if they are given a low rating, a reduction in trust is probable. We argue that the rating of these factors is associated with the rating of intangible assets such as reputation, intellectual capital, social responsibility, and legitimacy.

Despite the dearth of studies that empirically support the relationship between specific intangible assets and trust, the literature argues that there are conceptual links between them. For example, definitions of legitimacy suggest a positive connection to trust: legitimate organizations are more trustworthy to the extent that legitimacy is associated with meaningfulness, predictability, and credible collective accounts about what an organization is and does (Jepperson, 1991; Suchman, 1995). Therefore, by sharing these understandings, stakeholders have more certainty about the worth of granting the organization a discretional margin to decide about public resources. Similarly, public leaders who enjoy a positive reputation are also regarded as more trustworthy (Da Silva and Batista, 2007, pp. 590–591), whereas a poor reputation damages trust in public administrations (Wæraas and Byrkjeflot, 2012, pp. 188–189). The relationship between satisfaction and trust is as debatable as that between performance and trust. Nevertheless, the general assumption is that high-quality services lead to satisfaction and, subsequently, to trust. References for the relations between social capital and trust and between organizational culture and trust have been cited in the corresponding chapters.

The most empirically explored relationship is that between engagement and trust. Citizen trust in government and public administration has been generally argued to be an outcome of engagement, public participation, citizen involvement in public administrative decision making, and agencies' two-way communications (Wang and Wart, 2007; Yang and Pandey, 2011, p. 880; Thomas, 2013; Denhardt and Denhardt, 2015, p. 665). But there are also doubts about this causal chain (Uslaner and Brown, 2005, p. 872), and the more it has been explored, the more nuances have needed to be incorporated, and contingencies and contextual differences also have to be identified in order to fully account for the behavior of the trust variable. For instance, Fledderus (2015) finds that it is not coproduction as such but the way in which the latter is organized and managed by public officials that determines whether it ultimately produces outcomes such as trust in (local) government and generalized trust. Although participation builds public consensus, consensus building alone does not lead to public trust, for if done in an inauthentic manner, engagement efforts may lead to mistrust (Wang and Wart, 2007; Denhardt and Denhardt, 2015, p. 666). It has also been proved that public trust increases when public officials who focus on involvement efforts demonstrate integrity, honesty, and moral leadership (Wang and Wart, 2007).

The contingency argument that Yang and Pandey (2011) apply to citizen-involvement efforts also has relevance to trust and intangible assets: for each individual situation, a particular type of mechanism may be chosen, so in the aggregate, a variety of mechanisms should be in place so that trust is ultimately built. Different intangible assets can help produce trust in the public sector in different ways, and a specific organization should strategically develop the mechanisms to establish the intangible asset that it needs to eventually link with trust.

In Table 12.1, we relate each intangible asset dealt with in this book to trust. We look at them in both directions: an intangible asset as a source of trust, and trust as a

Table 12.1 Different intangible assets and trust.

Trust	*The capacity of an organization to be granted discretion in the use of public resources for the provision of public services within a context of uncertainty, and from which certain compliance emerges on the part of the other side*		
Intangible asset	What it tells us about	Rationale for the suggested positive impact on trust	How trust can affect this intangible asset
Satisfaction	Overall pleasantness in the public service experience	Higher satisfaction leads to the granting of a higher level of discretion to decide about public resources	Trust supports and enhances satisfaction
Organizational culture	The internal character of the organization	The stronger and more aligned the organizational culture, the more trust it generates	Trust enables a good culture by enabling flexibility and collaboration
Reputation	Records of the organization's past deeds and overall impression	The better the experience of past fulfillment of expectations, the easier it is to grant discretion to the other side	Trust turns to reputation in the same way that the present turns into the past; reputation is built on trust
Legitimacy	The capacity of an organization (and its functions) to be allowed to exist by its publics	The more solid the belief that an organization is needed, the easier it will be for it to be granted discretion	Trustworthy organizations are more likely to be allowed to intervene in public debates about legitimacy criteria, and thus more shared understandings are enabled
Intellectual capital	The capacity of an organization to manage knowledge well	In organizations with high intellectual capital, reasons to grant discretion (efficiency, efficacy, and competency) are more visible	In trustworthy organizations, there are better conditions for knowledge to be shared, systematized, provided, and enriched
Engagement	The capacity that a public organization has to make citizens involved in public administration processes	The more involved the other side is (in public administration processes), the higher the interdependence, and thus the higher the margin of discretion granted	It is easier for citizens to become involved in and follow processes run by trustworthy organizations
Social capital	The capacity of an organization to generate social cohesion	Bonding social capital fosters internal organizational trust, bridging social capital between citizens and organizations	Trustworthy organizations increase publics' willingness to become involved in larger social purposes

source of an intangible asset. Therefore, the questions that we attempt to answer are the following:

- How might a specific intangible asset help an organization to gain the discretionary power from the other side (that is, earn trust) to manage public resources?
- How might trust (the discretionary power earned by the organization) help the organization to earn the benefit of a specific intangible asset?

12.6 Trust and Communication: Building Trust

Hung, Dennis, and Robert (2004, p. 5) suggest three routes of trust formation: the peripheral route, the central route, and habitual trust. The peripheral route is based on third-party information, rules, categories, and roles that the situational contexts determine, but little weight is given here to the actual experience of the organization and its actions, or to collaboration and interaction with the organization and other publics. In this case, trust is formed on the basis of peripheral impressions and estimates that derive from organizational symbolic communication – that is, it is based on an image (a perception subject to manipulation and distortion). Therefore, trust formed in this way is less strong, and if discretion is granted, it can be easily removed from the organization. And when contextual uncertainty becomes even more acute, there is no reason to comply. The central route, based on perceived ability, integrity, and benevolence, involves experience of the organization; whereas images produce trust in the peripheral route, in the central route trust is produced by actual interactions between citizens and the public sector organization. Finally, structural trust is based on habitual trust (an ongoing granting of a discretional margin). The interdependence of the organization and its publics results in mutual collaboration and interaction, and the focus is on maintaining the relationship at a comfortable level of trust.

The process by which trust is built is progressive. During the first encounter, the initial impressions formed through the peripheral route form an image. Based on this image, a decision is made as to whether to trust or not. As more information and experiences are collected, the central route begins to gain ground. The accumulated experience and collaboration of the central route lead to trust. Trust formed through intangible assets is more stable than that formed through an image. Once established, trust based on intangible assets leads to a relationship if both parties so desire. As the relationship progresses, trust becomes habitual and ceases to be something that requires estimation and cognitive processes. The relationship does not, however, always progress through all possible levels, as demands and relationships vary.

Figure 12.1 suggests that trust is part of a virtuous circle in which intangible assets progressively feed trust. The figure conveys different levels of intangible assets, since, as was described in Chapter 4, there are intangible assets that are predominantly based on organizational knowledge, while others are based on stakeholder experience or mutual collaboration. The theory of generalized trust suggests that the public sector organizations in a society play a central role in brokering trust through the positive experiences of collaboration that they provide (Kumlin and Rothstein, 2005; Luoma-aho, 2009). As Figure 12.1 shows, all intangible assets contribute to trust, but a certain continuum can be distinguished. First, starting from the top, public sector communication builds on intellectual capital and organizational culture, which are

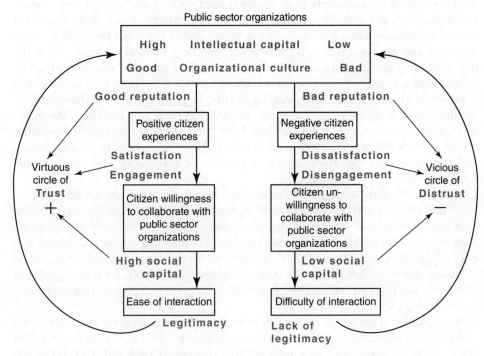

Figure 12.1 How public sector organizations' intangible assets contribute to either a virtuous circle of trust or a vicious circle of distrust in society. Source: Adapted from Luoma-aho (2005).

reflected through reputation. Reputation contributes to experiences, which in turn guide satisfaction and engagement and yield collaboration. Good collaboration produces social capital, and interaction produces legitimacy. This legitimacy in turn feeds trust into public sector organizations, which radiates to society at large, as Figure 12.1 shows.

Trust can thus be maintained and built upon. Dervitsiotis (2003) suggests that building organizational trust means cultivating quality relationships with stakeholders. These relationships are normally built up over long periods of time during repeated interactions and thus require constant fostering. Perseverance, however, is beneficial to the organization, as stakeholder trust developed in this way shields the organization from damage in times of trouble and legitimizes the organization. To some extent, trust requires a relationship to be formed, as in a relationship trustworthiness is under constant evaluation (Dervitsiotis, 2003).

12.7 Critical Issues and Further Research

12.7.1 Is There a Trend of Decreasing Trust in Public Sector Organizations?

There is a debate in the literature about whether there is a problem of low trust and of distrust in the public sector. This issue has been extensively explored by Bouckaert and

Van de Walle, 2004; Van de Walle, Van Roosbroek, and Bouckaert, 2008; Van De Walle, 2011), who have reviewed data from National Election Studies, World Value Studies, Eurobarometer, and Gallup, upon which the common assertion of a persistent global decline in attitudes about civil servants has been constructed. They conclude that this assertion may be based more on assumption than on empirical evidence. What the data support, these authors conclude, is constant fluctuations, a decline in trust in some countries, and an increase or no change in others. There is little empirical evidence of an overall long-term decline in trust in governments. Furthermore, the attention paid to attitudes toward public services has been very limited in the major international surveys, and at the national level, the bulk of survey material is rather recent (Van de Walle et al., 2008). Efforts need to be made in order to produce strong and consistent data that allows trends in trust to be determined and, more importantly, its causes to be explored.

This is particularly important in view of the fact that trust might be affected by a context of economic crisis. Uslaner (2010) argues that the economic crisis of 2008 led to a loss in confidence in financial institutions and in government more generally. He elaborates on the relationship between perceptions of inequality, generalized trust, and civic engagement, and concludes that "the legacy of the financial crisis and the economic inequality that it has left in its wake (both actual and perceived) is a hardening of both ideological and partisan lines, making it more difficult to enact legislation that might help the economic recovery" (p. 110).

An economic crisis seems to have an impact on the roots of generalized trust and confidence in institutions. Erkel and Meer (2016) have explored Eurobarometer data (21 waves in 15 European Union member states) between 1999 and 2011 to test the extent to which within-country variations in economic performance affect political trust longitudinally. They conclude that there is a relationship between economic crisis and trust: longitudinal changes in performance (growth, deficits, unemployment, and inflation) affect political trust; the impact of macroeconomic performance is stronger among the lower educated; and, finally, even in times of economic difficulty, budgetary deficits tend to undermine political trust.

A similar exploration has been conducted in relation to Spain, and its conclusion is that the economic crisis is modifying the way in which and the extent to which people trust the government. Based on an examination of the period between 1995 and 2010, the more recent the economic crisis, the more people base their trust assessment on experiential variables (the outcomes of public policies) rather than on inertial ones (ideology preferences). It seems that when an economic crisis has occurred, people in Spain tend to trust the prime minister if they have a job and if the economy begins to recover (Canel and Echart, 2011; Canel and García-Molero, 2013). However, in 2011, and partly as a result of a higher visibility of corruption scandals, Spaniards seemed to care more about the legitimacy of processes (honesty, transparency, and dialogue with public leaders) than they did about the legitimacy of outcomes (Canel, 2015). In the case of the United Kingdom, Whiteley et al. (2016) have found that the Great Recession, which started in late 2007, and the introduction of austerity policies by the incoming coalition government both served to undermine trust in government. Therefore, whether there is a crisis of trust and how an economic crisis affects it are issues for further research.

12.7.2 Debated Issues about Measuring Trust

Appraising institutions and organizations is a very difficult task, as it usually requires simultaneous estimation of actions on various scales of achievement, and the scales are often not commensurable. Taking trust as one of the indicators for determining the overall value of public relations, Grunig and Hon (1999) suggest that it can be measured through the three following components: *integrity* (the belief that an organization is fair and just, with survey items like "This organization does not mislead people like me"), *dependability* (the belief that an organization will do what it says it will do, with survey items like "This organization can be relied on to keep its promises"), and *competence* (the belief that an organization has the ability to do what it says it will do, with survey items like "I feel very confident about this organization's skills").

In measuring trust in the public sector (with the related objects of measurement, such as trust in government, in public services, in civil servants, or in public administration) scholars have identified several issues as critically important.

First, should trust be considered in an absolute or relative way? Bouckaert and Van de Walle suggest that to make meaningful statements, numbers should be looked at relatively, and that comparisons can take different forms – for example, between different levels of governments (for instance, trust in local government compared with trust in central government), across units of a same level of government (for instance, comparisons of trust in local government across towns), across countries (for instance, trust in the civil service across countries), and across sectors (for instance, trust in public sector performance compared with trust in private sector performance). These comparisons have complexities, since there are different understandings and cultural interpretations of what is to be measured – civil service, bureaucracy, state, public administration, and so forth – as well as of different ways of wording items, different thresholds of trust, and different ways of measuring the different influential institutional factors (Bouckaert and Van de Walle, 2001; Van de Walle, 2007; Bouckaert, 2012). Managing all these differences is a relevant challenge in advancing cross-national comparative research on trust in the public sector.

Second, should trust be measured based on evaluations that are retrospective (previous experiences and present observations) or on ones that are prospective (expectations about the future; Bouckaert and Van de Walle, 2001)? Sztompka's assertion that trust is a bet on future actions has to be complemented with knowledge as to whether the trust judgment derives from actual performance or from past experience.

Third, is measuring distrust equal to measuring a lack of trust? In responding to this question, Van de Walle and Six (2014) have argued against the conventional wisdom that trust and distrust are two polar opposites on a continuum, and they have stated that scholars should stop interpreting low scores on trust measures as indications of the presence of active distrust. Therefore, rather than using a trust-distrust continuum, these two constructs should be measured separately (distinguishing trust/no trust from distrust/ no distrust). As these authors show, their determinants are different, as are their consequences.

Fourth and finally, the question of causality is a perennial critical issue. What comes first? Is it the case that high satisfaction with public services leads to trust? Or, conversely, is it the case that trustworthy organizations tend to be given positive assessments of their performance? The literature has addressed this question and tried to suggest models for exploring causal relations, taking trust as a dependent variable as well as an independent one (see, for instance, Houston et al., 2016 and Kestilä-Kekkonen and Söderlund, 2016, to mention just some recent studies). The same can be said about the relations between trust and specific intangible assets (see, for instance, the analysis by Rothstein and Stolle, 2008, which attempts to determine the causal relationship between trust in government and social capital). Based on Table 12.1 in this chapter above, different research hypotheses can be elaborated for further research.

12.8 Summary of Trust

Table 12.2 summarizes the chapter and explains the value of trust as an intangible asset in the public sector.

Table 12.2 Trust as an intangible asset in the public sector.

Trust is the intangible asset that measures the capacity of an organization to be granted discretion in the use of public resources for the provision of public services within a context of uncertainty, and from which certain compliance emerges among other parties	
Tangible asset that trust enables	All physical capital associated with the different intangible assets that trust generates
Resource that trust generates	Citizen compliance and legitimacy in the performance of the public bureaucracy Efficiency, efficacy, professional pride, and collaboration Trust generates other intangible assets: organizational culture, intellectual capital, reputation, satisfaction, legitimacy, social capital, and engagement
Monetary expression	Costs savings, procedural time savings, and information Since distrust is associated with excessive oversight, overreliance on formal rules and procedures, it increases costs; distrust is also associated with low participation in policy implementation processes, which reduces efficiency
Value that trust provides to the organization	Trustworthy public organizations are better able to make binding decisions, involve public resources, fulfill aims, and guarantee fulfillment of public policies without the need to increase coactivity; they are also more capable of effective crisis management
Value that trust provides to citizens and stakeholders	Trust enhances public participation and empowers citizens; services provided by trustworthy organizations are more satisfying to citizens
Gaps that trust bridges	Trustworthy organizations enjoy greater compliance from stakeholders, and to the extent that different intangible assets build trust, their bridging of gaps helps trust to reduce uncertainty
Dependence on communication management	To the extent that communication helps to build intangible assets, communication is needed to make visible the reasons (values, experiences, and so forth) for granting a discretional margin to the organization Communication helps to transform the peripheral route to image-based trust into the structural route of an ongoing trusting relationship
Implied organization management transformations	For an organization to be focused on trust building, a new organizational distribution of functions, ethos, professional profiles, and attitudes is needed to bring about an orientation toward value creation
Measures	Quantitative and qualitative methods that embrace the range of different components of public sector: trust in civil servants, in public administration, in public services, and in public–private partnerships

References

Aggerholm, H.K. and Thomsen, C. (2016). Legitimation as a particular mode of strategic communication in the public sector. *International Journal of Strategic Communication* **10** (3): 195–206.

Andreassen, T.W. (1994). Satisfaction, loyalty and reputation as indicators of customer orientation in the public sector. *International Journal of Public Sector Management* **7** (2): 16–34.

Bentele, G. (1994). Public trust: normative and social foundations for public relations. In: *Normative Foundation for Public Relations* (ed. W. Armbrecht and U.J. Zabel), 131–158. Westdeutcher Verlag: Opladen.

Bouckaert, G. (2012). Trust and public administration. *Administration* **60** (1): 91–115.

Bouckaert, G., and Van de Walle, S. (2001). Government performance and trust in government. Paper for the Permanent Study Group of Productivity and Quality in the Public Sector at the EGPA Annual Conference, Vaasa, Finland (5–8 September 2001).

Bouckaert, G. and Van de Walle, S. (2003). Comparing measures of citizen trust and user satisfaction as indicators of 'good governance': difficulties in linking trust and satisfaction indicators. *International Review of Administrative Sciences* **69** (3): 329–343.

Bouckaert, G., Van de Walle, S., Maddens, B., and Kampen, J. (2002). Identity vs. performance: an overview of theories explaining trust in government. Second Report "Quality and Trust in Government." Leuven: Public Management Institute.

Brace, P. and Hinckley, B. (1992). *Follow the Leader: Opinion Polls and the Modern Presidents*. New York, NY: Basic Books.

Canel, M.J. (2009). El impacto de los sucesos imprevistos en la imagen pública de los gobiernos españoles. *Anàlisi: Quaderns de Comunicació i Cultura* **38**: 219–236.

Canel, M.J. (2015). Legitimacy and trust as intangible assets of the public sector: challenges for government public relations in times of economic crisis. Paper presented at the annual meeting of the International Communication Association 65th Annual Conference, Caribe Hilton, San Juan, Puerto Rico (21 May 2015).

Canel, M.J. and Echart, N. (2011). The role and functions of government public relations. lessons from public perceptions of government. *Central European Journal of Communication* **4** (1(6)): 109–123.

Canel, M.J. and García-Molero, Á. (2013). Comunicar gobiernos fiables. Análisis de la confianza como valor intangible del gobierno de España. *Zer-Revista de Estudios de Comunicación* **18** (34): 29–48.

Carmeli, A. and Tishler, A. (2005). Perceived organizational reputation and organizational performance: an empirical investigation of industrial enterprises. *Corporate Reputation Review* **8** (1): 13–30.

Chanley, V.A., Rudolph, T.J., and Rahn, W.M. (2000). The origins and consequences of public trust in government: a time series analysis. *Public Opinion Quarterly* **64** (3): 239–256.

Citrin, J. and Green, D.P. (1986). Presidential leadership and the resurgence of trust in government. *British Journal of Political Science* **16** (4): 431–453.

Cook, K.S., Hardin, R., and Levi, M. (2005). *Cooperation without Trust? The Russell Sage Foundation Series on Trust*. New York, NY: Russel Sage Foundation.

Covey, S.R., Merrill, A.R., and Merrill, R.R. (1995). *First Things First*. New York: Simon & Schuster.

Denhardt, J.V. and Denhardt, R.B. (2015). The new public service revisited. *Public Administration Review* **75** (5): 664–672.

Dervitsiotis, K.N. (2003). Beyond stakeholder satisfaction: aiming for a new frontier of sustainable stakeholder trust. *Total Quality Management & Business Excellence* **14** (5): 515–528.

Easton, D. (1975). A re-assessment of the concept of political support. *British Journal of Political Science* **5** (4): 435–457.

Edwards, G.C. III and Swenson, T. (1997). Who rallies? The anatomy of a rally event. *The Journal of Politics* **59** (1): 200–212.

Erikson, E.H. (1963). *Childhood and Society*. New York: Norton.

Erkel, P.F.A. and Meer, T. (2016). Macroeconomic performance, political trust and the great recession: a multilevel analysis of the effects of within-country fluctuations in macroeconomic performance. *European Journal of Political Research* **55** (1): 177–197.

Fiorina, M.P. (1981). *Retrospective Voting in American National Elections*. New Haven, CT: Yale University Press.

Fledderus, J. (2015). Building trust through public service co-production. *International Journal of Public Sector* **28** (7): 550–565.

Fukuyama, F. (1995). *Trust: The Social Virtues and the Creation of Prosperity*. New York: Free Press.

Gambetta, D. (1996). *The Sicilian Mafia: The Business of Private Protection*. Cambridge, MA: Harvard University Press.

García, E.G. and Fernández-Alfaro, M.T.L.P. (2014). *Tendencias Emergentes en la Comunicación de Instituciones*, vol. 28. Barcelona: Universitat Oberta de Catalunya.

Granovetter, M. (1985). Economic action and social structure: the problem of embeddedness. *American Journal of Sociology* **91** (3): 481–510.

Gronke, P. and Newman, B. (2003). FDR to Clinton, Mueller to?: a field essay on presidential approval. *Political Research Quarterly* **56** (4): 501–512.

Grunig, J.E. and Hon, L.C. (1999). *Guidelines for Measuring Relationships in Public Relations*. Florida: The Institute for Public Relations.

Grunig, J.E. and Huang, Y.H. (1999). From organizational effectiveness to relationship indicators: antecedents of relationships public relations strategies and relationship outcomes. *Theory and Practice* **36** (4): 644–667.

Gustavsen, A., Røiseland, A., and Pierre, J. (2014). Procedure or performance? Assessing citizen's attitudes toward legitimacy in Swedish and Norwegian local government. *Urban Research & Practice* **7** (2): 200–212.

Hamm, J.A., Hoffman, L., and Tomkins, A.J. (2016). On the influence of trust in predicting rural land owner cooperation with natural resource management institutions. *Journal of Trust* **6** (1): 37–62.

Hardin, R. (1993). The street-level epistemology of trust. *Politics & Society* **21** (4): 505–529.

Harisalo, R. and Stenvall, J. (2003). Trust management in the Finnish ministries: evaluation of management systems. *International Journal of Public Administration* **26** (8–9): 915–940.

Hosmer, L.T. (1995). Trust: the connecting link between organizational theory and philosophical ethics. *Academy of Management Review* **20** (2): 379–403.

Houston, D.J., Aitalieva, N.R., and Morelock, A.L. (2016). Citizen trust in civil servants: a cross-national examination. *International Journal of Public Administration* **39** (14): 1203–1214.

Hu, R., Sun, I.Y., and Wu, Y. (2015). Chinese trust in the police: the impact of political efficacy and participation. *Social Science Quarterly* **96** (4): 1012–1026.

Hung, Y.T.C., Dennis, A.R., and Robert, L. (2004). Trust in virtual teams: towards an integrative model of trust formation. Proceedings of the 37th Annual Hawaii International Conference on Systems Sciences, Track 1, Vol. 1, Big Island, HI, USA (5–8 January).

James, O. (2009). Evaluating the expectations disconfirmation and expectations anchoring approaches to citizen satisfaction with local public services. *Journal of Public Administration Research and Theory* **19** (1): 107–123.

James, O. and Moseley, A. (2014). Does performance information about public services affect citizens' perceptions, satisfaction, and voice behaviour? Field experiments with absolute and relative performance information. *Public Administration* **92** (2): 493–511.

Jepperson, R. (1991). Institutions, institutional effects, and institutionalism. In: *The New Institutionalism in Organizational Analysis* (ed. W.W. Power and P.J. DiMaggio), 143–163. Chicago, IL: University of Chicago Press.

Kääriäinen, J. and Sirén, R. (2012). Do the police trust in citizens? European comparisons. *European Journal of Criminology* **9** (3): 276–289.

Karens, R., Eshuis, J., and Klijn, E.H. (2015). The impact of public branding: an experimental study on the effects of branding policy on citizen trust. *Public Administration* **76** (3): 486–494.

Kestilä-Kekkonen, E. and Söderlund, P. (2016). Political trust, individual-level characteristics and institutional performance: evidence from Finland, 2004–2013. *Scandinavian Political Studies* **39** (2): 138–160.

Kim, S.-E. (2005). The role of trust in the modern administrative state an integrative model. *Administration & Society* **37** (5): 611–635.

Kim, P.S. (2010). Building trust by improving governance: searching for a feasible way for developing countries. *Public Administration Quarterly* Fall 271–299.

Kinder, D.R. and Kiewiet, D.R. (1981). Sociotropic politics: the American case. *British Journal of Political Science* **11** (2): 129–161.

Kumlin, S. and Rothstein, B. (2005). Making and breaking social capital: the impact of welfare-state institutions. *Comparative Political Studies* **38** (4): 339–365.

Lahno, B. (1995). Trust, reputation, and exit in exchange relationships. *Journal of Conflict Resolution* **39** (5): 495–510.

Lanoue, D.J. and Headrick, B. (1994). Prime ministers, parties, and the public: the dynamics of government popularity in Great Britain. *Public Opinion Quarterly* **58** (2): 191–209.

Levi, M. (1997). *Consent, Dissent, and Patriotism*. Cambridge: Cambridge University Press.

Lewis, J.D. and Weigert, A. (1985). Trust as a social reality. *Social Forces* **63** (4): 967–985.

Luhmann, N. (1988). The third question: the creative use of paradoxes in law and legal history. *Journal of Law and Society* **15** (2): 153–165.

Luoma-aho, V. (2005). Faith-Holders as Social Capital of Finnish Public Organisations. University of Jyväskylä, Studies in Humanities, No. 308, Jyväskylä, Finland.

Luoma-aho, V. (2008). Sector reputation and public organisations. *International Journal of Public Sector Management* **21** (5): 446–467.

Luoma-aho, V. (2009). On Putnam: bowling together-applying Putnam's theories of community and social capital to public relations. In: *Public Relations and Social Theory: Key Figures and Concepts* (ed. O. Ihlen, B. Van Ruler and M. Fredrikson), 231–251. London: Routledge.

van der Meer, F., Steen, T., and Wille, A. (2015). Western European civil service systems: a comparative analysis. In: *The Civil Service in the 21st Century: Comparative Perspectives* (ed. J.C.N. Raadschelders, T.A.J. Toonen and F.M. Van der Meer). New York, NY: Palgrave Macmillan.

Nadeau, R., Niemi, R.G., and Fan, D.P. (1999). Elite economic forecasts, economic news, mass economic judgments, and presidential approval. *The Journal of Politics* **61** (1): 109–135.

Nicholson, S.P., Segura, G.M., and Woods, N.D. (2002). Presidential approval and the mixed blessing of divided government. *Journal of Politics* **64** (3): 701–720.

Nye, J.S., Zelikow, P., and King, D.C. (1997). *Why People Don't Trust Government*. Cambridge, MA: Harvard University Press.

Ostrom, C.W. Jr. and Simon, D.M. (1988). The president's public. *American Journal of Political Science* **32** (4): 1096–1119.

Poppo, L. and Schepker, D.J. (2010). Repairing public trust in organizations. *Corporate Reputation Review* **13** (2): 124–141.

Poppo, L., Zheng, K., and Li, J. (2016). When can you trust "trust"? Calculative trust, relational trust, and supplier performance. *Strategic Management Journal* **37**: 724–741.

Putnam, R. (2000). *Bowling Alone: The Collapse and Revival of American Community*. New York: Simon & Schuster.

Quandt, T. (2012). What's left of trust in a network society? An evolutionary model and critical discussion of trust and societal communication. *European Journal of Communication* **27** (1): 7–21.

Robbins, B.G. (2016). What is trust? A multidisciplinary review, critique, and synthesis. *Sociology Compass* **10** (10): 972–986.

Rothstein, B., and Stolle, D. (2002). How political institutions create and destroy social capital: an institutional theory of generalized trust. 98th Meeting of the American Political Science Association in Boston, MA (29 August–2 September).

Rothstein, B. and Stolle, D. (2008). The state and social capital: an institutional theory of generalized trust. *Comparative Politics* **40** (4): 441–459.

Rousseau, D.M., Sitkin, S.B., and Burt, R.S. (1998). Not so different after all: a cross-discipline view of trust. *Academy of Management* **23** (3): 393–404.

Ruscio, K.P. (1997). Trust in the administrative state. *Public Administration Review* **57** (5): 454–458.

Ruscio, K.P. (1999). Jay's pirouette, or why political trust is not the same as personal trust. *Administration & Society* **31** (5): 639–657.

Scholz, J.T. and Lubell, M. (1998). Trust and taxpaying: testing the heuristic approach to collective action. *American Journal of Political Science* **42** (2): 398–417.

Seligman, A.B. (1997). *The Problem of Trust*. Princeton, N.J.: Princeton University Press.

Seyd, B. (2015). How do citizens evaluate public officials? The role of performance and expectations on political trust. *Political Studies* **63** (1): 73–90.

da Silva, R. and Batista, L. (2007). Boosting government reputation through CRM. *International Journal of Public Sector Management* **20** (7): 588–607.

Söderlund, P. and Kestilä-Kekkonen, E. (2009). Dark side of party identification? An empirical study of political trust among radical right wing voters. *Journal of Elections, Public Opinion and Parties* **19** (2): 1–81.

Suchman, M.C. (1995). Managing legitimacy: strategic and institutional approaches. *Academy of Management Review* **20** (3): 571–610.

Sydow, J. (1998). Understanding the constitution of interorganizational trust. In: *Trust within and between Organizations: Conceptual* (ed. L. Christel and R. Bachmann), 3–63. Oxford: Oxford University Press.

Sztompka, P. (1999). *Trust: A Sociological Theory.* Cambridge: Cambridge University Press.

Thomas, J.C. (2013). Citizen, customer, partner: rethinking the place of the public in public management. *Public Administration Review* **73** (6): 786–796.

Uslaner, E.M. (2010). Trust and the economic crisis of 2008. *Corporate Reputation Review* **13** (2): 110–123.

Uslaner, E.M. and Brown, M. (2005). Inequality, trust, and civic engagement. *American Politics Research* **33** (6): 868–894.

Van de Walle, S. (2004). *Perceptions of Administrative Performance: The Key to Trust in Government?* Leuven: Instituut voor de Overheid.

Van de Walle, S. (2007). Determinants of confidence in the civil service: an international comparison. *Research in Public Policy Analysis and Management* **16**: 171–201.

Van De Walle, S. (2011). NPM: restoring the public trust through creating distrust? In: *The Ashgate Research Companion to New Public Management* (ed. T. Christensen and P. Laegreid), 309–320. Surrey: Ashgate.

Van de Walle, S. and Bouckaert, G. (2003). Public service performance and trust in government: the problem of causality. *International Journal of Public Administration* **26** (8–9): 891–913.

Van de Walle, S. and Lahat, L. (2016). Do Public Officials Trust Citizens? A Welfare State Perspective. *Social Policy and Administration* **51** (7): 1450–1469.

Van de Walle, S. and Six, F. (2014). Trust and distrust as distinct concepts: why studying distrust in institutions is important. *Journal of Comparative Policy Analysis* **16** (2): 158–174.

Van de Walle, S., Van Roosbroek, S., and Bouckaert, G. (2008). Trust in the public sector: is there any evidence for a long-term decline? *International Review of Administrative Sciences* **74** (1): 47–64.

Van Ryzin, G.G. (2011). Outcomes, process, and trust of civil servants. *Journal of Public Administration Research and Theory* **21** (4): 745–760.

Wæraas, A. and Byrkjeflot, H. (2012). Public sector organizations and reputation management: five problems. *International Public Management Journal* **15** (2): 186–206.

Wang, X.H. and Wart, M.W. (2007). When public participation in administration leads to trust: an empirical assessment of managers' perceptions. *Public Administration Review* **67** (2): 265–278.

Whiteley, P., Clarke, H.D., and Sanders, D. (2016). Why do voters lose trust in governments? Public perceptions of government honesty and trustworthiness in Britain 2000–2013. *The British Journal of Politics and International Relations* **18** (1): 234–254.

Yang, K. and Pandey, S.K. (2011). Further dissecting the black box of citizen participation: when does citizen involvement lead to good outcomes? *Public Administration Review* **71** (6): 880–892.

13

Closing the Gaps

You can never please everyone with public sector communication
(Remarks by a head of communication at a large public sector
organization during a research interview)

This chapter summarizes the book and provides answers to the questions that we see arising in society and causing gaps between citizens and public administrations.

13.1 How Can We Close the Gap between Citizens and Public Sector Organizations?

What did we learn from intangible assets? In Chapter 1, we asked whether citizens are from Venus and authorities are from Mars. To answer this question, we could say that this still remains the case in many places. But the organized Martians are genuinely interested in understanding the changing Venusians better. Moreover, the Venusians are often more willing to collaborate when the Martians' processes are transparent and when they understand the logic behind the procedures.

To begin, we acknowledge that no matter how much information is provided, the public sector context often remains a very complex and politically sensitive environment, where major changes take time and some changes may even be impossible. Moreover, many of the changes necessary may or may not be related to communication, and attempting to fix them via communication alone may backfire. We expect that the intangible assets described in this book enable an increased mutual understanding between citizens and public sector organizations. Intangible assets provide a support system for authorities to obtain a better knowledge of citizens and their expectations, and they simultaneously provide citizens with a better understanding of the multiple constraints and interests to which public authorities are subject.

We will now briefly discuss some insights that could help to close the gaps identified at the beginning of the book. As assets continue to develop over time, the list of assets associated with each gap is not exhaustive.

Table 13.1 summarizes our understanding of intangible assets.

Public Sector Communication: Closing Gaps Between Citizens and Public Organizations, First Edition.
María-José Canel and Vilma Luoma-aho.

Table 13.1 Intangible assets and gaps.

	Satisfaction	Organizational culture	Reputation	Legitimacy	Intellectual capital	Engagement	Social capital	Trust
It measures:	The overall pleasantness of the public service experience	The extent to which the organization is aligned with certain core principles	The overall impression of the organization's past deeds	The acceptance of the organization and its functions by the organization's publics	The extent to which an organization manages knowledge well	The capacity of an organization to get citizens involved in public administration processes	The capacity of an organization to generate social cohesion	The capacity of an organization to be granted discretion in the use of public resources for the provision of public services
It generates:	Better life outcomes, social peace, organizational productivity, positive worth of mouth, employee efficiency, trust	Work flow, team efficiency, innovativeness, organizational flexibility, stability and effectiveness, increased productivity, collaboration, commitment, engagement, better service experiences, transparency of organizational processes, trust	Financial gains, faith in potential good interactions and experiences, guards against cutbacks, ease of interaction, positive attitudes, positive experiences, general citizen welfare, employee and citizen engagement, trust	Authority, rule following, unified popular will, less friction and conflict, decision acceptance, stability, support, credibility, loyalty, certainty, effectiveness, trust	Knowledge visibility, sharing, and systematization, quality and strategic management, good governance, well-built and consistent organizational culture, accountability, transparency, efficiency, networking, satisfaction, wellbeing, trust	Better distribution of resources, wider choices, active experience of service, shared authority, mutual understanding, enhanced relationships, support, dialogue, consensus, social cohesion, accountability, legitimacy, social capital, networking, trust	Goodwill, collaboration, less racism and discrimination, health, sense of security and belonging, citizen collaboration, sense of community, resilience, integration of diversity, reciprocity, satisfaction, welfare, empowerment, trust	Citizen compliance, efficiency, efficacy, professional pride, collaboration, a good organizational culture, intellectual capital, a good reputation, satisfaction, legitimacy, social capital, engagement

It bridges these gaps:	Misunderstanding, distance-related gaps, distrust-related gaps, gaps caused by bad experiences, lack of collaboration and engagement, the need for flexibility	Poor job satisfaction, low citizen satisfaction, poor service experiences, low efficiency, a lack of understanding of citizen needs and expectations	Lack of information about the organization's character; bad attitude and lack of engagement, where reputation helps to build a positive attitude; it lends the trust needed for interactions when there are no previous experiences to refer to	Lack of significance, lack of purpose, lack of understanding, lack of shared standards and criteria for judging, lack of collective accounts and rational explanations, lack of trust	The gap between real achievements and people's perceptions: it provides insights from public services and ways to measure and manage resources to meet citizens' expectations	The gap between the one-directional and static nature of traditional public sector communication and the need to more effectively meet citizens' needs and changing expectations; the gap between professionals and civil servants on the one hand and ordinary citizens on the other	Lack of trust and lack of collaboration between strangers; lack of facilitation between individuals, groups, and organizations	Trust contributes to almost all gaps between citizens and public sector organizations: trustworthy organizations enjoy greater compliance from stakeholders, and to the extent that different intangible assets build trust, their bridging of gaps helps trust to reduce uncertainty

13.1.1   Closing Gap 1: Speed: Bureaucracy versus Postbureaucracy

Although the scientific management paradigm's principles of efficiency and structure remain, there have been several attempts at improving citizen experience and speed of services. Despite this, it appears that citizen perceptions about speed remain tied to their previous views, which remain little altered by the actual changes. For this gap to close, we suggest building on the intangible assets of:

- *Organizational culture*: if the organization is well coordinated from the inside, it becomes more efficient and better able to meet changing citizen needs, and processes speed up through the removal of unnecessary procedures;
- *Satisfaction*: citizens who are satisfied tend to be more flexible with regard to timing;
- *Intellectual capital*: superior knowledge management helps the organization to respond in a timelier manner to its stakeholders' needs;
- *Engagement*: if citizens have been involved in the administrative process, they will have more realistic perceptions of the duration of the process.
- *Social capital*: as good experiences of collaboration accumulate, a reinforcing mechanism that speeds up processes and also increases interaction to diminish gaps in expectations is produced.

13.1.2   Closing Gap 2: Privacy: Public versus Private Communication

Because the boundaries between what is considered public and what is considered private are blurring, all public sector communication has the potential to be seen publicly. This gap will require a focus on intangible assets that embrace the similarly blurring boundaries between different stakeholders and yield the accountability and transparency that this public/private communication entails:

- *Organizational culture*: this aligns different (public/private) stakeholders toward certain core principles;
- *Legitimacy*: this creates common ground for elaborating explanations about what the organization is and what it does;
- *Engagement*: where citizens become involved in the provision of public services, they jointly manage the information that is produced;
- *Trust*: this will increase citizens' confidence in revealing information where government performance relies on their doing so.

13.1.3   Closing Gap 3: Viewpoints: Process versus Answers

The cause of this gap lies in different interpretations of the same situation: whereas the organization focuses on individual technical and procedural details, what citizens and stakeholders seek are answers to their problems. We could conclude that this gap can be closed by adding transparency to the process, but in such a way that doing so makes sense and yields an answer. Citizens may appreciate quick answers, but understanding the process can also help. Therefore, clarity and optimized communication can help people to rely more on information from the authorities. Intangible assets that might aid in this endeavor are as follows:

- *Satisfaction*: being focused on the end-user experience through service design will help misunderstandings to be avoided;
- *Reputation*: cumulative positive experiences for citizens indicate that they are receiving answers to their problems; if the reputation of the organization is built on expertise, citizens will trust the answers that they receive;
- *Legitimacy*: organizational messages will be framed in ways that better resonate with social and cultural standards, and they will therefore provide answers.

13.1.4 Closing Gap 4: Context: Single Events versus General Attitude

Public sector communication should be able to provide a long-term picture of the organization and its functions to provide stakeholders with an understanding of the context and environment, thereby generating realistic and collaborative attitudes. It is difficult to ascertain what influences attitudes toward public sector organizations and services, as such attitudes entail complex evaluative judgments (James, 2011). The following assets may help:

- *Organizational culture*: culture is reflected in every service encounter and hence radiates to citizen experiences;
- *Reputation*: although citizens may keep a record of all the problems related to public sector organizations, it is important to remember that the more positive personal experiences they have, the more they will cultivate a compliant and collaborative attitude;
- *Engagement*: the more engaged citizens feel in the process, the more they will be open to ongoing interaction, and the more flexible they will be regarding change in general;
- *Trust*: trust in the relationship that contributes to an attitude of compliance.

13.1.5 Closing Gap 5: Perceptions: Perception versus Performance

Perhaps the largest gap when it comes to public sector organizations remains that between perceptions and performance. Although closing it has been attempted many times through actions and policy, this gap is best closed via intangible assets, as it pertains to the relationship and expectations that citizens have regarding public sector organizations.

- *Satisfaction*: the more satisfied citizens are, the more they will also perceive positive signs regarding performance;
- *Reputation*: strengthening the reputation of the organization or service is central, since it enables acknowledging actual performance;
- *Intellectual capital*: intellectual capital provides insights from public services and ways to measure and manage resources to meet citizens' expectations; it helps to make real achievements (real performance) visible, thereby generating more adjusted perceptions;
- *Engagement*: when citizens are engaged in the provision of public services, their perception of performance will be closer to the actual performance levels.

13.1.6 Closing Gap 6: Roles: Obligations versus Rights

The original idea of bureaucracy as a protector of citizens has been severely challenged by the new communication environment, and some have even said that there is an information war taking place, in which narratives and counternarratives clash (Kuronen and Huhtinen, 2017). Public sector communication needs to take up the task of building and fostering the general atmosphere of the public sector, and central to this are clear roles and responsibilities. The intangible assets most capable of closing this gap include:

- *Satisfaction*: developing both internal and external satisfaction will increase the flexibility of the organization to adjust its obligations to its citizens' and stakeholders' rights;
- *Engagement*: more engaged citizens mean a greater shared authority, thereby harmonizing rights and obligations;
- *Social capital*: social capital will facilitate citizens' understanding of the organization's obligations to comply with the rights of different groups, and thus it will be easier for all sides to consider the full impact of individual choices for society at large.

13.1.7 Closing Gap 7: Media Use: Controlled versus Real Time

This gap is something that both public and private organizations must deal with. As with the other gaps, the process of closing it will occur over time and requires rethinking the organization's culture and processes. It can be argued that working on intangible assets implies an open attitude to new technologies, taking them as an opportunity to enhance interaction with stakeholders.

- *Organizational culture*: culture is reflected in every service encounter and hence radiates to citizen experiences;
- *Satisfaction*: the efficiency and efficacy associated with satisfaction can only be achieved by an organization that takes real-time interaction with stakeholders into account in the delivery of services;
- *Legitimacy*: an organization focused on legitimacy will develop the skills to undertake real-time communication to participate in the arenas where the standards and criteria used for judging are elaborated.

To the extent that all intangible assets are associated with trust formation (see the discussion in Chapter 12), trust is an intangible asset that can ultimately help to reduce all gaps.

As can be seen, many of these gaps actually occur on the level of perceptions. Perceptions result from expectations, and to manage perceptions, one must manage expectations. To conclude this book, we ask whether expectations can be managed and provide an example of how this expectation management can be done in practice.

13.2 Expectations Management to Build Intangibles that Bridge Gaps

For organizations wishing to bridge the potential expectation gaps between citizens and themselves, citizens' expectations must first be understood. Expectations matter, as they produce information that can be used as a basis for making policy decisions and weighing up alternatives (Rodrigo and Amo, 2006). The challenge of shaping citizen expectations is that most public sector communication and participatory practices remain top down and authority centered, mostly due to their political nature and bureaucratic processes (Alarcon and Font, 2014). Moreover, media and social media logics often emphasize negativity (Van Dijck and Poell, 2013; Fredriksson, Schillemans, and Pallas, 2015), biasing negative events as more important. This negativity bias has also been found in media reporting of public sector performance (Hood and Dixon, 2010), and citizen dissatisfaction rather than satisfaction is recognized as driving citizen action regarding public services (James, 2011). Utilizing citizen feedback is central, and "improved translation of those issues into performance specifications and delivery system design, and increased horizontal communication within the organization are likely to reduce the gap" between citizens' perceptions and expectations (Coye, 2004, p. 66).

Communication is understood to be the only intervention to bridge the gap between expectations and service in real time (Coye, 2004). The different cues that shape citizens' expectations are also important. Although public sector organizations may plan their own cues for citizens, there are always unplanned and external cues that shape citizen expectations; these can stem from the environment as well as from relationships (Coye, 2004, p. 66).

Expectation management is about listening to stakeholders and their needs before issues and problems emerge or escalate (Macnamara, 2016). In fact, organizational listening has many proven benefits, and governments and public sector organizations can "gain 'bottom line' results from better listening," including fewer complaints, reduced staff turnover, improved morale (which leads to increased productivity), reduced workplace disputation, and crisis avoidance (Macnamara, 2016, p. 310). To manage expectations, organizations must manage their own understanding of different stakeholders, as well as what these stakeholders wish for in relation to the organization (Luoma-aho and Olkkonen, 2016).

Much public sector communication has been accused of being inefficient, and citizens often fail to follow the desired public sector and government behavior recommendations, whether these relate to health, safety, or waste management. Behavioral economics suggests that several steps can be taken as far back as the planning stage of communication to ensure that people behave as expected (Kahneman and Tversky, 1979, p. 263). Building on Dolan et al.'s MINDSPACE acronym (Dolan et al., 2012), the following influences should be considered in planning for successful public sector communication that sets the desired expectations (Table 13.2).

For public sector communication to succeed, Dolan et al. (2010) suggest six Es that could actually ensure influence and desired outcomes.

1) Exploration refers to first understanding citizens or employee behavior that needs changing.
2) Enabling refers to designing the environment to support this.
3) Encouraging refers to applying the use of the aforementioned MINDSPACE influences to help individuals to behave in the right way.
4) Engage refers to gaining legitimacy and deliberation on the topic in public.
5) Exemplifying is about leading by example, thereby changing the public sector organization's behavior with a focus on consistency and transparency.
6) Evaluating is about finding out what actually works and halting what does not.

Table 13.2 The MINDSPACE model applied for planning public sector communication.

Messenger

Who communicates information to the citizens? Is it someone relatable? For example, instead of the minister or a spokesperson, who would be the best to promote a new antismoking policy to make the campaign resonate with citizens? A popular football player? A blogger?

Incentives

Citizens' mental shortcuts (such as loss avoidance) shape incentives: What is the reference point? And are there any quick gains to be mentioned to make the message more appealing? For example, citizens will return their public library books sooner if they experience a concrete loss, such as having to pay late fees compared to receiving mere warnings.

Norms

Citizens do what they see other citizens doing, so how can the right example be set? For example, if the norm is set to clean streets, citizen find it easier to not litter.

Defaults

Citizens follow defaults and preset options, so how can the right default be planned? For example, if the tax card is prefilled to the estimated right amount, citizens are more likely to finish it and return it than when they have to fill the entire card by themselves.

Salience

Citizen attention is drawn to novelty. What is relevant and new to citizens? For example, opening a new park will be perceived as more valuable in areas where clean air is scarce than in areas with cleaner air.

Priming

Citizens take in subconscious cues: How can these best be used? For example, if authorities clearly explain ahead of time which streets will be under construction and for how long, citizens will feel less need to complain about the inconvenience as they are mentally more prepared for it to happen.

Affect

Citizens' emotional associations matter: Which emotions can be activated? For example, how can the public sector organization's service department portray empathy better?

Commitments

Citizens seek to be consistent, so which promises can this be linked with? For example, recycling garbage is easier to achieve if citizens are reminded how successful they and other citizens of this particular area have previously been with recycling.

Ego

Citizens act in ways that make them feel better about themselves, so how can a coherence between the message and their ego be ensured? For example, enabling the citizens to take pictures and tag their location while donating to a water conservation campaign will ensure the citizens have a way of positively enforcing their decision.

Although changing processes may be more challenging than merely adding new ideas, some of these simple principles can be applied to ensure that expectations are set and behavioral outcomes are positive.

Case Study: The Fit-or-Fix Approach to Expectation Management in Public Sector Organizations

The fit-or-fix approach explains the process of expectation management handling in public sector organizations (Luoma-aho, Olkkonen, and Lähteenmäki, 2013, pp. 248–250). In 2012, the Finnish National Institute for Health and Welfare's (THL) communication department found its hands full with the daily practicalities of producing press releases and answering citizens' queries, but authentic expectation management required a more strategic approach and lacked commitment at a senior managerial level. Created by the organization's head of communication (M. Lähteenmäki), the fit-or-fix approach has allowed THL to be successful in bringing communication to the attention of senior managers and in giving them a fuller understanding of the contribution that well-planned communication can make to the organization. This work has already paid off in the form of higher reputational rankings and increased the employees' and stakeholders' satisfaction.

The fit-or-fix approach consists of five stages:

1) Communication professionals in public sector organizations sort through and identify expectation gaps that require attention based on monitoring and citizen, employee, or stakeholder feedback.
2) Top-level leaders and managers gather for a workshop where each of these gaps and feedback issues is examined in turn and decisions are made as to whether they should be placed in the fit category or the fix category. For issues that fall into the fit category, the organization will make changes in its practices and communication to better meet stakeholder expectations. The solution to issues in the fix category, meanwhile, is to repair stakeholder expectations to better meet organizational performance and responsibilities.
3) For each issue in each category, between two and five communication actions are formulated; these will be put into practice to improve the situation, both immediately and in the longer term.
4) Measures are set for evaluating the success of each change and for communicating with the feedback provider and those involved in identifying the gap.
5) The group adjourns to follow up on the results of the measures set, to enter into dialogue with those who identified the gap to begin with, and to evaluate and sort through new emerging issues. The process is a cyclical one, and as such the final stage is concluded by returning to the first step and identifying new and emerging expectation gaps. This process is illustrated in Figure 13.1.

Expectation management is the beginning of antifragility: it makes the foundation for what is known and marks the steps that should be taken.

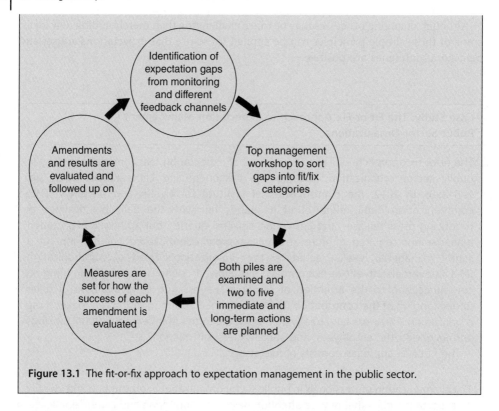

Figure 13.1 The fit-or-fix approach to expectation management in the public sector.

13.2.1 Concluding Remarks

The "intangibles movement" in the public sector implies a profound transformation in organizations and their actions. It transforms the way in which organizations build relations with citizens, and it allows organizations to both survive and plan ahead in dynamic and changing societies. The more the intangibles are strengthened, the better the relationships between citizens, stakeholders, and public sector organizations become. As has been discussed, intangibles are constructs, and much still needs to be done to find the formulas that best measure them. With better measures, all stakeholders as well as society at large will have precise information about what the public sector provides.

Although this book has introduced each intangible asset separately, we acknowledge that in practice all intangible assets overlap, and the strengthening of one may contribute to the strengthening of others as well. Organizations and communication professionals have to choose the gap(s) to work on according to their resources, needs, and capacities.

Public sector organizations range from fully public to almost fully privatized or outsourced service providers, and building intangible assets is dependent on the organization as well as its environment. Each public sector organization is unique, and starting to follow the intangibles movement will always begin one asset at a time. We recommend that organizations start with the one that helps bridge the largest gap, as doing so may allow improvements to become visible more quickly, thereby encouraging the organization to focus on other intangibles.

References

Alarcon, P. and Font, J. (2014). Where are the boundaries of deliberation and participation? A transatlantic debate. *Journal of Public Deliberation* **10** (2): 1–27.

Coye, R.W. (2004). Managing customer expectations in the service encounter. *International Journal of Service Industry Management* **15** (1): 54–71.

Dolan, P., Hallsworth, M., Halpern, D. et al. (2010). *MINDSPACE: Influencing Behaviour Through Public Policy*. UK: Institute for Government, Cabinet Office.

Dolan, P., Hallsworth, M., Halpern, D. et al. (2012). Influencing behaviour: the mindspace way. *Journal of Economic Psychology* **33** (1): 264–277.

Fredriksson, M., Schillemans, T., and Pallas, J. (2015). Determinants of organizational mediatization: an analysis of the adaptation of Swedish government agencies to news media. *Public Administration* **93** (4): 1049–1067.

Hood, C. and Dixon, R. (2010). The political payoff from performance target systems: no-brainer or no-gainer? *Journal of Public Administration Research and Theory* **20** (Suppl 2): i281–i298.

James, O. (2011). Managing citizens' expectations of public service performance: evidence from observation and experimentation in local government. *Public Administration* **89** (4): 1419–1435.

Kahneman, D. and Tversky, A. (1979). Prospect theory: an analysis of decision under risk. *Econometrica: Journal of the Econometric Society* **47** (2): 263–291.

Kuronen, T. and Huhtinen, A.-M. (2017). Organizing conflict: the rhizome of jihad. *Journal of Management Inquiry* **26** (1): 47–61.

Luoma-aho, V. and Olkkonen, L. (2016). Expectation management. In: *The SAGE Encyclopedia of Corporate Reputation* (ed. C. Carroll), 303–306. Sage.

Luoma-aho, V., Olkkonen, L., and Lähteenmäki, M. (2013). Expectation management for public sector organizations. *Public Relations Review* **39** (3): 248–250.

Macnamara, J. (2016). *Organizational Listening: The Missing Essential in Public Communication*. New York: Peter Lang.

Rodrigo, D. and Amo, P.A. (2006). *Background Document on Public Consultation*. Paris: OECD.

Van Dijck, J. and Poell, T. (2013). Understanding social media logic. *Media and Communication* **1** (1): 2–14.

Index

Public Sector Communication: Closing Gaps Between Citizens and Public Organizations, First Edition.
María-José Canel and Vilma Luoma-aho.